STRATEGIC RISK, INTELLIGENCE AND DIGITAL TRANSFORMATION

Digital Transformation: Accelerating Organizational Intelligence

Print ISSN: 2811-0552
Online ISSN: 2811-0560

Series Editor: Jay Liebowitz *(Seton Hall University, USA)*

According to a report released by Veritis in 2021 "the global digital transformation market size is anticipated to reach USD 1009.8 billion by 2025 from USD 469.8 billion in 2020. The demand for digital transformation services is expected to rise at a Compound Annual Growth Rate (CAGR) of around 16.5% over the forecast period from 2021 to 2025. The growing adoption of digital technologies, including Artificial Intelligence (AI), cloud computing, big data, the Internet of Things (IoT), and Machine Learning (ML), is driving the growth of the digital transformation market." To be competitive in today's fast-changing marketplace, organizations need to apply the "alphabet" of digital transformation.

The focus of the book series is unique and will cover the various perspectives on organizational digital transformation, namely business & management, technology, legal and ethics, and social aspects.

Published:

Vol. 6 *Strategic Risk, Intelligence and Digital Transformation*
by Eduardo Rodriguez

Vol. 5 *Digital Transformation for Entrepreneurship*
edited by Susanne Durst and Aive Pevkur

Vol. 4 *Digital Strategies and Organizational Transformation*
edited by G Reza Djavanshir

Vol. 3 *Doing Well and Doing Good: Human-Centered Digital Transformation Leadership*
by Cheryl Flink, Liora Gross and William Pasmore

Vol. 2 *Digital Transformation Demystified*
by Frank Granito

Vol. 1 *Digital Transformation for the University of the Future*
edited by Jay Liebowitz

More information on this series can be found at https://www.worldscientific.com/series/dtaoi

Digital Transformation
Accelerating Organizational Intelligence
– Volume 6

STRATEGIC RISK, INTELLIGENCE AND DIGITAL TRANSFORMATION

Eduardo Rodriguez
Wenzhou–Kean University, China
IQAnalytics Inc., Canada

World Scientific

NEW JERSEY • LONDON • SINGAPORE • BEIJING • SHANGHAI • HONG KONG • TAIPEI • CHENNAI • TOKYO

Published by

World Scientific Publishing Co. Pte. Ltd.
5 Toh Tuck Link, Singapore 596224
USA office: 27 Warren Street, Suite 401-402, Hackensack, NJ 07601
UK office: 57 Shelton Street, Covent Garden, London WC2H 9HE

Library of Congress Control Number: 2023039374

British Library Cataloguing-in-Publication Data
A catalogue record for this book is available from the British Library.

Digital Transformation: Accelerating Organizational Intelligence — Vol. 6
STRATEGIC RISK, INTELLIGENCE AND DIGITAL TRANSFORMATION

ISBN 978-981-127-859-4 (hardcover)
ISBN 978-981-127-860-0 (ebook for institutions)
ISBN 978-981-127-861-7 (ebook for individuals)

For any available supplementary material, please visit
https://www.worldscientific.com/worldscibooks/10.1142/13478#t=suppl

Desk Editors: Balasubramanian Shanmugam/Yulin Jiang

Typeset by Stallion Press
Email: enquiries@stallionpress.com

To Zhouping, Sebastian, Daniel and in memory of Marcela

About the Author

Eduardo Rodriguez, Ph.D., is a member of the advisory board of the new Finance, Innovation and Technology certification program from the Fields Institute of Mathematics at the University of Toronto, Canada. He is the Founder and Principal at IQAnalytics Inc., a research center and consulting firm in Ottawa, Canada. He is also an Adjunct Professor of Analytics at Telfer School of Management and Professor of Quantitative Methods for the Master of Healthcare Administration program at the University of Ottawa, Canada. Eduardo's previous books were *Risk Analytics: Data-Driven Decisions under Uncertainty* (2023, CRC Press) and *Strategic Risk, Intelligence and Digital Transformation* (2023, World Scientific). He was an Assistant Professor at the School of Mathematical Sciences at Wenzhou-Kean University in Wenzhou, China (Chinese campus of the Kean University). He was the Founder and Leader of the Risk Analytics Lab at Wenzhou-Kean University. Lately, he has been an active participant in the creation and development of the Data Science Program at the Inter-American University of Puerto Rico and a keynote speaker at multiple academic and professional conferences, including the CSAE International Conference on Computer Science and Application Engineering in 2021 and 2022.

Eduardo was the first Sentry Endowed Chair in Business Analytics at the University of Wisconsin–Stevens Point, USA. He has been a member of the corporate faculty of the MSc program in Analytics at Harrisburg University of Science and Technology, Pennsylvania, USA. He has created and developed the Analytics Stream of the MBA program at the University of Fredericton, Canada. He has been a Visiting Scholar at

Chongqing University in China and EAFIT University in Colombia (Master of Risk Management program).

Eduardo has extensive experience in analytics, knowledge, and risk management, mainly in the insurance and banking industry. He was a Knowledge Management Advisor and Quantitative Analyst at EDC (Export Development Canada) in Ottawa, the Regional Director of PRMIA (Professional Risk Managers International Association) in Ottawa, and the Executive Vice-President and Vice-President of Marketing and Planning for insurance companies and banks in Colombia. He was also a part-time professor at Andes University and CESA in Colombia. He has authored eight books on analytics, reviewed several journals, and published several works in peer-reviewed journals and conferences. He has also created and chaired the Analytics Think-Tank, organized and chaired the International Conference on Analytics ICAS, been a member of academic committees for conferences on Knowledge Management, and been an international lecturer in the field of analytics.

Eduardo holds a Ph.D. from Aston Business School, Aston University, UK; an M.Sc. in Mathematics from Concordia University, Montreal, Canada; a Certification from the Advanced Management Program, McGill University, Canada; and an MBA and a Bachelor's degree in Mathematics from Los Andes University, Colombia. His main research interests are in the fields of strategic risk, risk analytics, strategic intelligence development, and knowledge management applied to enterprise risk management.

Contents

Introduction

In this book, the study of strategic risk is not only oriented to understand its control and mitigation using analytics and digital transformation in organizations but is also about the analysis of strategic risks that digital transformation and data analytics/AI bring to organizations. Strategic risk control is one of the goals in creating intelligent organizations and, at the same time, it is part of the appetite for creating means to support organizations' development to adapt to changes in an uncertain business environment. A risk that emerges with new technologies is related to setting tech priorities in organizations. The Gartner (2023) technology trends report is a guide to develop capabilities to adapt organizations to new business environments where digital transformation is going from digital immune systems to Adaptive AI. Moreover, knowledge that is created by data analytics and the capacity to operationalize that knowledge through digital transformation can produce potential adaptive, sustainable, competitive advantages, and new risks will emerge as well. The core of the book is connecting data analytics and AI, risk management, and digitalization to create strategic intelligence as the capacity for adaptation that organizations need to compete and to succeed. Strategic Intelligence is a symbiotic work of artificial intelligence, business intelligence, and competitive intelligence. Strategic risk is represented by the probability of having variations in the expected performance results of the organizations that can limit their capacity to adapt and maintain sustainable competitive advantages. There is an emphasis in the book about the conversion of models that support data analytics into actions to mitigate strategic risk based on digital transformation.

Digital transformation, intelligence, and strategic risk analysis converge for the same purpose, that is, to provide means to organizations to succeed according to the organization's success definition. This is applicable from SuperAPPs, such as Wechat, Revolut, PayPay, Alipay, Omni, Rappi, and AirAsia, that are sets of connected apps in an ecosystem integrating services and providing the means to access and use those services through a unique platform, to talent development and upskilling for people to continue working and adopting new digital solutions. Thunström (2022), in a Scientific American article, exposed a special new challenge for organizations now and in the future: How can one deal with AI as a good means to grow and improve society's and citizens' lifestyle? She pointed out, "I'm a scientist who studies ways to use artificial intelligence to treat mental health concerns, and this wasn't my first experiment with GPT-3. Even so, my attempts to complete that paper and submit it to a peer-reviewed journal would open up unprecedented ethical and legal questions about publishing, as well as philosophical arguments about non-human authorship. Academic publishing may have to accommodate a future of AI-driven manuscripts, and the value of a human researcher's publication records may change if something non-sentient can take credit for some of their work." The issues here are about ethical capabilities of AI, possible misuse, and possible risks in a society. Good means in AI to work with humans can create new risk and humans need to be prepared to work on them: from regulations, identification of contingency methods for misuse, and more. This book will present several examples and discuss the concept of monitoring risks and how to guide risk management control.

The reader will find that everything in the book is based on the premise that strategic risk is different from other risks regarding not only the scope of all business processes, strategic and tactical, the same as decision-making and problem-solving, but also the capacity to use a combination of reason and intuition to develop risk management processes. The core of strategic risk mitigation is through the creation of strategic intelligence where data analytics is a pillar. Adaptation is a fundamental concept of intelligence understanding, AI is designed to help humans, risk is always present in any human and machine action with different levels of intensity, and data analytics leads to the creation of knowledge and intelligence.

Through the chapters of the book, there is a presentation of risk concept with reflections about technology use and human–machine interactions in organizations. This description includes a review of the evolutionary steps of organizations using technology that is connecting the data analytics modeling process and digital operations. This book reviews the process of moving from the use of statistical learning and machine learning for data analytics to the improvement and use of new technologies. The digitalization process is a potential opportunity for organizations to adapt well to new business environments; however, the results of digitalization are not necessarily good for everyone. There is a presentation across chapters about the influence, in strategic risk control, of cloud computing, blockchain, AI, and the creation of digital networks that are connected internally and externally to deal with internal and external customers, with suppliers and buyers, and with competitors and substitutes. The new risks appear once new knowledge emerges and is in use, but at the same time the new knowledge supports the initiatives to deal with risks of new ways of competing, collaborating, protecting, and growing the organizations' talents and customers as a means to move ahead and beyond. In summary, this book is not only about strategic risk but also about how it is mitigated and controlled using data analytics and digital transformation as important pillars in management. This book reviews factors affecting strategic risks, from the potential threats and perils on earth and in nature to the effects, development, and impact of business interruption, bankruptcy, changes of competitive positions, etc., that are crucial to the understanding of strategic risk mitigation. The integration of data analytics and digitalization is crucial in the way that new opportunities and risks appear because of the appropriate use of data and technology to transform business process and to create value through real-time data products and services.

Basic points to review Strategic Risk

Strategic risk study is a field that can be divided into layers, keeping in mind a couple of fundamental points: as mentioned earlier, new created knowledge brings new risks; data analytics and AI support the development of intelligence for solving problems but at the same time some of the risks are part of the use of these means of creating intelligence. Anderson *et al.* (2022) indicated an interesting issue when risk is analyzed in a mortgage business. The issue is strategic default. This type of risk is because of housing bubbles that in a moment can produce issues such as the asset for families being of a lower value than the debt in the mortgage. It is possible to search for better intelligence means to detect this potential behavior of debtors or to predict the occurrence of bubbles in housing that create these behaviors of the markets, financial services, and developers. Those are aspects where better AI can help improve prediction power to avoid crises that societies have experienced earlier. Nowadays, in 2022–2023, the risk of a housing bubble in China is spreading to economies across the world; many families are affected but do not yet know the gravity of the situation. The government of China, through the CCP, included risk assessment and mitigation through regulation and follow up of operations of financial markets and developers in its list of priorities.

Digitalization at the same time is a way to operate business, generate actions, service society, and is part of the solution for organizations to maintain competitive advantages because intelligence will depend on the capacity to use digitalization, for example, to maintain a competitive and relevant organization. However, digitalization can bring risk that organizations and society need to deal with: unemployment, misuse, dominance, unbalanced societies, etc. This means intelligence needs to be developed for serving the well-being of humans to create solutions for multiple problems and to deal with the risks that are emerging from the new knowledge. Groups of risk can be organized by layers according to expected losses and impacts caused in society, in a time horizon, and according to how humans and machines are going to interact. The following are some examples:

Layer 1: Humanity risk: water supply reduction, overpopulation and weight of the earth, growth of environmental issues, e.g., global warming, unemployment, wrong use of technology or AI, use of weapons of mass destruction, imbalance of wealth and power in society through groups and organizations, space threats, e.g., impact of astronomical objects, pandemics, waste management, etc. All these strategic risks frame strategic decisions in the sense that organizations (private, public, and social) are looking to mitigate those risks. Decisions about product development, for instance, are related to use of packages that can create additional waste, use of sources of energy such as cars with batteries (lithium, nickel, sodium, borophene, etc.), and how batteries can be disposed. These examples lead to the second layer of strategic risk that organizations face.

Layer 2: Socio-economic risks: This can be so wide such as thinking in the possibility to increase extreme economic powers, countries that can be with alliances dominators of human's life. It is possible to reflect in the Brexit case that at least three groups can modify or maintain balance in the world: North America, Europe, and Russia–China. It is possibly better to belong to a group like the EU than to be outside it because countries outside this group are more vulnerable to certain socio-economic threats. Similarly, societies are exposed to a lack of services in cities, which have limited capacity to support a good quality of living for citizens; moreover, changes in society can affect business performance. From the microeconomic point of view, strategic risks are associated with business bankruptcy, disruption, reputation, supply chain risks, energy use, employees turn over, and loss of knowledge.

Layer 3: Technological risks: There are cases when the management has been led by and based its decisions on best-selling books or others' ideas. The influence of this type of "fashion" in management creates issues for the development of people and machines, and the organization itself. Projects of data analytics and AI are built by blocks and require principles and steps of development with a vision that is reviewed in continuous manner, pointing to defined goals. A rigid view of what is valid today and a belief that is forever true are big issues; adaptation and calibration are required, but taking care of investing and leaving everything in the middle of projects development because of lack of clarity in what the transformations were looking for put at risk human actions in organizations. In the last 50 years, a lack of principle consistency and orientation created multiple issues in organizations: bankruptcies of companies that had once won prestigious awards for quality, changing from re-engineering to six sigma, lean analysis, and moving from analog to digital. Not everything is for everyone, and not everything that can improve businesses can be used in the same quantity and intensity.

Integration of conceptual models with knowledge creation and application are explained in the following chapters. The Knowledge Management Process in this book is important to understand because it is a link to structure the use of intelligence in creating solutions and support to making decisions under uncertainty. Knowledge is the mitigator of risk. Leoni *et al.* (2022) expressed that "Using a conceptual model validated using an empirical survey, the study sheds light on the relationships between AI, KMPs and SCR, as well as their impacts on MFP. In particular, the authors show the positive effects of the adoption of AI on KMPs, as well as the influence of KMPs on SCR and MFP. Finally, the authors demonstrate that KMPs act as a mediator through which AI affects SCR and MFP." The conceptual integration in the following chapters of concepts and ideas assumes that pillars of management are associated with good thinking, with principles of mathematical thinking, statistical thinking, and computational capacity under the business acumen is what keep potentially orientation for organizations.

The core of a data analytics project is the growing capacity to measure the impact of actions and processes, and to maintain the talent and human–machine interaction required for organizations. Human–machine interaction is changing, for example Google AutoML and similar options of predefined automated tasks that are performed by people and organizations such as creating models in Machine Learning to solve problems. The business environment could supply what talent development needs, upskilling, the same as maintaining challenges and providing opportunities to grow and learn; maintain management leaders showing the value of the data Analytics-AI and digitalization value, and so on. Those are examples of principles to mitigate risks in organizations; it is common to find that the new and fast-short life span management theories create confusion and lead to a loss of direction. Data science will change, digitalization will change, all aspects of technology will evolve, and adaptation will be part of the skillset and mindset to maintain growth in organizations.

This book is not comprehensive in the analysis of different types of strategic risks, but illustrates how the connection of strategic risk, intelligence development, and possible digitalization strategies can help to mitigate the impact of risk, control risk, monitor risk, and predict risk, during and after an adverse event. The reader will find an introduction to the current world of this discipline that contemplates the administration of companies immersed in a system that requires risk to be studied and managed in an organized manner and with strategic vision. To begin with, it is established that organizations seek to reduce the risk they run in their businesses and optimize their administration, but organizations will always live under risk, because they will not be able to reduce risk to zero.

Principles to study risk

A question in the study of strategic risk is how strategic risk coverage can be obtained. The answer is data-driven organizations. Coverage of risk is a data-driven decision and, as McKinsey (2022) noted, there are organizations using data for strategic and tactic movements. Data are assets that management and machines are taking care of to improve usage. Data potentially support the prediction of adverse events, and the selection of mitigators of risk will generate coverage that can be appropriate for good business performance. In strategic risk, the coverage of risk is about the organization's capacity to create the means to mitigate the potential losses of their operations. There is third-party coverage to certain strategic risks, but that is not enough. Risk Management and Enterprise Risk Management (ERM) are capabilities that create strategic competitive advantage for organizations. It is also considered that risk management seeks to control the value impact of potential losses, understood as loss reduction of value caused by the variation of an expected economic result. Losses may occur due to damage, socio-economic conditions, environment and natural, or other multiple factors. Organizations seek to protect themselves from these losses to which they are exposed by using insurance, derivative contracts, CDS (Credit Default Swaps), or self-funding their possible results. It is also assumed that companies are interested in covering risks to property, responsibilities, life, economy, price, interest rates, exchange rates, etc.

Within the perspective that arises in this book, it is considered that agents intervene in the process of managing the risk; reinsurers, insurers, financial institutions, technology organizations, governments, multilateral organizations, the owner of the risks, and several more are related because of coverage of the owner of the risk through contracts, which will have to be recognized as a premium in return. In strategic risks, business interruption insurance coverage exists, but strategic risks are mostly self-covered. In the cases of using derivative contracts made on an underlying asset that can be shares, bonds, tradable goods, indices, etc., hedges with derivatives use the contract to assume the risk and pay a contract price.

This book presents different conditions and ways in which risk is made explicit and its relationship with the success of a strategy in an organization. A balance has been observed between risks that affect the liabilities and assets of an organization and risks that can be applied both in the financial and industrial manufacturing fields. However, there is a greater emphasis on some points in the presentation of the book with reference to the banking business because of its development of risk management, digitalization, and the use of data analytics and AI. It is essential to emphasize that risk management and functional responsibility in a banking organization cannot be generated only in studying credit, which is a very narrow vision of all the development and control that must be carried out to reduce the loss in an entity of such high exposure. Banking risks include credit, liquidity, interest rate, market, foreign currency exchange, solvency, operation, physical resources, and human resources.

In general, an approach in strategic risk analysis uses the concept of portfolios: portfolios of markets, products, promotion, investments of technologies, etc. At present, the processes of portfolio management and asset and liability management are moving side by side, which simplifies portfolio analysis; the same must be done with credit and to ensure that the gap between assets and liabilities is as small as possible. All this within the perspective which establishes that to achieve a sustainable competitive advantage in organizations requires the possibility of controlling future imbalance in cash flow, which can only be done through adequate risk management, in order to manage an income and profits according to the organization's goals.

Other factors that risk analytics represents in this book are as follows:

(1) Risk analytics is a process that moves both from top to bottom and bottom to top in organizations. It requires political processes but also an understanding of the operation.
(2) Risk management is associated with all the functions of the organization; it is not a single problem of a single area, it is a general problem that is controlled centrally but is handled by areas of responsibility.
(3) There are different dimensions in portfolio management that contemplate the optimization of return as well as concentration, allocation of resources, and development of technologies to maintain an adequate information system.
(4) Risk management cannot be separated from the management of assets and liabilities, just as the relationship between business units, transfers, risks in resource allocation, and development of performance evaluation systems must be considered.
(5) Measurement systems require the construction of indicators, functions of distribution of probability of losses, calculations of variation, structuring of databases, creation of models, and an objective culture of risk that allows segmenting and directing of marketing efforts to find consumers and products most appropriate to fulfill the expectations of utility of the entity.

With this structure and foundation, it is possible to guides the reader to improve intelligence in organizations based on risk analytics. No traditional risk management is an orientation of strategic development, identifying and using critical variables of success that have always been latent. In a vast majority, variables are latent due to the administrative myopia, focusing on leaving organizations without structure in the short term to deal with risks that are not evident in the present.

Many risks influence decisions and operations at the same time in organizations

Some authors have presented the main concepts of risk management in financial institutions relating risks to avoid, transfer or manage, risk management goals, and communication challenges (Olfield & Santomero, 1997). To further organize the problem definition and scope of risk management and from that definition to seek solutions according to the risk and its relationship with the organization's risk processes have to be defined to act and create intelligence. One example is risk identification and assessment. In risk management related to the risk transfer, one can concentrate on the risks in which the company has competitive advantages and avoid the focus on minimizing non-relevant risks. Another example is to identify the actions of financial institutions and relate them to the risks to which they are part of the risk appearance and possibly impacted in case of adverse events emerge. It can start with risk analysis of a basic financial services organization, that deals with distribution, services, packaging, intermediation, and market generators. Those risks will be connected to threats that arise from systemic risk from changes in interest rates, prices of tradable goods, credit risk, transportation, and operational and legal risk. In a risk management system, it is necessary to establish standards and reports, impose positions, limits and rules, define investment guidelines, and relate incentive and compensation schemes. Some authors have presented the principal concepts of risk management in financial organizations as risks to avoid, transfer, or manage, the goals in risk management, and the challenges in communication.

These points show that, to the extent that financial institutions become more sophisticated as well as the markets in which they operate and that appear with a greater number of participants, they will produce new challenges of risk analytics, such as the following:

(1) Risk management should be comprehensive in the organization's business plan.
(2) Organizations must define the specific risks of each of the activities and develop ways to measure them.
(3) An organization should establish procedures such that risk management begins at the closest point to risk assumption.
(4) An organization must develop databases and measurement systems according to the way the business is oriented.

Kessler (2001) indicated that the risks of the 21st century, and how to anticipate and manage them, are associated with demographic changes in fertility and mortality, environmental changes, and new production systems. With each improvement in new technologies, specific risks are emerging. The universe of risks expands and the risks of nature have radically changed, leading to the requirement of new risk management techniques. The rate at which new risks appear is higher than the rate at which existing ones disappear. Kessler pointed out six factors in the process of risk expansion:

(1) New technologies
(2) New economic activities
(3) Accumulation of risks
(4) The service company has a poor relationship with the subject
(5) Economic and financial globalization
(6) Emergence of new epidemics worldwide

It is also important to note that risk management has to be conducted and the relationship between industrial and financial risks has to be assessed. Zech (2001) presented the following steps as part of an effective risk management process:

(1) Risk assessment
(2) Risk control
(3) Risk finance
(4) Administration and operation
(5) Risk communication

Risk management process development helps to concentrate the efforts of risk impact understanding that will connect risk and intelligence creation as indicated in the following paragraphs.

Connecting risk and intelligence in organizations

A first point is to observe three components of the topics presented in this book: first, identification of potential relationships of strategic intelligence creation through data analytics and AI, explaining the related theory; second, presenting exhibits with a mix of conceptual models and quoted pieces of observations and research results of multiple authors that open one's eyes to what is a risk and data analytics mindsets; and third, presentation of examples in the practice of cases of what is happening, has happened, and potentially will happen to organizations and the society. The content ahead reviews strategy concepts associated with the way to identify an organization as a system and how risks are present in the system components. In particular, the summary of concepts in this book takes into consideration several schools of strategy analysis and definitions of organizations:

(1) Strategy concepts
(2) Images of Organizations
(3) About Risk Management

Strategic risk is a complex concept given the extremely large number of factors interacting to create uncertainty and risks in organizations. Bankruptcies can come from many causes and there are unexpected results in organizations that were apparently covered. Examples include such as the Monitor consulting companies that was an experts in strategy but advised many organizations to file for bankruptcy, some of the biggest corporations in the world that filed for bankruptcy (GM, AIG, Lehman Brothers, etc.), and the owners of original and powerful organizations that created disruptive technology (BlackBerry, Nortel, etc.). Furthermore, strategic risks related to obsolescence or external risks, such as environmental, national, and security, are modifying business opportunities, limiting, in multiple cases, the chances to adapt and sustain strategies that provide benefits to stakeholders.

A connecting idea in the whole presentation of the topic is about the balance between compliance and conviction of using risk management as a pillar to build strategy and maintain capacity, creating capabilities to lead organizations that evolve sustainable competitive advantage under uncertainty. Conviction in developing risk management as strategic tool for organizations is a very important component in dealing with the top-down development of the path to follow in organizations and the bottom-up development to create what is required to lead strategic implementation. Intelligence will be present in the adaptation process of an evolving business environment that creates capabilities to achieve what the stakeholders desire.

A first step in this book to connect concepts of risk and intelligence is to align the understanding of an organization. This understanding is independent of the economic sector or activity, and it requires one to identify the strategy framework, to differentiate the strategic views and organization definition, and to observe how the organization's definition will affect all the analytics steps. Concepts such as Balanced Scorecard and Enterprise Risk Management lead to organizations being described as entities where there are four components: consciously coordinated work, social entities, identifiable boundaries, and goals (Robbins, 1990). These components are identified in various ways. For example, Etzioni (1964) defined organizations as "... social units (or human groupings) deliberately constructed and reconstructed to seek specific goals." Daft (1992) described organizations as "...social entities that are goal-directed, deliberately structured activity systems with an identifiable boundary."

Organization design (Stanford, 2007) is required to define how an organization will operate. One of the points of organization design is provide control (Burton & Obel, 1995). Control refers mainly to the process of observing how business processes are performing to convert resources into outcomes that an organization wants to achieve. Another point is work coordination given the need to support multidisciplinary and interdepartmental work in an organization, or as Burton and Obel (1995) state, "basically, organizations are formed to achieve a set of goals. For cost efficiency the work in the organization may be divided into a number of separate tasks. To obtain common goals the activities must be coordinated." Moreover, the purpose in the organization in moving from theory to actions is presented by Tsoukas and Knudsen (2003) and indicates that knowledge is converted into actions through the implementation of what is called the action cycle in an organization: diagnosis, invention, production, and evaluation. This action cycle goes from discovering a problem to evaluating the production of the solution (Argyris, 2003). Additionally, Alavi and Leidner (2001) considered organizations as interactions between people, environment, and knowledge systems, and introduced knowledge management processes as part of the organization design. Thus, organizational design is the "outcome of shaping and aligning all the components of an enterprise towards the achievement of an agreed mission" (Stanford, 2007).

Supplementing the previous view, Bolman and Deal (2003) took into consideration organizational components, the complexity of articulation, and the need to stay productive in order to survive and compete: "an environment filled with complexity, surprise, deception, and ambiguity makes it hard to extract lessons for future actions. Yet an increasingly turbulent, rapidly shifting environment requires contemporary organisations to learn better and faster just to survive." The analytics view was expressed as follows: "Organizations often struggle with how to formalize and communicate strategy so that employees understand which initiatives and objectives are key to the organization's success and how they can influence outcomes. Unfortunately, operating units tend to act in silos, which puts them at risk for misinterpreting strategic direction and, consequently, focusing on disconnected initiatives and inappropriate metrics."

One of the strategic risks is created because of issues in technology adoption, much like in data analytics and AI adoption, given the multiple barriers to overcome to provide value in organizations. On the one hand, alignment of priorities and goals of operating units can be in conflict with other areas, creating issues in resource allocation and difficulties in developing capabilities to support adaptive and sustainable competitive advantages. On the other hand, adoption is associated with how often and appropriately feedback is provided in an organization to share with analytics people about operations, customers, markets, plans, and strategies to be proactive rather than reactive. The process of preparing the organization based on reviewing what has been achieved is a component of creating intelligence using data analytics, measurement, and creation of metrics that can be understood and followed during the operation of the organization. In a complementary note, the SAS Fact Sheet indicated, "An executive team starts with a strategy that they believe has validity and worth; but without using statistical analysis, it could take months or even years before a flaw is uncovered, leading to unnecessary losses or reduced profitability. When you can't prove whether a strategy is working and which metrics and objectives are truly important, you risk following a flawed strategy with an incomplete mix of metrics."

The connection of strategic risk, strategic intelligence, and digital transformation is embedded in the definition of the business: Who, What, and How. Risk is the capacity to manage the business (Abell, 1980) in the intersection of the work (What — organization's offer) that people–machines do in the organization to satisfy the needs of the customers (Who — stakeholders) using different technologies (How — from production and delivery to payment methods). Intelligence is about the capacity development in each dimension and the capability to satisfy each dimension's needs. Digital transformation is when the three dimensions are changing to use digital technology. In the concepts ahead, the offer of the organization is defined as the connection of at least content (basic product definition), distribution channel conditions, and markets. This means that is not the same product or service to have the offer of toothpaste products, in units of one or units of dozens, with access online using delivery to home or in a store or any variation that digitalization can offer. This means any aspect of the three dimensions of business definition can modify the market offer. In that regard, evaluation and prediction of what organizations do bring about questions about performance management, that is, what tools and methods will support the journey to achieve what is desired by the organization: BSC, Six Sigma, etc., are not complete. There is a need to review the performance based on risk management about what affects the company performance and how to control and develop strategy based on uncertainty and risk.

The Balanced Scorecard (BSC) is one of the methods that organizations use for identifying results and designing strategy. The methodology of BSC was introduced by Kaplan and Norton (1992) by identifying four perspectives to balance performance evaluation: financial, processes, customer, and learning and development. Wegmann (2008) pointed out that the balanced scorecard is a means to support knowledge management, and Sears (2009) integrated concepts of Lean Six Sigma into the balanced scorecard, thereby supporting knowledge transfer. Additionally, the BSC has been applied to social organizations; for instance, Tardivo and Viassone (2010) summarize the application of the concepts of balanced scorecard to social assistance organizations. The BSC has been used as a means to understand the intellectual capital value for organizations. Boda *et al.*'s (2008) review of intellectual capital measurement systems opens a way to analyze the risk measure based on the changes of the expected results in the BSC. Additionally, Matin *et al.* (2010) pointed out that the balanced scorecard adds value in the knowledge sharing process when organizational objectives and people are matched, identifying roles and responsibilities. Keyes's (2005) approach of applying BSC to the IT area of the organization guides the identification of components that are required in the design of the BSC for service and realization of benefits for the users.

Review of Strategy Concepts and Organization's Brain

This section starts the strategy introduction to understand what an organizational brain is trying to do. The presentation of the terms of risk and risk management will be identified and organized based on the understanding of the concepts of strategic risk and operational risk. With that purpose, the understanding about strategy is required to present organizations as systems where risk management and analytics work will be part of the system control and orientation to achieve the goals. Strategy definitions will be used in the book as Alfred Chandler indicated, namely, that the identification of goals, actions, and resources used to achieve the goals defines the organization's strategy. Besides, Michael Porter indicated that a competitive strategy as a mix of activities in organizations provides value, maintaining differentiation. Another aspect is strategy study, which was conducted in a review of several schools by Mintzberg (1998) as presented in his work on the *Strategy Safari*. The following are his results:

- Design: planned perspective, cerebral, simple and informal, judgmental, deliberate — Selznick.
- Planning: plans decomposed into substrategies and programs, formal, decomposed, deliberate — Ansoff.
- Positioning: planned generic positions, analytical, systematic, deliberate — Schendel, Hatten, Porter.
- Entrepreneurial: personal, unique perspective, niche, visionary, intuitive, largely deliberate — Schumpeter.
- Cognitive: mental perspective, mental emergent, descriptive — Simon.
- Learning: patterns, unique, emergent, informal — Lindblom, Cyert, and March, Prahalad and Hammer.
- Power: political and cooperative patterns and positions, conflictive, aggressive — Allison, Pfeffer, and Salancick, Astley.
- Cultural: collective perspective, ideological, constrained, collective — Rheman and Normann.
- Environmental: specific positions, generic, passive, imposed, emergent — Hannan and Freeman.
- Configuration: any to the left, in context, integrative, episodic, sequenced — Chandler, Mintzberg.

In any of the possible views of strategy connecting and understanding organizations as systems lead to connect Intelligence with Morgan's (1997) work in the Images of the Organizations where he indicated about organizations as:

- Machines: mechanical thinking, bureaucratic.
- Organisms: discovering organizational needs, organization as an open system, adapting organization to the environment.
- Brains: information processing brains, creating learning organizations.
- Cultures: culture, shared reality, cultures and subcultures.
- Political systems: government and political systems.

- Psychic prison: trap of favored ways of thinking.
- People trapped by their own thoughts, ideas, and beliefs.
- Flux and transformation: rethinking relations with the environment, interaction as projection of themselves.
- Instruments of dominion: use and exploit employees, organization, class, control.

Morgan's view in his book is related to the perspective of organizations as organisms, brains, cultures, and flux and transformation. Data analytics and AI act in the brain and can be observed as a way to maintain the neuroplasticity of the "organization's brain." Data analytics and AI will provide opportunities to reorganize and develop the organization's components in new ways to maintain the aim to achieve goals. To start the strategic analysis, Exhibit I.1 provides a set of variables that will lead to a path to find data and relationships among those variables to build intelligence using data analytics, i.e., Machine Learning and AI.

With the previous concepts of organizations as systems, and identifying a brain, strategy, and "mind" in organizations, the next section is about basics of risk management.

Factors to review and organize guidelines for strategy formulation using intelligence systems:	Opportunity, Threat,Strength, Weakness, Score, Objective, Priority, Result
Current Organization • Main characteristics of the company • Suitability of the organization vis-à-vis the market • Marketing approach to business planning • Conducting market research • Customer relationship structure • Customer Awareness • Organized product development • Proper marketing organization • Strategy definition process • Communication process • Operational capacity • Adaptability to change • Knowledge system • Development of customer-oriented business processes • Production quality	**Production times** • Labor relations • Business atomization • Government Relations • Utility Center Development • Deepening in the client • Suppliers • Relationship with suppliers • Qualification system • Negotiation skills • Follow-up with suppliers

Exhibit I.1. Review of components to analyze in strategy formulation.

Target customers' people and organizations • Family • Large industry • Medium Industry • Medium-sized industry • Small industry • Employees • Merchants • Commerce • Freelancer • Foreigner natural person ---	**Substitutes** • Positioning • Importance • Market coverage • Quality • Volume • Development capacity • Acceptance • Development of the offer
How the relationship with the client is • Knowledge of the client's profile • Knowledge of customer potential • Knowledge of customer's buying habits • Sufficient level of services offered • Goodness of communication with the client • Information provided • Opportunity for care • Problem-solving capability	**Services** • Before purchase • After purchase • At purchase • Variety of offer
Operation • Conditions of the company's activity • Product Development • Customer Information System • Control Information System • Marketing Information System • Executive Training • Quality middle management • Business Training • Compensation of employees • Construction of information bases	

Exhibit I.1. (*Continued*)

About Risk Management

This section introduces risk management practice and it is supplemented in Chapter 1 with a more theoretical approach. The presentation of the topics given the interest in strategic risk is based on the vision of Enterprise Risk Management (ERM). The most generally accepted frameworks (COSO 2004, Conference Board of Canada 2003, Treasury Board of Canada 2001 & 2004, and Basel II, III Agreements) used for ERM implementation include guidelines that can be followed through implementation of risk processes. Brown (2001) describes the risk management processes as follows:

- Risk identification: This process refers to the group of actions developed in the organization to classify and map risks that can affect the organization in their current and expected business conditions.
- Risk measurement: Quantification and assessment of risk are important actions in RM, particularly the capacity to provide evaluation of the impact, frequency, and severity of risks in the business operation.
- Risk monitoring: These sets of actions represent the capacity to follow up on what has been designed for managing risks.
- Risk Control: This represents the capacity to evaluate and assure the adequacy of the RM actions, such as risk mitigation, risk transfer, and, in general, risk alignment of the policies and strategy.
- Risk application: Policies and solutions for the business processes and the required conditions to keep risk effects under control.

Additionally, in this book, a risk analytics process is considered as acting across all the risk management processes to create predictive, descriptive, and prescriptive models based on analysis of the vast amounts of data enterprise-wide and to support mitigation, control, assessment, etc., of risk. Risk analytics is a constant factor affecting the whole risk management process. The methods of dealing with risk are related to the organization's definition of business processes and strategy. Strategic actions and their evaluation of the contribution to the goal achievement are ongoing processes in organizations. All strategic initiatives are affected by risks, and organizations perform multiple activities to control these risks. Risk is differentiated from uncertainty in the sense that risk is at least assuming probability distributions to describe behavior of the variables and events, and uncertainty is no knowledge at all of the behavior of variables and events. At the same time, data are a source to support risk management practice functionality based on the data available and the identification of futures that the organization seeks to achieve. Risk is considered in the book as part of the strategic process and how Key Performance Indicators (KPIs) and Key Risk Indicators (KRIs) will be related in a good risk control. There is an assumption in the whole book that was mentioned earlier: risk management is converted into a strategic capacity in organizations that provides sustainable competitive advantages. The conceptual models in this book point to (Dicuonzo *et. al.*, 2021) risk mitigation supported by the use of regular and big data analytics in the risk management processes. However, in this book, the focus is on how strategic risk is mitigated or increased because of the limited use or misuse of strategic intelligence through data analytics or AI, and when it is appropriate or inappropriate to adopt digital transformation. The purpose is to support what an organization requires to perform well when competing in a market, such as the use of digitalization or a step forward when it is convenient to move in the direction of complete digital transformation. There is a reality that programs to improve efficiency lead decisions because digital leaders outperform their peers in nearly every industry. Ramesh & Delen (2021) indicated that organizations are spending around $1.3 trillion on digital transformation. However, efficiency improvement of digital transformations has not been successful in 90% of projects, creating negative impact in the performance of organizations and in some cases reducing capacity to innovate. In the same vein, Block (2022) in *Forbes* pointed out, "According to McKinsey, BCG, KPMG and Bain & Company, the risk of failure falls somewhere between 70% and 95%."

Figure I.1 represents the way that the loop goals of the organization, data analytics-AI, and intelligence. Figure I.1 also represents the way in which the loop goals of the organization, data analytics and AI, and intelligence creation are moving to mitigate strategic risk and maintain the organization in good shape, adapting and competing in the markets according to the circumstances that are emerging. However, risks and strategic risks are possible to predict in several cases but big decisions and many risk long tails of distribution of risk events are difficult to study. At the same time, certain risks are not possible to identify or predict, or to estimate impact in case of occurrence. In general, a rule to adopt in management is that variables that are not controllable should be kept in the administration radar, one should work on resilience in case events occur, and one should concentrate efforts on prediction and control of risks that are not black swans. Black swans and other risks coming from fashions, waves, or management are crises and failures of different types that have similar failure causes. Risk management and

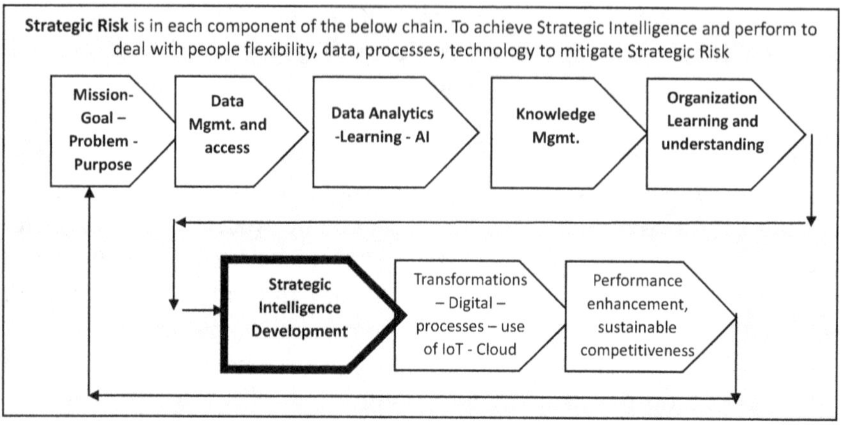

Figure I.1. Conceptual sequence to connect organization's goals and strategic intelligence through data analytics and AI use. Risk and performance.

digital transformation have similarities such as dedicated time to mathematical sophisticated models and less to assumptions understanding, learning from experience and experts in other knowledge domains to validate beliefs, and limited identification of how market conditions in risk management are connected to technology and not people development. Davenport & Westerman (2018) mentioned that "It happened with e-commerce, when companies like Staples and Walmart invested heavily in separate e-commerce units, only to have those units drain the company of resources. It happened with analytics and big data, when companies like Sears and Zynga invested millions in creating analytics units that never paid back their investments. And now it's happening with digital transformation."

In summary, Chapter 1 explains how to understand strategic risk, and the framework of general risk management, and how the concept of monitoring risk is crucial at the level of integration of all areas across the organization. The aim is to point out the concepts generated by intelligence improvement and solution implementation to mitigate strategic risks. In Chapter 2, the process of moving from business intelligence to strategic intelligence is presented where the crucial part is integration of human and machine intelligence to enable action transformations in organizations. Chapter 3 reviews the connection between data and analytics and digitalization, mainly from the perspective of what the data analytics process is and how models help to disclosure possible futures of the organization. Chapter 4 is dedicated to summarizing concepts related to techniques and technologies required in intelligence development and action implementation — everything from the perspective of strategy and not including all details of analytics techniques, but indicating the potential value that the technique can bring. Finally, Chapter 5 is about the challenges in this chain process of data analytics, intelligence, and action transformation to mitigate strategic risk, mainly paying attention to the business environment, internal and external, based on the human–machine interaction.

Cases for Reflection about Digital Transformation and Strategic Risks

A review of concepts in the book brings to the mind reflections about three different observations that appeared in real cases: First, certain organizations have been successful in digital transformation, while some are reporting failures but tried again and succeeded in most cases (Exhibit I.2). Second, it is important to identify what organizations are doing in the digitalization atmosphere. Not all are changing the business model but are adjusting their business dimensions to supplement the current know-how to move to learning and development of new capabilities (Exhibit I.3). Third, make note of examples of experiences with barriers and enablers to support organizations, because implementation and adoption of data analytics in organizations is a continuous process to develop analytics mindsets.

Exhibit I.3 contains a summary of points to discover digitalization initiatives in organizations of several areas, with three examples indicating the variety of possible digital solutions that mitigate strategic risk. In IKEA, creating distribution centers to be more accessible to customers; in AIRASIA, creation of a super-app that integrates many services; and in H&M, promoting the use of digital tools to provide service to customers in and out the store.

As a final point in this introduction, this book explains that experiences with management paradigms are always with barriers and enablers (Exhibit I.4). What is a constant is to manage under

Organizations	Failures	Success
Procter and Gamble		Thor Olavsrud, CIO. September 30, 2022: "In summer 2022, P&G sealed a multiyear partnership with Microsoft to transform P&G's digital manufacturing platform. The partners say they will create the future of digital manufacturing by leveraging the industrial internet of things (IIoT), digital twin, data, and AI to bring products to consumers faster and increase customer satisfaction, all while improving productivity and reducing costs." "The company has already undertaken pilot projects in Egypt, India, Japan, and the US that use Azure IoT Hub and IoT Edge to help manufacturing technicians analyze insights to create improvements in the production of baby care and paper products. For instance, the production of diapers involves assembling many layers of material at high speed with great precision to ensure optimal absorbency, leak protection, and comfort." "P&G is also piloting the use of IIoT, advanced algorithms, machine learning (ML), and predictive analytics to improve manufacturing efficiencies in the production of paper towels. P&G can now better predict finished paper towel sheet lengths.

Exhibit I.2. Observations of bad times in organizations trying to move to digitalization–digital transformation.

		Smart manufacturing at scale is a challenge. It requires taking data from equipment sensors, applying advanced analytics to derive descriptive and predictive insights, and automating corrective actions." From the CIO at P&G Mr. Vittorio Cretella, "We leverage AI across all dimensions of our business to predict outcomes and increasingly to prescribe actions through automation." "We have applications in our product innovation space, where thanks to modelling and simulation we can shorten the lead time to develop a new formula from months to weeks; in the way we engage and communicate with our consumers, using AI to deliver to each of them brand messages delivered at their right time, right channel, and with the right content." Guy Peri, Chief Data & Analytics Officer, P&G, pointed out, "In order for P&G to understand and best serve consumers, we need to drive a data-enabled culture and operationalize algorithms into every major business decision." https://customers.microsoft.com/en-us/story/1402016901008352804-procter-and-gamble-consumer-goods-azure

Exhibit I.2. (*Continued*)

Hewlett Packard		Form https://www.hpe.com/us/en/what-is/digital-transformation.html "As a recognized global leader, HPE delivers the expertise and experience to quickly implement digital transformations that efficiently adapt to rapid change. We help customers transform how they conduct their businesses by making their edge more intelligent and connecting it to the rest of the organization. Customers can then take advantage of this intelligence and create better experiences in the workplace — both for employees and customers." "HPE helps you to create a more intelligent edge with the following services: • Networking services: Build a communications fabric to support secure and efficient delivery of business outcomes. • Digital workplace services: Define how your employees and customers engage and conduct business. • Internet of Things services: Leverage data gathered from "things" on the edge to solve business problems."
Haribo	From James Sanders in Digital Transformation, January 15, 2019 https://www.techrepublic.com/article/how-a-troubled-sap-s4hana-migration-caused-a-gummy-bear-shortage-in-germany/ "German confectionery maker and gummy bear creator Haribo faced production constraints and missed deliveries to supermarkets due to a turbulent migration to SAP S/4HANA, according to a report in Handelsblatt.	

Exhibit I.2. (*Continued*)

	The unhappy IT department of Haribo began transitioning to S/4HANA in October 2018, converting 16 candy factories spread across 10 countries away from the heterogenous enterprise resource planning systems used in each region-some of which dated back to the 1980s."	
Hershey's	These are the three mistakes that led to the failure of ERP Solution. Hersheys ERP fail Source https://www.dfsm.com.au/erp-implementation-failure-a-case-study-2020/ "The operational team of Hershey's made a terrible mistake of sacrificing systems testing for the sake of convenience. So, no issues came into attention. By the time they get to know, it was too late. If you want to provide real-time experience to your clients, you must sure real-time testing process too. Second mistake of textbook implementation mistake. They tried to squeeze a complex ERP system into a short timeline. When you implement anything new, it demands some effort and not giving it the needed attention and effort is the sole reason for any kind of failure. So, it was an easy way to fail. The third mistake was to time the cutover period in a busy season. Halloween is the season of candy, and the staff was not trained for the ERP at that time. Hershey's ignored the fact and didn't reduce their orders. So, the ultimate reason for the failure was the non-qualified team as they were not proficient, but had to meet the deadlines and orders.	Michelle Buck, CEO, The Hershey Company: "We've been able to learn, frankly, from how some players went into that space and perhaps got into some issues where they weren't maximizing margins." "The consumer's shopper journey is not one of offline or online, it is interwoven, and so that's a place that we're very much focused." "The consumer wants, the consumer shops and the consumer buys. One constant is, there is a shelf, there is a basket and there's a checkout." Reported by Kate Silver https://www.thehersheycompany.com/en_us/home/newsroom/blog/hershey-shares-sweet-future-of-digital-commerce-with-analysts.html

Exhibit I.2. (*Continued*)

	Other than Hershey, Vodafone ERP implementation failure can also be used as a case study."	
Miller Coors	Josh Fruhlinger, Peter Sayer, and Thomas Wailgum, 12 famous ERP disasters, dustups and disappointments, CIO November 7, 2022 "In 2014, MillerCoors was running seven different instances of SAP's ERP software, a legacy of the years of booze industry consolidation that had produced the alcohol behemoth. The merged company hired Indian IT services firm HCL Technologies to roll out a unified SAP implementation to serve the entire company. Things didn't go smoothly: The first rollout was marked by eight "critical" severity defects, 47 high-severity defects, and thousands of additional problems recorded during an extended period of "go-live hypercare." By March 2017 the project had gone so far south that MillerCoors sued HCL for $100 million, claiming HCL had inadequately staffed the project and failed to live up to its promises."	
Revlon	In 2018, digital transformation was not going well. "Lessons learned: It has been cited that insufficient resource planning and internal collaboration had led to problems in change management that impacted this particular DX exercise. Other failures included lack of contingency plans to mitigate DX and related business risks; and ineffective management of the transition from their old infrastructure to the new ERP platform."	Stuart Lauchlan, August 10, 2021, Diginomica: "Back in February Debra Perelman, Revlon's President and Chief Executive Officer, talked up the importance of the firm's e-commerce efforts: Our net sales from e-commerce represent approximately 13% of our total net sales and grew 5% versus prior year quarter…Both North America and EMEA regions had double-digit e-commerce

Exhibit I.2. (*Continued*)

	From https://www.dfsm.com.au/4-lessons-learned-from-revlons-sap-implementation-disaster/ "Revlon revealed a couple of weeks ago that it was terrible to enforce its SAP. It was due to the inability to enforce the SAP that delayed financial reporting. Within 24 hours of publishing the story, its stock decreased 6.9%, triggering an investor's lawsuit. Not good for a well-established consumer product business, especially for publicly traded companies." "Revlon reported a lack of design as one of the problems behind the failure of ERP. As a result of its internal controls, the company suffered "material weaknesses."" "Revlon also announced that: In addition to a breakdown in its North Carolina Plant's operational controls and production problems." "Revlon endured delays in shipment and missed sales in North Carolina due to the production interruptions – the site of the first phase of its SAP live service." "Revlon clarified that they could impact their competitive position if such disruptions continue. Their client relationships, prospects, financial conditions, and cash flow may also influence them."	growth as did our elizabetharden.com business, which grew 25% over prior year quarter…We continue to focus on driving growth in this channel including across our own platforms, peer players and retailer dot com partners." Sharon Goldman July 23, 2021, businessinsider.com "Revlon began driving bigger investments in digital technologies related to e-commerce and social channels while moving away from a primary focus on the in-store retail experience, which had dropped off during the pandemic. The marketing organization also revamped its in-house creative team with a digital-first mindset, to test and learn on new platforms such as Clubhouse, a growing audio social network, as well as TikTok, which exploded during the pandemic."

Exhibit I.2. (*Continued*)

Nike	This is assignment of student Fioravanti (2020), Nike: Just do it. Differently!, Apr 30 "Just like many other companies in the consumer and fashion industry, Nike was heavily affected by COVID-19 lockdown. As a global brand with 1,100 stores, Nike closed more than half of stores in China as early as February to protect its employees; and decided, by mid-march to close all stores in the US, as the virus started to spread in the country. Even for stores that remained opened, the foot traffic has declined significantly."	Noah Basky, Nike's Earnings Calls Provide A Winning Digital Transformation Playbook, Forbes, 2021, July 27: "For instance, Nike forecasts that by 2025, over 50% of its sales will be direct-to-consumer. That's a staggering shift for a company historically so reliant on retail distribution." "With direct sales and digital revenue now accounting for more than one-third of its $45 billion in annual sales, Nike's technology investments are clearly delivering." "On Nike's FY 2021 Q4 earnings call, Donahue highlighted, "At the center of our digital ecosystem is our suite of apps, which in Q4 reflected over 40% of our owned digital business. This is the result of deeper consumer connections, fueled by compelling product and content."
GE	"The company created impressive digital capabilities, labeling itself a "digital industrial" company, embedding sensors into many products, building a huge new software platform for the Internet of Things, and transforming business models for its industrial offerings. GE also went to work on transforming internal processes like sales and supplier relationships. Some performance indicators, including service margins, began to improve."	From GE Digital, "Better operate, analyze and optimize industrial businesses. Our mission is to bring simplicity, speed and scale to our customers' digital transformation with software that helps them to better operate, analyze and optimize their business." "GE Digital sees data differently. People who see data differently, see the world differently. We're transforming the future of industry with software - now." Example of product: "GE created Predix, the operating system for the Industrial Internet, to help enable the digital transformation journey.

Exhibit I.2. (*Continued*)

		Predix provides the technical foundation necessary to power industrial apps that capture, monitor, and analyze machine data in order to improve throughput, reduce unplanned downtime, and increase operational efficiency."
Lego	"Lego successfully implemented a new multi-functional enterprise platform and launched a number of popular digital products." "However, it wasn't until the COVID-19 lockdown that Lego's digital strategy really started to take flight. As the pandemic pushed children towards indoor, independent play activities, Lego's sales soured despite retail closures. According to reports, compared to the previous year, the company's revenue grew 7% to 15.7 billion Danish krone ($2.46 billion) from January to June 2020. And the growth didn't stop there. The following year, from January to June 2021, revenues increased by 46% to DKK23bn (£2.7bn) as consumer sales grew by 36% In late 2021, Lego announced they would be capitalizing on the growth and entering the next phase of their digital transformation by investing in digital platforms, products and ways of working. This includes opening "digital talent hubs" in Shanghai, Copenhagen, Billund and London."	""The entire Lego ecosystem is actually, I think, only at the beginning. So, it's less about just creating an e-commerce store or an online store. It is really about this entire digital ecosystem and creating that future. And that's a long-term journey, that's a 10-year journey … And we're just a couple of years into this," Lego CEO Niels B. Christiansen explained to reporters in September 2021." From Lego.com "The LEGO Group set to nearly triple size of digital team to accelerate digital transformation" "COPENHAGEN, April 21, 2022: The LEGO Group today announced it has opened a new digital office in Copenhagen to support its long-term digital ambitions. The office, one of four digital workspaces around the world, will be a base for up to 400 colleagues. Digital offices in Billund, London and Shanghai will also be expanded to accommodate the growing team which will nearly triple in size over a three year period to more than 1,800 globally."

Exhibit I.2. (*Continued*).

	Elizabeth Mixson (2022) https://www.intelligentautomation.network/resiliency/articles/a-look-at-legos-digital-revival	Chief Digital & Technology Office, Atul Bhardwaj said, "Our digital transformation is one of the single largest investments the LEGO Group will make in a generation. We've been blending physical and digital experiences for many years and are excited by our progress. But, we have big ambitions so are accelerating our investment and expanding our digital team."
Burberry		From https://www.burberryplc.com/en/news/brand/2021/a-digital-experience.html "Digital innovation is a cornerstone of our strategy and our ambition is to remain the digital pioneer in luxury, building on our robust foundations and credentials in this area. It was our strong digital infrastructure that enabled us to continue to generate excitement around our new collections despite the challenges imposed by the COVID-19 pandemic. In order to safeguard our people and our communities, we transformed our shows and presentations into digital events and enhanced the online Burberry retail experience. In doing so, we brought our brand to audiences all over the world." "Digital continued to be a driver of growth during the year, with lockdowns and COVID-19 restrictions accelerating the shift online. As well as increasingly being the first step in our customers' inspiration journey, Burberry.com offered a virtual shopping experience for customers unable to visit stores shut temporarily due to the pandemic.

Exhibit I.2. (*Continued*)

		We provided the same exemplary service that is a hallmark of shopping in our stores through virtual conversations with our Sales Associates, who were on hand to assist with styling and sizing advice. We also enhanced Burberry.com with engagement-building tools, including virtual events and exclusive digital content, and we increased personalisation."

Exhibit I.2. (*Continued*).

uncertainty and that the search for mitigation and control of risk is a goal that is behind any management action. Risk management has had issues in implementation and definitions, just like data analytics. Learning from experience is a mitigator of operational risks and in the same line as strategic risks. Common areas of causes of failure are identified in planning for changes using new paradigms, identifying the reason for using the new approaches, participation and support from the top management, alignment with what is important in the value chain development and creation of impact through a good performance. Hershey offered recommendations for organizations in the process of digital transformation based on their experiences of trying and failing toward success.

Organization	Digitalization area — specific step
IKEA	Reported by the Agility Effect https://www.theagilityeffect.com/en/case/how-ikea-is-stepping-up-its-digital-transformation/ "Ikea is pursuing a large-scale transformation. In May 2021, the Swedish furniture giant announced that it was building a vast warehouse spanning 72,000 m^2 on a 16 ha site located near the port of Limay-Porcheville in the Yvelines department in France for an investment of €120 million. This future distribution centre, set for commissioning in 2026, will mostly be dedicated to online sales." Thomas Stackpole (2021): "How does going digital change a legacy retail brand? According to Barbara Martin Coppola, CDO at IKEA Retail, it's a challenge of remaining fundamentally the same company while doing almost everything differently." Bonnet & Wade (2022), introduced the interview with Barbara Martin Coppola, IKEA's Chief Digital Officer: "The vision and mission were built around three core elements: How do we become more accessible? Given our traditional out-of-town locations. How do we continue to be affordable? Serving our wide base of customers from India to China, to Germany. How do we become planet-positive? Contributing to the sustainability of the world we operate in."
Air Asia	SEPANG, 22 September 2021 — "As airasia's rapid transformation into a digital travel and lifestyle group continues to gain strong momentum, the group's engineering arm Asia Digital Engineering (ADE), ground handling division Ground Team Red (GTR) and logistics venture Teleport, are set to soar to new heights, leveraging the new technology revolution through digitisation and data. AirAsia Group Berhad (AAGB) President, Aireen Omar, who oversees digital operations, said embracing the digital revolution and driving innovation is a core focus across the entire airasia portfolio of companies." "While the pandemic has undoubtedly adversely affected our airline operations over the past 18 months, it has also reshaped consumer behaviour and we are really excited about the future of all of our digital businesses." "We're a group that continues to evolve based on consumer demand. A silver lining of COVID-19 has caused a huge surge in demand for cargo and online shopping deliveries and this is driving many new business opportunities and revenue streams. As a brand that has always had innovation in its DNA, we see huge potential, not only in our super app and fintech solutions, but also in our logistics, aircraft maintenance and ground services divisions."

Exhibit I.3. Looking for digitalization experiences.

	"Capital A (formerly known as AirAsia Group) is an investment holding company with a portfolio of synergistic travel and lifestyle businesses that leverage data and technology, including AirAsia Super App, fintech BigPay and logistics venture Teleport. Capital A's vision is to create and deliver products and services that focus on offering the best value at the lowest cost, underpinned by robust data accumulated over 20 years in operation and one of Asia's leading brands that remains committed to serving the underserved." "While our airasia Super App is already on track to become the platform of choice for everyday travel and lifestyle needs in ASEAN, ADE, is set to revolutionise the airline Maintenance, Repair and Overhaul (MRO) industry in Asia, our logistics venture Teleport is experiencing significant growth in line with overwhelming demand for cargo and online deliveries and GTR is preparing for strong regional expansion including with third party airlines as soon as travel restrictions ease and international borders reopen." From AIRASIA: "The AirAsia Super App is the one-stop travel, e-commerce and fintech platform business of Capital A offering consumers over 15 lines of products and services via the Super App as well as the airasia.com website. Powered by data and technology, the airasia Super App leverages its digital ecosystem of 51 million users and 40 million downloads to generate a personalised and seamless consumer experience. Users can also engage in real-time conversations, join like-minded communities, play games and much more. From travel needs to everyday lifestyle essentials, there is always something for everyone on the airasia Super App. Download AirAsia Super App via the Apple App Store, the Google Play Store and the Huawei App Gallery."
H&M	From the H&M Group corporate website: Helena Helmersson, CEO H&M Group, refers to "sustainability, AI and innovations in textile" as most important, when talking about H&M Group and rebuilding the industry of tomorrow. "Sustainability, AI and innovations in textiles are allowing us to rebuild the industry of tomorrow. This opens to lots of creativity and new opportunities. New technology allows us to engage even more with our customers and be more creative and fun. Who would have imagined a few years back that you would be able to scan yourself to get a pair of jeans with a perfect fit, especially made for you on-demand like the ones I am wearing today? That is now a reality." "In 2020, Alan Boehme was appointed Chief Technology Officer (CTO) at H&M Group."

Exhibit I.3. (*Continued*)

<table>
<tr><td></td><td>"Combining technology advancements will serve as a driver for H&M Group to become an even more customer-centric company where new growth opportunities are enabled. I'm excited about being part of accelerating H&M Group's digital transformation."
"H&M Group's human centered approach to tech is grounded in the company's heritage and values. Smart use of technology and data is integrated into everything the company does. H&M Group will continue, as we speak, providing its customers with a frictionless experience and empowering its designers and other employees, all the while using tech to make their operations more efficient, secure and sustainable."</td></tr>
<tr><td colspan="2" align="center">Pfizer
Integration business technology plan
Nitrex
Manufacturing
HEC
Teaching and Learning (Blackboard)
Bosch
Legal department
Estonia
E-government</td></tr>
</table>

Exhibit I.3. (*Continued*).

Risk Management issues • Mathematical models of only the truth, • Hubris without control, • Stubborn to change, • Limited orientation or silo based, no integral view, • Not understanding the success, • Believing the technology as the only crucial part of implementation, • Lack of risk monitoring — strategic.	Causes of failures in Analytics use (Strategy & PWC, 2012) Some common problem symptoms: • It is not clear which decisions need analytics and what decisions can have support from analytics (big decisions and less data, less analytics capacity in some dimensions). • There is no agenda-setting process for the development of big data. • The enterprise has big data capabilities but no consensus about how to use them. • Many decision processes are not driven by data, even with a big data system in place. • All facts come with a point of view — the data do not resolve differences of opinion.

Exhibit I.4. Risk and digitalization work together in the organization's evolution.

	• The IT department owns and manages the entire design process. • People with analytics talent are recruited but not enlisted in a strategic direction. • The enterprise does not retain those people. • The enterprise is still putting in place its success metrics for analytics talent. • Some departments "over-engineer" the processes; others "under-engineer" them.
Causes of failure in Digital transformation Davenport & Westerman (2018) and Davenport & Redman (2020) summarize the possible barriers/causes for good digital transformation projects: • Lost the support of top management, • no clear results, • CEO living in the process, which means losing the steward, • Reducing the funds.	Communalities of causes of failure: Lack of management support: bottom-up approach is not enough. Does top management really understand what new trends are using resources/technology, managing human and machine interactions, changes of customer habits, and needs of adaptation? Low integration and understanding across of the organizations of what is moving through the adoption of techniques, methods, and visions to be a smarter organization. Preparing people for changes, risk mitigation, acceptance of possible events, resilience, and proactivity to prepare the new steps in the strategy. Do things without a clear goal, problems to solve or how to evaluate when is good or bad the process and results of the adoption of new management perspectives-techniques-methods. To have expectations that are not realistic or with feet on the ground. Technology is a means to support strategy and adaptation but it is not the solution by itself.

Exhibit I.4. (*Continued*)

Recommendation for retailers in a digitalization process recommendations from Hershey's experience Kete Silver (https://www.thehersheycompany.com/en_us/home/newsroom/blog/6-tips-for-successful-digital-transformation.html) Six tips for successful digital transformation:

(1) The supermarket is not alone; it is a chain of steps in the decision of buying products, starting from the search on digital media to obtain the product in the store. The catalog and shelves in a store are extensions of one another.
(2) Integrate understanding of strategy in digital and physical spaces, permeating the full organization for good implementation and comprehension of what is required.
(3) Communication in terms of business orientation is always crucial but it has to be with clear observation of steps, barriers, and successes.
(4) Connecting the promotion with the distribution channels; all in the same boat; the media used for promotions with messages supporting both parts — producer and distributors.
(5) Close strategic experiences to support distribution channels, customer messages, and dealing with data at different levels, e.g., at producer and distribution levels, where customers have touch points.
(6) Go to the analytics process to have not only the proper data but also the appropriate analytics capacity.

Exhibit I.4. (*Continued*).

Chapter 1

Strategic Risk

This chapter is a theoretical presentation of risk concepts and it introduces the concept of risk, utility theory, risk aversion, and risk indicators construction. The general framework of risk management (RM) used in the book is aimed at managing the variability of the possible results of the company, especially in terms of developing data analytics, AI, and digitalization capabilities to mitigate and control risk. This chapter presents the concept of risk under a holistic view of the organization where it is possible to identify what strategic risk is and how to coordinate efforts to mitigate those identified strategic risks. The risk management processes are the roads to follow to obtain benefits of the risk efforts. In the coordination of efforts, utility theory helps to define where to find value. For example, this chapter presents how the coverage with insurance can be optimized, but at same time explains that there are more aspects to consider for protection–mitigation of the organization's risks. Risk management process development needs analytics tools, principles, and methods/techniques to deal with risk, to organize, and to align risk strategies with the business strategy. Strategic risk is presented in a joint explanation of what the organization needs to evaluate in its performance and how risk exists and is embedded in all organizations' activities. The end of the chapter presents examples on RM experiences and business process alignment.

1.1. Enterprise Risk Management (ERM)

The purpose of this section is to frame the analyses in the book using the Enterprise Risk Management (ERM) approach because of the need to study Strategic Risk as a risk of the whole organization when is exposed to multiple risks sources in the market-industry. Doumpos *et al.* (2023) pointed out that "We described six general topics that employ OR and AI methods to address various crucial banking issues: banking efficiency, risk management, bank performance, banking regulation, M&A, customer-based studies, and fintech in the banking industry. We also outlined the most widely used OR methods, including DEA, ABM, MC, fuzzy logic, and AI techniques, including SVMs, NNs, and ensemble methods." Banking by definition is a risk management and knowledge business that has a combination of digital and non-digital operations to perform well in the market. The number of applications and opportunities to develop capabilities in financial institutions is huge in areas such as RM; the same applies to other economic sectors. With these expectations of using AI and techniques in RM, the book is oriented to extend their practice to ERM. The study of ERM requires the understanding of the concept of risk, risk management processes, and the types of risks that are under multiple exposure conditions across the organization. In the following sections, a review of risk management concepts will be performed.

1.1.1 *The concept of risk*

The definition of the concept of risk has been a topic of discussion in multiple disciplines. Risk definition has been adapted to specific risk contexts where events can occur and that can modify what organizations and society are trying to do. Risk can be defined as the uncertainty that exists about whether an event will occur or not during a period and under certain conditions, reporting economic losses. Aven (2003) pointed out that risk is "the uncertainty about the world and uncertainty expressed by probabilities related to the observable quantities (Performance Measures)." For managers, the meaning of risk is more related to the concept of loss and there is no a clear identification of risk with the positive changes of performance (Tanriverdi & Ruefli, 2004). Tanriverdi and Ruefli (2004) define risk as the chance of loss and its magnitude; based on their analysis, they indicated, "In particular, we examine the notion that managerial interventions in the form of IT investments and activities can affect the risk/return profile of a firm. Such interventions would have the objective for a give level of return of reducing the chance of loss or the magnitude of loss-or both." They further note that "Risk, as chance and magnitude of loss, captures an aspect of performance that is not captured by return or by cost."

The Concise Oxford Dictionary (2008) defines risk as a "hazard, a chance of bad consequences, loss or exposure mischance." From scholars and practitioners such as McNeil *et al.* (2005), risk is "any event or action that may adversely affect an organisation's ability to achieve its objective and execute its strategies." Adding the quantitative component of risk to this definition, McNeil *et al.* (2005) say that risk is also "the quantifiable likelihood of loss or less-than-expected returns." McNeil *et al.* (2005) state that "any event or action that may adversely affect an organization's ability to achieve its objectives and execute its strategies." In that vein, Eppens *et al.* (1998) identified risk under the decision perspective and state that decisions under risk are those where it is possible to estimate the probability of the several states of nature that the decision-maker has to deal with. Likewise, risk has been defined as the variation of the possible returns or results that exist in a given economic situation. In addition, risk is the variation of the expected results under the conditions given in a period of time; it is considered that the variations are not necessarily in a final result but in the set of intervening variables that affect the result. In addition, the risk study involves the analysis of the consequences of the occurrence of the event, not limited only to the measure but to protection, prevention, and precaution in economic and social activities. In this book, risk is identified with the study of the variation (positive and negative results on what the organization is looking for and considers good performance) of expected results of factors influencing performance conditioned to previous knowledge.

Just as there are many possible definitions of risk, there are different types of agents and factors involved in risk analysis. Multiple risks and ways of analyzing them emerge according to any enterprise's activity, process, technology, and stakeholders. For instance, credit risk is possible to study according to operation, marketing, interest rates, and products, both for credit institutions and for insurance and industry. There are many kinds of risk that are involved in several actions and decisions in an organization. Van Greuning and Brajovic (2003) summarized the following kind of risks:

- Financial: credit, currency, market, capital, etc.
- Business: legal, regulatory, country, etc.
- Operational: fraud, damage, information, products, etc.
- Event: political, contagion, etc.

From the point of view of a risk study, the factors to consider are, on the one hand, the human–machine intelligence involved and, on the other hand, all the means and artifacts to analyze and manage risks. Individuals are classified according to their attitudes to risk in neutral; that is, when they keep their marginal utility constant, they are risk takers when marginal utility grows and risk adverse when marginal utility decreases. In each category, there are cases, such as investors who undertake risky projects for new businesses, which is a case of risk takers; but in the most generalized case, there is risk aversion in the business participants in industries. People will seek to reduce the possible variation of expected results in exchange for a payment for coverage, or additionally by the possible administration of the variables that optimize the process of selection and adoption of risk. Additionally, RM is a set of standardized methodologies, proven in many markets that also have their application at different levels of development of business results, as expected and their variations. However, quantitative risk management practices will never replace good common sense. This means there is a high requirement in the RM practice to answer the question of what good common sense is and how it could be complemented with the optimal risk assessment and mitigation.

Risk management must be objective independent and therefore able to define positions that can be different from the decision-making bodies. In case of conflict, the criteria of the risk manager must prevail (mistakes impact an organization more than successes). All activity is subject to risk; for example, accelerated growth in many cases exposes organizations to very large risk in almost all businesses. A risk study is through the RM process that has several subprocesses where data analytics can be involved and where the gains to an organization's intelligence and digitalization will be worth developing. Regarding these subprocesses of RM, Brown (2001) introduced a view of the processes such as risk identification, measurement, monitoring, control, and application, which is adopted in this book.

1.1.2 *Risk management processes*

In the introduction of this chapter, the definition of risk is identified and this definition is associated with the RM processes to follow. Brown's description of risk management processes is not unique and diverse

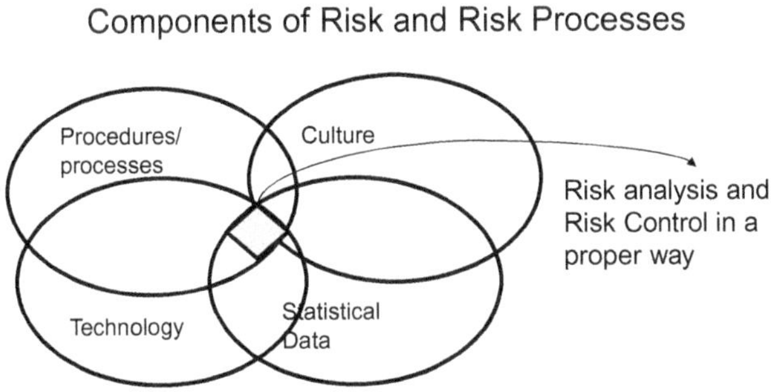

Figure 1.1. Intersection of factors for analysis of risk in an organization.

authors have included other descriptions. For example, Lam (2000) emphasizes governance, product line management, portfolio management, risk transfer, risk analysis, data technology resources, and shareholder management. Sharman (2002) indicates that the risk management processes are focused on strategy design, structure design, portfolio analysis and optimization, and measuring, and monitoring. Figures 1.1 and 1.2 show two aspects to consider in risk management process analysis: First, the external factors in risk analysis such as business culture, data, and technology are connected with risk control.

Second, using the risk management processes understanding for multiple risks in general through the use of knowledge that the organization obtained using data analytics/AI capabilities (Figure 1.2).

These two aspects of external factors and knowledge creation lead to RM process implementation as part of management development in business/projects supported by data analytics, AI, and digitalization; however, it has been identified that the attitude of the management and the mindset of the human–machine interaction influence what is required to strengthen a successful organization. Regarding risk attitudes, March and Shapira (1987) presented that a manager's risk attitudes and the way of dealing with risk are associated with the following statements: "They feel that a manager who fails to take risks should not be in the business of managing." "Managers look for alternatives that can be managed to meet targets, rather than assess or accept risks" (see Section 1.1.4, Risk Aversion). The next section connects risk processes and utility theory to understand principles of value creation in organizations.

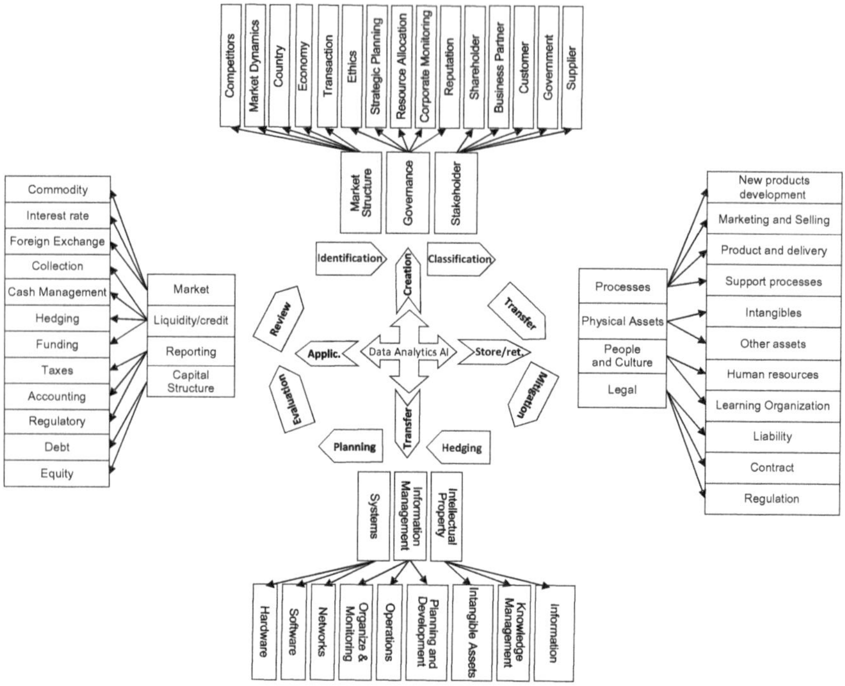

Figure 1.2. Risk management processes and the data analytics, AI, and knowledge management processes.

1.1.3 *Understanding risk concepts and processes using utility theory*

The concept of utility is represented by the preference that a person or company gives to the occurrence of certain events, considering the one that is preferred as the one that provides most utility. However, cannot be a preference on all occasions because in some cases there is indifference, which would give a decision for any of the options that are presented, and the options would represent the same utility. For the construction of utility theory, the assumption of the rationality of the decider is made. This is an assumption that has to be reviewed in an ongoing manner given the knowledge that in many cases rationality is not the factor supporting decision-making, but in this context of using data analytics and AI, the assumption aggregates value to the analysis of data and intelligence creation. Thus, the decisional problem becomes the analysis of utility, and utility is a function of the purposes that the company has set, because it is not only the obtaining of wealth in the short term but survival and enhancing competitiveness in the medium term.

Decisions are surrounded by uncertainty, as they involve utility analysis. In addition, there are conditions of compliance according to rules of behavior that are expressed in the form of a relationship or the occurrence of events/circumstances where the possibility of improving or reducing utility can show up. Additionally, it is assumed that an event is indifferent to itself, and if an event is indifferent to another and this in turn to a third one, the first will also be indifferent to the third. This rule is fulfilled for the case of the preference relationship; this is the condition of transitivity: If the first is preferable to the second and the second to the third, then the first is preferable to the third. Also, in the case where the first event is preferable to the second and the second indifferent to the third, then the first will be preferable to the third.

One way to achieve a solution to the decision that contains uncertainty is to study the *Expected Value and its variance* of the goal/factor, which in a project contemplates the randomness of the results, indicators of performance, or compliance. When the expected value is mentioned, it means that an organization is looking for the possible outcomes of economic conditions that are random. This concept is a fundamental element in all risk treatment because individuals can lose a sum X and would surely be willing to pay $E(X)$, the expected value, in order to save the possible loss. Likewise, this principle may not have all the validity because it also depends on the size of the loss and the relationship to the wealth that the decision-maker has, because sometimes for the decision-maker a loss become catastrophic and he/she can lose all assets. In this way, depending on the situation, the value that organization would expect to pay/bargain may be higher than the expected value.

Losses or gains in wealth are evaluated according to the comparison of expected values under the possible events that can occur. It is possible to perform the utility analysis denoting the random variables representing what can happen to the wealth at a time or under business conditions by X or Y, respectively. In addition, it is assumed that a utility function (***uti***) has been constructed that establishes for the individual the possible wealth that can be obtained when making a decision. $E[\boldsymbol{uti}(wealth + X)] > E[\boldsymbol{uti}(wealth + Y)]$ is the indication that X is preferred over Y. If there is indifference, the two terms are equal.

The form of a utility function can be given from the events, the preference relation, and the following axiom: If A, B, C are events such that A is preferred to *C* and this to *B*, then there exists an *r* in [0, 1] such that [*rA* + (1 − *r*)*B*] is indifferent to *C*. Then, there exists a function *uti* such that for any events ***uti***(*A*) > ***uti***(*B*) if and only if *A* is preferable to *B and* ***uti***(*rA* + (1 − *r*)*B*) = *r* ***uti***(*A*) + (1 − *r*)***uti***(*B*), with *r* at [0, 1].

These expressions mean that qualitative preference or indifference has the possibility of leading to numbers and maintaining consistency. Also, if there are two random variables *X* and *Y* that represent the economic values of the result, it is true that *E*(***uti***(*X*)) > *E*(***uti***(*Y*)) if it is given that the probability distribution of *X* is preferred to that of *Y*. In the case of indifference, they will be equal. The utility function exists, it is unique, and if there is another, this will be a linear transformation of it, so it can take a form such as

$$v(wealth) = \boldsymbol{a}\ \textbf{uti}(wealth) + b$$

where *v* represents another utility function that differs only in the values *a* and *b*.

$\textbf{uti}(wealth_2 - payment) = (1 - p)\ \textbf{uti}(wealth_1) + p\ \textbf{uti}(wealth_2)$ represents the amount that one would expect to pay for protection from maintaining the level of $wealth_2$ that is likely to be or having a lower level of $wealth_1$, but that occurs with probability (1 − *p*). In the case of a nonlinear utility function, Jensen's inequality is very important in this analysis. If *X* is a random variable and the utility function ***uti***(*wealth*) is under the assumption that the first derivative is greater than zero and the second derivative less than zero, then these inequalities emerge:

If ***uti***"(*wealth*) < 0, then *E*[***uti***(*X*)] ***uti***£(*E*[*X*])

If ***uti***"(*wealth*) > 0, then *E*[***uti***(*X*)] ***uti***³(*E*[*X*])

Also, in terms of risk and coverage of this situation arises: ***uti***(*wealth* − *payment*) = *E*[***uti***(*wealth* − *X*)] the right side of the equation means the expected utility of not buying protection when it is at a given wealth level. The left side is the expected utility of paying for full protection (*payment* by user of protection and *X* value of the loss): ***uti***(wealth − *payment*) = *E*[***uti***(*wealth* − *X*)].

Protection or coverage for risk events costs a premium price to the risk units according to expected values in the benefit of activities. Not all risk units accept or deal with risk in the same manner; some risk units can be willing to assume more risk than others. The next section reviews the risk aversion concept.

1.1.4 *The concept of risk aversion*

In the case of an individual, when the second derivative of its utility function is less than zero, it is said *to be Risk Averse*. Now, if it is observed from the point of view of who assumes the risk, the minimum payment value for assuming it is given by the following:

$$\textbf{\textit{uti}}(\textit{wealth of the one who assumes the risk}) \\ = E[\textbf{\textit{uti}}(\textit{wealth of the one who assumes the risk} + \textit{premium} - X)]$$

where the premium is the minimum that would be accepted for taking on risk X. So, for example, if the risk unit owns as wealth 1000 monetary units, if there is an event that affects that wealth, the wealth will be reduced to 800. If an individual buys coverage for 800 paying a premium of 100 or $E(X)$, then the final outcome can end up with 1000–100 if there is no event or with $1000-200+200-100$ if the individual buys the insurance and an event occurs. The other approach for covering a risk is using derivatives and hedging strategies that provide through specific contracts a protection to the variation of cash flows and returns in multiple financial transactions. The derivative contracts as they are future, options, etc., are obtained paying a price of the contract according to the conditions that each part will accept.

Equivalence of risk and *concept of coverage*: It is the process by which the quantity of a product, project, and transaction is reevaluated according to the terms of payment, maturity of the business, rates, activity, economy, inflation, and devaluation, which influence the development of the potential risk of the conditions in which it is presented. One way to make risk equivalent for the parties involved is to hedge some or all of the risk components. The concept of coverage has been studied in recent times in order to find the best options to perform it. It is observed in the theorems of Arrow (1963) and Mossin (1968) that studied the optimality of partial and complete coverage as well as coverage when there is a deductible. This applies in the first instance to insurance but can be applied to other fields. Likewise, the analysis has been treated using preference curves in a reference frame of mean and variance and in the reference framework of situation — claims or risk modification.

The curves that relate the mean return and the variability of the return in which the individual is indifferent are the curves of preference or indifference. Movements increasing variability and increasing average return can lead to a higher level of utility. The concept of diversification is represented, if it is assumed, for example, that there are only two assets, with their respective returns and variabilities, by relating the mean and variance of asset A and the mean and variance of asset *B*, and if an individual is forced to choose either *A* or *B* but not both, the individual will choose the point that is located on the highest indifference curve. If the individual is allowed a mix of the two assets *A* and *B*, the individual can get a return between *A return* and *B return*. The result will depend on the proportions of each of the assets and how these assets are related, that is, the value of a point between *A* and *B* when assets are independent and provide a convex curve representing diversification as a manifestation of risk aversion.

Optimization of coverage in RM can be observed in different ways as it could be in insurance: "If an insurance company is willing to offer any insurance policy against loss desired by the buyer at a premium which depends only on the policy's actuarial value, then the policy chosen by a risk-averting buyer will take the form of 100% coverage above a deductible minimum" (Arrow, 1963). It has been found that Arrow's theorem (1963) is robust and that it is maintained in any of the theoretical frameworks of analysis. Mossin's theorem (1968) is not maintained in general, especially when there is no smoothness in the preference curves, because the second-order differentiability is violated; however, if it is allowed that for some of the points of wealth the second-order differentiability is maintained, the theorem would remain in a general decision system.

Risk aversion can be interpreted as not wanting to preserve the average margin in the final distribution of wealth, and the individual having a strict preference for greater wealth under uncertainty. If risk aversion is studied in the reference framework of mean and variance of the distribution of wealth, these are considered as the levels of preference, if it is assumed that preferences comply with increasing with the mean and decreasing with the standard deviation. In addition, it is assumed that the preference is for diversification.

In the graphical representation of Figure 1.3, the indifference curves are of increasing slope due to risk aversion and convex due to the preference for diversification. It is assumed that if there are two random distributions of wealth that are equally preferable, the consumer prefers any convex combination of these to taking only *y* and *z*.

The representation of the triangle is given because in the case in which the *values y* and *z* are completely correlated they will be on the same line and in the case in which there is negative correlation they will be on the other sides of the triangle.

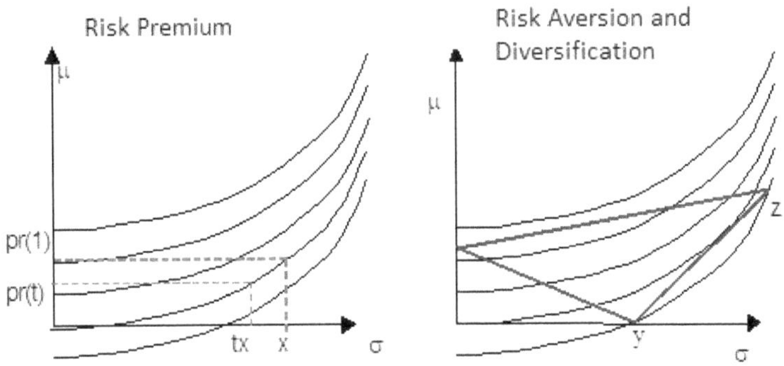

Figure 1.3. Risk premium and risk aversion.

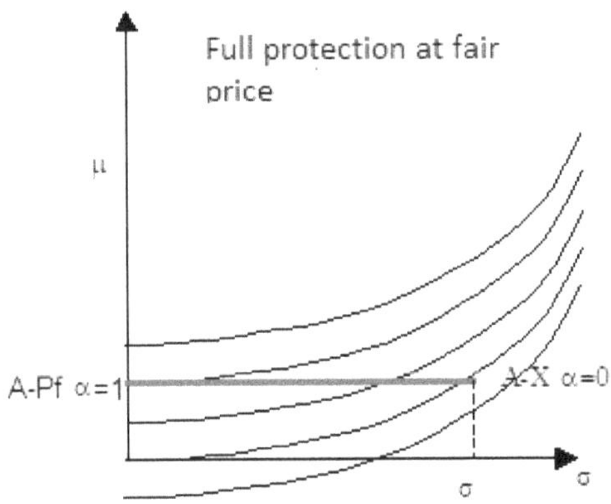

Figure 1.4. Mossin's theorem.

Likewise, the risk premium that depends on t between 0 and 1 generates the indifference curves of the positive slope with the characteristic of having a first derivative tending to zero when t tends to zero. Mossin's theorem, Figure 1.4, states that an individual who wishes to maximize his expected utility by being risk averse will choose full coverage or partial coverage depending on the percentage assigned to expenses and profit, with total coverage if this value is zero and partial coverage if the value is greater than zero. A value of α is estimated observing that identify the wealth to obtain if A is called the initial wealth, X the random variable that measures the loss, and P_f the premium that must be paid for full coverage, which will depend on the value represented by the percentage of compensation that would be received in case of loss. So when the value α is of

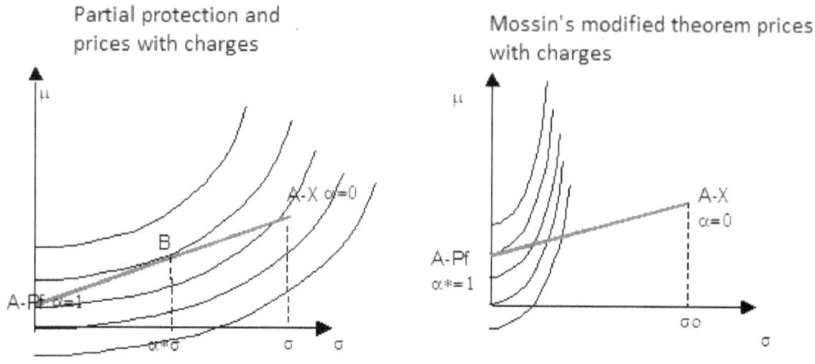

Figure 1.5. Modified Mossin's theorem.

one, it should have as wealth $A - P_f$ and in the case of the zero value, the wealth will remain in $A - X$. In the case in which the value of expenses and profit is included in the value of the premium, the previous graph is modified because the level of final wealth falls with the purchase of high levels of protection, seeking to balance with low levels of risk.

Mossin's modified theorem, Figure 1.5, states that an individual who is risk averse and does not necessarily maximize expected utility will choose full coverage when the expense and margin factor are zero, but in the case where the expense factor is greater than zero will take full coverage if the percentage of compensation is equal to one. In the case of being less than one, he/she will take partial coverage.

All these elements lead to the conclusion that individuals will be willing to pay something to avoid adverse risk outcomes depending on the level of compensation they will receive. Therefore, a fundamental principle in this book and, in general, in risk theory is to optimize the treatment of risk for the economic benefit of the individual and not as it is sometimes confused to seek to eliminate it, because risk will be present in economic activities. Likewise, the concept of optimizing requires RM, i.e., looking for mechanisms to improve the results of the company under a risk restriction that exists in each business.

1.1.5 *Decisions under risk*

In the previous sections, there was a presentation of the risk concept, risk processes, risk and utility theory, plus risk aversion understanding. This section presents the main points related to the effects of uncertainty in a

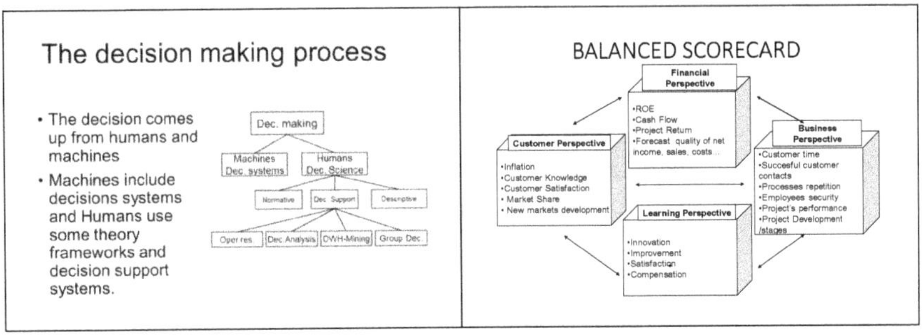

Exhibit 1.1. Decision-making process and balanced scorecard.

decision-making process. Uncertainty and risk are not the same in this book as indicated earlier. Less knowledge about process and outcomes means more uncertainty. Risks are identified and evaluated; looking for a better understanding of them will lead to better business decisions and actions. Analyses performed in strategic risk should contemplate the effect of randomness not only to identify the variations but also to study the distributions of the potential outcomes to provide analytical results to guide the problem-solving and decision-making processes. In this section, the important point to understand is how decisions and performance are affected by risk. The framework used is the Balanced Scorecard (BSC) and the variation of the results/metrics/indicators in each perspective of the Balanced Scorecard (BSC) is the core of the RM process.

Exhibit 1.1 presents the decision-making process involving human and machine intervention. Decisions in general are related to the Balanced Scorecard pillars. According to this view, every decision involves a risk, the decision-making process is related to RM (see Section 1.4 and Exhibit 1.37 for more details), and understanding result variation is a goal of RM. The stages of a decision-making process involve quantitative management that must include the development of risk assessment. The risk assessment will be through identifying steps in the decision-making process and their relationship to quantitative assessment and strategy according to the following:

(1) Definition of the problem.
(2) Search for alternatives.
(3) Evaluation of alternatives.
(4) Choice of alternatives.
(5) Determination of the action plan.

(6) Communication of the decision.
(7) Implementation of the decision.
(8) Monitoring and Evaluation.

These are the steps in the description of value search using data analytics, AI, and digitalization to guide decision-making. The following sections connect these decision steps with strategy and scientific methods to approach solutions or in general the analytics process to convert data into knowledge assets and actions. The next section starts with a definition of the context of strategy and risk where the problem definition will be crucial for strategic risk analysis.

1.1.6 *The context of the strategy and risk*

Strategy as mentioned in the introduction of the book has formulation and implementation steps. In both cases, data analytics is applicable. In formulation, the support of data analytics in monitoring, describing,

<table>
<tr>
<td>Steps of the strategy
• Analysis of the present situation
• Objectives
• Strategies
• Actions

Quantitative process
• Information system use
• Information of current realities
• Analysis and modeling
• Information to decide

Knowledge
• Information about the mixture of the market
• Prospective
• Actions
• Feedback to review each step</td>
<td>The problems associated with decision-making can be summarized as follows:
(1) The information available is not adequate or reliable.
(2) Data are presented in different forms and are defined differently.
(3) The criteria for analyzing the data are not sufficiently known; their reliability has not been tested.
(4) People and technology support is not available.
(5) The means of evaluation and accuracy may not be the most adequate.
(6) In the conditions of strategy, it is important that decision-making relates raw data with the attributes of customers, products, and processes; this means that answers are given to basic questions, e.g., what, who, how, when, where, why, how much, all seeking to clarify which is the most appropriate path for the development of the plan.</td>
</tr>
</table>

Exhibit 1.2. Strategy formulation steps, analytics process, and areas of action in RM.

Risk Manager Profile:
Risk management activities require a working group that is led by a manager who has many of the following competencies:

(1) Management of evaluation techniques; this is a tool for diagnosis and evaluation of risks in the organization.
(2) Organization of prevention measures and security systems for people and assets of the company.
(3) Understanding of legislation and jurisprudence concerning risk and its consequences.
(4) Management of principles and practices on the use and determination of risk coverage.
(5) Knowledge of business administration.

Statistical and systems knowledge to turn technical tools into reality.

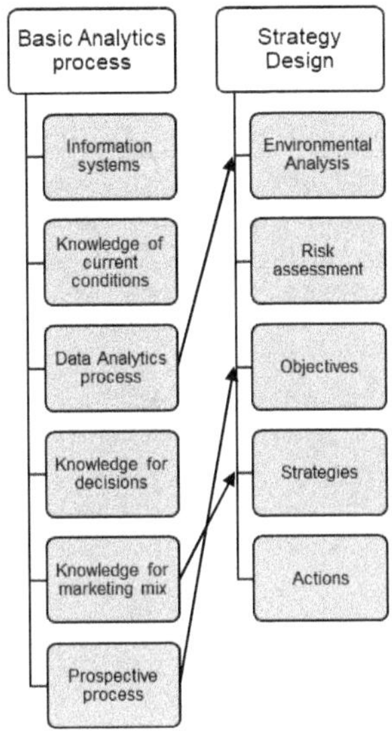

Exhibit 1.2. (*Continued*)

Field of action of RM:

(1) Generate risk promotion and awareness programs.
(2) Risk analysis, evaluation, and control.
(3) Review of the principles of business behavior *vis-à-vis* the different actors of economic activity.
(4) Ongoing review of the elements of risk in business processes.
(5) Modeling of processes and their specific risk conditions to evaluate and control their impact.
(6) Search and identification of risks.
(7) Analysis, classification, and diagnosis of risks.
(8) Quantification of risks and economic valuation.
(9) Measures to counteract risks.
(10) Risk prevention policy.
(11) Risk hedging policy.
(12) Development of a RM and start-up program.

Exhibit 1.2. (*Continued*)

predicting, and identifying opportunities is crucial; the same is true in management control systems to implement and learn about the strategy outcomes, errors, opportunities to improve, and identify possibilities to define actions in the business operation. Exhibit 1.2 is a summary of steps of strategy that are connected to decision-making to solve problems. Strategy at the end is a means to organize how to solve problems. In the business context, the core problem to solve is how to deal with the risk of being not successful in an enterprise. This means how to maintain performance that provides value to stakeholders. In this regard, the analytics process and RM provide support to strategy design not only in providing insight but also in providing a mindset to organize what is required in following logical steps to feed and maintain good operation of an organization.

Moreover, Exhibit 1.2 looks for the reader's reflection comparing the common aspects in each process of decision, strategy, and data analytics, which need to flow across the organization in the way that is a commonly perceived that depicts an understanding of thinking and structuring solutions. Decision-making includes analysis about projects, daily routines, process development, or improvement, and many other ways of presenting and promoting decisions. The decisional processes are in essence the same; the difference lies in the levels, intensity, and impact of the decisions, the possibility of using tools, methods, and technologies to support the processes, the speed with which the barriers are overcome, the quality of information available, and the time

Risk management program background:	Examples of strategic work and RM across activities and products in organizations that help to design RM systems.
(1) Risk can be modified by making changes to customer selection standards and the way activities associated with the company's primary function are controlled. The same applies for RM of portfolios and for changes in economic and environmental conditions. (2) The goal given to RM is to maximize an adjusted rate of return by maintaining exposure to risk, for example, credit in the case of the financial institution, within established parameters. (3) In a financial institution, credits are the most important source of risk; however, there are other actions such as acceptances, interbank transactions, foreign currency transactions, operations, or control of transactions, especially if there are derivative operations. (4) Institutions have been provided with tools to achieve greater competitiveness in the market and achieve a higher expected benefit, which requires one to maintain it in an appropriate environment of credit risk and all sources of risk in the organization. (5) It is important to operate in a scheme in which there is a process of generating policies, controls, measurements, and administration adequate to meet the complexities of credit activities or other elements of risk. The conditions of supervision, analytics, and adjustment of transactions, as well as aspects of asset and liability management are important.	(1) The identification of the characteristics of customers and the understanding of them should lead to a clarification of the conditions for the payment of debts and behavior for the selection and segmentation of markets. (2) Attribution limits generate an identification of exposure levels, but the rationale focuses on risk underwriting conditions. (3) Processes of approval of new and extension of credits must be well identified through methodologies that allow the company to generate sustainable competitive advantages and not only transform an indicator that does not generate organizational growth. (4) Controls are part of the day to day because it is the monitoring of the clients, which generates adequate results. (5) Creation of a system of provisions and reserves, its technical design, and its adjusted definition serves for control.

Exhibit 1.3. Risk management and its information systems.

Relations with information systems and the concept of risk and its management require the constitution of an information system from data management to the formation of indicators . A methodological structure has the following steps:	**Building the basis of a Risk Analytics Systems**
(1) Identify the scope of the plan. (2) Define the commitment of the administration. (3) Understand the business. (4) Evaluate current systems. (5) Identify processes, create an entity model of relationship versus risk. (6) Perform problem analysis and goal improvement. (7) Establish critical success factors. (8) Identify the general IT requirements for the planned strategic developments. (9) Evaluate the impact on technology of both models and computing and access. (10) Administrative identification and application identification are required.	A. Establish processing and information requirements through interviews with management, business projections, identify what current applications and databases contain. B. Evaluate sources of information. C. Establish what information projects are in process. D. Establish the areas contributing to risk management. What are the information needs. E. Identify technological support. F. Convert information needs into systems projects. G. Give priorities to the set of applications. H. Determine computer conditions and client server applications. I. Define office requirements, communications, in terms of control and sources of information. J. Budgeting and impact assessment.

Exhibit 1.3. (*Continued*)

horizons with which processes are carried out. Relationships with other areas in RM move in many directions and with direct and indirect influences on the functional areas and operations. For example, RM is part of the decisions and strategies relating to the purchases or supply chain that the organization has, customer information system design and use, financial capabilities, management of contracts and guarantees, production and operation standards, legal conditions in which legal processes are carried out, development of human management, behavior and management of staff members, knowledge, and development of outsourcing standards. This means that most business activities will have to be considered in a RM program, in different conditions and involvement intensities for planning and execution of the program. Exhibit 1.3

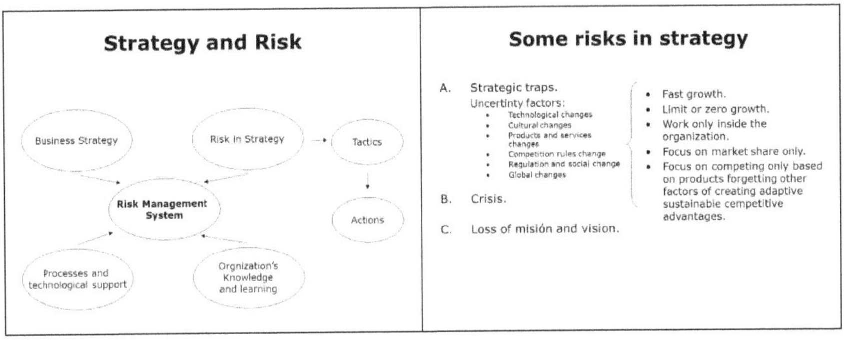

Exhibit 1.4. Risk and strategy.

presents points about how a RM program can be associated with certain activities such as product development, relationships with other business areas, and what a risk analytics system requires. The best way to say is that in the context of strategy implementation and the efforts of implementation will be around mitigating risks limiting to achieve the organizations' goals.

A systematic way of looking at the problem of risk information and management is based on coordination and alignment of what is presented in Exhibit 1.4. Strategy components need to be connected to strategy and operation actions through RM systems that create knowledge to support with evidence possible roads to take to successfully compete. In the paths of strategy implementation, multiple risks are going to appear and the capacity of the organization will be used in a continuous manner. A risk to observe and study is that the organizations can be confused because of strategy traps or a limited vision of what is potentially affecting a business model and threats in a business environment. A good example of mitigating this risk is when organizations take the time and resources to live the present and future of possible operations: One organization is the current operation and the other is a prototype of what could be in ten or more years after planning with the purpose of designing scenarios to operate according to behavior changes of markets. Data analytics and AI help immensely in this regard because it is not necessary to stop for analysis; analysis on the fly can be conducted to adapt the organization according to monitoring of market conditions results/trends, early warning systems, simulations, and a combination of processes to obtain outcomes. Limitations in terms of strategic risk and strategic intelligence development are disruption and events that are not in the radar. As mentioned in the introduction of the book, there is always the possibility of black swans, but the capabilities of RM will depend on resilience and loss minimization after adverse events.

Actions and tactics are responses to the translation of actions of a risk information system that represents business strategy, risk in strategy, processes and technological and statistical support, and training and learning conditions. It should be noted that the entities participating in each of these components are different in hierarchy and functional level, which will create certain limitations to knowledge transfer, but this is where digitalization can help. For example, training supply is required in human–machine resources, knowledge transfer in processes and technology use where software and hardware support are required, or for risk controls and guide board level designed under a business strategy conditions by the general management of a company. A relationship between strategy and risk focus on the identification of factors generating variation in the three dimensions of the business is introduced in the next section.

1.1.7 *Principles of Enterprise Risk Management (ERM)*

With the previous concepts of strategy and risk relationship, it is natural to move to the holistic view of RM across the organization as presented in this section, and it is the core of RM approach in this book. RM evolved to ERM as a strategic step and a way to create strategic intelligence. Lam (2003) pointed out, "As a topic, strategic or enterprise risk management … is really just plain, good risk management practice suited up … risk management didn't arrive on the scene as a holistic practice. Rather it lapped up on our shores in waves." Dickinson (2001) defined ERM as "a systematic and integrated approach to the management of the total risks that a company faces." Bowling and Rieger (2005) indicated that ERM can be presented as support to the governance process, better administration of RM costs, and "Through increased communication, RM leads to broader understanding and recognition of risks." ERM has many benefits related to the reduction of risk profile. In the first quarter of 2023, Silicon Valley Bank shut down operations. It was one of the biggest banks in the USA (historically, the second-biggest bankruptcy in the US market), with a focus on entrepreneurship — start-ups and innovation economy support. The organization could not get the capital resources required to operate, selling securities at a loss, which created panic, producing massive withdrawals from the bank. Another bank that failed is Silvergate, which concentrated on products related to digital-crypto currency transactions and fintech in the digital currency industry. Bankruptcies originate from liquidity issues because of massive withdrawals from the banks. Under the pressure of low expectations due to how innovators and crypto currency organizations were performing, the shares plunged in a very short period of time. Those are examples of ERM failures because of potential issues of strategy and observations of asset–liability management in the organizations. FTX was one of Silvergate's customers and FTX's failure happened a few weeks before Silvergate's default.

ERM as the integral study of risk across the organization involves a variety of people–machine interactions, knowledge, processes, and technology–machines use. This variety can create difficulties for ERM implementation because one needs to identify and coordinate risk control actions across the organization for implementation. The expertise in RM is not the same across areas or applicable to different kinds of problems (Dickinson, 2001; Warren, 2002; Shaw, 2005) but the organization needs common approaches and principles to align strategies and tactics for risk control. The most generally accepted ERM frameworks to support implementation are found at the Treasury Board of Canada 2001 & 2004, Conference Board of Canada 2003, COSO 2004, and Basel II–III Accords 2004 and 2010.

Strategic risk is a subject of ERM and, according to Simons (1999), the causes of financial losses are expansion, cultural pressures, reduced controls, lack of communication of business values, learning systems, and concentration on information. These causes are strategic risks and are influenced by an increment of business complexity, transaction creation, lack of control, information management, concentration in niches and investments, and the use of cost as the only important factor to manage. Business complexity and the cost of knowledge show the need to provide more meaning to the information and better KM (Sutcliffe & Weber, 2003) to build actionable answers to risk threats. This means the search of better knowledge and strategic intelligence creation to protect organizations against strategic risks through the use of data analytics and AI.

Risk threat measurement and understanding are part of the RM practice. Cumming and Hirtle (2001) define risk measurements as the quantification of risk exposures and RM as "the overall process that a financial institution follows to define a business strategy to identify the risks to which it is exposed, to quantify those risks and to understand and control the nature of the risks it faces." Financial institutions have transformed a reactive RM into a strategic discipline, which adds value through the learning, risk analysis, and solutions as part of the day-to-day business (Meulbroek, 2002; Sharman, 2002; Liebenberg & Hoyt, 2003; Banham, 2004). However, the strategic view has had to deal with some issues in RM practice, generating the introduction of a general regulation framework, known as Basel II, III (2004, 2010) Capital Accord, which has several implications in RM and information systems decisions.

Even though there are benefits of ERM concepts, there are organizational issues to solve as well. Lam (2003) noted that the benefits of ERM are based on the concept of integration: integration of risk organization, integration of risk transfer practices, and integration of risk practices in the business processes. Besides, he indicates that based on the preparation of the organization for ERM, the expected benefits are "... increased organisational effectiveness, better risk reporting, and improved business performance."

From SAS product brief, resource integration and auditing are considered part of the ERM process that "Demands for transparency and reliability continue to increase for corporations. These demands flow from the shareholders and regulators directly to boards and executive management — roles that now have codified duties to ensure the ongoing efficacy of company systems and processes, as well as the overall governance of the enterprise. As a result, the internal audit function is evolving beyond its roots as an investigative function and emerging as a true corporate management instrument. Chief audit executives (CAEs) and the expert auditors who work for them must now generate more than just a past-performance retrospective; they need to operate as a process-oriented, forward-looking group with international perspectives that can provide education, assurance and insight beyond traditional annual audit plans." According to these concepts, a summary of basic general steps in ERM is as follows:

- Defining the value of ERM.
- Finding the relationship between strategy and risk.
- Designing risk control.
- Performing steps in risk analysis.

- Hedging equals investment in an asset to reduce the risk of a portfolio.
- Diversification is a means to control portfolio investing in a wide variety of assets.
- Covariance and correlation in portfolio analysis.
- Covariance is how much the return of risky assets is moving together and correlation is the measure put on the scale of −1 to 1.

These steps are followed in an organization and applied to components owned by the company which are part of the elements of risk that the entity must manage in the ERM vision. This means that there are elements that constitute part of the components of risk, such as the following:

(1) Physical assets of the company.
(2) Properties, machinery, equipment, land, furniture, appliances, vehicles, and recreation areas.
(3) Intangible assets of the company, which are the most important in the new economy.
(4) Markets, suppliers, image, transport, human capital, relations with the state, communications, training systems and maintenance of culture, research and development, operating methodologies, rights, agreements, and treaties.

With these concepts of ERM and risk and strategy, the next sections supplement the understanding of variables that compose risks and how uncertainty in business appears. The purpose is to analyze the general aspects that will influence RM decisions.

1.1.8 *Factors that affect ERM implementation*

This chapter has presented an overview of factors that represent risk in organizations. Reference has been made to the financial sector, which is one of the most advanced in RM practices and digitalization in a business that is not a tech company. This chapter also considers how deregulation, uncertainty, and risk affect business results. Risk is present in different situations in organizations from many internal and external conditions, wrong decisions, and multiple other sources. Examples are very interesting to study, such as Orange County's investment pool which lost 1.7. Trillion dollars in repo operations because everything was focused on inadequate information management. Barings Bank lost 1.5. trillion dollars because the trader made an improper decision on futures and options. Daiwa Bank did not report losses in bonds for ten years. Sumitomo Corp. had heavy unreported losses due to unauthorized negotiations.

In all cases, the event that generated the loss was an individual situation; it could have been prevented by creating control elements through RM. The economic instruments with which they work today are numerous and the exposure has increased, because there are derivative operations, repos, loan securities, and many other instruments that have risks. The problem is not in the instruments or in the financial products generally; a large part of the risk problem is found in the people or machines that use the tools. Additionally, risks associated with liquidity, credit, operations, and legal aspects are increasing the participation in business management, always within the orientation to improve organizational performance. Likewise, government organizations are interested in developing methodologies to adequately manage risk conditions, create, and place control systems to protect public interests. Activities are carried out that show the risk conditions explicitly, RM is promoted, capital levels are verified, and risk conditions are reduced; finally, it seeks organizations are dealing with a factor of a very high incidence of risk in results and business decisions.

The concept of risk includes components such as risk determination and evaluation which highlight the difference between seeking to avoid risks, control risks, managing risks, optimizing risks, and communicating the modifications that arise in the operation. Some risks are likely to be avoided or eliminated, although as mentioned earlier, in reality organizations live with risk, so it is important to try to reduce the incidence of some factors. Likewise, the transfer of risks, on the one hand, must be developed as a mechanism to reduce the economic variations of a loss or the occurrence of an adverse event. On the other hand, there are risks that must be managed continuously, of which we must know the distribution and develop control mechanisms. In an ongoing management process, it is identified that "Risk Management is frequently not a problem of a lack of information, but rather a lack of knowledge with which to interpret its meaning" (Marshal *et al.,* 1996). Risk management comprises "the overall process that a financial institution follows to define a business strategy to identify the risks to which it is exposed, to quantify those risks and to understand and control the nature of the risks it faces." The lack of knowledge is linked to the measurement or assessment of risk capacity that "entails the quantification of risk exposures" (Cumming & Hirtle, 2001).

ERM reviews risk for the whole organization (Exhibit 1.5), which implies centralized risk support under the culture of individual risk responsibilities and actions to control them; at the same time, there are steps to converting data into plans of actions that use statistical and machine learning to understand risk conditions. The support for ERM information and technology is in a risk management information system (RMIS). Olfield and Santomero (1997) presented a guide to build an RMIS for a financial institution, indicating the required establishment of standards, limits and rules, investment guidelines, and incentives and compensation. Each step includes specific knowledge and process identification and is complemented by (Crouhy *et al.*, 2000) "information collection and normalization, storage and dimensioning, analytics processing,

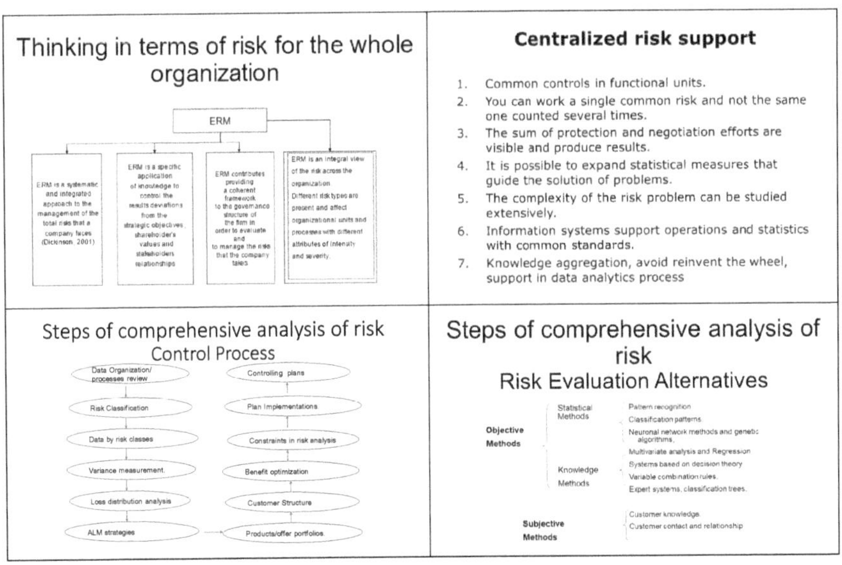

Exhibit 1.5. Risk in an organization requires the observation and analysis of individual parts and the aggregated whole organization.

information sharing and distribution". However, RMIS implementation has two main barriers: the cost vs. priorities, with similar costs and the flexible integral view of different factors and controls required in the ERM (Levine, 2006), such as data management, structure of documents and reports, and the use of data analytics (Jones, 2001; Hormozi & Giles, 2004).

As already mentioned, risk exposure continuously appears and requires multiple resources to monitor and evaluate impact in the organization. Risk exposure is given by the different components of the organization that can be affected by adverse events to generate possible losses of the occurrence of those events associated with a risk. These are cases of exposure to losses because of risks that generate direct damage to the organization that are not controllable, such as those that come from natural phenomena, and social, economic, and political situations in an environment. Risks associated with controllable events represent damage to the company's property or operation. Examples include equipment failures, damage to assets, incompetence, negligence, bad behavior of employees, transportation, dishonesty, inventory losses, deterioration, and obsolescence. From an indirect point of view, there are multiple cases of exposure: extra expenses, extra costs, changes in the forces that move competition, concentration of assets, managerial errors, responsibilities acquired by the company, changes in style, purchasing processes, negotiation conditions, normativity, bad practice, management irresponsibility, lack of knowledge, financial values, data, and reduced capacity to develop organizational intelligence.

In summary, factors influencing ERM development are associated with the differentiation of having a RM practice based on individual risks and having a treatment of risk that is aggregated with multiple sources of risks and courses of mitigation actions (see the differences RM and ERM Exhibit 1.6). This differentiation between RM and ERM shows the ERM practice as a means to create a competitive advantage in organizations observing a balance among managing the basics, innovation, integrity, and simplicity (Galloway & Funston, 2000). However, in order to perform ERM activities, it is necessary to do the following: first, to have information and technology supporting risk quantification and integral risk analysis across the organization (Olfield & Santomero, 1997; Cumming & Hirtle, 2001; Degagne *et al.*, 2004); second, to take into consideration three elements: the people–machines involved, processes and scope, and ERM processes, i.e., risk

Differential attributes between RM and ERM (Meulbroek, 2002; Lam, 2001; Cumming & Hirtle, 2001; Dickinson, 2001)	
Risk Management (RM)	**Enterprise Risk Management (ERM)**
• Silo, individual view of risk • Specific risk analysis • Tactic orientation • Related to control and minimization • Organization specific, department, or business unit. Concentrated on business events • Disaggregated methods for risk analysis • Responsibility on the functional managers • Performance evaluation concentrated on the particular problem solved • Protection of adverse financial effects of bad events. Earnings volatility protection from the source • Reactive • Specific control of section or division expenditures • Individual risk analysis • The priority is the portfolio and individual sources	• Global, holistic view of risk • Risk analysis across the organization • Strategic orientation • Related to competitiveness • Individuals, business units and the complete organization. Corporate view • Aggregated methods • Governance/stakeholder responsibility • Risk performance evaluation enterprise-wide and based on risk • Organization stability protection. Decision-making process based on risk • Proactive • Reviews and reduction of duplication of RM expenditures • Interdependent risk analysis • Priority can be portfolio structure, asset modification, or strategic movements

Exhibit 1.6. Comparison between RM and ERM.

identification, measurement, monitoring, control, and application (Brown, 2001); and third, to include in the ERM scope the enterprise risk or the risk seen across the organization, composed of financial, operational, and strategic risks and hazards.

Digging in the set of strategic or tactic factors that are associated with an ERM and Strategic Risks, it is possible to detect them using the forces of competence that Porter (1980) introduced: Environmental conditions in the level of competence that an organization possesses represent a component of risk that alters the results of the organization; if the forces that move the competition are observed, each of them represents an element of risk. Additionally, macroeconomic factors are potential sources of variability in results. In addition, the bargaining power of buyers, to the extent of customer concentration, represents levels of difficulty in placing the rules of product supply and demand, which becomes more difficult to manage and can determine the difficulty in achieving organizational goals. When not only concentration but also fidelity is observed, the development of methodologies is required to reduce the risk of loss of customers — churn — low customer loyalty to brands, etc. Customer acquisition involves many activities such as promotion, advertising campaigns, and vendor training, which involve important investments and therefore more points in which there is potential risk.

Moreover, suppliers are another type of organization's customer and partner with bargaining power and additional supply chain risks involved. Suppliers also play a preponderant role when considering the costs of the company because price competitiveness can be lost if it is known that the concentration or low availability of suppliers leads to the rules of the game being defined by them. Likewise, the supplier ceased to be an independent part of the value chain to become a partner of the company, which means that compensation and supplier development systems are on the list of improvement of risk exposure. Another contributor to risk is the group of distributors. They are very powerful when they concentrate on who can or cannot keep the distribution service, how they are going to pay the suppliers, or how the distributors will evolve, from stores to digital, from changes of original products to customized ones, from the stability as it has occurred with traditional retail that has threated economic conditions, etc. This is one of the most difficult sources of risks to overcome in the growth stage of the company, because defining which distributors should be involved can be equivalent to delivering one of the critical variables of success to a third party. In the digital world, the option to go directly to customers is practiced and it is intensified because of the reduction of using cash for payments through superapps. The decision to keep a product among its offering portfolio represents a continuous activity of maintenance and development of portfolio that can be competitive every time.

Nevertheless, defining the arena of competition and the members of the strategic groups according to business definitions is fundamental in dealing with risk. Concentration of efforts in strategic risks is related to where the organization is positioned in an industry and the kind of resources committed to maintain that position. There is a difference between receiving the payment by a distribution channel after 90 days when an SME is trying to achieve the goal of being in the same distribution channels as the most important brands, and an organization that has already organized a portfolio of distributions to manage cash flow in a better way thereby compensating unbalanced in and out cash. An interesting case involves academic institutions, as several universities are competing to be recognized research institutions, and the transition has been based on what type of leagues the institution would like to be in. A time frame is fundamental for investment and modification of the university capabilities. It is not just about stating to all faculty that they need to publish in the best journals tomorrow; it is about what is possible and the positioning in terms of what universities, students, and faculty can do to evolve and sustain a great and attractive set of options to upskill stakeholders. Possibly for certain institutions to have concentration on efforts to compete with research institutions can distract them in the search of creating and maintaining good and strong mix of programs and education for moving students to the society with required skills. In that view of competition, the selection of who to compete with or current competitors' identification has multiple ways of generating changes in the structures of the organizations, through the design and implementation of their strategies, new presentations offered to the market, and the commercialization of their products. In the same way, potential competitors can enter a market at any time; the levels of profitability and participation can be affected, but fundamentally the lack of sustainable competitive advantages and differentiating elements on offer can generate inconvenient changes in the development of the organizations.

Furthermore, strategic risks are affected because of the market of substitute products. It is a reality that affects organizations due to the infidelity of customers, the rationalization of customers, or simply the goodness of products or services that are presented as an alternative to meet their needs. Access to technology and resources/technology is another risk and competition factor that generates changes in the competitive environment. Nowadays, almost all participants in an industry have access to the same technology resources; development of talent and machine interactions are possible ways to maintain stable conditions and continue inventing performance. These factors of competition and risk lead to a greater penetration in the customers' minds or improvement of positioning, as well as a greater approach by the client to remain loyal to the organization.

Access to resources can be a constraint in multiple dimensions in a business, but in data analytics, AI capabilities, and digitalization, it is not a barrier; it is more about use adoption and capacity to deal with scope economies — do more with what is available.

In short, risk across the organizations should be seen as individual or aggregated risk, which is a fusion of two components: the frequency with which it can occur and the value that can be generated when an event occurs, i.e., severity. Thus, each of the aforementioned factors can have a greater or lesser intensity as well as a greater or lesser occurrence, with the possibility of presenting cases that are very infrequent but of a high cost which can greatly affect the results of the company. In the same way, it is necessary to contemplate the supply capacity and the way to prevent or manage the occurrence of events. Within this aspect is the management of financial assets. Therefore, the management of a portfolio is part of RM and does not focus solely on the proper management of this single variable. In ERM, a level of complexity is the multivariate view of frequency, severity distributions, metrics evaluation, and predictive models. Following the concepts associated with ERM, a fundamental aspect in the process of developing organizational intelligence is to understand more about uncertainty effects in business as explained in the following section.

1.1.9 *Uncertainty in business*

The previous section related factors that influence the ERM analysis and strategic risk analysis. In this section, there is a presentation of the perspective of how uncertainty influences businesses. As noted in the previous paragraphs, the factors and components of risk are interrelated to the expected results. Nowadays, it is not possible to conduct an analysis only of the pure risks, i.e., risks that affected the assets of the company and that were measurable and controllable through insurance. In RM, all business risks are a constituent part of risk analysis, which involves the study of the techniques and methodologies of the way processes are operated in the organization, for example, production, distribution, and technology related to social, economic, political, and human resource conditions and the flow of goods and services that involve the company and the client.

Management of activities that yield results in the assets and liabilities of the company is subject to risk analysis. It is not possible to just review certain aspects or areas of risk, as used to be the case in the development of actuarial science, more on the liabilities side than on the investment/ assets or business development side. That is the role that data analytics plays these days. Analysis of both assets and liabilities requires identifying administration and organizational structures, capabilities and constraints, and evaluation criteria. The concentration of pure risk is limited vision. Risk described as pure or random risk according to the event occurrence affecting people and organizations can be classified as follows:

- Personal: Affects people in their integrity and heritage.
- Physical: Affects assets and heritage.
- Civil liability: Affects third parties in the development of an activity.
- Financial losses: Identified with financial results.
- Political or social: Business environment-context and their effects due to the occurrence of risk events.

However, there are other risks affecting business, depending on the business definition. A good example of risk in business is the article by Oldfield and Santomero (1997) where they grouped the risks of financial institutions in five classes:

- **Systemic Risk:** it is the risk of changes in the value of assets associated with systemic changes, which may come from changes in interest rates, changes in asset values, and changes in energy. In time, these risks cannot be diversified.
- **Credit Risk:** it comes from debtors who do not make proper use of their credits, due to the inability to pay or a breach of contracts.
- **Operational Risk:** it is associated with the security of processing, the transactions of obtaining or delivering titles, the registration of data, or the way in which the processing of systems is carried out within the entity.
- **Legal Risk:** it is represented by regulation, the creation of contracts, or the development of protection and guarantee mechanisms.
- **Counterparty Risk:** it depends on the possible deterioration of who has carried out the business with the financial institution.

Each of these is applicable to both financial institutions and service companies.

Business risks are identified according to the consequences in losses or gains: technical, economic, profitability of new investments, new processes, or new strategies:

- Marketing, new competition, new product launches, higher product prices.
- Socio-economic, fashion changes, social, environmental problems.
- Financial banking, credits, collection difficulties, payment difficulties.
- Political, legislative, nationalization, change of rules and negotiation structures.

A principle across businesses is that risk can be analyzed to reduce the impact or risk appearance, but it is not possible to reduce it to zero. Optimization presupposes a series of operating conditions that seek to maintain a balance between risk and performance in support of the development of the organization. Organizations need to complement the conditions imposed by state agencies/regulators or industries with their own rules that support the changes in business conditions that they are exposed to. That is, the organization must be more proactive in forming its own control mechanisms against risk, such as the following:

1. Allocate a budget for the implementation of a risk management program, with the participation of top management.
2. Balance the development of the implementation of a risk management program, technology with the recognition of the capacity of people and machines that will execute their jobs properly, and the criteria to identify technological support.
3. Identify the points where technology will support the organization, but do not leave everything in the hands of the technological response. Technology is a means not an end. First identify the conceptual model then develop the technological support, not the other way around because it would be like starting aimlessly but with a large investment.

This general view of risk in business leads to a detailed analysis of identifying and differentiating strategic and operational risks, monitoring them, and identifying and evaluating risk indicators as explained in the following section.

1.2. Strategic and Operational Risks

A fundamental point in the analysis of risk is to discover the relationship between risk and strategy as it was presented in the previous sections. There are multiple types of risks, and they affect strategies and tactics in various ways: they are concentrated on individual tasks or they have ramifications in multiple areas as shown in Figure 1.2. General risks in an organization are correlated and affect the organization performance in several ways. The view of the organization as a system helps to understand what is happening in a particular area and how risks can affect the general organizational system. In this book, the emphasis is on the observation of risks that affect the organization as a whole. Exhibits 1.7 and 1.8 show different types of risks that can have multiple levels of impact on the competitive position of an organization. A good example is the risk related to knowledge assets in organizations: The impact is strategic if the core capabilities can be lost, thereby reducing the possibilities of enhancing organizational performance. At the same time, human–machine interaction is a reality that has to be very well managed to stimulate organizational competitiveness. Policies about upskilling and protection of human, logic, digital, and more intangible assets are

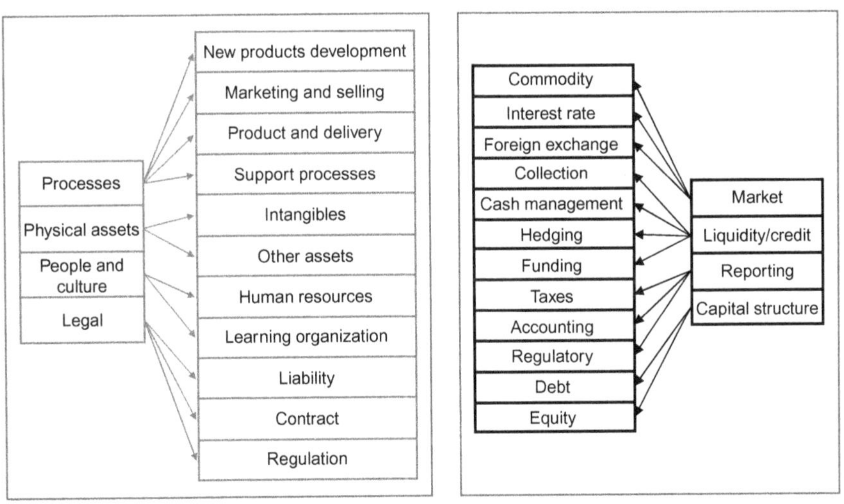

Exhibit 1.7. Different types of risks.

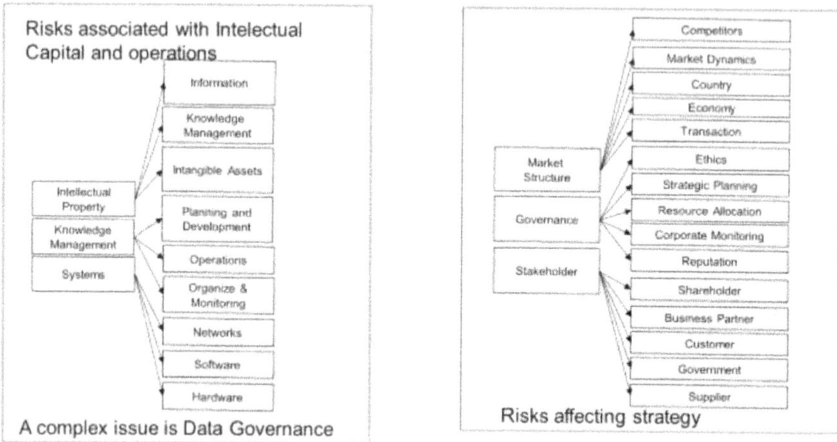

Exhibit 1.8. Different types of risks.

priorities because they consolidate positions to sustain the business in good shape.

There is a difference between identifying risks according to components of the organizations analyzed as a system (Figures 1.7 and 1.8) and identifying risks by specific problems to solve or conditions to deal with in a market. For examples, an important analysis to perform is the terms of application of digitalization as a means to mitigate strategic risk. Strategic risks in a new business perspective are associated with intellectual capital and operations if a big component of the strategy depends on people's creativity, data analytics, and development of AI. Threats against those assets in the organization will be a priority for evaluation to adapt to new competitive game conditions.

At the same time, strategic risks are related to what is happening in the business environment, which can be described as follows:

- Instability that is fed by multiple crises: financial, socio-economic, political, humanitarian, environmental, etc.
- Risks are correlated, there is a connection in risk appearance and there is a possible chain of events when one adverse event appears to generate a chain effect to new adverse events. Thus, exposures and risks in multiple dimensions can be related.

- A risk management process requires proactive, predictive action for resilience plans and actions after events. Plans require the evaluation of most likely events and impact, the minimum and the most complex situations. Plans and assessment are an ongoing stress testing process. To sustain or maintain an organization's healthy performance and survival, scenario simulations are required in multiple circumstances to maintain competition capacity and differentiation in organizations.
- More now than ever before, exposure analysis is a crucial engine to tune up in the management of organizations. Monitoring the exposure is what can be a differentiation means in creating sustainable competitive advantages. Volatility of resources is part of the daily industry game and the greater the understanding of the possible variability of results, the better the decisions and actions to take.
- A silo-oriented view of risks is not sensible because of the interconnected risk nature, and in that regard the value of data analytics is to support the observation of risk and impact according to predictions and possible outcomes of simulations. The value of data analytics and AI is to have a better understanding of variability of the factors to compete and what to do to create differentiation of organizations in markets.

Organizations develop strategies in search of their goals. Strategies can be formulated very well, and they can be assumed to be winning strategies for all stakeholders; however, the results cannot be what organizations expected. The risks are not only present in the identification and formulation of the strategy but also, and mainly, in the implementation of the strategy. In this book, strategic risk analysis is part of the design of management control systems. Strategy under uncertainty is considered as the key point to prepare organizations to compete or perform well in a market, in society, or in general to achieve their mandate. Once the organizations are prepared to develop the strategy, they must deal with risks that can modify the expected results, during the implementation. The presentation of a strategy mindset in this book takes into consideration the analysis of the factors that can affect good strategy implementation and the learning process to deal with the future.

Exhibits 1.9–1.14 and their tables have been taken from work conducted at the Risk Analytics Lab by the author and a student assistant, Mrs. Shuyi Yao, at Wenzhou-Kean University using Deloitte Insight

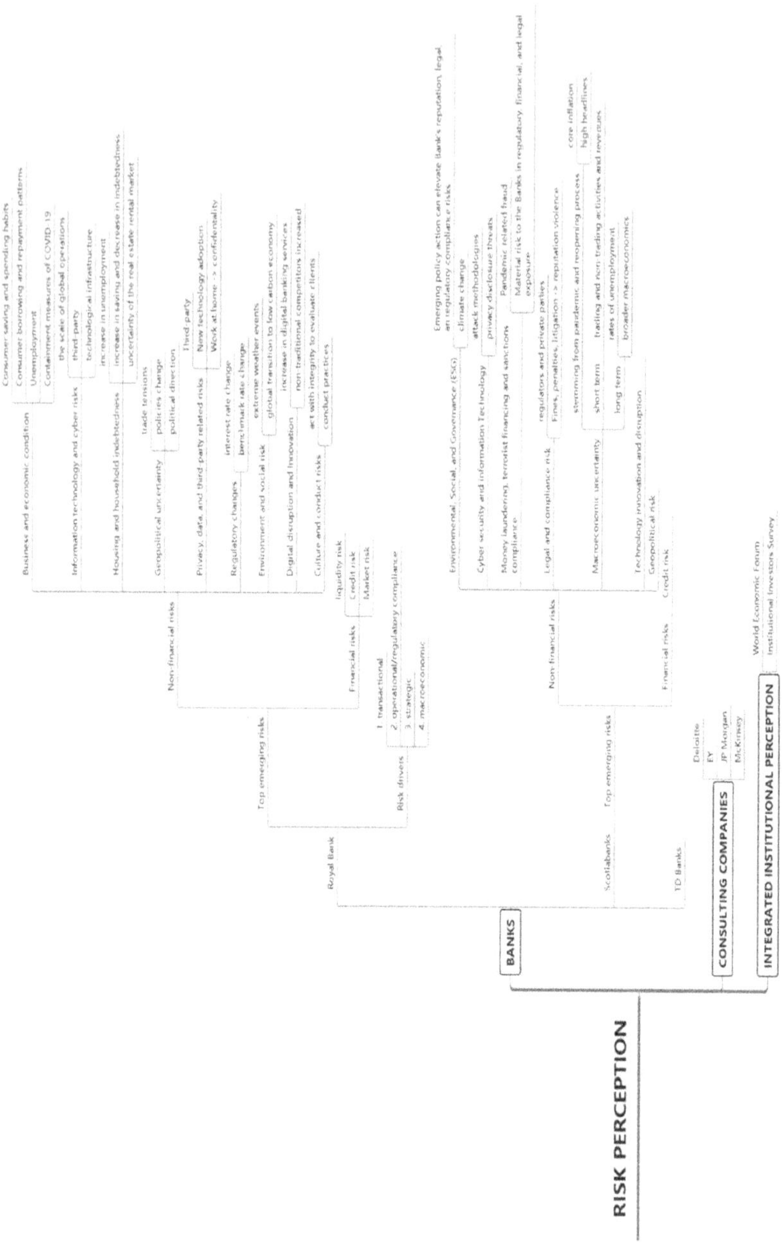

Exhibit 1.9. Risk perception form different observers of the market-banking perspective.

reports 2013–2021 as the data source. The aspects reviewed in the production of risk perception are provided in Table 1.1.

Exhibit 1.10–1.14, which are built based on the Tables 1.2–1.6, show the importance of what management finds for implementing a good risk

Table 1.1. Aspects to review in the construction of perception maps.

Aspects reviewed in the reports	Detail
Risk appetite	How challenging is each of the following in defining and implementing your organization's enterprise-level risk appetite statement?
Risk management measures	Over the next two years, how much will each of the following be a priority for your organization in risk management?
Stress tests	To what extent are the results of capital stress tests used by your organization for each of the following purposes?
Aspects of implementation	For your organization, how challenging is each of the following aspects of implementation of the new Basel Committee market risk rules (resulting from the Fundamental Review of the Trading Book (FRTB), including the new market conditions.
Investment management	In managing risks in your organization's investment management business, how challenging is each of the following?

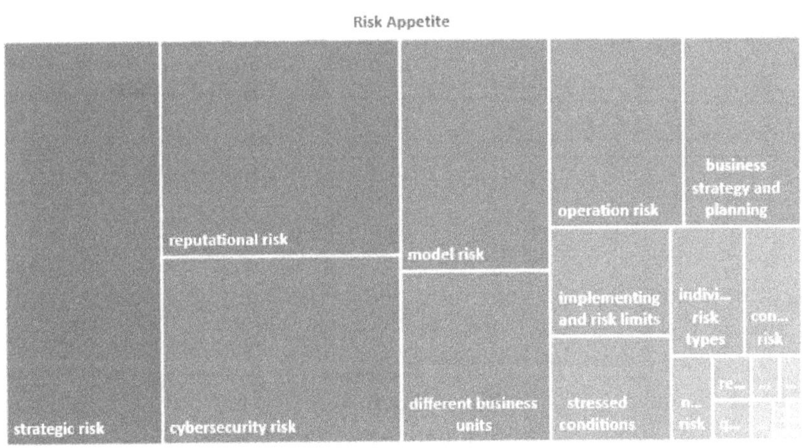

Exhibit 1.10. Strategic risk has a high importance in organizations similar to risk related to strategy and its implementation (Deloitte reports 2013–2021).

Table 1.2. Scores of perceived risks by executives (Deloitte's reports 2013–2021).

Type of risk	Aggregated score
Strategic risk	8.5429
Reputational risk	6.9944
Cybersecurity risk	6.0854
Model risk	4.7062
Different business units	3.4844
Operation risk	3.4109
Business strategy and planning	2.9967
Implementing and risk limits	1.7859
Stressed conditions	1.7066
Individual risk types	1.2708
Conduct risk	1.0047
Nonfinancial risk	0.4612
Regulatory expectations	0.2380
Quantitative risk	0.2200
Gaining the active participation of business units in implementing the risk appetite and risk limits	0.1694
Market risk	0.1352
Liquidity risk	0.1189
Third party investment management	0.0618
Credit risk	0.0554
Concentration risks	0.0400

management practice. The highest score appears in adoption, understanding, and creating risk culture in the organization where data and in general technology for RM support should be enhanced.

In an additional form, it is possible to review reporting to the board in the same manner as reporting to the senior management to create understanding of what policies in RM represent in decision-making and capacity to perform better in the market.

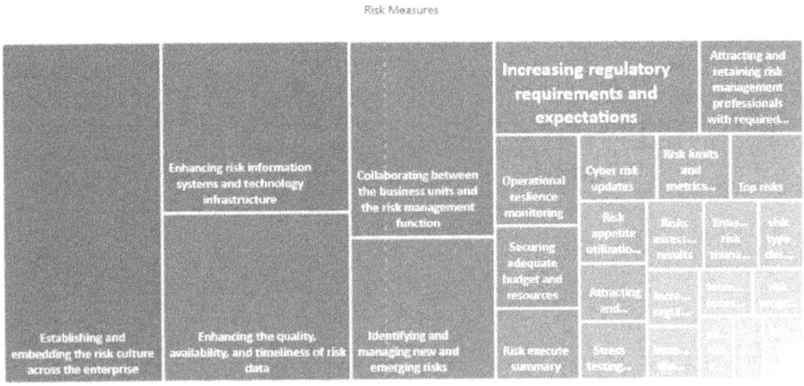

Exhibit 1.11. Priorities to improve adoption in an organization.

Table 1.3. Priorities for adoption enhancement of RM in an organization.

Risk measures	**Aggregated score**
Establishing and embedding the risk culture across the enterprise	7.160
Enhancing risk information systems and technology infrastructure	4.244
Enhancing the quality, availability, and timeliness of risk data	4.170
Collaborating between the business units and the RM function	3.751
Identifying and managing new and emerging risks	2.731
Increasing regulatory requirements and expectations	2.553
Attracting and retaining RM professionals with required skills	1.282
Operational resilience monitoring	1.000
Securing adequate budget and resources	0.915
Risk execute summary	0.779
Cyber risk updates	0.683
Risk limits and metrics trend analysis	0.633
Top risks	0.633
Risk appetite utilization vs. risk appetite	0.563

Table 1.3. (*Continued*)

Risk measures	**Aggregated score**
Attracting and retaining RM professionals with required skills	0.525
Stress testing results	0.517
Risk assessment results	0.517
Enhancing RM capabilities	0.488
Risk type dashboard	0.414
Increasing regulatory requirements and expectations	0.391
Increasing the role and involvement of senior management	0.368
Increasing focus on strategic risk	0.330
Risk program updates	0.325
External risk environment	0.275
Capital and liquidity	0.247
Increasing the efficiency	0.147
Agile management	0.078
Increasing the role and involvement of C-suite	0.055
Increasing the role and involvement of the board of directors	0.055
Aligning compensation and incentives with RM	−0.043

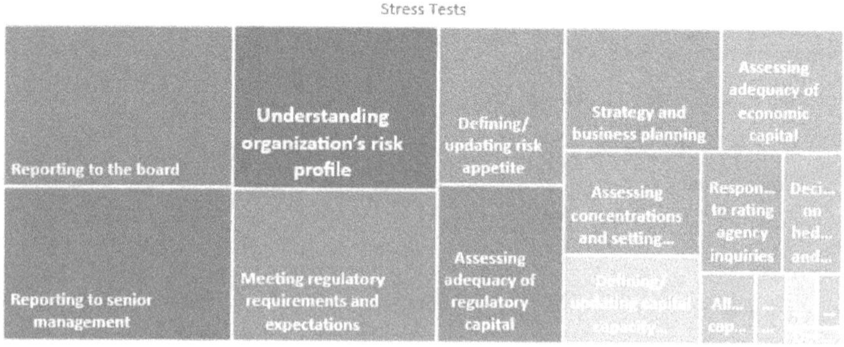

Exhibit 1.12. Map of aspects that require improvement to generate adoption and enhancement of RM.

Table 1.4. Identifying aspect scores that require improvement to generate adoption and enhancement of RM.

Stress tests	**Aggregated score**
Understanding organization's risk profile	19.653
Reporting to senior management	21.086
Reporting to the board	22.352
Assessing adequacy of regulatory capital	11.879
Meeting regulatory requirements and expectations	18.391
Defining/updating risk appetite	11.923
Strategy and business planning	11.349
Assessing concentrations and setting limits	8.410
Responding to rating agency inquiries	5.870
Assessing adequacy of economic capital	9.036
Deciding on hedging and other risk mitigation strategies	4.279
Allocating capital to businesses and products	2.312
Pricing products or benefits	0.816
Merger and acquisition decisions	1.361
Defining/updating capital capacity requirements for risk	7.175
Determining triggers for recovery plan actions	0.585
Assessing adequacy of regulatory capital	0.970

Once the general management aspects that require attention to enhance RM the operation aspects appear. Data and technology are identified as crucial for implementation of risk strategy the same as the clarity about what a compliance process will be based on regulation requirements.

And as a final observation, the reports through the years have shown that enhancement in RM implies investment in data, information technology, and compliance capacity.

According to the Global Economic Forum 2021, the top ten most important risks based on two-factor likelihood and impact are the following: Digital power concentration, digital inequality, and cybersecurity

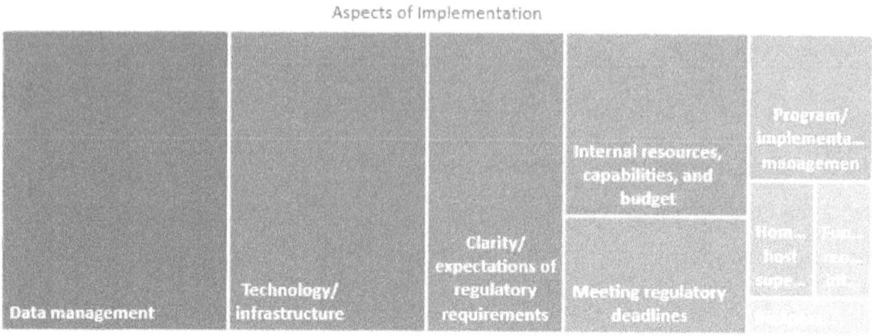

Exhibit 1.13. Operational aspects to consider as priorities for implementation of RM enhancement.

Table 1.5. Operational aspects to consider in implementation or RM enhancement.

Aspects of implementation	Aggregated score
Data management	5.313
Technology/infrastructure	4.624
Clarity/expectations of regulatory requirements	3.210
Internal resources, capabilities, and budget	2.594
Meeting regulatory deadlines	1.651
Program/implementation management	1.418
Home/host supervision	0.615
Functional reorganization/integration	0.519
Business realignment	0.356

failure are part of the top risks, but those more likely to occur are extreme weather, climate action failure, human environmental damage, infectious diseases, biodiversity loss, interstate relations fracture, and livelihood crises. In terms of impact, the top ten risks include IT infrastructure breakdown, natural resources crisis, and debt crises and the following a six risks classified as most likely: infectious diseases, climate action failure, biodiversity loss, human environmental damage, extreme weather, and

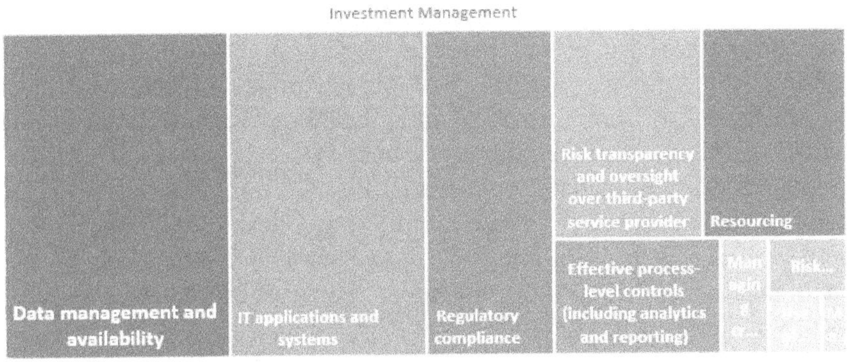

Exhibit 1.14. Investment map for improving RM practice.

Table 1.6. Investment for improving the practice of RM across time.

Investment management	Aggregated score
Data management and availability	6.964
Resourcing and information systems supporting RM	2.849
Regulatory compliance	3.920
Effective process-level controls (including analytics and reporting)	1.813
IT applications and systems	6.057
Risk transparency and oversight over third-party service provider	2.954
Risk governance	0.415
Managing credit and liquidity risk and its impact on portfolio construction risk	0.524
Managing investment risk and its impact on portfolio construction risk	0.139
Use of alternative data in investment and operational process	0.300

livelihood crises. This means six of the top 10 risks by likelihood are at same time top ten risk by impact. Only one digital-related risk was mentioned and classified as high impact and high likelihood — cybersecurity failure.

Risks in a society are observed through the lens of a silo view, i.e., studying risks in independent way and individual risks, or through the lens of integral risk management, i.e., ERM view. Possible issues of complexity of integrating data, computation, analytics, and mathematical capacity appear to create value such as the model risk itself, capacity to learn how to mitigate risks, or as Lebovitz *et al.* (2021) pointed out, "Discovering the disconnect between ML-based AI's know-what and human experts' know-how enabled managers to better understand the risks and benefits associated with each AI tool."

Observing what the perception of risk is and what the priorities are according to that perception depends, as well, on the type of organizations. Risk is not the same from a holding organization point of view or from specific business units (BU) in specialized or very well-defined markets. All risks are linked to the development of competitive advantages at different levels as investors of operators. There is evolution in markets from a single industry to diversified industries (unrelated and related) where business unit (BU) strategies will be related to and dependent on the portfolio position (BCG portfolio analysis matrix) for the whole organization. Those competitive positions have aspects to analyze regarding the sharing of resources in a manner similar to core competencies that can be upgraded and developed for the good of the BU in an industry. BU analysis can be through the following tools: maps of market growth relative to market share, attractiveness and strengths, Porter's Forces, generic competitive strategies (low cost — differentiation), value chain analysis, BSC Kaplan, and Norton. At the same time, the analysis of different strategies in continuous development with a risk appetite to grow has implications on the following:

- Organization structure
  - Decision-making process/authority
  - Management familiarity with industry
  - Driver on operation and financial planning
  - Culture building
- Management control and strategic planning
  - Budgeting
  - Transfer pricing — resource allocation

- Compensation — incentives — HR mobility
- Resources management — synergies — scale and scope
- Starting with mission, vision, value proposition
- Based on the mission to review the factors associated with planning process, formalization of capital expenditure and evaluation, capital investment analysis, project development, compensation, budgeting review
- Structure of the BSC properly defined to support the BU portfolio

RM is considered important in the strategic management process (Meulbroek, 2002), and an integral view of RM (Brown, 2001; Froot *et al.* 1994; Banham, 2004) has the capacity to create value in order to develop a competitive advantage (Galloway & Funston, 2000). The competitive advantage of industrial organization can be limited because of the risk of potential losses caused by expansion, cultural pressures, reduced controls, communication of business values, learning systems, and concentration on information (Simons, 1999). From a social organization perspective, development can be limited because of the lack of capabilities to support the required communities' growth through the programs or projects. With these points in mind, Exhibit 1.15 shows a guide to reflect how strategic risks are affecting strategic management. Strategic management cannot be separated from what strategic risks are. There is no clear path on where to go if strategic management is only based on assumptions of growth or opportunities; the analysis of strategic risk provides guidelines to design and implement strategies. This is where strategic intelligence plays the main role in identifying the paths required to evolve and succeed in the market. This means creating formal systems to measure, creating financial and non-financial indicators that will help organizations with product definition, revenue management, dealing with issues of markets growth, and possibly, the most important, reducing the probability of falling in strategic traps because of limited truth about the organization's performance. As presented earlier, Exhibits 1.9–1.14 show several of the risks from internal capabilities that are not providing what organizations need, such as permeating risk management culture across the organization.

In the introduction, general points were presented to connect strategy, and RM, and decision-making. In this section, based on risk perception, additional observations of RM and strategic management are uncovered.

<table>
<tr>
<td>Improvement of strategic management
Carenys (2010) pointed out, "Therefore, the current trend in management control research is to combine the use of formal systems, having financial and non-financial indicators, with informal systems, to create a 'control package', because it is considered that through sole use of cybernetic systems it is impossible to control the relevant variables for an organisation to achieve its objectives." This is exactly the integration that is required. Nothing can be separated from people's behavior but the cybernetic/analytics approach is contributing to complementing and developing routes to achieve better performance. Carenys (2012) continues, saying, "In other words, the current trend is to combine the use of formal systems, having quantitative and qualitative indicators, with informal systems, because it is considered that through the sole use of mechanistic systems it is impossible to control the relevant variables for an organisation to achieve its objectives."</td>
<td>Improvement of strategic risk management ... financial plan strategy

• Products with better margin. Option the best market with high price in hiker weekenders. High level of retain earnings — 40%
• Change term of debt. 70% long term
• Continue improvement in production, reduction cost. 5% for 2002
• Maintain cost structure. Margin 15%
• Investment of $550,000 in plan. Equipment, design, and product development</td>
</tr>
<tr>
<td>Improving strategic risk management — strategic problems
• Growth reduction. High level of liabilities. Strong foreign competitors
• Low market share in interest segments
• Change of customer
• Distribution channels are attacked by competitors. Plant constraints
• Seasonal market
• Design or style
• Branding</td>
<td>Improving strategic risk management

Some principles:
• Avoid strategic traps
• Do not avoid hard facts, avoid half truths
• Reject seeing risk as bad things. Ask why is the organization doing well — Time, market, changes
• Maintain redundancy as a good friend.
• Start from the end, from the expected results, and go back to build a solution process
• Only one view, only one kind of people, only one way to think
• Alignment of goals
• Formal and informal organization (Culture, management style, work ethic, perceptions and rules, budgets)</td>
</tr>
</table>

Exhibit 1.15. Improvement opportunities of strategic and RM.

External and internal factors in the organization structure • Functional • Business units • Matrix	For instance, in the controller function to refer continuously to: • Best value to add • Ways to see the role • Adapting the management control system

Exhibit 1.15. (*Continued*)

A review of strategy and risk concepts leads to the definition of strategic risk in terms of the probability of losing rank position with regard to the other firms in the reference set (Collins & Ruefli, 1992, p. 1709). Strategic risk can take different forms such as reputation, industry margin reductions, economic efficiency, environmental issues, energy issues, geographical hazards, threats and terrorism, citizen or customer dissatisfaction, and distribution of justice (Young & Hasler, 2010; Gates, 2006). The rank position in a market is associated with decisions about factors that produce uncertainty, decision-making traps, and selection of wrong directions. Part of the strategic risk is because the organization itself is oriented to goals and processes that are not appropriate for it. It is here that strategic intelligence has a considerable value and where decisions will be based on evidence and intuition according to data and development of capabilities of AI and digitalization when and where required (see Exhibit 1.16). In light of the possible causes of strategic intelligence, it can be clear that several of the operational risks can be converted into strategic risks.

Moreover, strategic risk and operational risk are directly connected to competitive advantage development and the use of data analytics and AI as means to fuel and maintain the engine of the benefits of strategic intelligence enhancement. The following concepts are required to understand the contexts of the analysis and the differentiation among strategic risk and operational risk. In the integration of KPI and KRI, the strategic and operational pain points must be considered and studied properly. Slywotzky and Drzik (2005) consider strategic risk the biggest of all risks for an organization. These authors identify the following factors that have incidence in strategic risk: industry margin squeeze, technology shift, brand erosion, competitors' strengths, customer priority shift, new project failure, and market stagnation. Furthermore, strategic risk is observed as a lack of capacity to achieve goals, reducing the possibility of supporting community development. Young and Hasler (2010) pointed out that

<table>
<tr><td>Factors which produce uncertainty:
• Technological changes
• Cultural changes
• Product and services changes
• Competence rules changes
• Political and operational condition changes
• Global environment changes</td><td>Wrong directions
• Fast growth
• No growth
• Internal focus alone
• To be just worried for the market share
• To forget the other dimension of competitors different from products
• Crisis
• Vision and mission loss</td></tr>
<tr><td colspan="2">Avoid falling in decision-making traps according to Hammond et al. (2006)
• Bias of last information
• Maintaining status quo
• Justifying past choices
• Supporting instinct
• Problem-solving methods affecting decisions
• Lacking forecast feedback</td></tr>
</table>

Exhibit 1.16. Uncertainty factors in organizations.

reputational risk, which is part of strategic risk, is the risk affecting reputational capital, which includes concepts related to honesty, responsibility, objectivity, and fairness in the outcomes and processes. In contrast with strategic risk, operational risk is "[t]he risk of loss resulting from inadequate or failed processes and systems, human error, or external events" (Ong, 2006). A way to relate operational risk and stakeholders is presented by Sadgrove (2005), who indicates different types of hazards depending on the business value chain; this is related to suppliers, processes and internal risks, distribution, and customers.

Based on the above observation about value chain and risk that can be illustrated using the work of Young and Hasler (2010), strategic risk is indicated in the case of international trading organizations. Operations in international trading organizations offers services and products which increase exposure to risk because of local market factors as well as the international landscape with increased possibilities of variation in multiple dimensions of transactions: risk related to country, socio-economic risk, customers knowledge, and competitors in local markets. An example of how these types of factors can affect risk is Target arriving in Canada. Target opened a large number of stores but had to leave the country a few months later because the business was doing very badly, losses accumulated, and there was no possibility of recovery, leading to the closure of 133 stores and losses amounting to more than a billion dollars. Target's expansion in Canada failed. Furthermore, the development of the capital market is a fundamental element in the change in risk conditions because of different contracts that are negotiated. Information structures about risk conditions need to have an administration with better control and training of people in charge. Foreign investment in different countries brings new ways of doing business, changing the levels of technology, the ways of local operations, and the way of reaching consumers. Marketing needs to be more developed, segmentation is more precise, there is greater focus on organizations, a lower level of intermediation is sought, and products become more sophisticated, all of which are components that lead to the vulnerability of the results. Successful market structures and marketing practices can quickly achieve better treatment of possible outcomes, but the level of speed of change and the difficulty in the strategy development process require more organized control and execution of projects. In particular, and using international observations, strategic risks are mainly described as follows:

Reputation: For example, international trading organizations have goals that involve responsibilities with three main stakeholders: the international organization that is supported by the government of the originating country, the country where the organization is working, and the users and beneficiaries of the programs and projects.

Trust: Comprises two main aspects: reliability and credibility (Maister *et al.*, 2000). Reliability is identified in the sense that the local country can be confident that the programs are supporting areas where the local country is not able to act to solve certain community problems. Credibility is identified in the sense that the organization has the expertise to accomplish the responsibilities that the local government and users expect to be performed.

Funding: There are limited funds around the world for development organizations. The reduction of budget and access to resources can be a barrier to developing and finishing projects.

Organizational adaptation to changes: Changes that appear from the new country's regulation, organizational morale, and internal adoption of the new government's requests. The strategy to be adopted by the organization for the coming years is under an ongoing process. As such, it must be assumed to be a constraint. It is required to initiate an awareness-raising campaign of the corporate culture that is expected and desired. It is important to create and maintain an environment for developing staff competencies (knowledge, attitudes, and skills) over time to ensure the success of projects, even with new members of the organization. The work on the organizational culture must be maintained over time to take effect.

Deregulation factor: Concentrating on the management of integral risk affects the possibility of providing more services, development of capital markets, foreign investment, new financial businesses, better supervision, technical patrimony condition, segmentation is more strongly attacked, growing disintermediation, margin reduction, and greater distribution costs. This leads to the possibility of more sophisticated and analytical customers, more sophisticated products, more sophisticated but more complex technologies, more marketing through focus, greater technology analysis, an increase of communication media and presentation of services, and greater economic difficulties and continuous changes (Exhibit 1.17).

Deregulation as a factor to tune-up risk management and to move from compliance to strategic visión of risk management

Changes to review the effects:

- Possibility of providing more services.
- Capital market development.
- Foreign investment.
- New financial business.
- Better supervision.
- Conditions of technical heritage.
- Segmentation more strongly attacked.
- Increasing disintermediation.
- Margin reduction.
- Higher distribution costs.

- More sophisticated and analytical consumers.
- More sophisticated products.
- More sophisticated but more complex technology.
- Increased marketing by focus.
- Greater information analysis technology.
- Increase in media and service delivery.
- Greater economic difficulties and ongoing changes.

Exhibit 1.17. Changes can come from regulation.

Changes in marketing structures: Changes can occur in distribution channels, access to distribution networks, outsourcing structure, and redefining the roles of companies. Thus, new risks are presented to be analyzed and different values are introduced in the results since the affected variables can be extensively modified.

With the previous review of some of the strategic risks, the next point is to think about the nature of operational risks illustrated with an example of services in social work in communities based on knowledge use:

Effectiveness: Self-confidence of the different teams is great. However, officials report that daily work does not leave much time for fundamental processes of knowledge management: Neither knowledge creation nor the actions or process tips are recorded or documented; even the systematization of experiences is not done. There are only progress reports and final project presentations, with no supported storage on the intranet or the Web (which can be public) to share knowledge with other teams and ensure implementation at different levels (not only in the area where it was created). The silo culture is a direction that organizations require to review given the need to create multidisciplinary teams and projects to study and deal with risk and problems that require multiple perspectives to achieve a proper solution.

User/beneficiary satisfaction: There are different kinds of users: communities and external organizations that are involved in several programs. They can be public or private. The volume of document exchange is high and the subjects very diverse. The contacts with organizations are also diverse. The interviews show the need for improvement regarding the users or beneficiaries.

Efficiency of resource use: One of the limitations in operation is the budget and the access to resources. Good management of the resources is a priority in order to accomplish the proposed goals. There is a challenge in managing resources given the nature of the activities and interaction with the users. Poor resource management can jeopardize the service delivery.
Lack of knowledge: Information and documents are produced in a high volume mainly associated with the government-related organizations. However, their production and distribution are not standardized, their storage is very time consuming, and retrieval is difficult.

Collaboration: Inter-area work or networking with users is informal. It should be facilitated and systematized. This is without doubt the area where people are looking for solutions. Although there is interaction, the experience is not recorded, stored, shared, and communicated in a formal and systematic way.

Training or upskilling process: Given the time constraints for training, it is usually conducted through basic virtual means or learning by doing.

Given the more frequent crises and the presence of short periods where disruptions can appear, leading to faster impact on performance, there needs to be assessment, monitoring, control, mitigation, and post-event action plans to guide organizations to navigate with better identification of potential outcomes. Data analytics and AI help in the prediction, simulation, and definition of guidelines and actions but human–machine interaction will show if there are strengths to guide people to lead solutions and orientation of results, regulation adjustments, market collaboration, etc., with evidence to maintain a good societal standard of living.

To summarize, strategic and operational risks have to be linked to the development of competitive advantages in organizations, dealing with the concept of risk in the whole organization, different types of risk, components of risk and risk processes, corporate risks and decisions under risk, steps involved in comprehensive analysis of risk, a review of the quantitative outcomes, and good practice of real options analysis, simulation, and optimization tools in the search for intelligence development (see Exhibit 1.18).

In real options analysis, the NPV of cash flows and the present value of the fixed costs are supplemented by considering a time frame where opportunities are valid, the possible events that affect the outcomes, the length of time when the project or action will be performed, and how the

Real Options

- Projects – strategies risk analysis
- Based on Call Options and under the assumptions of Black-Scholes' model
- The main question is to proceed or differ a project
- $O = f(I, C, V, T, R)$
- R risk free interest rate, T time to differ the project exploitation), V variance of the value, C project capital(strike price), I investment value

Exhibit 1.18. Basic concept of real options.

market conditions are in reviewing risk-free assets. The idea is that projects can improve the option value before exercising an option when it is possible to increase a present value of positive potential inflows, reducing the present value of the outflows, create uncertainty, increase the duration of the opportunity, increasing risk free interest rates and reducing the waiting time to use the right to exercise the option. Real options are in general classified options to expand the operation, to abandon or to sell some assets at a depreciated value, to wait to perform the actions in a time in the future, to contract or not proceed with the project if conditions are not as good as expected, and to switch to another project in case the original conditions are potentially less attractive than the conditions. At the end, the project value has three terms: one is associated with the NPV, another is associated with the cost of not continuing with the project, and the third maintains the volatility of revenues and costs.

In the next section, there is supplement to the risk identification presented in this section. The way to identify a risk in a complete manner depends on how to evaluate, assess, and monitor it. The next section introduces a risk monitoring system that starts identifying general strategic circumstances generated by productivity, strategy, and risk traps, and looks for variables and their relationships to observe possible variations or risk in expected results. The section shows how the analysis is performed based on segments or clusters identified though data analytics and the qualitative way connected to the offer and operation of the organization.

1.3. Evaluating and Monitoring Risks

This section seeks to guide the evaluation and monitoring of risks using concepts from a general review of factors to include in a design of risk monitoring information systems and management control systems. A monitoring system is presented through the concepts of risk classification, RM practices, risk curve level analysis, and relationships of RM and identification of business areas and problems in organizations. Several concepts are illustrated using a setting of banks and their credit risk conditions. Qualitative tools of monitoring risk are included in the following paragraphs which can be converted into quantitative pieces of risk monitoring systems. These pieces of the systems are related to credit analysis traps, strategic traps, and productivity traps. It is considered that an organization that assumes risk as a fundamental part of its business, such as insurance companies, banks, and other companies, may have exposure to decisions about what the best competitive position can be. Exhibit 1.19 shows multiple examples of traps in strategy, operation, and risk that require resource evaluation. This is the case of having goals but with levels of liabilities that can asphyxiate the organization. The problem of the thought process that growing is always the best is that it can generate risks that require attention. In general, the concept of traps is subject risk analysis because a trap is a possible event or decision that creates potential negative effects in an organization.

The concept behind Exhibit 1.19 is that, to meet a strategic objective, it is necessary to overcome multiple traps that are open along the way to achieve the goals. The first difficulty is to identify traps as risks to take and then to find the way to avoid them when they potentially appear at every step of the strategic process. The enumeration that is presented seeks to introduce a guide to the key points in which an organization can identify priorities of monitoring potential risks that can affect future operation. For example, in the case of credit (Exhibit 1.20), the issues can occur/appear when there is no relationship between price and risk; this suggests that it is possible to fall into the trap of not knowing how much to risk, strategic blurring, reduction of the objectivity of the evaluation, etc. Another example is when a bank like Silvergate or Signature in 2023 is connected to the markets of risk operations in cryptocurrency organizations; traps in this case that are generated because of cash flow and effects of combinations of traps such as believing that technology is an enabler for everything good. Exhibit 1.21 shows the example of traps in credit risk as a combination of other traps, and in the example of the bankruptcy of the two banks, it is about concentration of deposits and investment that created issues in the cash flow.

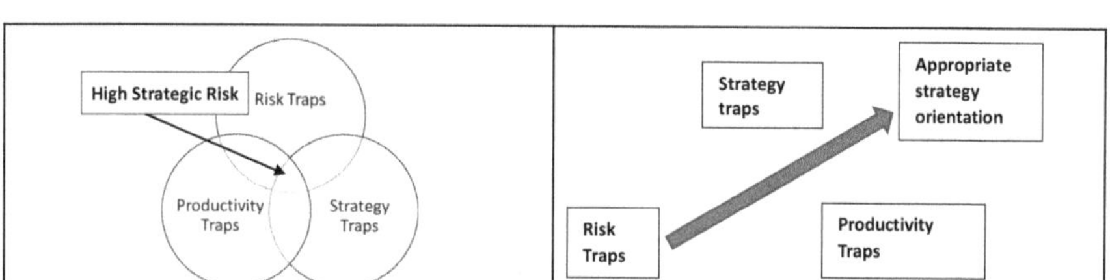

Exhibit 1.19. Strategic risks and productivity traps in organizations.

Risk Traps are associate with the lack of analysis of aspects such as the following: • Do not risk more than you are willing to lose. • Consider random events. This means that the search for probability distributions that describe risk is fundamental. You cannot let everything be spontaneous without having a behavioral orientation. • Do not risk much for little. • Believe that everything is solved with technology. • Not having clarity on how to manage data. • Consider only the asset at risk exposure or only engage in analyzing the elements of the liability.	**Strategy traps** They are those that the approach to the strategy seem to take the organization on the best path to follow. However there is an illusion, misunderstanding and confusion to obtain appropriate results. For example, in the concept of "being the largest is the best," there are countless concepts that would make it possible for this to be false. For example, if the organization is a leader in size and also in cost structure, possibly being bigger will be better. But if on the contrary the organization is very large with a poorly organized cost structure, it is possible to lead to total failure. • Making the operation of the business too narrow. • Stay in the middle. • Not be aimed at the consumer. • Being cheaper is better. • Underestimating the competition. • Today's success will be tomorrow's success. • Only the highest levels of the organization know the strategy. • Superficial communication. • Consider eloquence to be everything. • To be placed in the situation of excellence of yesterday more than tomorrow. • Reaching today's figures tomorrow. • A good athlete can run in any business. • Analysis paralysis. • Match corporate culture.

Exhibit 1.19. (*Continued*)

Productivity traps

These refer to processes and procedures that may prevent compliance with an adequate performance structure that must strengthen the company at its competitive level. This enumeration contemplates elements that affect both people–machines and the results of automatic processes, all with the same orientation of being possible productivity reducers.

- Inadequate development of internal policies.
- Consider that everything is handled on the basis of good relationships.
- Believe rumors and encourage them.
- Reduce the objectivity of the evaluation.
- Consider that every person must give results in the same way.
- Maintain poor communication.
- Generate preferences among managers/employees.
- Maintain an unmotivated work group.
- Generate bias culture.
- Not expressing things clearly.
- Feed the condition first as individuals and/or after the organization.
- Pursuit of power first and foremost.
- Do not make decisions but leave things to the own free will of the member of the organization.
- Generate little authority.
- Poor planning.
- Believe that profitability is achieved without developing the business, plans, structures, etc.
- Take a different orientation from the market.
- Build organizations on the basis of belief and not based on evidence.
- Show incongruities between duty and being.

Exhibit 1.19. (*Continued*)

When a combination of all these elements is presented as poor planning, with poor communication, underestimating competence, and little identification of responsibilities, what can be expected? Within a credit institution, one would simply not know what market group is the objective; therefore, if the organization wants to follow a road, it would not be possible, nor would it be able to choose which are the competitors with which the organization first has to dispute the market, and worse still the

1. There is no relationship between price and risk.
2. The cost of capital is set aside.
3. It plays with the antiselection.
4. The price has not been studied, only regulation matters.
5. Emphasis is placed on portfolio growth.
6. You don't look at the balance of the credit portfolio.
7. Perform a low scan.
8. Managerial evaluation is not in terms of final results but sales.
9. Authority without powers.
10. Inadequate customer search.
11. Relate status with attributions.
12. Relate hierarchy with the ability to grant credit without having the skills.
13. Loss of history, learning of the entity.
14. Little identification of responsibilities.
15. Believe that politics is the same element that guides good results.
16. Not supporting the process in good systems.
17. Generalize the practices without knowing the fields where they will act.

Exhibit 1.20. Traps in credit risk.

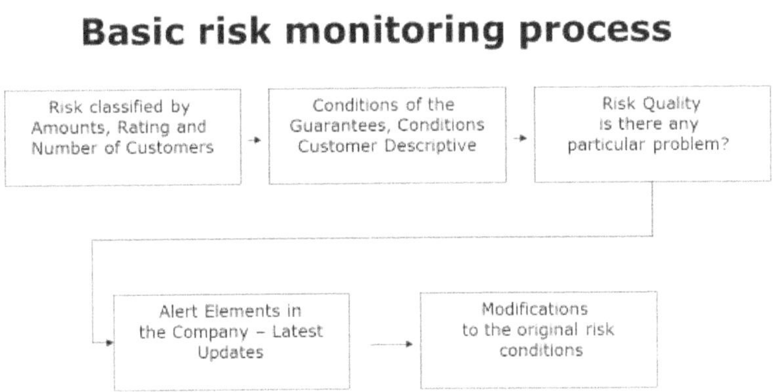

Figure 1.6. Sequence for risk monitoring.

organization's management would not know what kind of responsibility the officials have — each could go in a different directions.

Now, with the understanding of possible traps in the radar of risk study, the possible sequence to monitor risk is given in Figure 1.6 where the assumption is that risk classification has been done to move through the next steps in creating intelligence. A surveillance/monitoring process is fundamental given the observation of how businesses are evolving, how industries are affected by markets conditions, etc., and this monitoring process is implemented through an information/knowledge management system. In the following paragraphs, there is a brief description of pieces of the system that help guide what to do according to segments defined through a clustering process — unsupervised learning.

A first step is to review how risk exposure segments are linked to objectives and goals of organizations. Each of the boxes in Exhibits 1.21–1.25 can be filled in with an understanding of what is an expected value of indicators such as revenues, profits, and ROI. Once these elements are clear, the search for variations of the expected value of where the organization can help and its causes can be the way to identify risks and areas to concentrate and to work on for risk mitigation purposes.

The mix of business components dedicated to the risk exposure segments is fundamental to measuring the impact of risk realization on the bottom line of the organization. Products, distribution channels, and several other factors are assigned according to optimization goals from management. For instance, the Winners segment can be a generation of profits in high percentage, but it is not growing as expected; the revenue management strategy can help to compensate profits expectations using specific strategies with other segments. Those strategies will help to mitigate strategic risks regarding profit generation.

From the point of view of data analytics, clustering analysis will help though a multivariate view of the risk exposure segments with the possibility of including priorities of targets to generate the AI applications to maintain adjustment according to predefined and continuously reviewed thresholds for setting priorities. Variables used in the process of connecting risks, segments, and variables in a bank setting can be used for branch offices. For many years, banks have identified the digitalization/automation projects as priority, including special solutions as ATMs or automated teller machines supporting human work inside branch offices, using telephone banking, or creating apps for online banking. However, customers have multiple needs and habits and depending on how profitable the solutions are certain decisions can be made. Branch offices did not disappear and in several cases grew, possibly because certain transactions and services are not possible to transfer to other service systems. Strategic risk is presented if no adjustment to the service offer is done and at same time if changes are abrupt and only a type of system is offered. Different can be

Segments	Objectives — general/global
Winners	
Opportunity	
Commons	
Basics	

Exhibit 1.21. Aligning risk exposure segments and objectives.

Segment	**What is the priority**	**Which products**	**In sales**	**In distribution channels**
Winners				
Opportunity				
Commons				
Basics				
Others				

Exhibit 1.22. Aligning risk exposure segments and components of marketing plan.

the situation of banks that are from the beginning totality digital and that grew the business with customers adapted and adopted new technologies (see Section 4.4).

Another level to monitor risk is connecting risk exposure segments and strategy. Exposure is the fundamental piece of risk analysis. Exposure represents the business interest where an organization can be affected because of the appearance of risk events. Identification of relationships between the risk exposure segments and business strategy components is a crucial step to monitor and control strategic risks. Exhibit 1.24 shows examples of a combination of what an organization is offering to risk exposure segments and how an organization like a bank can translate pieces of strategy to reach and maintain those risk exposure segments in good shape, creating value. Complexity appears given the variability of the options in each category and that is how part of the strategic risk analysis and possible mitigation solutions will provide value as well.

<table>
<tr><td></td><td>Variable 2</td><td colspan="9">Age</td></tr>
<tr><td>Variable 1</td><td></td><td colspan="3">Young</td><td colspan="3">Middle</td><td colspan="3">Retired</td></tr>
<tr><td rowspan="4">Revenue</td><td>Category</td><td>Branch</td><td>ATM</td><td>Phone</td><td>Branch</td><td>ATM</td><td>Phone</td><td>Branch</td><td>ATM</td><td>Phone</td></tr>
<tr><td>High</td><td></td><td></td><td></td><td></td><td></td><td></td><td></td><td></td><td></td></tr>
<tr><td>Medium</td><td></td><td></td><td></td><td></td><td></td><td></td><td></td><td></td><td></td></tr>
<tr><td>Low</td><td></td><td></td><td></td><td></td><td></td><td></td><td></td><td></td><td></td></tr>
</table>

Exhibit 1.23. Aligning products, customers, and revenue.

It was indicated before the business definition What, Who and How dimensions are the bases where offer of the organization will be and the business dimensions where risk exposure will appear. What Exhibit 1.25 shows is how risk exposure can be different, similar to risks, which means identifying mitigants according to transactions, customer profiles, and methods/technologies for customers to use. A good example is with risk related to regular checking accounts in a bank. If there is a withdrawal in the office, using telephone banking, or using only payments, risks can be about teller knowledge, telephone security methods, or communication/transaction hacking in an online environment. All risks are tied to an equivalent transaction type, but solutions come from multiple technologies, teams, knowledge/experiences, etc.

Building a score tool to maintain consistency and compare criteria results is a possible way to prioritize the intervention in risk mitigation, Exhibit 1.26 shows a simplified view of intuitive scoring that can be upgraded when more data are available to obtain three main aspects to work on: competitiveness, attractiveness, and opportunities. One can evaluate how factors affecting each of these categories are associated with risk exposure segments. This means that actions for mitigating risks will be under the logic of exploiting opportunities, being competitive, and where there is market attractiveness and risk appetite.

In general, risk exposure segments shown in Exhibits 1.27–1.31, and using a bank example, show how these matrices can guide the identification of areas where risks are present or emerging, with a clearer definition of metrics to evaluate risk and control them. Key risk indicators will be identified, and the monitoring information system will develop

Risk exposure Segments and marketing mix relationships	Products and prices	Commercial actions	Distribution	Service	Intangible assets	Customer knowledge systems
Segments	Offer characteristics	Communication	Offices	Contact	People	Innovation
A	Price	Promotion and public relations	Cards	Knowledge	Local and global image	Transference
B	Risk		internet	Training		Collaboration
C	Appeal	Network development and database management	Phone	Complexity levels	Positioning	infrastructure
…	Improvement opportunity		Peripheral			Business process
…	Differentiation					Structure knowledge system
N						

Exhibit 1.24. Alignment of risk exposure segments and marketing mix.

<table>
<tr><td rowspan="2">What and who</td><td colspan="4">Customer profiles</td></tr>
<tr><td>Age</td><td>Income</td><td>Equity</td><td>Complexity</td></tr>
<tr><td>Needs</td><td colspan="4" rowspan="5">Who is offering it? What is the financial institution? With what intensity or effort? Is it the strength of competitors?</td></tr>
<tr><td>Transactions</td></tr>
<tr><td>Basic Information</td></tr>
<tr><td>Consumption</td></tr>
<tr><td>Asset Management</td></tr>
</table>

Exhibit 1.25. Alignment of customer profiles and customers' knowledge according to risk exposure.

capabilities to be proactive in RM to contribute to the construction of adaptive, sustainable advantages. The process starts with the reviewing of risk exposure segments and product types.

Then, it is worth dividing risk exposure segments and product use by attributes, by revenues, profitability, volume use, transactions, and so on.

Once products and attributes of those products are related, a review of risk exposure segments and transactions will provide knowledge about operations.

Operations are internal actions in the organization that can be observed in competitors of market participants of get a benchmark in terms of risk exposure segments and profitability — segment analysis vs. competitors — industry — by cluster of industries represented groups of variables to generate actions by segments.

If the segments are considered using any analytics method, the next step is capacity and capability evaluation to support them.

Exhibits 1.32 and 1.33 are examples of how to combine that knowledge created from data analytics and how it can be translated to specific organizational objectives and its performance evaluation as part of the management mandate. These exhibits present items that can be adapted to any organization based on the macro categories of knowledge creation to use, business objectives, and resources, and process use and enhancement. The survey of these elements helps to organize a map to find where

Main factors	Competitiveness			Attractiveness			Opportunity					
Specific factors	Differentiation possibility	Competitive intensity	Entry barriers	Capacity adjustment	Capabilities	Maturity	Market share	Knowledge score	Profitability	Total competitiveness	Total attractiveness	Total opportunity
Weight	15%	10%	5%	10%	15%	5%	15%	10%	15%	30%	30%	40%
Risk exposure segments												
1	2	1	5	4	2	4	2	4	2			
2	1	5	3	5	1	4	3	5	2			
3	2	5	5	3	4	3	5	4	3			
4	4	4	2	4	3	3	5	1	4			
5	5	4	5	5	5	4	2	3	5			
6	2	1	5	4	2	4	2	4	2			
7	1	5	3	5	1	4	3	5	2			
8	2	5	5	3	4	3	5	4	3			
9	4	4	2	4	3	3	5	1	4			
10	5	4	5	5	5	4	2	3	5			

Exhibit 1.26. Creating scoring methods of segments according to competitiveness, attractiveness, and opportunity.

Risk exposure segments	Liquidity	Basic	Credit	Insurance	Transactions special	Transactions general	Balance profitability	Demographic	Risk
Winners									
Opportunity									
Commons									
Basics									

Exhibit 1.27. Aligning segments and type of products, transactions, volumes, and risk.

Risk exposure segments	Accounts by products and customers			
	chequing	saving	Cred.card	Investment
Winners				
Opportunity				
Commons				
Basics				

Exhibit 1.28. Aligning risk exposure segments and products.

Risk exposure segments	Transactions per month per product / services				
	ATM	Branch	Phone		
Winners					
Opportunity					
Commons					
Basics					

Exhibit 1.29. Aligning risk exposure segments and services.

Risk exposure segments	Expected growth	Purchases growth	Indicator consistency
Strong			
Moderate			
Potential			
Complex			
Attention			

Exhibit 1.30. Aligning risk exposure segments and expectations of the organization relationship.

Risk exposure segments	**Capabilities**	**Observation**
Massive and personal/families	Scoring methods	
	Low-cost operation	
	Standard products	
	Fast changes	
	Centralized services	
Private	Personal loans	
	Investments	
	International	
Small business	Standard products	
	Documentation	
	Low-cost operation	
	Automated surveillance	

Exhibit 1.31. Aligning risk exposure segments and capabilities of the organization.

certain needs exist and where the process capacity can be limited because knowledge development of data analytics has not been well defined and improved.

Exhibit 1.33 illustrates the use components of a BSC for monitoring system design for slicing and dicing objectives, processes, and resources. Exhibit 1.33 is a visualization of a problem that has to be solved in several dimensions related to the organization's operation and strategy. The main actions inside the organization will be to connect data and metrics according to the vector, objectives, business process, knowledge process, and resources used. Near the scores that are aggregated (Exhibits 1.34 and 1.36) by business process and by knowledge process are guides to review where enhancements can be performed.

Risk management processes will provide answers to risk assessment and how an organization's governance needs to be prepared for creating and communicating risk capacity to maintain and improve the stakeholder's value. A clear case is the strategic risk related to the position of the organizations in a competitive environment. Figure 1.7 identifies that the system that is looking for right actions in efficiency and effectiveness

Evaluation Advancing Strategic Intelligence

		Perception of advances of using data analytics knowledge creation, access, storage, transfer, and application					
Definitions		Indicators					
			Nothing	Poor	Acceptable	Good	Excellent
Risk Knowledge Creation	1	In systematization of explicit knowledge, experiences, and learning at work				X	
	2	In the use of participatory methodologies to share knowledge with other officials and groups		X			
	3	In the efficiency of operation	X				
	4	In the effectiveness of operation					
	5	In the innovation and processes					
Risk Knowledge storage and access	1	Information storage					
	2	Information quality					
	3	Knowledge of user's needs					
	4	Access to information and knowledge					
	5	Knowledge interdisciplinarity					
Collaboration Risk Knowledge transfer	1	Knowledge exchange					
	2	Activities with diverse teams					
	3	Results' quality					
	4	Business environment					
	5	Talent development					
Risk Knowledge Application	1	Experience automation					
	2	Result and experience visibility					
	3	Use of innovation					
	4	Satisfaction of users					
	5	Brand equity					
Learning and Development		**People learning and development**					
	1	Organization planning					
	2	Internal web channel use					
	3	Skills development					
	4	Best result management					
	5	Working environment					

Exhibit 1.32. Evaluating Knowledge process, learning, and capabilities to use data analytics.

Internal processes development,	**Processes** 1 Identification and value 2 Execution 3 Follow-up and evaluation 4 Experience automation 5 Communication development
Resource use	**Resources** 1 Operational use 2 Time for using 3 Time to obtain access 4 Compliance of operation rules 5 Financial efficiency
Users/beneficiaries/customers	**Users / customers / beneficiaries** 1 Satisfaction stakeholder 1 2 Satisfaction stakeholder 2 3 Satisfaction stakeholder 3 4 Satisfaction stakeholder 4 5 Satisfaction stakeholder 5

Exhibit 1.32. (*Continued*).

needs to be aligned at multiple levels in the organization identifying when it is possible cause and effects relationships using diagrams that describe process steps.

In addition, it is required to have a combination of the risk exposure segments and how the vector of objectives, processes, people, etc., are related to what organizations are able to do and are currently doing. A risky competitive position is built, as mentioned before, based on a strategy and its implementation; hence, a SWOT analysis helps to define what to use and what to do. However, many of planned movements are exposed to what other organizations are doing and to the business environment conditions. Creating a competitive position requires the review of factors such as processes, products, people, machines, and technology. These factors require an ongoing review of potential threats and opportunities. A competitive position will be based on attributes that can have variation, and variation of those attributes will create indication of risks to evaluate. Changes in competitive position can be summarized as the following changes in factors:

Organization objectives	Knowledge Processes / Business Processes	Identificación	Formulación	Valoración	Ejecución	Seguimiento	Evaluación	Comunicaciones	Sistematización de Experiencias	Total
	Knowledge Creation									
	People									
Objective 1	Promotion of the development of new solutions for beneficiary problems	5	1	1	1	1	1	1	1	12
	Encouraging the participation of officials in solving problems	5	5	5	5	5	5	5	5	40
	Encouraging the implementation of new solutions	5	5	5	5	5	5	5	5	40
	SUBTOTAL	92								
	Processes									
	Use of the Intranet for the creation of new knowledge	5	5	5	5	5	5	5	5	40
	Existence of an innovation plan	5	5	5	5	5	5	5	5	40
	Promotion of new solutions	5	5	5	5	5	5	5	5	40
	SUBTOTAL	120								
	Resources									
	Improvement of allocation of economic resources and operating guidelines of the organization	5	5	5	5	5	5	5	5	40
	Understanding new rules or changes in legal areas	5	5	5	5	5	5	5	5	40
	Support for compliance with project deadlines	5	5	5	5	5	5	5	5	40
	SUBTOTAL	120								
	Users/beneficiaries/customers									
	Improved effectiveness of solutions to user problems	5	5	5	5	5	5	5	5	40
	Methodological improvement for program and project development	5	5	5	5	5	5	5	5	40
	User involvement in responses and solutions to problems	5	5	5	5	5	5	5	5	40
	SUBTOTAL	120								
	Knowledge Storage/Access									
	People									
Objective 2	People can find the content	5	5	5	5	5	5	5	5	40
	People can retain the content history	5	5	5	5	5	5	5	5	40
	People can reuse content from multiple areas	5	5	5	5	5	5	5	5	40
	SUBTOTAL	120								
	Processes									
	Existing technology supports the creation of new solutions to problems	5	5	5	5	5	5	5	5	40
	Access to documents is easy	5	5	5	5	5	5	5	5	40
	The process of access to information is adequate	5	5	5	5	5	5	5	5	40

Exhibit 1.33. Scoring the relationship of objectives and organization's knowledge capacity according to processes and resources available.

	SUBTOTAL	120								
	Resources									
	Budget data are comparable over different time periods	5	5	5	5	5	5	5	5	40
	The budget data control structure is adequate.	5	5	5	5	5	5	5	5	40
	The budget structure encourages the creation of new solutions to users	5	5	5	5	5	5	5	5	40
	SUBTOTAL	120								
	Users/beneficiaries/customers									
	Shared analysis of beneficiaries' needs encourages the development of new solutions	5	5	5	5	5	5	5	5	40
	User information is easily accessible in archived documents	5	5	5	5	5	5	5	5	40
	Users actively participate in the identification and execution of solutions	5	5	5	5	5	5	5	5	40
	SUBTOTAL	120								
Objective 3	**Knowledge transfer**									
	People development									
	Our colleagues are willing to share knowledge	5	5	5	5	5	5	5	5	40
	Meetings to discuss solutions are appropriately collaborative	5	5	5	5	5	5	5	5	40
	Activities in which knowledge sharing is promoted are appropriate	5	5	5	5	5	5	5	5	40
	SUBTOTAL	120								
	Processes									
	The use of systems that allow working with other officials is appropriate	5	5	5	5	5	5	5	5	40
	Existing technology for inter-communication and collaboration is adequate	5	5	5	5	5	5	5	5	40
	Today's technology helps us get better results	5	5	5	5	5	5	5	5	40
	SUBTOTAL	120								
	Resources									
	Training for the use of resources is adequate	5	5	5	5	5	5	5	5	40
	Financial resources to support knowledge transfer are adequate	5	5	5	5	5	5	5	5	40
	The execution of the budgets to support joint work is adequate	5	5	5	5	5	5	5	5	40
	SUBTOTAL	120								
	Users/Beneficiaries/customers									
	The collaboration of different people from diverse groups appropriately supports users	5	5	5	5	5	5	5	5	40
	Adequate use is made of existing means to better understand other institutional issues	5	5	5	5	5	5	5	5	40
	Sharing what they know with other officials and users is appropriate	5	5	5	5	5	5	5	5	40
	SUBTOTAL	120								
Objective 4	**Knowledge Application**									
	People									
	The interest of officials in applying knowledge is adequate	5	5	5	5	5	5	5	5	40
	The application of knowledge is done in a timely manner	5	5	5	5	5	5	5	5	40
	Institutional conditions for applying knowledge are right	5	5	5	5	5	5	5	5	40
	SUBTOTAL	120								
	Process									
	Existing technology fosters the application of knowledge	5	5	5	5	5	5	5	5	40
	Institutional processes foster the application of knowledge	5	5	5	5	5	5	5	5	40
	The capacity for change and improvement of processes is adequate	5	5	5	5	5	5	5	5	40

Exhibit 1.33. (*Continued*)

SUBTOTAL	120								
Resources									
Incentives for the application of knowledge are adequate	5	5	5	5	5	5	5	5	40
Project execution capacity has improved due to the application of knowledge	5	5	5	5	5	5	5	5	40
Resources dedicated to applying knowledge to do better work are adequate	5	5	5	5	5	5	5	5	40
SUBTOTAL	120								
Users									
The knowledge accumulated in the institution supports users very well	5	5	5	5	5	5	5	5	40
The ability to develop new projects and solutions is getting better	5	5	5	5	5	5	5	5	40
The application of institutional knowledge to the solution of user problems is adequate	5	5	5	5	5	5	5	5	40
SUBTOTAL	120								
Total	240	236	236	236	236	236	236	236	1892

Exhibit 1.33. (*Continued*)

Scores of the objectives	
Summary Indicators	
Knowledge processes	
Creation	452
Storage and Access	480
Transfer	480
Application	480

Summary BSC	
BSC	
People	452
Process	480
Resources	480
Users	480

Exhibit 1.34. Aggregation of scores according to knowledge processes.

Business process	
Identification	240
Formulation	236
Valuation	236
Execution	236
Follow-up	236
Evaluation	236
Communications	236
Experience automation	236

Exhibit 1.35. Aggregation of scores according to business process.

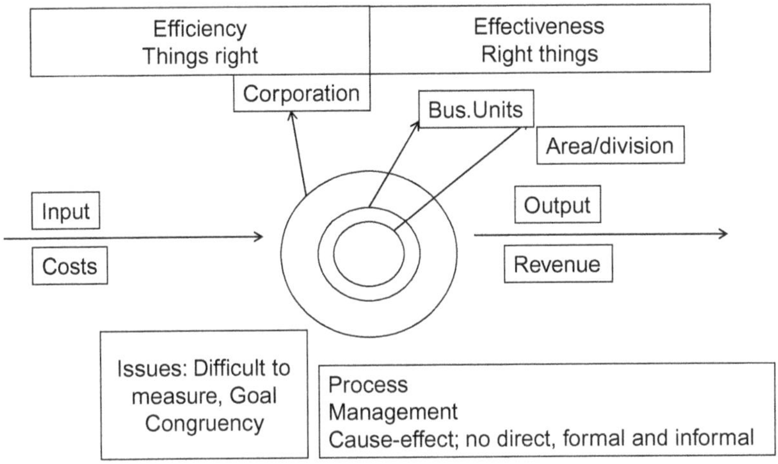

Figure 1.7. RM functions and generation of risk capacity.

- The possibility of offering more services.
- Capital market development.
- Foreign investment.
- New financial businesses.
- Better supervision.
- Technical equity restrictions.
- Weak segmentation and aggressive competence.
- Less intermediation.
- Margin reduction. Concentration
- Higher distribution costs.
- More sophisticated and analytical customers.
- More sophisticated products.
- New technology and more complexity. Digitalization and access to use it.
- Higher focus marketing. Niches with high risk.
- More advanced information analysis technology. Speed of information dissemination.
- Communication media and service increment.
- Permanent changes and bigger economic difficulties.

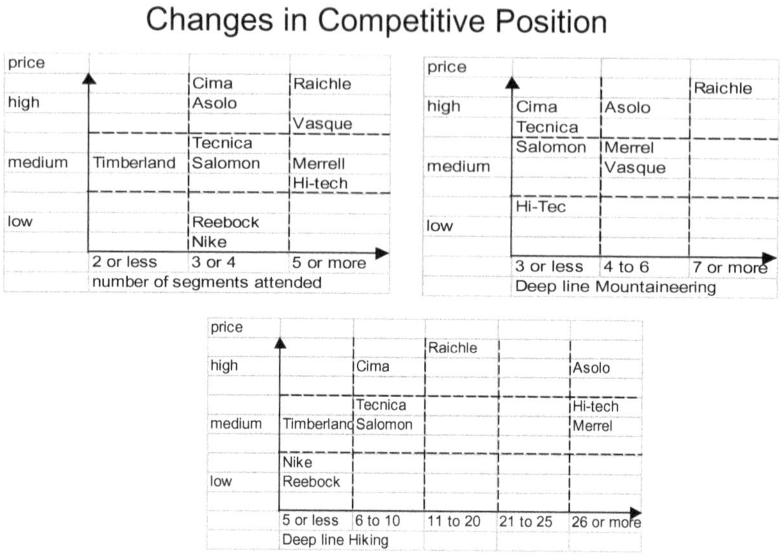

Figure 1.8. Using maps of competitors to evaluate positions according to the dimensions of business product, customers, and technology.

From the previous list, it is possible to state that currently, and based on the digitalization of transactions in the financial services market, panic because of potential issues in banks can have major consequences such as bankruptcy. In March 2023, three banks declared bankruptcy, and six more were in poor condition, including Credit Suisse. The speed of communication and reactions to withdraw money from banks demonstrate levels of risk, such as selling assets with losses or having high concentration in certain sectors in the asset, deposits, and investment sides. The plunging value of the shares and very fast flow of "negative" information took the three banks out of the market in less than a week. The list of factors that can affect a competitive position can be represented and evaluated using a Cartesian diagram, measuring distances on planes or radians as shown in Figures 1.8 and 1.9, or by using data analytics methods such as Correspondence Analysis as described in Section 4.2.

As mentioned, change in business dimensions is a potential risk in terms of variability of expected results in each business axis of customers, technology, and offer. The capacity of organizations to

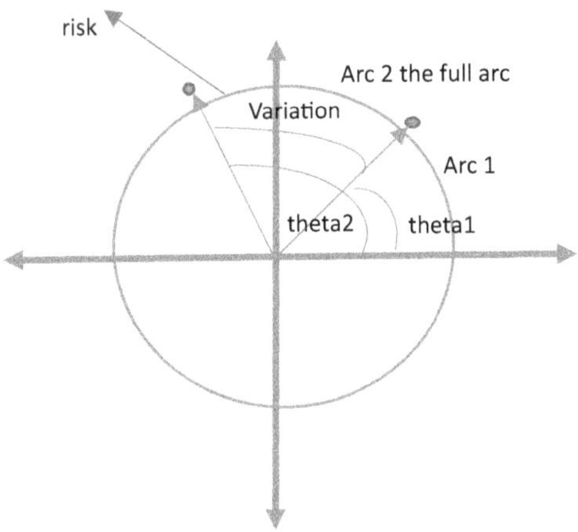

Figure 1.9. Strategic risk evaluation is about the change in competitive positions represented by change in angles.

develop barriers to protect themselves from certain changes is a mitigation strategy. This means creating contingency strategies. In that regard, confrontation strategies are required to reduce potential losses because of strategic risks. Confrontation strategies (Exhibit 1.36) means the design of answers to compensate the effects of opponents/competitors' strategies, when they are appropriate. An example is product design and launching certain products to balance the offer that a competitor has. In the current car industry environment, EV (Tesla) cars are pioneers. There are organizations in the process of changing the portfolio of combustion cars for EV cars. There are organizations that want to be in the hybrid segment (Toyota). There are others that are looking for cars based on different sources of fuel (hydrogen, for example, in the case of car makers in Germany). All these strategic movements are under the assumption that combustion cars going to decline, and regulation will affect the demand. These strategies are risky if the implementation is not controlled because they are directly affecting the business definition of organizations. Digitalization projects are part of confrontation strategies. New strategies need technology. New technologies increase capacity to reduce the failure or cost in operation, support competitiveness, and at the same time increase risks.

All in the direction of enhancing the dimensions of the business: • New products • Customer focus • Sales development • Evaluation of customer profitability • Development of customer knowledge • Better segmentation • Improved process analysis • Permanent customer evaluation • New distribution channel development • Cost evaluation • Implementation risk	Changes in Competitive Position — New technologies and risk as presented in Chapter 4. • IoT • ML and Data Analytics process • AI systems design • Use of repositories of Non — SQL • Managing Cloud computing parallel computing capacity
All above on top of the systems and technologies that supports operations where it is required such as: • AI technologies • IoT technologies • Disruptive technologies • Digitalization solutions • Client–Server development • Relational databases • New statistical packages • CASE methodologies • Outsourcing systems • Images processing • Voice processing • Operation without paper • Delivery systems • Statistical technology • Communication	Costs and Benefits from tackling use and maintenance risks: • Better service level • Better customer relationship • Marketing efficiency • Cost reduction • Better cross selling • Customer accessibility

Exhibit 1.36. Possible factors generating changes in competitive positions.

Those contingency actions to protect organizations with regard to competitive positions deserve a meticulous exam of risks associated with new technologies. A common issue with new technologies is not only the creation of the technology but also the requirement of talent to use the new technology or capacity to maintain operation of new technologies. Aligned with the example of the cars industry, there are important aspects

Changes in Competitive Position - Each new technology has specific risks

- Automatic teller machines.
- Teller-Office integration.
- Point of payment.
- Home banking.
  - By phone.
  - Internet.
- Data bases.
- Office platforms.

Associated risks:

- Vandalism.
- Non communication.
- Communication interceptions.
- Waste and garbage data.
- Bad use.
- Process cost.
- Security system violations.
- Non follow up and control.

Exhibit 1.37. Illustration of competitive position according to basic banking technology and associated risks.

to review in EV cars that are beyond the vehicle itself. Risks appear in terms of capacity to provide service to charge cars, possibly requiring mobile electric chargers, issues with disposal of batteries, issues with chemicals that are used in battery construction, new competitors that are very aggressive in the market, or markets where regulation can be stronger for combustion cars. The main point is that technology can potentially affect strategic risks under multiple agents and their own risks and possible individual changes (Exhibit 1.37).

As a summary of this section, strategic risk analysis is about possible changes in competitive positions; factors that can affect those positions are internal and external and related to what Miller and Bromiley (1990) indicated — there is convergence to three factors to be considered in risk analysis: income stream risk, stock returns risk, and strategic risk. The authors indicate that nine measures of risk are associated with strategic management: systematic risk, unsystematic risk, debt to equity ratio capital intensity, R&D intensity, variations of ROA, variations of ROE, stock earning forecast, and variation of stock earning forecast. This can be a limited view of the financial aspects and possibly a reduced integral view of the organization because of the aggregation of the variables used. Strategic risk goes further because its analysis requires the life development, survival, and strengthening of capabilities and capacity of the organization. There are risks related to the strategy formulation and implementation. The proposed work in this book defines the KPI and KRI, and reviews the creation of metrics, analysis, and meaning that comprise people–machines, processes, and technology. The main reason is that indicators cannot be only numbers; they need to be followed by people initiatives to mitigate risks and to improve the performance of the organizations. Miller and Bromiley (1990) concluded, "The results demonstrate that income stream risk reduces subsequent performance and that this influence exists across industries and performance levels. On the other hand, the influence of strategic risk on performance varies across industries and performance levels. Additional work on strategic risk, particularly the connections among financial strategies, operational strategies, and performance, appears to be needed."

Strategic risk is associated with managing cash flows. Bankruptcies occur because of reduced capacity of managing cash flows and at the same time a lack of capacity/capabilities to have muscle to defend and improve the competitive position that is coming from a not-so-solid funding management. The process of cash flows includes the good management of accounts payable and receivable, the ways to manage methods of payment, the conditions of the distribution channels for managing financial resources, and of course the appropriate management of liabilities. An interesting aspect in strategic risk is to consider the business units as investments of a holding organization. The flow of resources of the holding is based on the dividends that business units bring to the holding. The issues that affect these business units are the issues to consider in the analysis of strategic risk and the way that funding for the holding can be modified (see the example of Holding Organization from Fan *et al.* (2002) SAS for Monte Carlo Simulations).

The next section supplements the view of monitoring risks through the review of what the analysis of structures for management control systems should be. A management control system is a means to implement and evaluate how a strategy has been applied.

1.3.1 *Note about strategy analytics and integration of concepts in management control systems*

Changes in competitive positions and risk control require Management Control Systems that connect the dots: management control systems analyze goals and their relationships to scorecards and the use of data (analytics capabilities development) to improve strategy implementation. In this book, the assumption is that it is not only an accounting approach or human resources approach that can be used for designing good management control systems but also adequate use of analytics, mainly prescriptive analytics. Taking some points from management control systems theory, Anthony and Govindarajan (2007) pointed out that management control systems correspond to "The process by which managers influence other members of the organization to implement the organization's strategies." These authors continue stating that management control systems will "Facilitate management control, primarily focus on strategy execution, encompass both quantitative and qualitative performance measures, Concerned with broadly defined activities" and that the good management control system will "Achieves goal congruence by aligning: Organizational goals and Individual goals." These aspects require a good understanding of what is influencing performance. This understanding requires more than descriptions; an exploration of factors is required for the combination of data, analytics, and interpretation to supplement the beliefs of humans in management.

As noticed, in general, management control systems require data analytics that be applied on regular or big data that combine variables, models, and iterations of models' outcome for production and development of solutions. The data analytics process includes the use of constraints related to operations, conditions of regulation, management bodies of process and results of data analytics processes, use of appropriate methods or techniques for problem resolution, and possible implementation of those solutions by embedding them in the operation information systems. This is the beginning of adopting in the changes toward digitalization, involving preparation of people and process to overcome the barriers of strategy implementation, in most of the cases human–machine related because of wrong interaction, planning, and training. A strategy can be very strong in formulation and poor in implementation that will require the following components of a control system (Antony & Govindarajan, 2007):

- Detectors
- Assessors
- Effectors
- Communication

Management control systems are designed to support strategy implementation. These systems are from cost accounting to knowledge management and RM systems. The crucial aspect in the management control system's design is that strategy is formulated based on the support of data analytics or AI, and the implementation systems, control, follow-up, and prediction will be through data analytics or AI as well:

- The Committee of Sponsoring Organizations of the Treadway Commission (COSO) states that "Risk appetite is the amount of risk, on a broad level, an organization is willing to accept in pursuit of value. Each organization pursues various objectives to add value and should broadly understand the risk it is willing to undertake in doing so." Risk appetite is the definition of how much risk is part of the strategy definition. It needs measurement system definitions and management control systems design.
- The COSO continues, stating, "ERM is not isolated from strategy, planning, or day-to-day decision making. Nor is it about compliance. ERM is part of an organization's culture, just as making decisions to attain objectives is part of an organization's culture." Managing risk is not just to align the organization's actions to the regulator's expectations; it is the way to compete. Competition or good performance in a market is based on a good plan and control of the organization's uncertainty/risks.
- Management control systems in some cases are focused on areas; they are not seen as integral systems. Data analytics work is part of the integral view from data to people's actions/decisions. There is a work to do that is to describe a strategy implementation (SAS Strategy Management view), regardless the performance management framework that organizations have chosen. There is a need to align the actions of an organization to optimize strategic outcomes. In any case, the organization needs to define, plan, execute, and validate strategy:

    - **Define:** Formalize strategy and goals and the relationships between key performance indicators using strategy maps and diagrams.
    - **Plan:** Set targets, thresholds, priorities, and weights associated with strategic objectives and metrics. Align strategies to support those of the organization.
    - **Execute:** Monitor progress toward targets and goals. Receive alerts to areas of underperformance. Visually depict impact between leading and lagging indicators. Share feedback and commentary.

- **Validate:** Prove that a strategy delivers expected results. Statistically quantify impact, priorities, and relationships and perform what-if analysis.

Organizations create early warning systems and control systems to provide the following help during and post action:

Strategic Goals: The definitions of what to do, where to go, and how to achieve the goals are the bases of any good performance plan. Merchant (2012) pointed out, "Objectives are a necessary prerequisite for any purposeful activities. Without objectives, it is impossible … to assess whether the employees' actions are purposive, to make claims about an organization's success … Objectives can be: financial vs. non-financial, quantified, explicit vs. implicit, economic, social, environmental, or societal."
Equity and Capital Structure: In strategy, the concept of capital structure involves how to use financial resources to pay for acquiring and using assets or for everything that is part of the organization's operations. Key risk indicators are associated not only with the allocation of resources in the organization's strategy implementation but also to map risk actions and priorities based on defined objectives such as searching to maximize the value of the firm, minimizing the weighted average cost of capital, and maximizing the market value of the common stock.

Strategic goals as a creation of balanced risk scorecards are a way to explore and review movements ahead in organizations. Exhibit 1.38 indicates examples of strategic goals according to what is required to align performance evaluation and risk strategy map development.

Figure 1.10 represents strategic goals and how an organization needs to develop management to support/develop capabilities to achieve goals through appropriate implementation of the strategy. The concept to keep in mind is that there are continuous processes to connect what is desired, what is required, and the way to align and coordinate multiple roles and conditions of the business operation. Strategic risk will emerge if the continuity of improvement and review of results and their variances regarding KPIs and KRIs (key risk indicators) are broken.

As an example, the following paragraphs describe a case of strategic risk in financial institutions (Exhibit 1.39), as an approximation that can be made in the search for expected profits according to the destinations of the credit, the activities of the sectors, the geographical location, and the expected conditions of utility that the companies analyzed possess.

Strategic goals: How to get where the organizations want to go? Keep in mind: Known, Unknown and Unknowable options: Possible future, desire future, feasible future use processes of: • Planning • Coordinating • Communicating • Evaluating • Deciding • Influencing	**Strategic goals: How to get where the organization wants to go?** • Clarify where to go and where to start. Decide what to measure • Create the systems to measure • Be sure that you can measure data and capacity to add value to the raw data • Perform Analytics — knowledge — understanding — Study what you get and what you wanted to achieve … Answer the Why question about potential value added. • Find root causes — and cause — effect connectivity Communicate — horizontally and vertically
Financial increase: Shareholder value • Strategic Objective • Key Performance Indicator • Strategic Initiatives • Key Risk Indicators • Actions/controls	Customer increase: Market share • Strategic Objective • Key Performance Indicator • Strategic Initiatives • Key Risk Indicators • Actions/controls
Internal processes: Improve marketing • Strategic Objective • Key Performance Indicator • Strategic Initiatives • Key Risk Indicators • Actions/controls	Learning and growth: Optimize work force • Strategic Objective • Key Performance Indicator • Strategic Initiatives • Key Risk Indicators • Actions/controls

Exhibit 1.38. Aligning strategic objectives and BSC factors.

Likewise, a policy could be associated with the conditions of the environment, which constitutes a continuous activity of RM. The identification of what the new projects are and the new expectations of the clients greatly influence the risk exposure.

Fundamental elements include the premise that risk is not only studied at the end of the business process; for example, sometimes the risk is looked at in the final result of granting a loan, but the risk associated with the stages of the processes is forgotten. This is the case with credit

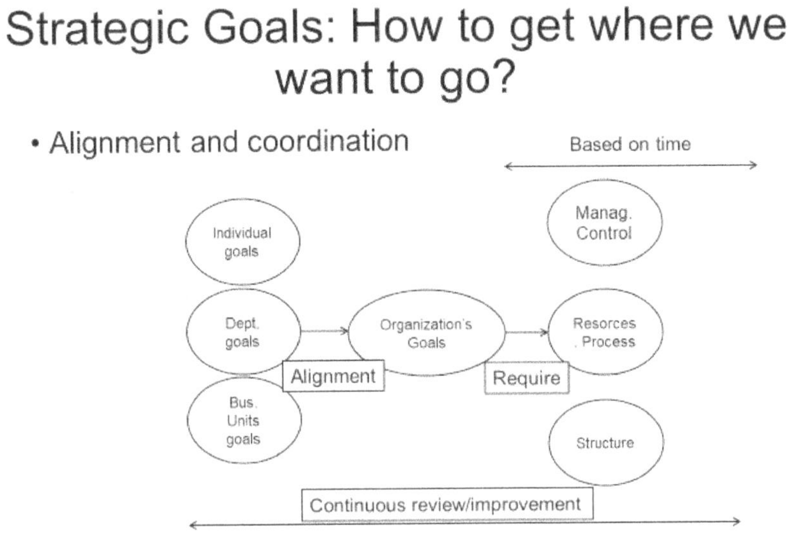

Figure 1.10. Aligning goals across the organization and use of organization's capacity.

as well where the pre-sale has a risk as well as the sale achieved through bad information and bad prospecting. The filing of credit also has the operational risks of bad input of data, bad diligence, inadequate analysis by choosing bad subjects for credit, incompletely disbursement, or unsatisfactory constitution of the guarantee. Thus, from this perspective, it is observed that there are risks prior to the client initiating the payment of its obligation, and this affects the soundness of the business. The subsequent steps also have their level of risk associated with the stages of the processes. The severity, frequency, and deviations of each stage are different and can lead to a modification of the value given to the credit study or any other process that considers risk. From a strategy standpoint, RM can become a financial and operational strength, a means of assessing achievements, and an appropriate framework for risk taking.

RM as part of the management control system is the guide to find solutions to the risk problem of generating an adaptive sustainable competitive advantage. It consists of elements of technology, which support policy, and a guide for improvement. The quality of RM is a real advantage if done properly. A business is defined on the basis of the knowledge of the client for adequate management of the company risk, which is

<table>
<tr><td>The risk profile can be constructed with elements that lead to identifying:
• Purpose of credit and source of payment.
• Integrity and reputation of the applicant.
• The client's risk profile and sensitivity to economic and market developments.
• Applicant's payment history, the current ability to pay, based on cash flow trends and projections.
• A look ahead that establishes the ability to pay, on several scenarios.
• Legal conditions of the client to be able to assume the debt.
• Economic conditions of the client.
• Credit conditions and possibilities of change in the future.
• The requirements of collateral and guarantees.</td><td>Likewise, a strategic plan must contemplate the changes to which the entity is exposed and how to affect a result:
• The interest rate generates adverse effects on the price if the interest rises; if it goes down, they are favorable.
• Favorable effects on investments when interest rates rise; if it goes down, they are adverse.
• The effect on deposits, for example, higher interest rates generate high withdrawals; design of new elements of customer attraction.
• If the rates go down, there will be prepayments due to refinancing; the credits will be placed at a lower rate.</td></tr>
<tr><td colspan="2">Some of the risks that must be considered in the financial institution are not studied in traditional risk management; however, they are of great importance, Some of them are as follows:
• Risks derived from the standard operation.
• Risks arising from criminal acts.
• Risks of people.
• Risks of fixed assets.
• Risks by processes, results, and activities.
• Risks of administrative policies.
• Market risks.</td></tr>
</table>

Exhibit 1.39. Possible sources of risk in projects.

represented in credit risk, information, relationship of assets and liabilities, etc. A healthy balance is achieved when solving the sequence segmentation problem, location and sale problem, supply problem, and utility problem. In a financial institution, a general problem is studying clients, liabilities, or assets only on one side. From a data analytics point of view, data warehouses support a view in multiple faces: customers, products, transactions, customer behavior and possible answers to: which can generate a pre-agreement banking scheme to handle payments and credits: What/how do customers pay? schools, utilities, leases, credit fees, services, ATM, mobile, and POS transactions. Another big question to solve is whether entities have their own parameters of behavior and definition of results. Do the regulatory measures coincide with those of the entity? This implies the review of adjusted prices, deadlines, and other variables to know which level of mixture is most appropriate for the entity and at the same time complies with the standard and not vice versa. This implies that part of the strategic activities is connected to risks and variables of the business understanding such as the following:

(1) Knowledge of the price of products and services is required.
(2) Differentiation by interest rates or the value of products with orientation to the constitution of reserves and management of different risk conditions.
(3) For total risk, weighting assets alone is not appropriate. Risk quality analysis is required, which is found in the client of the financial institution and its potential.
(4) Establish capital allocation vs. concentration limits, credit services, portfolio exposure, and asset and liability structure.

The heart of the business in general is risk; it represents a joint evaluation of the business, the information system, the operation, competition, the client, the regulation, the control, and fundamentally, the creation of value by the adequate risk management. In the example of a financial organization, a credit process has a design in order to consolidate risk actions through objective risk assessments, improving evaluation models and data, differentiation on RM not only because of size of operations, and investing in the credit completion process. This is behavioral analysis, representing a great element of value in the process, and adding value in terms of loss prevention. This means that the costs of resources used for mitigating risks must be taken into account in the process. The variation of massive supply by segmented selective supply is also required, in order to seek as a priority the possible credit profiles. This implies opening the market in groups of high homogeneity but the greatest possible difference between the groups, similar to balancing a portfolio with multiple levels of risk levels.

This section connected strategy and management control systems, including RM. Exhibit 1.40 revisit aspects of strategy and RM that, for example, are connected to a revenue strategy in particular and how it can be monitored and followed in strategy implementation: evaluation, treatment, financial analysis, operational analysis, etc., including the risk reports aligned to the goal of the strategy.

Likewise, from the data analytics point of view, control and prevention of losses require the identification of a probability density function,

The design can be represented in three main elements:	The sector study should include the following:
• An increase in the value of permanent risk assessment (control). • Separation between decision-making based on price and relationship management (How much risk is desired, the presence of the service, and at what price), • The business is differentiated based on risk and not on variables such as size or product.	• Common indicators, growth, participation, profit, margin. • Surveys of the behavior of the sectors. • Forecasts of specialists of macroeconomic indicators. • Identification of critical variables in the competition of the sector studied.
The business risk report comprises the following: • Review of the minimum operating requirements of the business. • Risk profile through models. • Evaluation of plants. • Key indicators • DOFA. • Sector profile.	A business view of risk is about following: • **Evaluation:** Includes the methodologies for estimating the risk in a company and its activities. • **Treatment:** Refers to how a system will be developed to care for the conditions and possible outcomes of the risk. • **Financial analysis:** Identification of the impact of risk on results from the financial perspective. • **Operational analysis:** Identification of the incidence of risk in the perspective of internal processes.

Exhibit 1.40. Organizing a study of strategic risks regarding external factors.

emphasizing the differentiation between value payable for credit losses and uncertainty in credit losses. This indicates that a margin and revenue analysis is required in order to provide an adjusted measure of return on equity by risk conditions. In any case there is a process for the following: (1) For data collection, numerical or categorical data can be used. The sample should be defined to better reflect the characteristics of the data. (2) For classification of customer groups, two different types of problems are presented; one is the definition of the groups and the selection of the variables and the other is to classify a new client in one of these groups. (3) Cross-validation of the classification with current data. (4) For new data, assign each of the new prospects to the classification group with more similar characteristics. (5) Review the results and perform an erroneous classification analysis.

In the next sections, there are conceptual models that allow the estimation of the probability of finding loss of a certain value, as well as what the expected value of loss is for a specific portfolio observation. Risk measure models are associated with classification and risk management processes, similar to how an organization's departments will be related to risk. In the data analytics side, *aggregate models* will be used: These are top-down approaches that seek to infer total risk (sum of credit, market, operating) from competitive reviews and volatility of cash flows. In the variance of loss rates side, *structural models* will be used: These can be evaluated with top-down and bottom-up methods. Assumptions of homogeneity are made, and the probability density function is estimated from the volatility of historical charges. For the bottom-up case in financial services, there is an analysis of internal credit systems and their definition of losses, evaluation of loans, credit relationships, determination of parameters, probability density function, and capital placement rules.

1.3.2 *Some observations about risk classification*

The first component in analysis of strategic risk is the understanding of risk exposure. Risk exposure analysis implies many dimensions to review and each one with potential complexity. A way to start is providing a better understanding of risk classification as a support to know how risks can be connected and potentially mitigated with an organization's initiatives. The following points bring aspects to identify and to work on in risk classification:

- The task of classification is very important in RM fundamentally because many of the tools that will be used in the analysis are better adapted to some risk types than to others; for example, insurance coverage represents an example in which certain risks can be transferred to insurance companies.
- RM must include both resources/means of risk analysis and means of RM, maintaining independence between markets and experts and adjusting results for interpretation and understanding through experience.
- RM involves a level of independence and guidance in decisions that produces a balance between heuristic and continuous search of the path of good result.
- The search for organizations' objectives achievement is a risk management process.
- Risk classification should take into account that risk can be classified relative to frequency. Events can be related to repetition, for example, having good or bad incidents /customers /suppliers /investments at different times in a business operation. In addition, the intensity or severity of a risk can change, and a small number of large possible losses might occur even though frequencies are low. A combination of frequency and severity is required to evaluate expected losses. This means in terms of the model a different set of variables to make decisions about each of the groups; variables based on risk event occurrence.
- Classification methods require complete data including structured and unstructured data.
- Loss distributions are usually long tailed, implying that they are not very similar to a normal distribution and are generally mixed distributions. The effect of weather is very important; irrigation is good today but might not be so tomorrow.
- Some of the variables in risk analysis are categorical and it is necessary to create dummy variables to include them in the models.
- Some products can be measured as packages or studied as each presentation separately. This means that the risks can be good or bad depending on the groups of products, portfolios, or resources taken.
- There is a difference between individual, aggregated, and business risk. Each one contemplates different variables and possibly different methods of analysis.

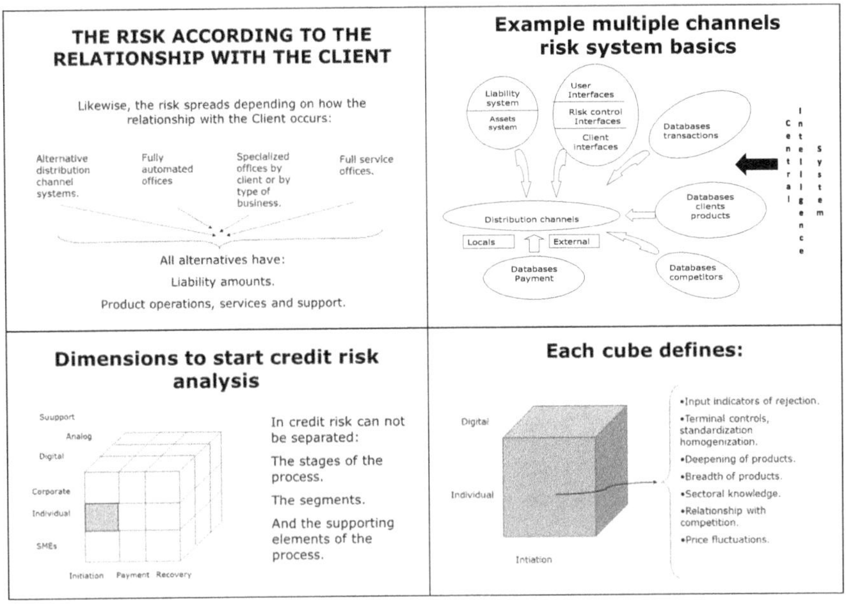

Exhibit 1.41. Illustration in credit risk factors and relationships to review.

In the development of a strategy, implementation, and verification, it is necessary to identify what is happening with respect to the definition of an offer generated by an organization (Exhibit 1.41). For example, it is essential to know if one should locate the organization in the graphic near of the variable referring to the use of conditions of high relationship with the client or where the homogenization of the contact processes is pre-established and determined. Risk analysis will be related to questions and answers on aspects of relationships to customers. As indicated in a previous section, offering digital solutions is not a matter of having the technological capabilities associated with the offer; there will be other sources of risk to review such as risk rates for loans in the case of banks depending on limits and access. Credit cards are expensive because price is associated with fast credit access that presupposes not applying to certain risk mitigation filters. The general problem of risk assessment and classification contemplates diverse decisions about collection of data, the definition of the selection criteria, and the selection of various individuals, according to established risk factors. The entire strategic process of RM that involves risk with the analysis of the target market, for example, requires the development of controls of the points of contact between clients and entity. Thus, different channels can have routines that offer greater control than others in important aspects of the risk relationship with the customer. For example it is not same to control a credit card as a distribution channel as an office with full service. The risk modification in exposure and assessment is clearly different. Distribution channels can modify risk conditions in the offer of organizations. At the end, offers in organizations are the full package of the marketing mix; it is not only the essential content but also the packages, channels of contact, people of the organizational environment, etc.

The risk control in each case is different when there is a high relationship and a greater variety of situations in which the change is more likely to occur. In the case of standardized channels, products, or services, the variance is reduced. So, it is essential to establish the production and delivery line at which the organization will be located. With this in mind concentration risk on transactions (credit), physical assets or people's risks, taken individually or as a mix will demand different risk controls and management information systems. Exhibit 1.41 depicts that distribution channels enclose data interrelationships inside the organization, since the transactions, products, and historical elements of the organization will be linked. It should be noted that for these statistical bases to be successful, they require user interfaces, risk interfaces, and customer interfaces that coordinate their use. In the case of credit risk, the focus of management is that the statistical system is not separated from the process stages, segments, and supporting elements of the process.

Variables and outcomes of analytics classification methods will guide the development of indicators and means of evaluation of the outcome of RM associated with the strategy. For example, if the organization measures the number of rejections of customer applications in a credit process as well as in a portfolio of products and what competitors offer, it will establish how vulnerability can appear in certain areas of the organization. Risk and income in a pro forma financial statement simulation go further than just observing scenarios and studying effects on risk indicators for operation, the flow of funds, fraudulent situations, possible losses that arise in business operation, in management of unbalance assets–liabilities equilibrium in a portfolio, and recovery management in case of adverse events. All components of risk analysis can be affected by risk classification and the organization's components and their relationships to risk. The next two sections provide a simplified description of what these relationships mean.

1.3.3 *Organizational components of RM*

In the context in which organizations work to achieve business integration around risk intervention, it is necessary to achieve results about procedures that minimize risk, describe processes, and adjust activities as accurately as possible. It is important to understand technology and how software development, methodologies, computing, and analysis must contemplate the use of deterministic and random conditions in models on which they are based. It is expected that the improvement in knowledge will become part of the technology with which the new strategic design is carried out or the existing one is sustained, using appropriate statistical data, not accounting data. This is related to the concept of technology, but it becomes a priority because data are the food of all risk management processes. If data do not work properly, a lot of time and effort can be lost. Another aspect is risk culture, which is a difficult concept to concretize. It represents the collective feeling of the value of actions undertaken to achieve a goal about risk expectations. RM must be part of each area in an organization from its conception to its development and realization, based fundamentally on the fact that administrative risk becomes a sustainable competitive advantage and therefore part of the company's assets. The intersection of these concepts helps to ensure that RM is associated with good profitability and not with adverse outcomes. Risk is not the same in all levels of possibility of adverse event appearance, just like it is not the same in the economic impact; risk level curves help to connect risk and organizations.

1.3.4 *Curves of the level of risk and relationships of RM and organizational areas*

Exhibit 1.42 represents a reference system that combines volume of dollars and volume of units in risk analysis. The concept is that an

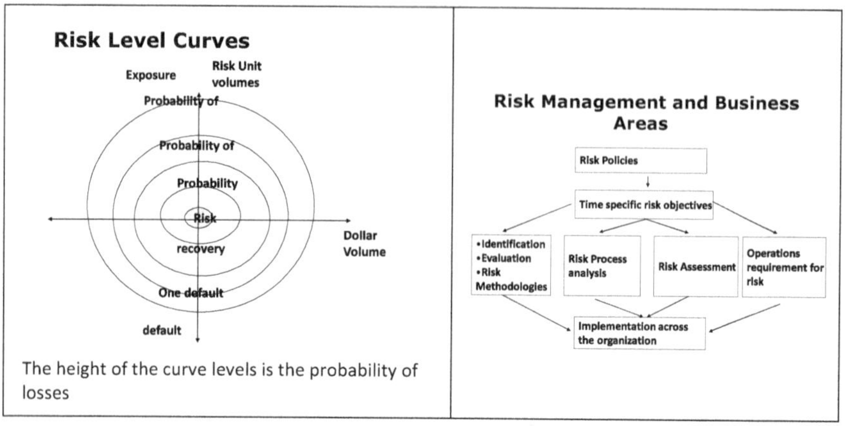

Exhibit 1.42. Risk levels according to frequencies, severity, and areas that risks affect.

organization is exposed to risk and each time an organization approaches the center, the levels of variables that affect potential losses show the mix of one or several events, with low or high severity and with low or high potential recovery. These risk levels are associated with the risk taking, assumption, and management in any area of the organization.

The relationship between risk management processes and areas of the organization represents the conditions and constraints that define excellent RM. It all starts around a RM policy condition as part of the company's strategic development. Once the connection between business and risk management processes is clear, it is necessary to identify a set of objectives that are supported by the evaluation, treatment, and financial and operational analysis of risk. Each of them produces specific responses for the organizational development of risk policy. Functions in organizations and relationships of actions and organizational processes of RM are essential to consider at each stage of the definition of structure and responsibility inside organizations. In the case of illustration in the banking business, the main axis of credit is clearly observed, but there may be many more that must be integrated into the same risk vision. This means it is appropriate to create matrices related to monitoring the development of strategic intelligence as a combination of the who and what of the business definition in terms of customer profiles. The observation of attributes of customers on clusters identifies segments. Those segments are categories in dimensions of the who–what–how of the business definition as well. Each segment as mentioned before has risk differences, and business processes operation will be affected by how one deals with those risks. An example is the levels of filters that are used in underwriting in insurance or banking, where risks differently affect intensity steps in business processes and filters that are converted into internal tasks or assignments in the organization. The underwriting role is about filters, possibly to automate and substitute with AI solutions, leaving human capacity for complex cases out of regular market conditions, such as accepting risks because of commercial agreement. Operation of RM will have an effect on how to use technology, what to automate, and how digital solutions can help. Human intervention will be fundamental in calibrating model learning and the way that results can be assigned to provide answers to needs of segments through multiple possible combinations of an organization's circumstances that are not yet analyzed because of the novelty of the practice.

1.4. Performance and Risk Indicators

This section introduces concepts regarding risk indicators and how they guide what to perform in risk management processes. Dealing with risky conditions is part of the daily decision analysis of organizations and risk indicators support the creation a roadmap for actions, creation of contingency strategies, and building an organization's capacity based on risk analysis (Exhibit 1.43). A strategic vision of risk is to identify what leads actions and strategic movements to mitigate risks to which the organizations is exposed to. For this reason, having a more adequate product offer, achieving a better sales capacity, and attending to processes with more controlled work systems are means of facing possible business variations. It is important to know that an approach within a RM methodology is to work hard on what is controllable by the organization, so that the risk is being reduced to the variations that are presented by uncontrollable and external factors that belong to uncertainty. In any condition, a measurement system is required and the next section states what measurement will represent.

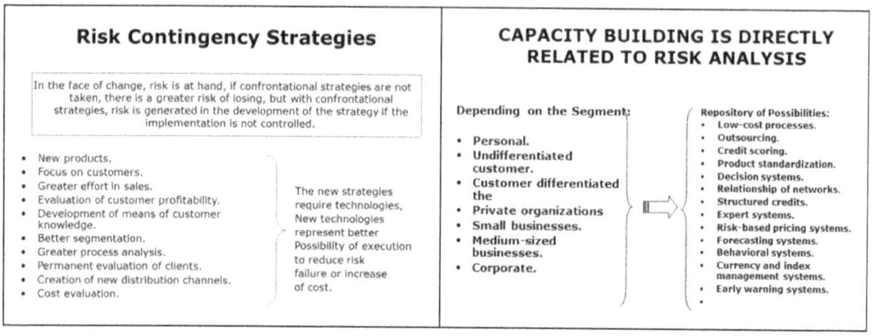

Exhibit 1.43. Varied strategies to deal with strategic risks.

1.4.1 *Basic concepts of risk indicators and measurement*

In this section, the topic is the basic measurement process. The aim is to find fundamental means to describe risks. Organizations support all risk analyses on the variation of targets, similar to identifying how key performance indicators can be affected by risk and how to define key risk indicators (KRIs) associated with these expected KPI values and results. Organizations observe variation of expected results which can be on the negative and positive side of results and performance. The main reason is that in strategy and strategic risk analysis, one is required to realize that the explanation and understanding of outstanding results are because the organization is consciously oriented toward achieving them (capabilities oriented and obtaining good results) and it was not simply a random result. The purpose at the end is to find explanations to behaviors and to learn from them, and to identify the reasons and potential replication of the strategic process. In banking, after Basel II and III, authorities demanded more accurate work on data quality to assess and develop risk control solutions. It is important to conceptualization that the vision of data cannot be only limited to the current tactics or operational business development. RM data require more specific datasets, more categories, more often observations that are continuous and come from streaming, working not only with structured data but also data coming from social media or any other network source. The cost of data infrastructure needs to move to use published data from multiple sources, organizing repositories based on AI search engines of data, API use, etc. Creating new data from raw data will feed new models and will support the risk monitoring systems.

With this general view of data issues, the following question should be asked inside the organization: How can an organization measure strategic risks? To answer a question like that, there are pieces of business operations to organize around data to build risk metrics, such as the following:

(1) Description of a required system and technological support of risk measurement.
(2) Risk capacity and RM functions building a performance measurement system based on risk.
(3) Changes in competitive position and benchmarking.
(4) Strategy analytic tools: growth vs. investments.
(5) Forecast and time series review: longitudinal and panel data.
(6) Differentiation between key performance indicators and key risk indicators.
(7) Models and creation of risk indicators; rate of interest random models; some expected interest rate measures, duration, convexity, volatility, and so on. All cases using multivariate approach.
(8) Statistical fitting of data to probability distributions.
(9) Tree structure of risk indicators and models to support the organization's RM and business processes (Exhibit 1.45).
(10) Evaluation of variance of results; forecasts vs. real.

According to the list above, to build capacity in an organization to deal with risk that is based on the evidence of indicators in the risk monitoring system requires what is presented in the next section based on a BSC structure.

1.4.2 *Enterprise's capacity and risk*

When a capacity analysis is carried out in an organization, in many cases, the bottlenecks are studied, and it is emphasized that the maximum capacity is related to the minimum possibility of attending activities in the business processes. A decision-making process comprises more than just what is known. This is the risk part of decision-making, which will determine what is the margin with which the organization will operate without problems. If the strategy in an organization is about segmentation and it makes a differentiation of segments for easy identification, with good potential in number and reduction of overlapping segments, a risk management process could have a higher level of focus and capacity developed according to groups of stakeholders.

This is how decisions according to segments of massive banking markets are oriented to deal with small amounts and high-volume of operations, which is totally different in terms of risk conditions in corporate banking where the volume of cases is small, but value is high. If in a massive business what has been done by an entity is not controlled with the business standards of operation, it is possible that services can have operational or product risks, while in the corporate case, operations, controls, and development of evaluation methodologies would change according to the customer–business nature.

Classification systems require that data are correct in volume and quality and that their manipulation is carried out in a simple way through automatic systems and models. Automation is a crucial part of the game. In the case of high-value or corporate banking, the situation will be different since each operation will be individually analyzed and will not go through the same automatic processes that exist in other segments; risk controls will be in different steps of the commercial contact, type of projects analysis, experiences, etc. With these decision criteria that are observed, including the concept of risk as a part that contributes to the most accurate analysis, a step can be taken to understand how RM is related to other functions of the company. In corporate analysis, a lot of data will have multiple external data sources that require a different set of capabilities for creating what is required in risk analytics. A foundation for the evaluation of the performance of the organization is centered on the concept of balanced scorecard (Exhibit 1.44). This evaluation

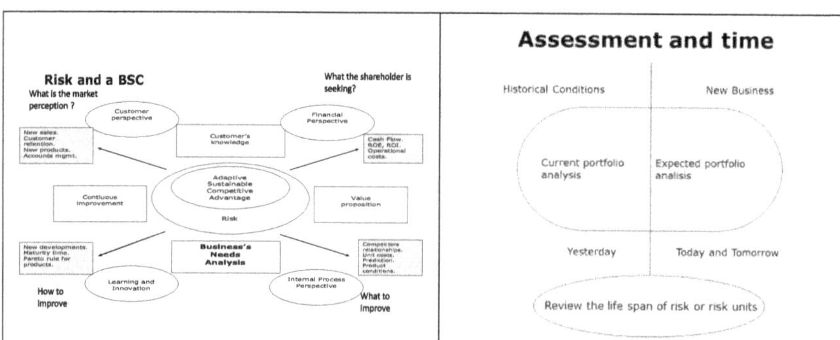

Exhibit 1.44. Risk and BSC relationship for strategic risk understanding.

system seeks to integrate the following different organizational points of view that require evaluation into a cause–effect relationship:

- Customer perspective.
- Financial perspective.
- Internal perspective of the business.
- Innovation and learning perspective.

In the context of strategic risk analysis, each of the BSC pillars of analysis needs a review of what risks are associated with them. This is a process of connecting risk to each perspective, which will provide a way to evaluate them defining the associated risk indicators. The following questions need to be answered: How does the client see the organizations? How is a shareholder optimized? How can one improve and in what? Individual evaluations produce indicators, and indices can be built with them. For example, the relationship must be made to improve the ROI and productivity of the organization, which requires a better definition of processes and the development of customer knowledge through a human–machine well-trained force that provides the support to most of actions.

In the case of financial organizations, a full performance can be assessed by observing risk or variation in ROE caused by the variability of net income, equity, net margin, or capital cost. The net margin changes can come from interest rate variability, volume variability, a mix of product variability, and so on. It is the same as studying a return on equity separated as return on assets and assets used according to the level of equity. To achieve a better view of performance, the balanced scorecard that defines a cause–effect relationship should be measured: financial perspective, customer perspective, internal business perspective, and perspective in terms of innovation and learning. From the customer's perspective, satisfaction, retention, and loyalty must be observed in front of the attributes of products and services, the relationship with customers, and the image and reputation. All these are related to the objectives and their measures. Before the concept of a good risk, one must have a good client who is loyal and who grows with the organization. This includes utility analysis for each client. Furthermore, as noted, in a financial organization, the development of RM methodologies constitutes a sustainable competitive advantage. Fundamentally, it requires customer knowledge, a value proposition, and business analysis on requirements for development of continuous improvement methods to optimize risk and improve business profit. When evaluating and measuring business performance, it is necessary to have a perspective of the historical condition and new businesses. The historical condition represents that the organization must have methodologies to address what already exists, and for everything new, the experience will help as well as the factors that affect the selection of markets and adaptation of policies.

The four variables of the BSC, financial perspective, customer perspective, internal business perspective, and perspective, are required to observe in the present and in the future with an eye on creating innovation and learning.

A relationship discovered between risk and business through a BSC helps to clarify the integration of three business aspects: process improvement, competitive position, and a better measurement system of the organization's performance. The capabilities to build business capacity are based on creating business simulation of results and better portfolio management understanding. From marketing-strategy portfolios (markets, products, promotion) to investment portfolios. The main point to make is that causality is not evident and the relationships that the organization uses between KPI and KRI need to be validated and observed/monitored all the time. Precipitated conclusions can lead the organization to wrong decisions. Miller and Bromiley (1990) concluded the following in their study: "In summary, this study evaluated the measurement properties of some of the most common risk proxies used in strategic management research. We applied the three underlying risk factors derived from this analysis to the study of risk-return relations in corporate data, demonstrating that differing risk factors provide different substantive results. The results indicate that income stream risk has a negative influence on subsequent performance. Other findings from the application were not readily explicable with the theory developed here and merit further study. These results can be seen as a prelude to more detailed and sophisticated tests of the causal mechanisms and logics presented for risk — return relations."

As an illustration, an indicator of the risk of the financial institution can be constructed taking into account the following:

- The expected return on $E(\text{ROA})$ assets.
- The relationship between capital and CAP assets.

- The standard deviation of return on assets, which identifies the relationship between return, use of investment, and deviation of return, meaning that the greater the deviation, an adequate result in the management of the entity and risk can be lost.

$$\frac{[E(\text{ROA}) + \text{CAP}]}{\sigma_{\text{ROA}}}$$

Apart from the time component, it is essential to include risk indicators about expected values of loss, individually or in groups, that take into account the frequency of occurrence and the possible value of the loss. Searching the best fit of probability distribution that describe potential losses. Losses can consider direct and indirect cost associated or specific definitions of events consider positive/negative for a good organization performance.

1.4.3 *Tree Structure of risk indicators*

Exhibit 1.45 presents multiple facets related to the creation of risk indicators, starting from a tree relationship to define each strategic objective potential risk affecting the objective, metrics, data use models, and strategic solutions required. There are different approaches to develop risk indicators in an organization using financial statements, stock market behavior, benchmarking, etc. The most important is to follow the sequence related to strategic objective — key performance indicators, risks associated with the indicators, and key risk indicators. Creation of dashboards to describe data and observe the methods with technologies is fundamental to the data analytics process that supports the model's understanding. The models presented in Section 4.2 require data organized in ways to apply models like ANOVA or classification/regression trees. In any case, the organization and cleaning processes of data are crucial no matter the level of model sophistication. For example, regressions and neural networks can be affected by missing values, which would decrease the amount of data to use in the models and lower their predictive power. Additionally, the data preparation contemplates, in several cases, transformations of input variables to make the usual assumptions of regression more appropriate for the input data.

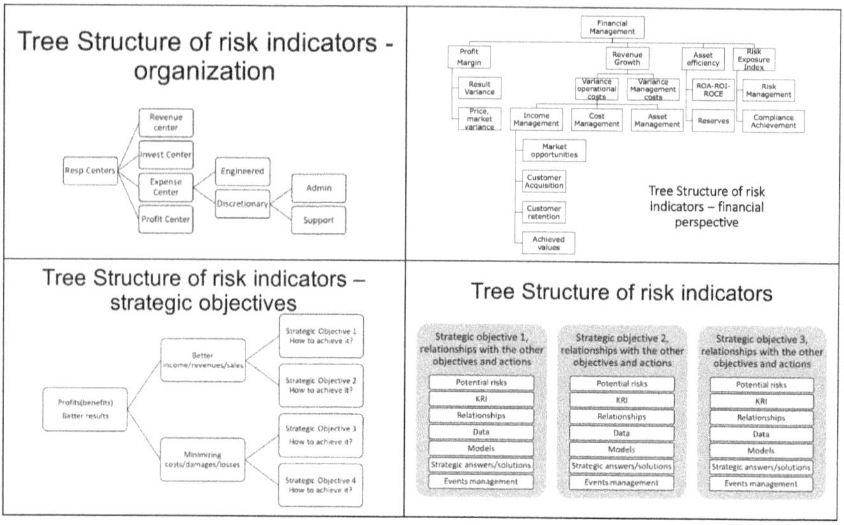

Exhibit 1.45. Structure to review risks across functions and organizational areas.

A key performance indicator (KPI) is a metric that shows whether an organization is progressing toward its stated goals. In creating dashboards (see Section 3.2 using R and Shiny), KPIs can be visualized by speedometers, thermometers, tachometers, sliders, dials, arrows, traffic lights, and other types of gauges. In any representation, the purpose is to find how to visualize KRIs based on the expected behavior of the KPI and the factors than can affect the KPI; identification of risks that can affect KPIs leads the definition of the KRI, which is a good practice in building multivariate risk indicators as it could be the result of tree separation/unification of the indicators or through the use of outcomes of multiple regressions or ML results. For example, probabilities of KPIs variation given values of variables used to describe the KPI. A final comment is about integration of KPIs and KRIs (Exhibit 1.46), for example, connecting the following:

(1) **Risk metrics:** Order statistics and percentiles. Risk model VAR model CVAR operation analysis of portfolio.
(2) **Use of scenarios and simulation:** Testing internal and external factors that affect the organization.

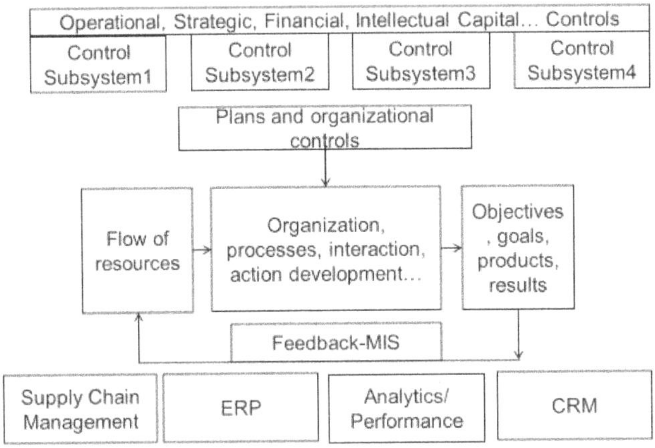

Exhibit 1.46. Relationship components between KPIs and KRIs to support RM systems.

Using concepts associated with probability distributions, simulation, and scenarios, the following trends are created:

- Econometric simulation models outlook indicators and Monte Carlo simulation
- Linear programming in portfolio analysis
- Markowitz portfolio analysis measures risk profile for business units, products, and regions
- Resource allocation methods
- Portfolio analysis approach for products, business units, and markets

The relationship between KPIs and KRIs represents links to define operations, financials, marketing, etc., to the organizational controls and means for activating the flow goals and resources including technology use. At the end, the connection will be prioritized by reviewing risk limits, creating behavioral indicators, and building exposure management tools to understand the potential impact of adverse events in the performance of the organization.

To dig deeper in the creation of metrics, the next section introduces the way to connect KPI and KRIs to monitor and assess risk. The use of these indicators can be individual or multivariate. The multivariate approach is desirable because of the possibility of using relationships that exist in the metrics.

1.4.4 *Connecting KPIs and KRIs*

This section looks to explain how key performance indicators (KPI) and key risk indicators (KRI) are related. The basic concept is that once an organization defines a metric and a value for that metric according to business conditions, it can be modified which can also affect the achievement of results. KRIs are based on the risks that organizations identify that can represent variability of the KPI targets. In this book, it is important to keep in mind that as an assumption, organizations need to reflect on the business results and reformulate goals based on the analysis of the previous period's results through time. This means that one of the purposes is to create time series of values of KPIs and results (outcome data of business process are new data to feed data analytics and AI processes), to study these times series, and at the same time to review if the risk identified had events that modify the organization's results. However, having time series is not enough, and organizations need to understand the root causes of the variations and understand the distribution of the results. In that order of ideas, key performance indicators are metrics and values to align strategy and implementation performance. It is required to work on strategy formulation indicators and implementation or performance, and from them key risk indicators are designed based on the following two questions: What can affect the key performance indicators? How can one measure the variability of the key performance indicators?

Differences of KPIs and KRIs regarding time are by period of evaluation; for example, KRIs are mainly for early warning systems and prediction. This is, KPIs are identified and KRIs are going to be estimated according to variation analysis. The variation can be because of inflation or changes in significant variables, and the forecast or prediction is the expected value of where KPIs can be. As in any measurement system, it is required to know the definition of dimensions and scales of the metric, for example, time, units, and economic metrics (currency). Each level of key performance indicators can have a number of factors affecting the result. See the example of Exhibit 1.47.

Differentiation between KPI and KRI

As it is in any measurement system it is required the definition of dimensions and scales of the metric. For example time, units and dollars etc. Each level of Key Performance indicators can have a big number of factors affecting the result

Key Performance Indicator	Key Risk Indicator
Net of new customers	Metrics associated with: Complains without solutions, returns, defects, reviews. Example: Number of customers that did not buy anymore, did not renewed ...
Proportion of bad debts to total revenues	Metrics associated with changes in the status of accounts receivables. Example: probability of moving from 30 days payment to 60 days
Market share by products and regions	Many factors can influence

Exhibit 1.47. Illustration of creating KRIs for each KPI.

KPIs and KRIs are linked and used under many perspectives of performance evaluation of organization. A method is directly based on a BSC or through a combination of factors as the following: (see Exhibit 1.48 for relationships to use in building metrics):

- Benchmarking and changes in a competitive position
- Variance of results
- Forecasts vs. real
- Creation of risk indicators using multivariate approach
- Building a performance measurement system based on risk

Exhibit 1.48 illustrates how concentration metrics of revenues/sales do not necessarily have the same distribution of profit concentration. In each component of a BSC, risk can be differentiated, one organization could have a business model based on a small number of customers with high contribution to profits, another different risk will be when sales and profits are atomized across the customers and products portfolio. In the same manner to achieve return on equity or on assets or investment, risk

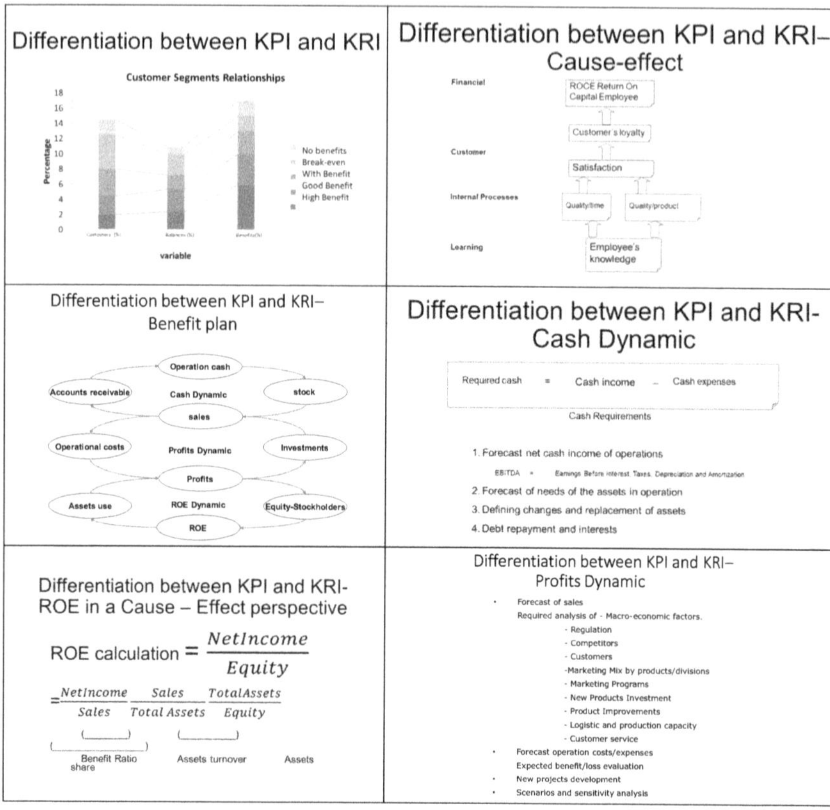

Exhibit 1.48. Structure of financial relationships for the definition of KPIs and KRIs.

will be related to the behavior of the variables involved in those indicators calculations for example the return of equity can be a sequence including return on sales, sales by assets and assets used to equity. A return on Investment in a NGO can be related to number of satisfied beneficiaries served divided by resources used to promote programs of social development. Each metric has the required definition for example what the meaning of satisfaction will be and how to identify and review the behavior of factors defining satisfaction. Another way to see the effects of potential changes is connecting operations where cash dynamic, profit dynamic, and return dynamic are related to one another and each one can have a direct effect on each of the factors affecting the

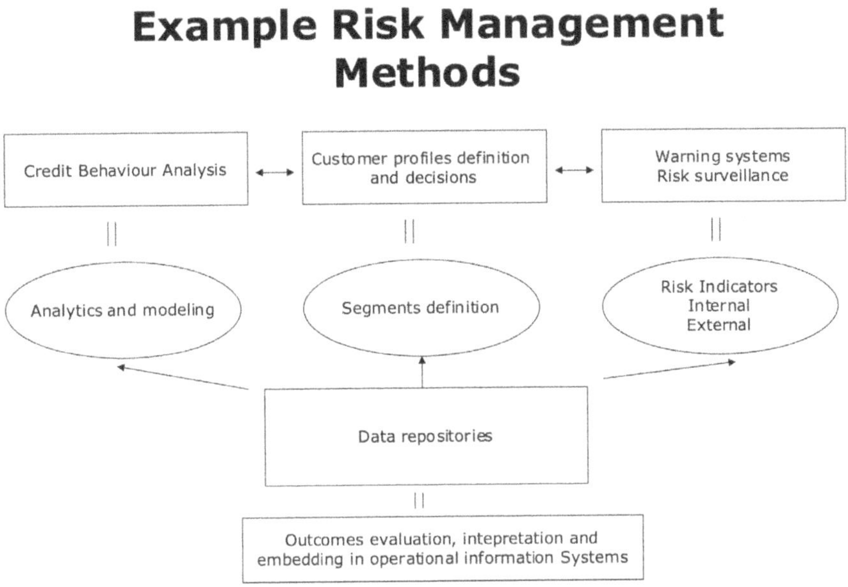

Figure 1.11. Illustration of methods in RM applicable to ERM and strategic risk.

dynamic behavior. In the end, multivariate analysis is required, the cause–effect (Fishbone diagrams, influence diagrams with support of correlation analysis, structural equations, and causal inference) behavioral diagrams or conceptual models and analytics relationship tools used as regression methods will provide a better understanding of what will help to control risk and avoid the highest losses in case of adverse events. A good example is in bankruptcy analysis; once the decision is made for filing bankruptcy, the organization proceeds to optimize and arrange inventory reduction, negotiating leases, finding how machines and assets can be sold, dealing with locations, employees, etc., all of which have to be planned to reduce loss and have the possibility of returning to the business with a new restructured organization if that is the purpose. Some examples are Delta Airlines, Apple, General Motors, and Chrysler.

Once the decomposition of metrics is done, the variables and data needed for measurement will appear and will be clearer to guide the design of KPIs and KRIs. Figure 1.11 is an illustration of how RM methods can be observed in three levels, each one with risk indicators to control. The top level is about questions to answer regarding behavioral analysis of risk, definitions of risk profiles, and creation of warning systems. Those are supported by analytics, segmentation, and risk indicators — internal and external. All of them are supported by data and operational information systems. In terms of KRI decomposition and data selection, the sequence to analyze is from top-down and bottom-up to clarify data availability and possibility of using the indicators in a connected way to solve analytics questions.

In light of the search for data availability to obtain metrics and feasibility to use them a RM system leads to the construction of a well-founded information system that studies risk processes, evaluates them and can control them. The risk management information systems is a means to guide-support the course of actions to perform in risk management. Figure 1.12 indicates that in the center of the creation of risk indicator will be the identification of frequencies and severity distributions analysis, which will be performed through the identification of the composition of the distribution to obtain loss evaluation and distribution.

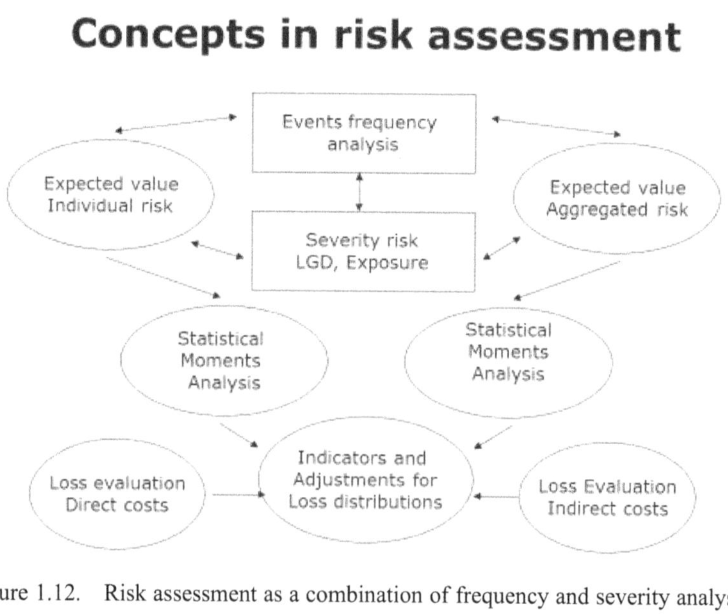

Figure 1.12. Risk assessment as a combination of frequency and severity analysis.

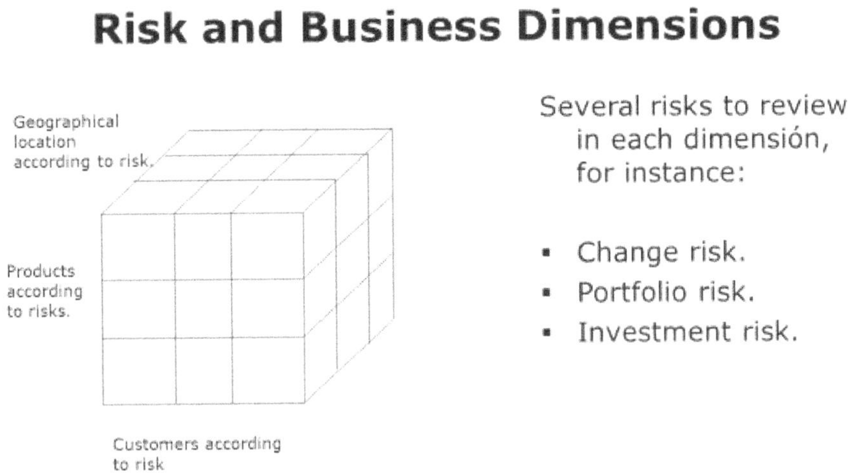

Figure 1.13. Review of risk by business dimension.

Risk indictors and KRIs will appear according to priority and requirement in the strategic risk analysis and monitoring system development. More work on each measurement process will provide the capacity to recognize impact of risks on performance and evolution of the organization.

The following section is a presentation of how the contents of the previous section can be organized to achieve the goal of RM systems that will feed strategic risk analysis to prepare organizations to handle risk according to the business conditions. One of the most important applications in risk analysis is to make marketing more focused. The focus is mainly on the initial identification of the risk profiles of interest and then looking for the attributes that the segments must possess to be served under the known risk conditions. Section 1.1 presented several concepts related to how business definition needs to be used to ensure ERM understanding. Figure 1.13 shows the three dimensions represented by customers, product, location of the offer that are analyzed under risk with the purpose of obtaining metrics according three factors acting together, and not observed and analyzed independently. In terms of probability principles in data analytics, it is the problem of having probability joint distributions and multivariate analysis. This indicates the possibility of obtaining factors that are potentially affecting the risk structure of each of the variables (factors) or each dimension. For example, low-risk products can be made in different presentations to customers of different risk profiles with clarity of which location is expected to be served. The risks in each dimension are analyzed according to internal and external conditions, e.g., business environment change, portfolio, and investment.

In today's organization, corporate risk and senior management policies influence business units and therefore the structure that generates synergies and management of shared resources. A rationale for this relationship is that risk policies cannot be independent of shareholder interests, and, fundamentally, the elements of RM will be common although business units may assume different forms of risk. This means that tasks will be undertaken and policies will be defined, leading consistent to optimization of RM in the business units.

1.5. Study Cases of Risk Types: Basic Observations

This study case is a simplified illustration of how to start building a risk monitoring system to structure strategic risk analytics and develop data analytics/AI to deal with uncertainty and threats. The company's name is First Data Inc. and the time frame for the example is consistent with the data used for presenting the concepts. This company is competing in a market of technology, mainly providing solutions to organizations based on business analytics. First Data Inc. is similar to other organizations, but for this case only three companies are used as competitors: Microsoft, Hewlett Packard, and Accenture. Data of three periods per company have been gathered. Data are based on financial figures and adapted scores of what a company could perceive of its performance in a market. In the example, RM concepts are used in the real case of competitors and socio-economic conditions affecting First Data Inc. Data are gathered from Yahoo Finance, but the scorecards and qualitative parts are fictitious with the purpose of illustrating the process. Data are of two types: Qualitative (SWOT analysis) and Quantitative (financial Indicators, financial statements, and stock prices). Everything is based on a hypothetical balanced scorecard and its strategy map (see Exhibit 1.49).

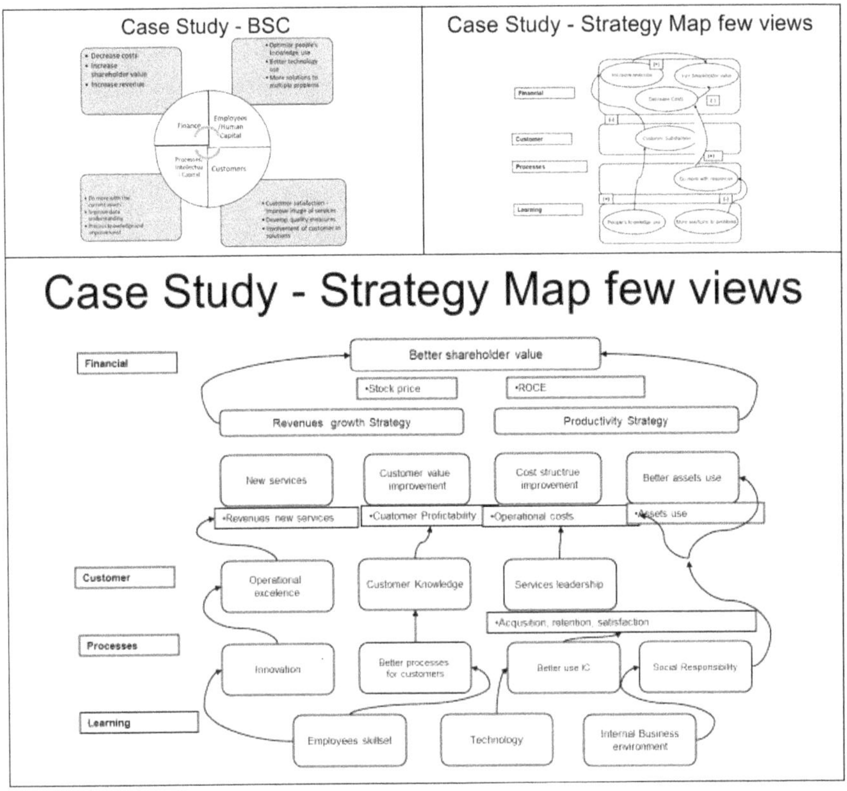

Exhibit 1.49. Samples of BSC and connecting the factors to determine risks that affect each connection.

Table 1.7 provides the main financial data and summarizes the financial indicators of results and ratios.

In addition, data from competitors are provided in Table 1.8. This table shows important differences of how companies define their strategies based on the fact that thc inference of KRIs will be associated with the impact of the bottom line of First Data Inc. For example, operational and gross margin in First Data Inc. are the second highest after MSF, placing it, at least in terms of that goal, in the same group and in different strategic groups to ACN and HPQ. According to what was indicated in the

Table 1.7. Example financial indicators.

Financial indicators			
Fiscal year		**Management effectiveness**	
Fiscal Year Ends:	31-Dec	Return on Assets (ttm): Return	10.27%
Most Recent Quarter (mrq):	31-Mar-15	on Equity (ttm):	107.73%
Profitability		**Balance sheet**	
Profit Margin (ttm):	13.27%	Total Cash (mrq):	8.81B
Operating Margin (ttm):	21.40%	Total Cash Per Share (mrq):	8.95
		Total Debt (mrq):	38.83B
Income statement		Total Debt/Equity (mrq):	315.95
Revenue (ttm): 9	0.15B	Current Ratio (mrq):	1.3
Revenue Per Share (ttm):		Book Value Per Share (mrq):	12.33
Qtrly	90.83	**Cash flow statement**	
Revenue Growth (yoy):	−11.90%	Operating Cash Flow (ttm):	17.15B
Gross Profit (ttm): 4	6.41B	Levered Free Cash Flow (ttm):	12.50B
EBITDA (ttm)6: 2	3.61B		
Net Income Avl to Common (ttm): 1 Qtrly Earnings	5.64B		
Growth (yoy):	-2.30%		

Table 1.8. Financial comparison of competitors.

Direct Competitor Comparison	**DATA Inc.**	**ACN**	**HPQ**	**MSFT**	**Industry**
Market Cap:	164.44B	60.76B	57.44B	374.01B	850.52M
Employees:	379,592	323,000	302,000	128,000	1.95K
Qtrly Rev Growth (yoy):	−0.12	0.05	−0.07	0.07	0.12
Revenue (ttm):	90.15B	30.90B	108.28B	94.78B	697.18M
Gross Margin (ttm):	0.5	0.32	0.24	0.65	0.27
EBITDA (ttm):	23.61B	4.89B	12.94B	33.71B	40.44M
Operating Margin (ttm):	0.21	0.14	0.08	0.3	0.06
Net Income (ttm):	15.64B	3.04B	4.69B	20.00B	N/A
EPS (ttm):	12	4.71	2.51	2.41	0.37
P/E (ttm):	13.92	20.58	12.68	19.14	18.45
PEG (5 yr expected):	2.37	2.06	4.46	2.7	1.62
P/S (ttm):	1.84	1.97	0.54	3.99	1.02

earlier sections, strategic risk as a competitive position changes a multivariate cluster analysis can help to determine which companies are constituting the strategic groups.

From the point of view of using qualitative data, SWOT analysis helps to consolidate quantitative observations and guide the understanding of possible reasons for changes in indicators. In First Data Inc., these are data aspects to consider. The following information is from EBSCO SWOT source with a modified company name:

(1) **First Data Inc. Strengths**
Source Fortune 500 list with mega customers, including many of the world's largest enterprises.
Weaknesses: A tardy arrival to the cloud computing party.
Opportunities: Offering customers a secure hybrid cloud model.
Threats: Cloud computing platforms like Amazon, Microsoft, and Google.

(2) **Microsoft Strengths**
Surface revenue was up 44 percent in the company's last earnings report, which indicates that the tablet is gaining traction among users. Microsoft's cloud computing platform Azure is growing and continues to catch up in share to rival Amazon's AWS service.
Weaknesses: XBox revenue is down, as sales for Sony's PlayStation 4 US consistently outpace those of Microsoft's gaming console.
Opportunities: As virtual reality continues to gain traction, the company's Hololens could be the next big innovation in gaming. The company's mobile operating system Windows 10 mobile is set to be released this summer and could be Microsoft's Hail Mary to compete with Google Android and Apple iOS as a dominant mobile platform.
Threats: The personal computer market continues to slide downward, which is less opportunity for Windows to reach consumers on desktops.

(3) **Hewlett Packard Strengths**
In the wake of many cyber attacks on big corporations, HP's security software business has grown. HP's acquisition of Aruba Networks could potentially bring in an annual revenue of $729 million.
Weaknesses: HP was forced to write down a majority of its $10.3 billion acquisition of Autonomy due to accounting misrepresentations by the latter company and is in the process of suing Autonomy's co-founder and former CFO.

Opportunities: Developing innovative hardware lines for the HP Inc. business: HP's line of powerful, Zbook Workstation laptops debuted earlier this year, aimed at power users such as product designers or engineers. HP's first move in 3D printing, Multi Jet Fusion, was expected to hit the market in 2016.

Threats:

- Massive layoffs to the company could cripple hiring. HP expects to fire around 55,000 employees leading up to and during the separation.
- Mounting labor costs in China could erode the company's profitability.

(4) **Accenture Strengths**

- Operating model focused on growth.
- Diverse presence across various industries and geographies with strong client relationships.
- Robust alliances network.

Weaknesses: High dependence on consulting business platforms.

Opportunities

- Increased adoption of cloud computing services.
- Strategic acquisitions further strengthen Accenture's market position, with growing demand for enterprise mobility.
- Strong pipeline of contracts.

Threats:

- Volatile and uncertain economic conditions and intense competition
- Revenue may be adversely affected by currency exchange rate fluctuations.

This comparison shows the need to use numerical and non-structured data. The next example is related to bank business and credit risk.

1.5.1 *Banks as data analytics, knowledge, and risk organizations*

How does the organization influence good RM? In the banking business there are multiple structures of services and products that lead to managing different risk conditions. Depending on the product and the operation–risk relationship (see Figure 1.14), risk methodologies can be generated to support the strategic development of RM in a bank. For example,

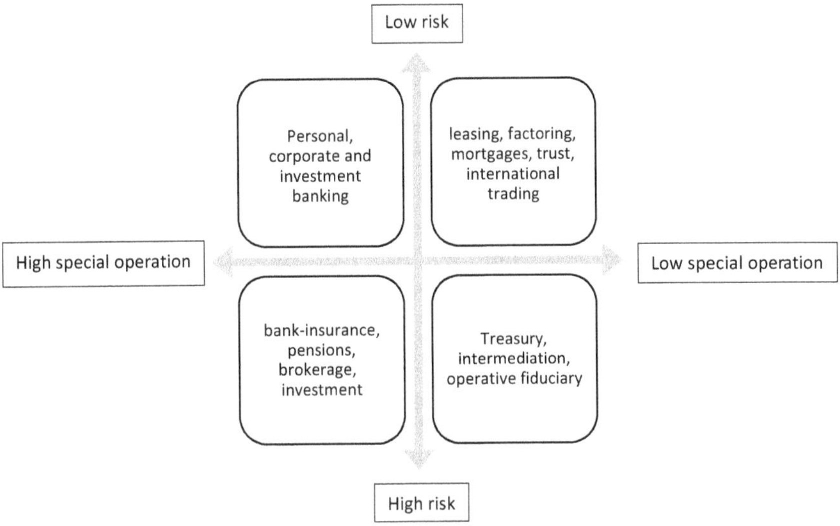

Figure 1.14. According to operation and risks, multiple organizations activities/products/service can be classified.

high-level trading products and services with high management risk conditions have been introduced to banking and generate new controls and new knowledge. For products and services of special operation but known and experienced presentation, the management risk is reduced since it is better controlled.

It is possible to say that a lower level of administrative risk difficulty would arise when there are complementary but already experienced products to the bank's basic offers. This is also associated with the conditions of heterogeneity and homogeneity that are generated in controlled operational processes, in addition to methodologies that offer objectivity to the risk selection process. Additionally, the structure of the product must be oriented to mono product with multiple standardized presentations that comprise the variables: interest rate, term, use of services, amortization system, rotation, associated expenses, and amount or quota. In the risk analytics process, a differentiation must be made between credit management and RM. The first comprises the management of assets to maximize profit according to risk conditions. The second comprises the organization of the conditions so that the asset, liabilities, transactions, customers, and technology will be a source of maximum benefit reducing uncertainty. This means that RM includes credit management and not the other way around.

A complete analysis includes the review of customer sources, relationships analysis using analytics models, the structure of data repositories, etc. It also represents the need to study the behavior of liabilities. From the knowledge of the asset clients of the bank, it is possible to look for clients of the liability side that fit the most appropriate profile for credit, and in turn for clients of liability, it is possible to locate who are the ones with the best potential profit results. The customer selection of the bank products and asset uses search filters within a data warehouse or data repository. In the presence of current customers, the tactic work is concentrated on understanding customers' behavior and increasing penetration of product/service use for each customer, plus a relationship study between asset and market, where customer knowledge influences possibilities to achieve goals in market share, organization's growth, etc. The work in portfolio management, control, operations, and offer development is simultaneous. For example, an approval program in a release scheme for an asset product and liability linkage is based on the client's profitability. This includes a reorientation of some functional areas and development of competencies in price management, constitution of reserves, policies, information systems, statistical models, monitoring, control, follow-up, administration, operational, etc. It must also be linked to the management of risks associated with liquidity, operations, commercial, definition of acceptable returns, etc. Credit areas risk analysis states that policy be consensual, which also identifies price and distribution of portfolio and relationship with the market. A level of policy that becomes operative develops the means to execute procedures, make manuals, review, and follow-up.

1.5.2 *Illustration of a value chain and other business processes*

The following paragraphs illustrate the forms of interrelation between risks, activities, and processes of the entire organization, starting from product and the other management variables of the organization. Continuing with the example of financial institutions, risks in a value chain analysis can come from supply chain risks or from resources to create value as it is liquidity management, which can be seen as static or dynamic in business. A dynamic approach is the most appropriate for observing cash flows, inflows, and outflows as random variables and therefore using forecasting techniques and simulations. The properties of the time series of deposits and credits are the determinants of liquidity needs. This must be tied to obtaining model results for interest rate, inflation, and devaluation, among multiple indicators. Reserve position is another concept of risk assessment. A methodology can be established with the following structure for the analysis of reserves:

Total reserves are equal to required reserves + excess reserves (if any)

Required reserves are those developed on loans plus non-loan reserves. All this is within the framework of minimizing interest expenses for the financial institution, maintaining an adequate relationship with the client, and complying with regulations. This means that in a new orientation of financial institutions, it is common to constitute reserves according to the possibility of failure that is foreseen in different processes of an organization. In the case of credit and within product analysis, a mono-product structure that contemplates different variables of the financial business is especially considered, with each of the variables that make up the product constituting a source of risk to be contemplated. For example, interest for the savings account or type A credit is not studied, but interest as a fundamental variable, and how it affects all the combinations of products that depend on it, is studied.

Concept of mono-product presentation according to market and channel becomes multiple standardized products:

(1) Interest rate.
(2) Term.
(3) Use.
(4) Services.
(5) Amortization system.
(6) Rotation.
(7) Associated expenses.
(8) Amount or quota.
(9) Source, process, and use relationship.

Likewise, organizations could use a multiplicity of growth options, with one of them being the creation of associations. In this aspect, there are some possible changes or variations that require organizational clarity. In the case of a credit portfolio, the question arises of how much risk organizations want to accept. This is related to investment levels, asset management, portfolio, policies, and provision management. In particular, the management of provisions seeks to introduce in financial institutions a risk reduction criterion that requires a greater organization of the variables that make up the risk, in order to meet risk levels that may occur in different events. Specifically, the level of aging of the portfolio represents a risk of failure and it must be known what its structure is in the future and how it may affect the company's results.

Other risks related to daily organization development are marketing risk in terms of studying what could happen in market segments that are misidentified, loss of effort in sales and advertising, and estimation of future sales, with the risk of being above or below; the loss is represented in facilities investments, advertising, and sales personnel. In addition, there can be issues in adoption of sales compensation systems, risk possibility of high turnover of sellers, loss in what is invested in training, bad image, decreased prices of a production line, risk uncertainty of elasticity of demand, loss of sales revenue, and demand problems.

Exhibit 1.50 indicates the need for risk monitoring with factors that are affecting risks from various sources.

Sectors: • Number of establishments • Industrial value added participation • Participation in industrial production • Employment generated • General concentration • Apparent consumption growth • Effective protection • Average tariff • Dependence on the specific foreign market • Sales • Percentage of companies with operating loss • Number of companies in concordat • Assets • Import penetration • Export orientation	• Liquidity, current ratio • Indebtedness financial obligations and total liabilities Reason for indebtedness • Leverage: net debt/equity • Working capital assets • Inventories / sales *365 • Accounts Payable/Cost of Sale * 365 • Accounts Receivable/Sales *365 • Yield • Operating/Asset Sales • Sales/total assets • Cost sales/sales • Operating/sales expenses • Net margin • Operating margin • Growths • Opinion polls • Prices and costs • Foreign trade

Exhibit 1.50. Factors affecting risk appearance required to surveil for strategic risk monitoring.

All these elements provide answers to the following:

(1) Competitive structure.
(2) How the market is distributed and under what conditions growth is expected.
(3) Strategic groups in which the organization develops.
(4) Development of markets that are substitute or complementary.
(5) Development of technology for this type of sectors.

In the following chapter, some methodological elements are introduced for creating strategic intelligence based on a first analysis of what RM is and in particular what strategic risk represents, actions to mitigate it through knowledge creation using quantitative, qualitative key risk indicators, following risk management processes, and managing data as an asset, and creating means to move from business analytics to integrated strategic intelligence.

Chapter 2

Building Organizational Strategic Intelligence

This chapter is about the integration of concepts and paradigms in organizations that lead to use of strategic intelligence development and digital support to mitigate strategic risks. The chapter covers basic concepts related to the structure of strategic intelligence based on ideas and tools that organizations use in strengthening data analytics and artificial intelligence capabilities and capacity. Organizations need to clarify the understanding of the meaning of strategic intelligence and data analytics, given the misinterpretation of having technology as a goal and not as means to achieve what organizations are looking for. A good example is the use of big data and the confusion of big data with the concept of big data analytics. Big data are another kind of data that require management under certain conditions; big data are a type of data to use in information system analysis and design. This means big data form an information systems problem to solve; this could be from the point of view of storage, access, or related to what is possible for transforming or using data in applications. Meanwhile, Big Data Analytics (BDA) is about the application of data analytics techniques and methods to obtain value from big data, to create actionable knowledge; that means if big data exist without analytics, big data are probably not going to give the organization the value that is expected.

Organizations sometimes believe that big data are something new; but big data are not new, they have always been present in society and business in different ways and different fields. For instance, big data come from radio astronomy signals and have been generated by organizations in terms of production processes that involve several steps like chemical processes for creating and developing factories. The difference is how nowadays organizations are looking to use data as a valuable asset. This means organizations are looking to connect everything that is part of internal and external data sources with a variety of data types to influence an organization's strategy and tactics based on evidence, creating intelligence and operations based on AI, where models, technology, and talent together provide support for what the organization needs in operations or answers to questions that the organization wants solved. In the case of paper manufacturing, quality control could be based on the traditional approaches of total quality management and chemical engineering; however, the purpose in current conditions of manufacturing is to be able to do something more with data that just collecting it continuously for monitoring of the paper manufacturing process; it is more about prediction. Organizations required more than reports of past and present conditions of the performance; they need data analytics to achieve strategic intelligence. Strategic intelligence is related to developing methods or techniques to use available resources smartly to improve current and future capacity in organizations. This capacity leads to the creation of capabilities to support decision-making, answer to business questions, generation of meaning to feed a complete process, where human intelligence–machine intelligence are engines, and to guide an organization in the creation of adaptive sustainable competitive advantages to improve performance.

In a very simple way, using intelligently data as an asset, and big data analytics as means to solve organizations problems, is what organizations are trying to improve; it is an opportunity to use knowledge, technology, and data to create value. Quantitative methods have been used from the second half of the 20th century to solve problems in organizations. The evolution has been from the specific solution of problems and very particular data using statistical and operations research techniques to the wide use of descriptive, predictive, and prescriptive methods to guide organizations in identifying possible futures, solve more general problems than before, and to generate actions accordingly. In terms of business intelligence (BI), data use from internal sources of the organization was limited to report production and to indicate the instant observations in time of what an organization was living or lived in the past. However, reports were not enough to guide organizations to make better decisions or solve more problems. Adaptive business intelligence conceptualized the use of knowledge creation using techniques to obtain outcomes that provided insights in decision models and methods. Data analytics is the process where data are used for moving information to actions through statistical and machine learning techniques. In this context, strategic intelligence is considered as a combination of business intelligence, competitive intelligence, and artificial intelligence. This means a way to obtain appropriate knowledge to create intelligence with a wider spectrum of observations and the means to understand those observations and apply them in the organizational context. What is clear is that intelligence is about finding ways to adapt the organization system to maintain and improve a performance that is appropriate to the stakeholders.

Business intelligence uses ML and several models (data analytics) to generate inference — planning insights more than just reports of static and present-past observations in cases where that is part of the BI mandate in the organization by people working in BI. In certain cases AI is used for helping to organize, clean, and prepare data. AI is part of supporting the outcome creation of BI and its processes. This is a matter of scope because BI has been limited to internal, descriptive, and explorative knowledge creation in organizations. Nevertheless, data analytics goes further and applies the same processes and additional techniques to different types of problems in multiple areas of organizations. When data are external, and metrics are related to the conditions of sectors and industries, a competitive intelligence level can be obtained and problems internal and external require the analysis of data to solve certain problems such as classification of risk units. In the case of classification, data analytics as a process requires both data and techniques to concentrate on problems, producing intelligence that understands how factors affect variability of target variables or values that the organization wants to achieve.

The next sections will guide the reader to link BI, competitive, intelligence, and artificial intelligence to understand what is expected in integrated strategic intelligence for performance improvement in an organization. The backbone of the conceptual link is the use of analytics methods and mindset to create knowledge to mitigate strategic risk.

2.1. From Business Intelligence to Data Analytics

To understand the reasoning behind business intelligence (BI) development and how it evolves to data analytics processes, one must start with the processes of the search for evidence-based decisions in management. In management, an important step ahead during the last seventy years was the use of a set of theories as evidence to support answers to organization's problems. This search follows the use of scientific methods that were described by Feynman (1968) in one of his lectures: "Now I'm going to discuss how we would look for a new law. In general, we look for a new law by the following process. First, we guess it (audience laughter), no, don't laugh, that's the truth. Then we compute the consequences of the guess, to see what, if this is right, if this law we guess is right, to see what it would imply and then we compare the computation results to nature or we say compared to experiment or experience, compare it directly with observations to see if it works. If it disagrees with experiment, it's wrong. In that simple statement is the key to science. It doesn't make any difference how beautiful your guess is, it doesn't matter how smart you are who made the guess, or what his name is … If it disagrees with experiment, it's wrong. That's all there is to it." Business intelligence and data analytics are aligned with the desire of management to find clues or insights to support a course of actions and decisions. Business intelligence and data analytics use new technologies based on advances in science: mathematics, statistics, computing, etc. Those advances use the interaction of science and technology according to what is described by the Understanding Science website run by the University of California Berkeley: "Science and technology feed off of one another, propelling both forward. Scientific knowledge allows us to build new technologies, which often allow us to make new observations about the world, which, in turn, allow us to build even more scientific knowledge, which then inspires another technology … and so on." In general, the process in management to be more scientific or methodical is described as a sequence of steps (Figure 2.1) that starts with complete uncertainty, developing into some tasks based on questions to solve for knowledge/evidence, moving to an internal view of possible solutions/answers to guide decisions, moving to solve questions about future and possible outcomes of decisions, and then moving to use that generated intelligence to mitigate risk in organizations.

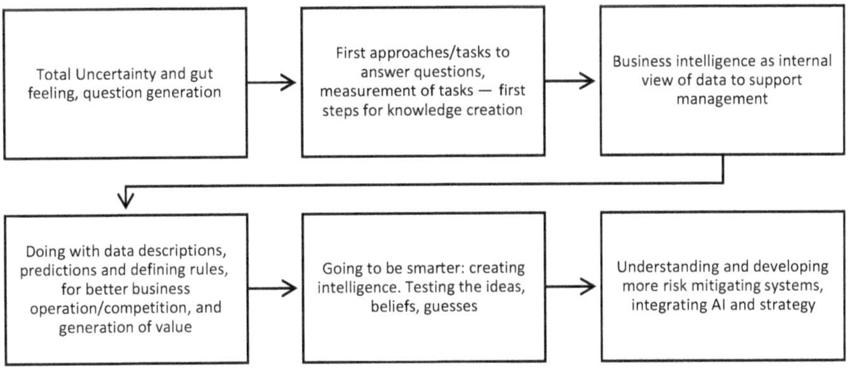

Figure 2.1. From total uncertainty to creating knowledge, intelligence, and mitigating strategic risk.

These efforts in using a more scientific approach promote BI processes oriented to answering questions in the following strategic decisions areas:

- Definition, organization, and design of goods and services, answers to customers' demands, analog or digital.
- Leading quality and control under the analog or digital operations — customer's experience and satisfaction.
- Assessment, design, strategy, and development of process capacity and capabilities.
- Delivery, promotion, and production of the offer, using delivery systems, physical locations, digital location, design of presentation (digital/physical means and their layouts).
- Human and machine assignment, job design, interactions, people and machines complementing one another.
- Supply chain management operation and risk control.
- Scheduling according to continuous or discrete times, digital or with limited access to production and operation processes.
- Control, learning, prediction, planning, simulation of the operation with and without maintenance.

Therefore, the strategic areas need structures of BI systems to provide ongoing value creation in the organizations. As Trieu *et al.* (2022) presented in their review of business intelligence, BI comprises BI system quality, data integration and data cleaning, and orientation to use evidence to support decisions and actions. In their study (Trieu *et al.*, 2022), a BI context includes dimensions and elements as follows:

- BI system components: reports dashboards, analysis, and queries.
- Data components of a BI system: data dictionary, business rules and data logic, data checking, and validation actions.
- Organization's culture: unit of BI functions and adoption by the organizations to use in decision-making.

Operations research and BI started a line of work for evidence and scientific method application to guide organizations. Exhibit 2.1 summarizes aspects related to implementation of the scientific method in management as associated with the following: first, understanding what a system is about. The system concept is used explicitly and implicitly in this book: explicitly in the description of what a system should have and implicitly in the way that all processes are connected though the systems of organizations. The value of understanding the organization as a system is that it allows the identification of strategic intelligence and strategic risk control as an outcome of several processes performed previously based on data analytics/AI. As mentioned, the search for using the scientific method and analytics way of thinking is not new as Bursk and Chapman (1963) indicated. In addition, the search for answers using disciplines associated with analytics, or solving paradoxes. Those situations appear in a kind of questions–answers that can affect a business creating $N \times N$ relationships between problems and models that will lead to improve strategic intelligence.

The use of a scientific method is appropriate for understanding the transition from no business intelligence to business and strategic intelligence. Exhibit 2.2 indicates a brief of the work done in science, what having more intelligence represents in a business environment, and how to connect intelligence and decisions under constraints and realities as Goldratt (1986) and Ackoff (2007) indicated. Ackoff's reflections open the windows to define and use strategic intelligence as finding solutions to problems that generate strategic risk and observing that more internal barriers and lack of understanding could be trouble for defining the degree of digital transformation that is required in organizations to adapt and use to compete properly.

Organizations want to understand how to set goals and objectives based on evidence. This is the first step in creating intelligence using the

Ackoff's System definition (Ackoff, 1981, pp. 15–16):

"A system is a set of two or more elements that satisfies the following conditions:

- The behaviour of each element has an effect on the behaviour of the whole.
- The behaviour of the elements and their effect on the whole are interdependent.
- All possible subgroups of elements also have the first two properties."

We use component instead of the element Knowledge Discovery/Creation plus Innovation and Actions to intervene in Reality Creation. It is more than adaptation; it builds the Reality! Silos of knowledge should be part of the past!

"In the years since the mid 1950's a trend toward a new and more scientific approach to the solution of business problems has been developing. It stems from methods first suggested by the advocates of "operations research." But, it is already apparent that by drawing in depth both on mathematics and on social sciences, and by utilizing intensively the high-speed electronic computer, researchers are beginning to give to the decision-making process a scientific base akin to the established methods which have long provided the bases for research in physics, biology, and chemistry."

New Decision-Making Tools for Managers. Edited by Edward Bursk and John Chapman, The New American Library, New York 1963.

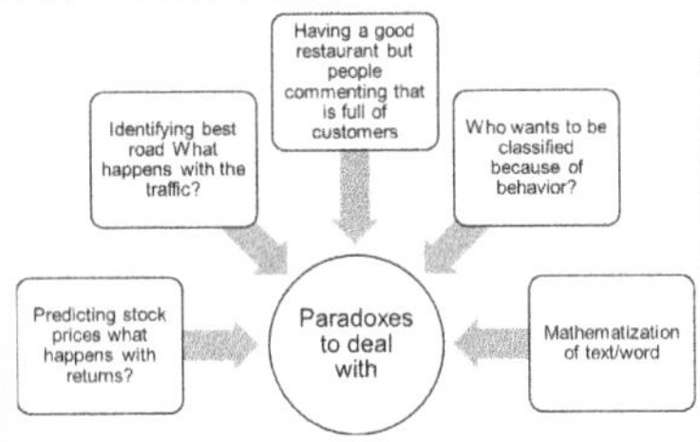

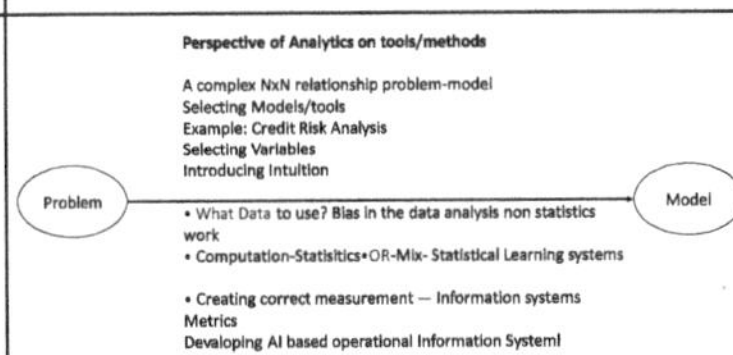

Exhibit 2.1. Systems and scientific method in management.

capacity and capabilities based on analytics techniques because intelligence is related to the understanding of what is happening now, what happened in the past, and what could happen tomorrow, and what to do

What we do in science

Alpaydin E, 2014, Introduction to Machine Learning, Third Edition by The MIT Press ©

- "Almost all of science is fitting models to data. Scientists design experiments and make observations and collect data. They then try to extract knowledge by finding out simple models that explain the data they observed. This is called *induction* and is the process of extracting general rules from a set of particular cases.
- We are now at a point that such analysis of data can no longer be done by people, both because the amount of data is huge and because people who can do such analysis are rare and manual analysis is costly. There is thus a growing interest in computer models that can analyze data and extract information automatically from them, that is, learn."

There are more elements to include in the Learning System - coordination is crucial!

But, be intelligent in which sense?

1. Business
2. Strategy
3. Artificial
4. Sentient
5. Security
6. Multiple Intelligences (Gardner 1983)

I thought about constraints and making decisions

To be more intelligent is to deal with constraints

Goldratt(1986) pointed out

- "I view science as nothing more than an understanding of the way the world is and why it is that way. At any given time our scientific knowledge is simply the current state of the art of our understanding. I do not believe in absolute truths. I fear such beliefs because they block the search for better understanding... Knowledge should be pursued, I believe, to make our world better-to make life more fulfilling."
- One big constraint is in ourselves. Mosterin(1978) pointed out that the world is not structured in a unique way but the structure is based on the projection of our concepts on the world

To be more Intelligent: Making Better Decisions

- Simon (1977) notes that a decision making process comprises intelligence (problem/opportunity definition), design (model formulation and validation), choice (selection solution to model) and implementation
- Different models/ DSS can be designed according to the decision making process
- Raiffa (1968) decision under uncertainty proceed by a construction of a list of viable options available, list events that can occur, consider time, evaluate possible results of the options, put some measure of uncertainty, select a strategy

The Learning System requires clear identification of intelligence criteria

Understanding more some realities - Ackoff

Ackoff indicates that problem solving implies selection of possible paths to achieve one or more objectives or results. Some of his F-Laws (2007) are more and more contemporary (Ackoff RL, Addison HJ, Bibb S 2007 Management F-Laws: How Organizations Really Work):

- 19. "The only thing more difficult than starting something new in an organization is stopping something old."
- 23. "Business schools are as difficult to change as cemeteries, and for the same reasons."
- 29. "The amount of time a committee waste is directly proportional to its size."
- 36. "The less important an issue is, the more time managers spend discussing it."
- 38. "Administration, management and leadership are not the same thing."
- 40. "Business schools are security prisons of the mind."
- 61. "It is very difficult for those inside a box to think outside of it."
- 64. "Most corporations and business schools are less than the sum of their parts."

The Learning System requires understanding a SWOT of each element the same as the whole elements set

Exhibit 2.2. Science work and management requirements.

according to different futures. The study of various types of problems requires development and design of strategies to understand and organize what data analytics will provide to the creation of internal organizational systems. Data analytics (Exhibit 2.3) contributes to a good development of the processes in strategy to understand how results will help to avoid traps and mistakes for validating hypotheses, assumptions, and interpretation of outcomes. An issue is that if management does not improve the capacity to use information and knowledge created by analytics in a solid way, it could reduce the capacity to achieve goals and the capabilities to compete.

To start thinking in terms of strategic intelligence under the frameworks of risk management and knowledge management, the first step is to link business intelligence and competitive intelligence. A way to

"Data mining involves extracting interesting patterns from data and can be found at the heart of operational research (OR), as its aim is to create and enhance decision support systems. Even in the early days, some data mining approaches relied on traditional OR methods such as linear programming and forecasting, and modern data mining methods are based on a wide variety of OR methods including linear and quadratic optimization, genetic algorithms and concepts based on artificial ant colonies." Author(s): B. Baesens, C. Mues, D. Martens and J. Vanthienen, *The Journal of the Operational Research Society*, Vol. 60, Supplement 1: Milestones in OR (May, 2009), pp. s16–s23.	"In our view, analytics is the rational way to get from ideas to execution." R. Saxena and A. Srinivasan, *Business Analytics, International Series in Operations Research & Management Science 186*, DOI: 10.1007/978-1-4614-6080-0_1, © Springer Science+Business Media New York 2013.
"We will use two different perspectives to lay out the characteristics of analytics: one is related to how business value is achieved and the other regards how it is implemented … the business perspective of the analytics definition deals with future action and any technology, product, or service that contributes towards the action can qualify to be part of analytics solutions …The technical implementation perspective describes the characteristics of analytics in terms of the techniques used to implement the analytics solution." *Implementing Analytics A Blueprint for Design, Development, and Adoption*, Nauman Sheikh, Elsevier, 2013.	"Bounded awareness can occur at various points in the decision-making process. First, executives may fail to see or seek out key information needed to make a sound decision. Second, they may fail to use the information that they do see because they aren't aware of its relevance. Finally, executives may fail to share information with others, thereby bounding the organization's awareness." Max H. Bazerman and Dolly Chugh, Decisions Without Blinders, Harvard Business Review January 2006, pp. 88–97.

Exhibit 2.3. Concepts from data mining, OR to data analytics and how decision making can be affected by limited analytics use.

manage knowledge is integrating a search for the answers and how the use of analytics resources is going to add value to what the organization is doing to improve and maintain the performance, to survive, and to grow better in the market. This means the question is how to connect isolated concepts, and for that a first point to keep in mind is that knowledge is a means for being smarter, i.e., trying to use data analytics to measure, to estimate, to predict, describe, and to generate an understanding of what is happening and could happen with the organizations. Second, organizations' knowledge creation through analytics mitigates risk, and the most important concept is that intelligence is about adaptation; it is about designing and acting in the way that organizations with humans–machines are able to tackle to overcome barriers to compete and win.

Exhibit 2.4 indicates some aspects on the evolution of business intelligence to data analytics. First, evidence construction is about dealing with a combination of intuition and reason, the same as using quantitative and qualitative data and methods. Knowledge creation is not only about reason or quantitative variables analysis but also about the mix of all those components to understand and foster actions. Second, there is a need to use knowledge properly. In several cases it is required to use by organizations the formal updated academic research. Third, moving through a modeling process requires a clear view that models are just "models", and they provide clues to answers but are final solutions; they require calibration and improvement, which means analysis of the outcomes, assumptions, techniques, levels of accuracy required, and a balance between cost of new accuracy level and the value added to the bottom line of the organization. Fourth, moving from BI to data analytic implies the search for scope and learning inside the organizations to solve more problems and discover and tackle causes, issues, and promotion of adequate changes.

An example of transforming BI to data analytics is a decision made in the Scotia Bank, Canada, where management was engaged in training to understand how the organization could use data analytics for operations in all corners from legal to commercial departments moving through risk management as part of the bank culture. Management was motivated to learn, improve, and develop competitive capacity using data analytics. Capacity and capabilities that are not just to assess risk but to know how to answer questions like: what the potential losses to deal will be and how using risk analytics it is possible to mitigate and to allow market expansion creating a customer-oriented culture. The bank's strategy not only permeated the analytics process throughout the organization but it also

"Of course the gut/brain dichotomy is largely false. Few decision makers ignore good information when they can get it. And most accept that there will be times they can't get it and so will have to rely on instinct. Fortunately, the intellect informs both intuition and analysis, and research shows that people's instincts are often quite good. Guts may even be trainable, suggest John Hammond, Ralph Keeney, Howard Raiffa, and Max Bazerman, among others. In the Fifth Discipline, Peter Senge elegantly sums up the holistic approach: "People with high levels of personal mastery… cannot afford to choose between reason and intuition, or head and heart, any more than they would choose to walk on one leg or see with one eye." A blink, after all, is easier when you use both eyes. And so is a long, penetrating stare." A Brief History of Decision Making, Leigh Buchanan and Andrew O'Connell Harvard Business Review, January 2006, pp. 32–41.	"Why Don't Practitioners Know about Research That Academics Think Is Very Important? Managers need not be exposed to scientific knowledge about management to practice their craft." Evidence-based management and the marketplace for ideas, Wayne F. Cascio, *Academy of Management Journal* 2007, Vol. 50, No. 5, 1009–1012.
"The Confirming-Evidence Trap: You'd better not let that conversation be the clincher, because you've probably just fallen victim to the confirming evidence bias. This bias leads us to seek out information that supports our existing instinct or point of view while avoiding information that contradicts it. The Estimating and Forecasting: Traps Making estimates or forecasts about uncertain events, however, is a different matter. While managers continually make such estimates and forecasts, they rarely get clear feedback about their accuracy." John S. Hammond, Ralph L. Keeney, and Howard Raiffa The Hidden Traps in Decision Making Harvard Business Review January 2006.	"The problem is that most companies are not succeeding in turning data into knowledge and then results. Even those that do, are doing so only temporarily or in a limited area." Thomas H. Davenport, Jeanne G. Harris. David W. De Long, Alvin L. Jacobson, Data to knowledge to results: Building an analytic capability, California Management Review, Vol. 43, No. 2 Winter 2001.

Exhibit 2.4. Transition to using scientific methods and reason/evidence in management.

connected and enhanced leadership and employee participation to prepare for digital transformation in order to improve customer experiences and customer relationships.

According to the above ideas, to be more intelligent implies goals aligned with the search of delivering the best results for the stakeholders; this means it could be a problem of cost control or how to create new capabilities and new capacity under uncertain conditions and constraints to produce expected results. Evolving from BI to data analytics is oriented to make better decisions but approaches to generate more value are used; for instance, moving from scenario analyses to Monte Carlo simulation, can create difference in the understanding of data and possible guides for decision-making. The same is applicable when it is the case of moving from heuristic solutions and inductive conclusions to the level of finding optimal solutions or general and inferential results applicable according to certain assumptions. Exhibit 2.5 illustrates what the aim of analytics is and how analytics is a component of BI for organizations to be smarter, indicating that data analytics will be possible to use if management lead the analytics use transformation. For example, in Monte Carlo simulations, the idea could be to make decisions according to the distribution of NPV of cash flows under the uncertainty of the cost of capital, the possible structure and relationships of variables that constitute a net income, or the uncertainty around the changes through time. The metric NPV will not be studied as a fix value; it will be studied according to its probability distribution and decisions will be made at least based on expected value and variances. Another important aspect of the analytics process as part of evolution of BI is understanding the learning process. The search for solutions to problems requires analysis of a reasonable error approach according to learning improvement that is connected to human understanding of a business situation and its potential implementation. In several cases, the search for solutions is about confidence intervals where metrics will be located with higher probability; tolerance is a kind of acceptance of certain levels of risk and is connected to good-enough solutions to guiding business strategies.

The answers to questions about risk and about the use of BI and data analytics are not necessarily good in the first round of analysis, that is, it is not possible to answer these questions without sophisticated methods that require more elaborated work. It does not mean that a good answer requires sophisticated models; the principle of parsimony and simplicity will help obtain good answers. The ongoing search for answers to questions motivates the movement from BI to data analytics use. Exhibit 2.6 introduces three aspects to observe in a transition or transformation from BI to data analytics-based organizations. The first point is about the need to

<table>
<tr>
<td>"The goal for analytics is to make better decisions. However, while many organizations collect data and some organizations engage in analytics, few organizations link their analytics activities to their decision making." How to make better decisions and get better results, Tom Davenport February 2010 Harvard Business Review</td>
<td>"The term intelligence has been used by researchers in artificial intelligence since the 1950s. Business intelligence became a popular term in the business and IT communities only in the 1990s. In the late 2000s, business analytics was introduced to represent the key analytical component in BI (Davenport, 2006). More recently big data and big data analytics have been used to describe the data sets and analytical techniques in applications that are so large (from terabytes to exabytes) and complex (from sensor to social media data) that they require advanced and unique data storage, management, analysis, and visualization technologies. In this article we use business intelligence and analytics (BI&A) as a unified term and treat big data analytics as a related field that offers new directions for BI&A research." Business Intelligence And Analytics: From Big Data To Big Impact, Hsinchun Chen, Roger H. L. Chiang, Veda C. Storey MIS Quarterly Vol. 36 No. 4, pp. 1165–1188/December 2012.</td>
</tr>
<tr>
<td colspan="2">"In our work with dozens of companies in six data rich industries, we have found that fully exploiting data and analytics requires three mutually supportive capabilities ... First, companies must be able to identify, combine, and manage multiple sources of data. Second, they need the capability to build advanced analytics models for predicting and optimizing outcomes. Third, and most critical, management must possess the muscle to transform the organization so that the data and models actually yield better decisions." Making Advanced Analytics Work For You A practical guide to capitalizing on big data by Dominic Barton and David Court Harvard Business Review, October 2012, pp. 78–83.</td>
</tr>
</table>

Exhibit 2.5. Data as asset that are processed to generate more value.

review scope and quality of procedures, techniques, and results. During the financial crisis in 2008–2010, a leading research paper had points to review and correct. Second, a data analytics process, as presented in Chapter 3, requires a continuous feedback and review in each stage. Another important aspect in the transformation to data analytics is that there are reactions to the data truth, or more than that several barriers can appear to use results because organizations would like to keep the status quo, maintain the beliefs, and confirm the current conditions and decisions made in the past. What this means is that data analytics transformation is not only about learning techniques and data management to create knowledge but also about how organizations are able to deal with truth. A third point to review is that the evolution of BI to data analytics is not only because of the sophistication of questions and models used to answer them, but also because of the capacity to organize thoughts and problem resolution logic to get answers. It is about what the organization could do to infer from and interpret data, starting with a clear review of options for solutions. It is possible that some models are doing a very good job to guide organizations with their outcomes as they are not complex in their structures or implementation. In this line of ideas, moving from BI to data

APR 16, 2013 Mike Konczal: "In 2010, economists Carmen Reinhart and Kenneth Rogoff released a paper, "Growth in a Time of Debt." Their "main result is that … median growth rates for countries with public debt over 90 percent of GDP are roughly one percent lower than otherwise; average (mean) growth rates are several percent lower." Countries with debt-to-GDP ratios above 90 percent have a slightly negative average growth rate, in fact." "In a new paper, "Does High, Public Debt Consistently Stifle Economic Growth? A Critique of Reinhart and Rogoff," Thomas Herndon, Michael Ash, and Robert Pollin of the University of Massachusetts, Amherst successfully replicate the results So what do Herndon-Ash-Pollin conclude? They found "the average real GDP growth rate for countries carrying a public debt-to-GDP ratio of over 90 percent is actually 2.2 percent, not −0.1 percent as [Reinhart-Rogoff claim]."" [UPDATE: To clarify, they find 2.2 percent if they include all the years, weigh by number of years, and avoid the Excel error.] Going further into the data, they are unable to find a breakpoint where growth falls quickly and significantly.	"[t]oo much common management "wisdom" isn't wise at all, but instead is based on flawed knowledge of best practices that are poor, incomplete, or outright wrong — not to mention hazardous to an organization's health." Hard Facts, Dangerous Half-Truths And Total Nonsense: Profiting From Evidence-Based Management (2006) Pfeffer and Sutton, HBP.

Exhibit 2.6. Data Analytics capacity is not only modeling but also a mindset for exploring what data can say to support management.

[*The Guardian*, Thursday July 20, 2006]

Gavyn Davies Does the Maths: How a Statistical Formula Won the War: "By 1941–42, the allies knew that US and even British tanks had been technically superior to German Panzer tanks in combat, but they were worried about the capabilities of the new marks IV and V. More troubling, they had really very little idea of how many tanks the enemy was capable of producing in a year."

"One solution was to ask intelligence to guess the number by secretly observing the output of German factories, or by trying to count tanks on the battlefield. Both the British and the Americans tried this, but they found that the estimates returned by intelligence were contradictory and unreliable."

"The basic idea was that the highest serial number among the captured tanks could be used to calculate the overall total. The German tanks were numbered as follows: 1, 2, 3 … N, where N was the desired total number of tanks produced. Imagine that they had captured five tanks, with serial numbers 20, 31, 43, 78 and 92. Call the sample size S and the maximum serial number M. $(M-1)(S+1)/S$

By using this formula, statisticians reportedly estimated that the Germans produced 246 tanks per month between June 1940 and September 1942. At that time, standard intelligence estimates had believed the number was far, far higher, at around 1,400. After the war, the allies captured German production records, showing that the true number of tanks produced in those three years was 245 per month, almost exactly what the statisticians had calculated, and less than one fifth of what standard intelligence had thought likely."

Exhibit 2.6. (*Continued*)

analytics in strategy could pose question such as how much risk is going to be accepted or what is going to be the system or systems to control the effects of uncertainty in the organization. These questions will require a set of data analytics steps to form an assessment of exposure to the simulated potential outcomes and their variation of the strategy.

BI is moving to a data analytics environment with the purpose of creating data analytics structures that will be oriented to maintain awareness of potential business issues/risks and potential adverse events in terms of customers and other stakeholders. Measuring systems need to be created under principles of consistency, precision, accuracy, and security in terms of being able to protect data source, human and machine resources, and algorithms for creating the knowledge and learning required in the organization. Data analytics requires details about experiment design, data collection, and analysis in order to understand how, for

(1) Strategic Intelligence (2) Digitalization–Digital Transformation (3) Strategic Risk Li *et al.* (2021) "Navigating the opportunities and risks associated with AI implementation requires firms to develop a strategic AI orientation." Main Concepts — Strategic Intelligence Convergence of • Business Intelligence • Competitive Intelligence • Artificial Intelligence — Russell and Norvig (2021)	• Using Data Science/Analytics to develop and properly use intelligence to deal with risk • Intelligence as the capacity for adaptation by humans, organizations, societies to solve problems, achieve goals, use actionable knowledge to control, mitigate risk • Data Science/Analytics creates knowledge, knowledge reduces uncertainty, and provides means to deal with risks.

Exhibit 2.7. The opportunity is an appropriate transition for the use digitalization and AI for the good of humans.

example, a distribution channel will generate revenues and profits according to the knowledge of customers and the volume of the customers' purchases. These components of the problem go further than BI and are part of the data analytics aim.

A summary for this section is as follows:

- BI is not only using data for reporting; it is possible to use data analytics to create adaptive business intelligence and to expand the understanding of what data are saying to the organization. BI has been limited in scope; the concept should be more about adaptive BI.
- BI and knowledge creation to develop intelligence depend on the definition of targets, orientation to listen to the data, and to be open to a continuous review of how results are obtained and the meaning creation of those results in the context of business.
- To move BI to a data analytics transformation requires more on the human side than on technical side of data management and the modeling process; the transformation is about interpretation and analysis of the problems to be solved to find solutions that are not necessarily sophisticated but good and have the potential to evolve and improve. It is about creating actionable knowledge that mitigates risks in an organization.

In the next section, the emphasis is on how competitive analysis contributes to intelligence development and how intelligence is orienting strategy design and implementation. In the section, there are examples about the value of integration: first in telecommunication, second healthcare, third supply chain risk analysis, and fourth management awareness and actions in risk-related settings (see Exhibit 2.7).

2.2. From Competitive Intelligence to Intelligence-Driven Strategy

Competitive intelligence is the capacity to create intelligence based on data from industry analysis to understand how participants in the industry act according to a business environment. Not all members of a market are considered competitors with the same intensity. Some clusters of multiple attributes of the members of the market will define the groups where the organization has the first challenges to achieve better performance (see examples at the end of Chapter 1). This means a strategic intelligence development process is going to be in the chain of starting with data, identifying how management is using the knowledge created to design the systems that integrate knowledge and potentialize digitalization (Exhibit 2.7). Competitive intelligence uses data about external sources that can be structured data from markets, financials, customers, and other socio-economic dimensions of generating knowledge about market attractiveness and possible risks. The fundamental aspect to move in the direction of organizing an intelligence-driven strategy is to develop systems that take data and transform that in a multi-faceted view of what is happening in the market. It is not only about ratio metrics but also about how time series of an indicator of the whole market are evolving vs. the same indicator in the organization for direct and related competitors in the industry. At this level, the application of the competitive forces with an analytics system to capture the market behavior, plus methods like BSC for measuring what is happening internally, will provide means to generate intelligence.

From competitive intelligence to intelligence-driven strategy, the use of balanced scorecards (BSC) is to find the best way to improve actionable knowledge of customers, employee–machines interaction, business

Digitalization/Digital Transformation	*Strategic Risk:*
• Differences among digitation/digitalization and digital transformation: Data-driven decision-making. • Opportunities: Business Application, Competitive Advantages. • Risks/Perils: Weak implementation of the strategy, measurement, systematic approach, misuse of resources, centralization–decentralization. • Use of data, improve the process, create offer and connect the business transformation.	• Variation and its measurement process. *Two points:* • Performance: expected results. What can affect the expected results? • How can the organization affect the world and the consequences in performance? There are important aspects in the treatment of risk when the need is to integrate and not to study silo risks. Problem of bankruptcy, disruption, reputation.

Exhibit 2.8. Connecting risks and digitalization.

processes associated with income, or net income results. The metric values as target can change depending on the organizations and the metrics used to measure success: Benefits, users served, profits, social indicators, etc., will be comparable with the same concepts in the industry. The creation of knowledge will be oriented depending on how specific risks are identified in each BSC dimension. For instance, in the case of the customers, risks could be about losing customers or dealing with the investment portfolio of promotion or a full marketing mix. In terms of Exhibit 2.8, as an example, there are transformations in organizations that create challenges in risk management processes as in the case of digital transformation that plays the two roles of mitigating strategic risk and opening new risks such as using new technologies and means of operations as the cloud services.

In general, a problem, in the relationship of competitive intelligence and intelligence-driven strategy, to solve from the risk perspective and intelligence development, is about resource allocation for improving performance of organizations in a market maintaining and improving levels of returns for the shareholder. Resource allocation refers to portfolios of products, investments, markets, promotion, etc., that the organization is looking to administer. In Section 1.4, the explanation was about moving from KPIs to KRIs, and within the current discussion the point is that competitive intelligence connects KPIs and KRIs in the organization. Moreover, competitive intelligence contributes to the improvement of the organization with regard to human–machine knowledge creation, learning to create value, and maintain relevance and impact in the market with a solid performance. The time of having only market shares as the indicator of performance is in the past. The size of the organization is not the goal; it is about the health, growth, and evolution/adaptation.

The steps for transformation into an intelligence-driven strategy require enhancement in intellectual capital, talent, human–machine interaction consolidation and AI/data analytics that create actionable knowledge with orientation to make better decisions and competitive sustainability that deals with good and bad conditions of uncertainty. Adaptation of strategy is part of the intelligence, and involves overcoming the misconception of the 70s and 80s about strategic intelligence or strategic planning as a static process with results instead of a dynamic course of actions to adapt to changes according to the conditions of the market. The business dimensions explained in the introduction of this book (offer (What), technology (How), and market (Who)) indicate how to distribute the intelligence and risk analyses and how those analyses should be integrated in strategic risk mitigation. Digital transformation is part of the HOW dimension in a business definition, depending on the conditions of offer or markets. In banking, many years ago, digital transformation started with the use of plastic cards as distribution channels for credit, payments, cash, etc. Offices were equipped with more technology to support customer transactions, and some management groups believed that banks should be all digital and online. The reality is that nowadays banks have a combination of branch offices that are fully digital, with ATMs, and call centers with humans and chatbots, as well as online services. There are different types of bank businesses even though they having similar services; the way that they manage human and technology portfolios, markets and products is where the differentiation is and where intelligence development plays the role of creating value. Data-driven strategies and intelligence-driven strategies are about how to get the best of what the organization needs to do with data analytics to exploit market opportunities with a mix of human talent and machine capabilities. Technology will not be a differentiator; as for example, ATMs were differentiators in banking but they years later converted into a must for having a banking service business. The ATM was not a competitive advantage, the combination of personal customer contact and ATM was highly appreciated by several segments and under certain transactions, thereby improving and promoting the business.

Another interesting review of creating intelligence is observing communications and healthcare. In the case of telecommunications, Exhibit 2.9 shows that data analytics is adding value not only in the optimization of network service but also by creating intelligence to deal with strategic factors in the industry: device design, use, selection, types of customers, new offer of services, maintaining operational risk at a controllable level, dealing with regulation, competitors, new technologies adoption, pricing, etc.

In the healthcare industry, many new opportunities are appearing in order to provide a more intelligent-driven strategy approach to the industry. Exhibit 2.10 shows two examples of using data analytics under the definition of learning concept. The learning process in healthcare has multiple levels: learning from diseases, learning from administration of hospitals, learning from using certain types of quantitative models, causality analysis, etc.

The previous examples of communications and healthcare prepare the reader to see that data science and risk understanding are connected in practice (Exhibit 2.11); risks related to customers, patients, devices, data source creation (devices for diabetes, Parkinson's, or in hospitals for diagnostics), learning from the users, etc., are all types of solutions directed to improve quality experience of stakeholders and maintain the organizations in good shape. These examples illustrate that when isolated solutions are observed in a holistic way, what is created prepares the organization to integrate strategic intelligence, which is the topic in the next section.

However, the capacity and capabilities on the technical/technology side are only one step from integrated intelligence generation. Human and machine interaction requires a high level of concentration in management. Intelligence from machines is meant to be a support to the intelligence from humans to leverage each another and produce the increment of value delivery. Exhibit 2.12 shows how, in industries, this interaction is the engine to grow applications and mitigate risks in the practice to advance technology, which is in the best way to support performance improvement.

In Telecommunications: From processes: user-related problems up to technical/engineering problems

Monte Carlo Simulation: Dale Lehman, Huybert Groenendaal, Greg Nolder: Practical Spreadsheet Risk Modeling for Management

"One of the major business decisions that cellular phone service providers must make is how much to subsidize the consumer's acquisition of the phone and what long-term contract terms to incorporate to recover these costs over time."

Optimization: Optimal Product Bundling using several approaches from bundling call/waiting, voice mail, caller ID, etc., up to Internet of Things

Mix of tools: Segmentation and Pricing for a subscription-based service

"The service provider will use the information to optimize network performance and provide a higher quality of service. It will also enable Vodafone Ireland to perform capacity management and root-cause analysis quicker and more cost-effectively." Note from Vodafone Ireland (2012).

In Telecommunications:

Many questions appear that are not marketing related:

- Why are companies always buying storage?
- Why are companies using many servers?
- Why are backups taking so long?

How can one measure service satisfaction and provide incentives?

How can one develop new product/service options?

How can one optimize the traffic of messages?

Or there are trends to review that are related to product/service design and customer and strategy design in other fields. For example, the use of telecommunication solutions for healthcare. These are opportunities for telecom firms — collaborative work with complementary organizations.

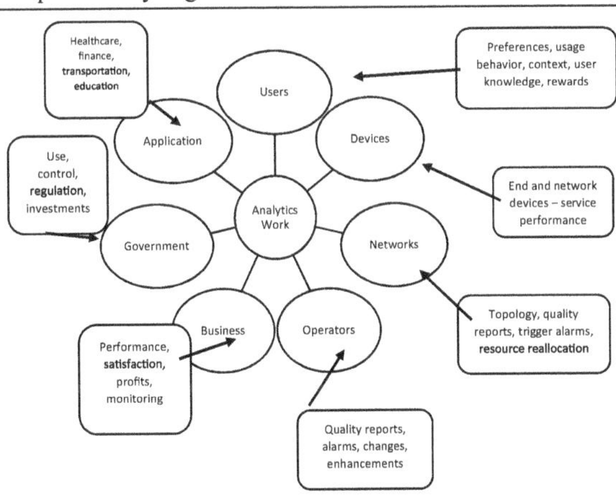

In telecommunications, as in most industries, there is an issue of perspective for analytics use according to multiple human–machine–artifacts interactions in the business.

Exhibit 2.9. An illustration of analytics applications for improving Telecommunications.

Analytics in Healthcare — Support to organizations • Using analytics for improving organizational measurement systems, management control systems, and risk management systems o Integrating key performance indicators and key risk indicators o Developing data structures connected to analytics capabilities to add value to decision-making and problem-solving processes o Developing the bridge between computation capacity and interpretability of outcome capacity o Patient experience improvement: networks, mobility, prediction, control, ambulatory, etc. o Processes improvement using optimization-based benchmarking • Particular solutions — examples o Exploration of data-driven hospital strategies o Using the cloud for data collection, aggregation, analytics, and decision-making o Integrating data from disparate sources for population health management o Turning knowledge into practice for patient care in and out of the organization o Using predictive analytics to improve quality and efficiency of care o Deployment of mobile devices for population health management, and harnessing the big data produced by them	Dyagilev and Saria (2016) Learning (predictive) risk scores in the presence of censoring due to interventions, Machine Learning, Vol. 102, pp. 323–348 "We propose a novel ranking based framework for disease severity score learning (DSSL). DSSL exploits the following key observation: while it is challenging for experts to quantify the disease severity at any given time, it is often easy to compare the disease severity at two different times. Extending existing ranking algorithms, DSSL learns a function that maps a vector of patient's measurements to a scalar severity score subject to two constraints. First, the resulting score should be consistent with the expert's ranking of the disease severity state. Second, changes in score between consecutive periods should be smooth. We apply DSSL to the problem of learning a sepsis severity score using a large, real-world electronic health record dataset. The learned scores significantly outperform state-of-the-art clinical scores in ranking patient states by severity and in early detection of downstream adverse events. We also show that the learned disease severity trajectories are consistent with clinical expectations of disease evolution. Further, we simulate datasets containing different treatment administration patterns and show that DSSL shows better generalization performance to changes in treatment patterns compared to the above approaches."

Exhibit 2.10. Learning about learning for machine and human interactions.

Ustun and Rudin (2016), Super sparse linear integer models for optimized medical scoring systems, Machine Learning, Vol. 102, pp. 349–391 "Scoring systems are linear classification models that only require users to add, subtract and multiply a few small numbers in order to make a prediction. These models are in widespread use by the medical community, but are difficult to learn from data because they need to be accurate and sparse, have coprime integer coefficients, and satisfy multiple operational constraints."	Tom M. Mitchell pointed out "A computer program is said to learn from experience E with respect to some class of tasks T and performance measure P, if its performance at tasks in T, as measured by P, improves with the experience E." "Nice to think about not correct or wrong answer. Many decisions are related to define as good or bad the answer based on the variance of performance metrics." *Machine Learning at Carnegie Mellon University. Author of the book Machine Learning (McGraw-Hill, 1997)

Exhibit 2.10. *(Continued)*

Computer and Data Science in the risk landscape (1) AI — Development and Use (2) Operational and non-operation risks related to AI, IT, people (3) Data product creation (4) Fintech, Insurtech, Healthtech, etc. (5) Errors, bias, misunderstanding (6) Sustainability (7) Risk intelligence development (8) Computer science involvement in strategic risk and strategic intelligence. Bank Example: Nova Scotia Bank, Canada • Digital adoption has accelerated changes/Analytics use/Human–Machine interaction • Global regulators look for open banking and non-traditional new participants • New participants are disrupting the traditional operating model	• Increased customer demands, needs, and expectations require multi-year digital transformation • About artificial general intelligence, strong intelligence, general intelligence. IBM in its main web page about AI indicates, "If researchers are able to develop Strong AI, the machine would require an intelligence equal to humans; it would have a self-aware consciousness that has the ability to solve problems, learn, and plan for the future." Development and offering based on • Creation of data products • Supplement of the current offer • Reports dynamic, interactive, shareable • Interactive applications • Presentations

Exhibit 2.11. Moving in the direction of data analytics in risk understanding.

People and Machine Interaction and Development will be stronger for instance: • The underwriter work concentrated on the tails of the distribution of cases • The medical doctors dedicated to special cases. • Professor for not repeating content but concentrate on special topics/students, etc. Sturm (2021) "… second, adjustments to ML systems made by humans are largely beneficial, but this effect can diminish or even become harmful under certain conditions…"	• Fintech, Insurtech, Healthtech, etc. • Intermediaries are potentially in observation stage • Product changes are redefined • Errors-, bias, misunderstandings • Starts with data and continues with its analysis • How to deal with the "Fake" diffusion of messages • The excess of not formal references to support knowledge creation • Sustainability cost/responsibility — Smart Cities • The issue of enterprise value vs. the attraction of investors because of social responsibility • The problem with risk is that an event can happen • We need to do more to mitigate effects, enhancing risk intelligence Black swans will appear forever! Non-predicted catastrophes will appear

Exhibit 2.12. Moving in the direction to understanding people and machine interaction.

The reality is that convergence between what is real potential risk and what is possible to do to mitigate adverse effects is something that organizations require to work on as a priority. Learning and using the new knowledge to advance mitigating risk is a priority (Exhibit 2.13). In Chapter 1, the types of risk that are priority in the minds of organizational leaders was illustrated; the reality is that the two most probable creators of losses because of impact and likelihood on the technology side are cybersecurity and digital transformation. Identification is the first steps: the process from the risk management point of view is what organizations around the world are working on, and a common denominator is that humans can be the enablers and at the same time barriers and sources of risks. Human and machine interaction in terms of intelligence development is about what humans are doing with the potential of AI/data analytics and the way that organizations learn to use the new acquired knowledge.

(1) Organizations cannot stop because of COVID-19 (2) Organizations need to ask themselves • What they learnt for the next time • What organizations did to reduce society effects • What organizations did in terms of experiments to solve prove problems • What organizations did in terms of production improvement	What to expect? What to do? The ongoing change at a high speed and with high impact implies faster and more accurate work in the orientation of efforts, societies, and organizations in using our intelligence capacity

Exhibit 2.13. Risks are always present, and their analysis is a continuous process.

Capacity to learn What did we learn from some examples? (1) Financial crises (2) BBC Four experiment with the Spanish Flu (3) The airlines industry and the September 11, 2001 event (4) Nuclear energy in Fukushima, Chernobyl (5) Water, Global Warming, etc. Sturm *et al.* (2021) pointed out they are looking to understand "how organizations can coordinate human learning and ML to learn effectively (i.e., accumulate high levels of knowledge) as a whole." https://www.ey.com/en_us/global-board-risk-survey; https://www.pwc.com/us/en/library/risk-management-leader.html	Model Risk is part of our daily concern. Van Deventer *et al.* (2013) state, "The list of the models that failed under the duress of the credit crisis is a long one,…" and included the following aspects that affect the work in risk management: (1) What happens to others will not happen to me (2) Silo risk model view (3) Everyone is using the same model, so no problem (4) Everyone is using the same assumptions (5) Models are better if they are mathematical: issue of assumptions to find a formula, number of risk factors, independence, normality, etc. (6) Banks have to follow the practice of banks in North America and Europe

Exhibit 2.14. How to learn to deal with risk.

The capacity to learn (Exhibit 2.14) from competitive markets and what has happened in previous experiences with adverse events helps to create aligned human–machine interactions. An earthquake in Turkey and Syria in 2023, with more than 20 thousand casualties and many families without houses, is an example of learning and using technologies to warn, rescue, and organize people efforts, supplies, etc. Intelligence is about what to do to avoid the worst losses, to create contingency barriers and resilience. It is not about concentrating on predicting events that will have a high probability of occurring. It is about reducing impact with the intelligence created because of integration of many individual solutions using data analytics/AI and human interaction, reviewing models, understating results, communicating findings, etc.

After reviewing the BI and data analytics relationship and observing competitive intelligence and intelligence creation, the following section illustrates the connection between artificial intelligence and an integrated strategic intelligence view.

2.3. From Artificial Intelligence to Integrated Strategic Intelligence

The concepts in this section are organized according to the understanding of intelligence evolution in organizations as shown in Figure 2.2.

This diagram (Figure 2.2) represents the connection of what organizations are doing to create strategic intelligence using techniques and data plus human and machine capabilities that create understanding and

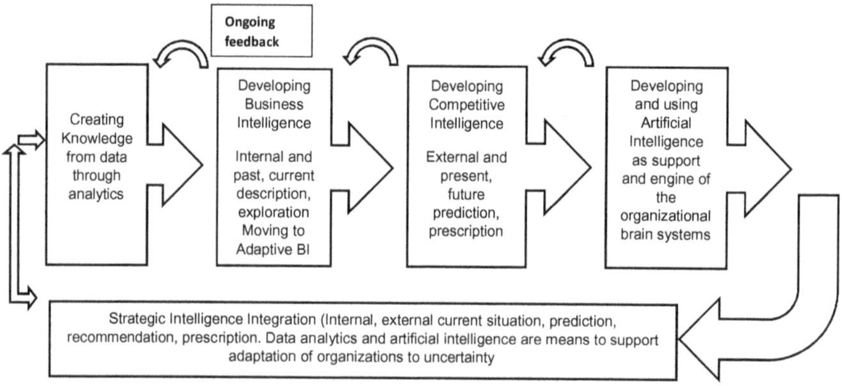

Figure 2.2. The system to generate strategic intelligence though data analytics and AI, with feedback in each step moving at multiple levels on intelligence evolution.

propagate actions in multiple forms — actions that are able and oriented to navigate in the uncertainty of the business operation. The degree and speed of transformation in terms of organization knowledge maturity are part of the decisions. Part of the advantages of using data analytics in practice is to have experimentation measurement before completing the changes. There are different types of risks, multiple knowledge sources, and a variety of solutions from the technical and technological point of view that can bring extraordinary and powerful benefits if they are aligned with the organization's orientation. In organizations, a point to understand is that not everyone has to be Airbnb in terms of daily rent in the hospitality industry, not everyone has to be related to the services for transportation intra cities-locations using self-driven trucks or drones. Organizations compete according their capacities/capabilities with technology. Now, the question is how to develop means for moving from a traditional process of improvement with automation to intelligent and digital-based process. The evolution is under the principle that, first, the analog and human process must work well before being automated. Intelligence creation and smart automation of processes require intelligence development not only on the technical side but also in how to lead the efforts to provide capabilities that organizations require to successfully operate in light of current and future changes. In the development of data analytics and AI applications, a point to consider is that intelligent is about prescription — to determine rules of operation and select the best alternatives under the constraints in any market/industry conditions but with the targets in mind to obtain benefits for all stakeholders.

For instance, in a hospitality organization, it might be important to continue with the current hotel services or offer packages or services using data products for the customers. The decisions analysis starts with the traditional tools, observing if the marginal costs of change are not so high and the benefits can be attractive, meaning the improvements can be converted into better value or impact. However, once results of marginal analysis are released, a new intelligence challenge emerges because the pressure of being more digital is huge in several markets and industries, and not all paradigms in management are applied in the same way to every organization. This means a higher level of strategic intelligence needs to be reflected in feedback analysis of each step in a data analytics/AI process implementation, that is, a continuous back and forth of questions and answers of how data analytics/AI and digital transformation provide the value that is required in an organization's strategy.

In terms of strategic risk, the integration of intelligence provides solutions for what issues and barriers in business performance improvement. In general, to advance and create awareness and capacity for risk management, it is valuable to observe that, first, "Risk Management is frequently not a problem of a lack of information, but rather a lack of knowledge with which to interpret its meaning" (Marshal *et al.*, 1996); second, "... banking is an information and knowledge-based business" (Fourie & Shilawa, 2004); and third, "... once a risk is identified new knowledge is required" (Shaw, 2005).

As an example, financial institutions are mainly operations, services, and contracts associated with people and machine interactions, and those organizations need to manage different kinds of information and knowledge in order to deal with risk exposures. These differences in information and knowledge influence the data analytics/AI application to ERM practice to align information, people, and ERM processes (Warren, 2002). In that regard, first, human interaction is part of the risk knowledge sharing process and is involved in the process development of ERM; second, technology provides the support for business processes, knowledge and information systems, and required tools to make decisions and develop strategies; and, third, business processes act in parallel with ERM processes during strategy implementation.

Another illustration of creating strategic intelligence as a means to improve risk management is in the supply chain risk analysis. There are specific risks related to credit and operations in international trading and local supply management. In supply chain, credit risk is associated with the issues of country knowledge and the way that organizations deal with risk mitigation through two main concepts in country analysis: political, socio-economic conditions for trading and competitiveness in/of the markets. The business dynamic to manage supply chain requires strong coordination and synchronization, particularly in the search for risk control and analysis. Given the nature of the business, a country as a risk unit of analysis is crucial because risks are exposure increase in different countries by volume of business in international trading. To create strategic intelligence and deal with country and credit risk according to the experience, one needs the following answers about required adjustments in the organization:

- Emphasis on suppliers, not only on transactions.
- Improvement of intra-knowledge sharing.

- Value and use of expertise within organizations.
- Dealing with risk knowledge, means for risk control, and value generation.
- Working on the use of the digital means to transfer knowledge from content to scrapping the web and managing capabilities for content mining and organizations, access, and storage. Reducing the silo orientation in the organization and creating more problem resolution communities.
- Changing the reaction to vents for prediction of possible outcomes of events and how to deal with potential losses.

In the process of mitigating supply chain risks, the following intelligence development is needed: risk assessment/judgment, problem-solving, business intelligence, international participant relationships, market knowledge, mitigation knowledge, modeling process, proposals and business solutions, technical advisory, and sector knowledge. Furthermore, risk knowledge using analytics and communication capabilities with suppliers can be, for example, dependent on country knowledge transfer involving economic, political, and social aspects, that is, related to all kinds of risk exposure of the organization — operational, financial, strategic, physical, and marketing. Country knowledge resides in multiple locations, people, data marts, data warehouses, intranet files, Internet, credit agencies, etc. In the practice of duplication of information and conflicting messages, the effort to locate and obtain information and knowledge is significant; the information format is not easily accessible, the information is not kept up-to-date, and the information is not tied to achieving the company's objectives and supporting several areas and business drivers. To achieve goals or implement strategy, being more intelligent is about integration of several aspects, data, multiple sources, analysis of documents and reports, transactions and market conditions, outlook from risk and possible economic results, etc., all to the mutual benefit of suppliers and organizations to achieve a mutual goal to deliver to the market on time and under competitive conditions.

Construction of solutions that integrate intelligence retains the basic attributes of risk analytics systems that start with what Crouhy *et al.* (2000) and Levine (2004) indicated: integration capability, flexibility, access to the data and outcomes, data management, time management, data and process requirements, and sharing and distributing risk knowledge. In intelligent solutions, focus is on country knowledge, which allows consolidated access to all country knowledge in one centralized area that distributes value to the organization at multiple levels of needs.

Data transformation as a process having valuable effects of building by blocks the Strategic Intelligence capabilities can fall in potential barriers to overcome that limit a successful Strategic Intelligence development, such as:

- Contradictions of knowledge sources such as documents, similar content from different authors, no updating process, different messages are unhelpful. Users have to get a uniform message in order to avoid confusion and misinterpretation.
- Different sources of data and report issuers are part of the source input. This identifies the need to create standards to share content to get consistent results.
- Different kinds of users, and diverse users and needs are part of intelligence solutions. This means the capacity to provide independent answers to different risk knowledge consumers and to create diverse solutions.
- Selection of explicit knowledge is the first option to work with. Tacit knowledge is based on the trust and the definition of a person with better expertise.
- Review the value of the documents for the users. Many of the explicit knowledge documents are not used and many of the documents used are not written in a way that the user needs or with the possibility of sharing with others.
- Formats and structures for documents, data products, reports, and the presentation using markup languages will be adjusted for identification and extraction of pieces/sections of these artifacts.
- Naming conventions —Taxonomies — variable definitions, data dictionaries, means to facilitate the dissemination of data and results are important. Intelligence requires memory and appropriate semantics in data organization to store and retrieve documents, reports, and data products. In these areas, the appropriate use of markup languages and tools helps immensely. The use of visualization, plotly, markdown, shiny, and other great means solves several issues of knowledge transfer/sharing.
- Change factor as related to the mindset of users and issuers of knowledge is also important. Organizations of outcomes according to the users and not based on the objects (artifacts) used only.

- Prototyping and the agile principles approach are crucial to support iterations in solution development in order to define/develop answers to problems and to effectively communicate within developers and users of solutions in search for strategic intelligence enhancement. The agile principles are key, more so than the methodology because the data analytics/AI process is continuously reviewing data availability and appropriateness of techniques to obtain small but important outcomes where the parts developed can be separated to test hypotheses to observe the model's fit calibration.
- Strategic intelligence is about human and machine interactions in the following multiple levels:
  - Developers and users working together in the process of prototyping to introduce a smooth procedure to reduce the possibility of rejection of the developed solutions.
  - Business rules through the presentation of the prototype. The identification of the application and the need for changes can be communicated easily. Validation of assumptions and identification of gaps in understanding and resource identification (data being one of the crucial ones) can be powerful advantages for a successful project.

Another example of transition to integrated strategic intelligence is the stakeholder's preparation for adoption of what intelligence will provide. In the frameworks of enterprise risk management (ERM) and data analytics/AI, the top-down and bottom-up approaches look to improve strategy, policies, risk appetite definition, the decision-making process, and business processes, among many others. The capacity to transfer risk knowledge affects all stakeholders, and understanding the risk knowledge about the enterprise's value is a key requirement to identify protection strategies for business sustainability. There are various factors that affect this capacity to transfer and understand risk management. Communication among groups appears to be a significant variable in improving risk control but appears to be a weak factor in improving the perceived value of ERM. However, the ERM mandate requires a clear understanding of risk management policies, actions, and results, and the use of the integral view of risk management as a governance and compliance program to support the value-driven management of the organization. Furthermore, ERM implementation demands better capabilities for unification of the criteria of risk analysis, alignment of policies, and protection guidelines across the organization. These capabilities can be affected by risk knowledge sharing between the risk management group, the board of directors, and other executives in the organization.

Risk is a factor influencing the organization's results and needs better understanding, or as Doherty (2000) said, "Moreover, we need to understand these disruptive effects of risk because appropriate risk management strategies can be formed effectively only if we understand the precise effects of risks." Lam (2003) quoted, "The risk management process does not stop at promoting risk awareness or measuring risk exposures. The ultimate objective is to optimize the risk-return of the business; or to put it slightly differently, to effect real change in the risk profile of the company." Risk knowledge sharing has barriers as well. Risk knowledge sharing is related to people's interaction and willingness to collaborate and use knowledge from different people or sources. This point of the human–machine factor is then aligned with the work of Bosua and Scheepers (2007), who said, "Knowledge sharing is a more subtle concept, and is seen as a dual process of enquiring and contributing to knowledge through activities such as learning-by-observation, listening and asking, sharing ideas, giving advice..." In particular, risk knowledge sharing has its foundation in the culture and trust of the organization in order to develop an informal learning process (Singh & Premarajan, 2007).

The differentiation between knowledge transfer and knowledge sharing can start with the vision of Nonaka and Takeuchi (1995) that relates knowledge creation and knowledge sharing and indicates that knowledge is amplified and internalized based on the interactions between individuals in an organization. Nowadays, it is not only about humans but also about humans and machines transferring knowledge. In 1997, Davenport expressed the idea that knowledge sharing is a volunteer process and distinguished it from formal actions like reporting or structured knowledge-related interactions. Von Krogh *et al.* (2000) complemented Davenport's (1997) point, indicating that sharing tacit knowledge requires action from internal people through conversation, fostering the development of a capacity for analyzing problems equally through conversation, and creating context for the knowledge sharing process. These two observations showed a clear indication of knowledge sharing as a support to other processes and related to people's interactions. This is an important point because knowledge sharing refers to the exchange of ideas which do not have to be codified.

The results of previous studies (Rodriguez *et al.*, 2012) indicate that communication among executives in risk management must be improved in terms of flow and integration of risk policies to improve the board's understanding. Communication is the basis of knowledge sharing and the knowledge management program (Te'eni, 2006; Rollett, 2003; Zack, 1999). Additionally, the search for effective methods to communicate risk management to the board is fundamental for the decision-making process as Samoff and Stromquist (2001) pointed out: "Decision-makers have very short attention spans and they are unwilling or unlikely to read more than a few sentences on a topic. If so, for knowledge to be useful it must be presented succinctly." This is complemented by Uzzi and Lancaster (2003), who indicated, "learning, like knowledge transfer, is a function of the type of relationship that links actors." In organizations' the understanding of the board of director is not associated with the effectiveness of means used to communicate the risk policy and results. The flow of communication top-down appears to be unassociated with the board's understanding; however, there is a positive association of the policy integration and the board's understanding. Furthermore, there is a relationship between communications of the risk appetite and the board's understanding of the risk policy. In terms of strategic intelligence development, the value of working on increasing the board's understanding is shown through the capacity of the board to communicate risk appetite and policy integrations. This means a positive step of alignment as Kaplan and Norton (2006) indicate. However, the means of communication used appear to not have a positive effect on the board's understanding of the risk policy, suggesting an improvement in the search for different approaches for communication and risk knowledge transfer. A more systematic approach could be used based on specific needs and requirements of the board.

In summary, integrated strategic intelligence depends on risk knowledge and data analytics/AI knowledge transfer across organizations. The challenge is to overcome the limited understanding of technical components of using risk and data analytics techniques . Experience suggests that integration of policy and business process with the results of data analytics/AI creation helps to put what is discovered into context to guide the way to facilitate decisions to adopt new means of implementing strategy. A good example is when OpenAI promoted ChatGPT, which is a powerful potential tool for creating organizational intelligence. Companies in the same industry are looking for solutions as in the case of Google

BARD. Other economic sector companies are also thinking about how to be more efficient and effective using human resources or solutions that can be fed by those new technologies, codes, methods, etc.

The next chapter is about connecting data analytics and digitalization. The aim of the chapter is to survey concepts and methods to understand the data analytics process to produce valuable and actionable knowledge to creating model outcomes, prototypes, and final solutions.

Chapter 3

Data Analytics and Digitalization

This chapter describes the data analytics process and the steps to obtain digital solutions and potential digital transformation means for organizations. The chapter is divided into four sections: Data Analytics Process from Data to Valuable Actions; Data Analytics Integration to Digital Transformation; Models, Prototypes, and Solutions; and Case Studies of Strategic Risks. The aim of this chapter is to guide the reader to the comparison of the data analytics process and the data mining process, and how they are integrated into the general business strategies and AI and digital transformations. The last section introduces an example to explain required stages, after data are organized, for connecting models, prototypes, and solutions. It is important to keep in mind that agile principles are behind the concepts presented; however, the agile principles are suggested to work on data analytics and AI, but agile development cycle is not the suggested for AI and digital transformation because of the following reasons: Data Analytics and AI processes require continuous feedback in each step of the analytics process where there is an ongoing loop of data, model, and solution; modeling that can be from mathematical development, computing and conceptual sources, inductive (data mining) and deductive (mathematical models) processes; review of the good relationship among data, model, possible implementation, understanding and adoption. In AI and digital transformation, the processes integrate the stages and discovery of inputs and outputs based on the partial outcomes that are created in each step.

3.1. Data Analytics Process from Data to Valuable Actions

The premise of this book is that given strategic risk and opportunities, there is a need to create knowledge to mitigate risks and achieve goals. The search of actionable knowledge that leads to adaptive, sustainable, and competitive advantages is performed with tools, techniques, and solutions from Statistical and Machine learning, such as AI and mathematical and computational models. Once knowledge is created, the management of it is crucial to learn and to develop new steps in business processes and innovation engines that will come from the appropriate management of human and machine interaction (Figure 3.1). In all these steps, knowledge is a component to organize and promote the achievement of answers and to identify how to improve assumptions and methods. The generalization of model results can depend on the assumptions, theory, time, and data available. For example, time is a factor affecting whether a model can be discrete or continuous. The learning process in modeling, calibration, and interpretation has a big impact in implementation of risk management processes. Uncertainty cannot be avoided magically; uncertainty has layers that can be revealed and tackled but risk will always be present.

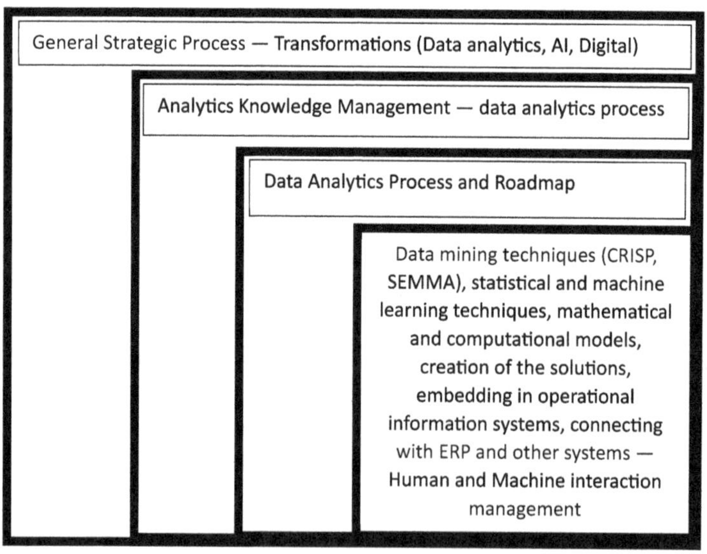

Figure 3.1. From strategic process and data analytics to use data mining techniques.

A challenge in organizations is the coordination of resources under the understanding that organizations have knowledge workers and problem-solvers and not workers and jobs. This means organizations require a new vision of talent management that is about the interaction of human and machine talent (intelligence of machines and humans moving in the same direction) according to problem resolution. The old silo view and functional separation in organizations is less effective and less efficient for organizations in dealing with uncertainty. Projects development in data analytics is a combination of several perspectives and capabilities of the team that includes people and machines. Furthermore, organizations have problems to solve and not just tasks to do, which implies that organizations have managers and analytics professionals working together and this requires the organization of strategic risk modeling knowledge and the ability to use common knowledge in mathematical modeling.

In the implementation of the data analytics process, the knowledge management (KM) processes applied to analytics are crucial, in particular, how to support the use of common knowledge in risk management processes. Knowledge that is created by the analytics process will be useful for solving, promoting, and implementing actions inside organizations, for example, with regard to the migration of strategic risk, dealing with educational institutions, or managing the introduction of a product in a new market. In a simplified way, there are stages for knowledge creation where knowledge is represented by strategic risk assessment; knowledge storage repositories and retrieval through data support for external and internal users, including regular or big data and explicit knowledge (documents, reports, recommendations, etc.); knowledge transfer using the experiences of many people in known cases (providing means for interactive, shareable, and dynamic capabilities of results use–reuse, comments, adjustments, etc.); and knowledge applications to discover business process opportunities and deployment of results and actionable knowledge are created. These KM processes support the complete system of data analytics, i.e., AI and digitalization. In the context of Strategic Risk and Integrated Strategic Intelligence creation, KM processes include the following:

Risk Analytics Knowledge creation: This involves identifying assumptions, conceptualizing processes, recognizing and selecting techniques to use to solving risk-related issues, selecting risk management processes, developing collaboration, finding solution, prototyping models, and testing. Risk knowledge involves developing new models, replacing existing models, promoting new solutions, participating in problem-solving, and organizing product development and risk evaluation for innovation. From the technology side, risk knowledge is created to provide access to models and results, to manage technological support like AI tools, networks, intranets, to develop external solutions/answers methodologies for problem-solving, to increase the sophistication of solutions, to manage data/quality, to analyze multiple risks, and to select solution development and accessibility.

Risk Analytics Knowledge storage and retrieval: Many different components exist in risk modeling to store and retrieve data, such as documents, raw data, created data, taxonomy, metadata, and structured and unstructured data. The action of storing and retrieving implies cleaning data, developing and implementing documentation process, structuring information, and codifying human knowledge with comments of tacit knowledge from individual and groups. Metrics as a form of risk analytics knowledge are needed to identify the quality data repository, data volume, codified documents/indexed/structured processes, and metadata structure, and to conform with data repositories, documentation incentives, technology used for repositories, processes to populate data, document standards, and processes to access and use data repositories.

Risk Analytics Knowledge transfer: Risk modeling knowledge can be transferred through networks, blogs, presentations, portals, meetings, discussions, collaboration activities, content management designs, distribution, testing reporting, and so on. There are differences to consider when transferring risk knowledge between individuals, from individuals to groups, between groups, across groups, and from groups to organization. All these groups for risk knowledge transfer require actions among the participants to improve communication processes and the willingness to share by fostering the existence and richness of transmission channels such as unscheduled meetings, informal seminars, coffee breaks, quality of knowledge transfer channels, taxonomies, metadata, forums, bulletins, interdisciplinary solutions search, feedback sessions, and discussing forums.

Risk Analytics Knowledge application and learning: Application of risk modeling knowledge is represented by decisions, business processes, and can be modeled in other organizational areas by impact analysis, evaluations, new developments, new solutions of strategy, and tactical decisions. Application is involved in the process of organizational performance evaluation, testing results, defining and implementing directives, organizational routines, process and technology updating, accessibility, work flow automation, training and experience support, business understanding, results interpretation, speed of application, and risk cases access.

Davenport *et al.* (2006) presented that organizations can have and develop analytics as a strategic capacity for competing. Analytics work requires information systems support. However, risk management information is based on a risk context and risk process use, involving assessment, classification, and interpretation; this means designing and developing a risk information system. Information without knowledge of the context could be dangerous. For example a risk can be the similar for many organizations but the likelihood and impact can be different, frequency and severity can be different, and the data available can be different as well. The problem with risk management involves not just the information but the interpretation and communication of its meaning. Organizations are competing to optimize their performance on analytical capabilities, which means getting access to quantitative expertise, capable technology environment, and appropriate data. Analytics capability supports what Pfeffer and Sutton (2006) called the craft of managers that needs to be learned by practice, experience, and the use of evidence as a means to constantly update assumptions, knowledge, and skills. As Apte *et al.* (2002) said, the problem is not just to describe what the organization needs or request; it is to predict, to optimize, to classify, and more.

There are three attributes to the holistic view of strategic risk management challenging processes and technology: integral, comprehensive, and strategic views (Abrams *et al.*, 2007). This complexity is observed when the modeling process is looking for aggregation analysis when each organizational section can have different performances, problems, and resources. Analytics processes require a dynamic bridge between KM processes and ERM processes passing through people–machines, business processes, and technology. This step means getting answers to questions such as how to measure, interpret, and discover directions of the organization performance connecting risk metrics with risk management processes. There is a search, in this step, for cause–effect indicators related to the risk modeling process and other risk management processes.

The use of AI–data analytics process and digital solutions goes further into the relationship between the four types of organizational capital (Fairchild, 2002): intellectual, human, social, and structural. One is required to move and consider the machine and human interaction as creators of intelligence. The analytics process (Rodriguez, 2017) indicates the steps and the emphasis on data, use of data mining as components of a sequence of steps that creates knowledge form data. The analytics process (Figures 3.2 and 3.3) starts answering questions such as what the organizations is looking to measure. The concept is that the definition of what to measure brings a reflection of the alignment of strategy and the concrete purpose of the organization's operation in terms of a definition of key performance indicators and key risk indicators. Moreover, the definition of strategy and goals, and the measurement of methods and means lead one to define the control of strategy implementation and how the operationalization or required transformation will lead one to achieve is the objective. The third component to organize the analytics process is to clarify that no measure, or measurement process on strategy, will be static, and changes in metrics (see the concept of risk as variation evaluation in Chapter 1) will be present through time; this means the concept of risk analytics needs momentum to identify how strategic risks will be

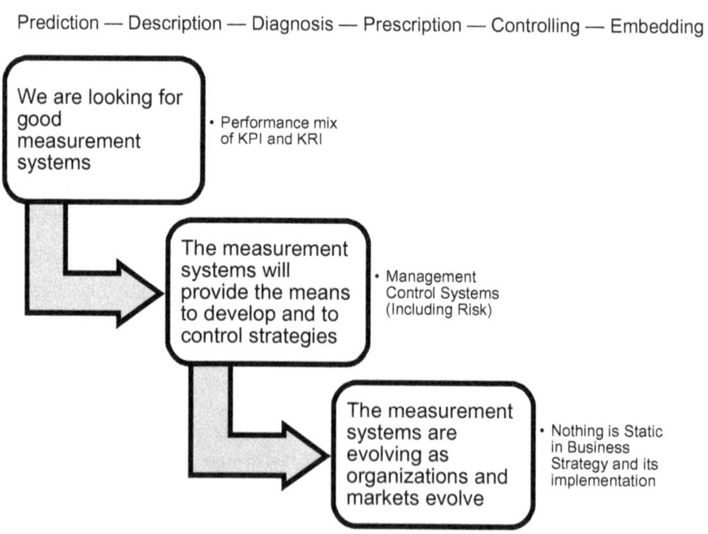

Figure 3.2. Sequence to build the data analytics process.

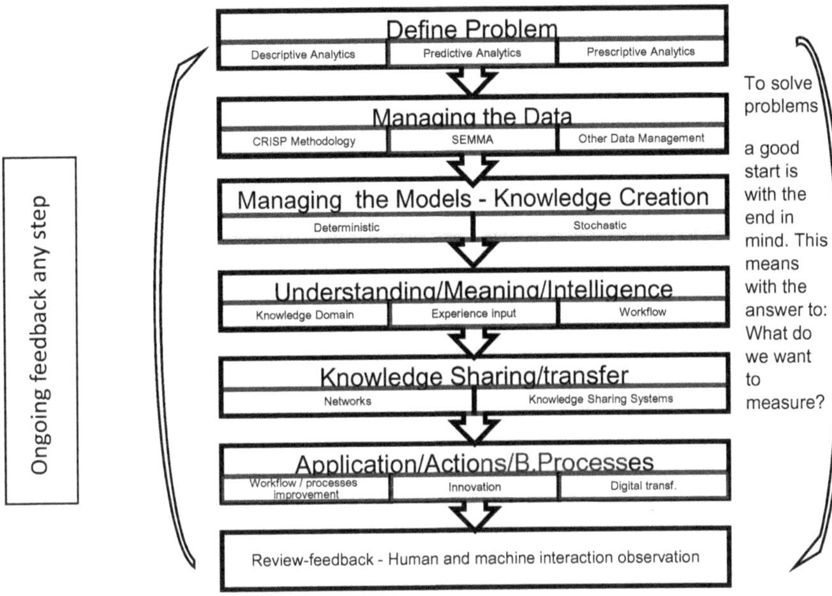

Figure 3.3. Data analytics process.

monitored, assessed, and mitigated to maintain competencies and capabilities in organizations.

The description of the analytics process (Figure 3.3) is as follows:

- *Definition and delimitation of the problem and problem scope through the needs of the business*: The main subprocess is understanding the problem in terms of the descriptive analytics, prediction, and prescription to discover the real root cause, i.e., to find the problem to solve, generate questions to answer, and define the possibilities to approach the problem resolution by blocks. This mean after observing the past and current situation, the question is about analyzing potential futures. Once the futures and orientation of results could be defined, the question will be how to optimize processes to reach the desired and feasible futures. The search for understanding of the problem will be performed using statistical descriptions, visualization, forecasting, classification, optimization, and simulation. The ongoing feedback refers to the back-and-forth steps with models, the data available and their organization, and potentially emerging issues that need to be solved. This stage has the following questions to answer: What is the company trying to accomplish? How is the corporate performance measured? What are the data needs to support the measurement system? What are the analytical steps and how can the analytics projects support the planning and control of strategy design and implementation?

- *Managing data and using data mining tools to start an inductive process of knowledge discovery*: This is the step of producing a usable dataset, where variables can be original raw data or new created, defined data according to the problem to solve, where data are clean, and the garbage has been reduced. However, the link of data and problems is where the issue begins as questions about data are going to influence the scope of the problem, and the problem to solve will dictate the variables and data to use. In this stage, the following questions appear: Are all variables that the analyst would like to have in good shape? Are data balanced with regard to a target? How is the combination of variables? What is the required level of structured and unstructured data to solve the problem? How will data be fed to maintain the updating of models?
- *Managing models and knowledge creation*: Models in general can be identified as conceptual models or models where the framework for the problem's resolution is to simply tackle the problem. Mathematical, statistical, and computational models are static and dynamic, deterministic, and stochastic. The purpose of these models is to describe variables and their relationships as facts, random behavior, or ways that when combined can produce results usable to answer questions or solve problems. Another type of model is the structure for the calculations that can be a combination of deterministic and stochastic models, which is a common way to move data through different stages. A good example is what appears in influence models and translations to spreadsheet structures for calculations. For instance, in the beginning stage, data can show the main statistics and feed the analysis of probability distributions that can be used to describe the behavior of variables. Those results of the distribution will be used as a guide to describe potential results, obtain approaches to the answer to problems of classification problems, or feed a simulation process.
- *Developing Understanding and Meaning by developing Intelligence*: Intelligence is when the meaning arises in any data analytics process; it is when the users and their reasoning accept and use what the insights are saying. The directions can be improving the sense-understanding of the problems, the possible dimensions-shape-scope of the problems

and the problems themselves from the technical point of view. It involves a review of the context and knowledge domain. This refers to the work of creating meaning that is based not only on the results interpretation but also on the initiation of the data selected and the model construction. Materialization of intelligence will appear once the workflows are permeated by the understanding of new knowledge and its powerful input for better knowledge domain development.

- *Analytics Knowledge Sharing and Transfer*: Analytics work is in most of cases multidisciplinary and across multiple areas of organizations. The analytics process is not completed when the results are obtained. The results need to create actions. Results need to be embedded in the organization through their adoption in business processes. The work of the analytics process is creating an analytics knowledge management system to transfer what is discovered to multiple stakeholders that will build on that knowledge with actions. In principle, the analytics process will use networks and systems for communication and sharing to promote prototypes and their potential to create functional results and new capabilities.
- *Application, actions, and business processes under a permanent plan*: The analytics process requires a strong and permanent back-and-forth flow of teaching and learning. Contextualization of the results is crucial. Improvement and innovation of the workflow are part of the objectives in analytics knowledge creation.

As a supplement of the analytics process, in the following paragraphs, roadmaps are presented. Chambers & Dinsmore (2014) pointed out the roadmap for developing a data analytics process. These authors' roadmap is a guide for organizations from the beginning to the end, from the current situation to future competitive conditions, and to link several projects that organizations have in process. Strategic risk is implicit in organizations having a silo view and separated from a digital orientation of the organization, while a data analytics process is connected to a digitalization process or complete digital transformation using the intelligence created by the data analytics process. The steps in the roadmap are the guidelines to create the actions in the organization implementation and data analytics transformation. A roadmap has to embed the data analytics process in the operational plan and execute the organization's mission and strategy. A roadmap has to improve the business process. The roadmap and the data analytics process are continuously updated and enhanced to create an evolving sustainable competitive advantage. The analytics roadmap must be aligned to the whole organization's strategies and goals. The following is a way to start the analytics roadmap:

- Identification of objectives of the data analytics project transformation:
  - Identify the areas of work for project development in which the organization needs to improve, e.g., threats in the industry.
  - Give priority to areas of work and problems to be solved, i.e., pain points to study.
  - Clarify the concentration of problems to be solved in the project, i.e., scope and building blocks.
- Observing the aspects to be measured at the managerial level and clarifying which of the pillars of the organization's strategy are allocated to the project(s) to develop in data analytics, such as:
  - Sustainability and growth, e.g., increase revenues to a certain limit.
  - Simplicity, e.g., digitalization efforts.
  - Customer focus, e.g., delivering new customer experience platforms.
  - Future-proofing, e.g., implementation of compensation and merit-related initiatives.
- Defining data analytics scope:
  - Is the work to be developed part of current initiatives in data analytics projects in the organization? If so, in what area?
  - If the project is new, which data analytics group(s) would the organization want to connect?
  - Is there any appetite to use data analytics in a specific functional area, e.g., risk? Is there interest in functional areas such as marketing, finance, talent, and technology?
  - For example, in strategic risk is valid to ask for:
    - Is it a priority to work on internal or external risks or a blend?
    - Is any internal functional risk a priority? Like credit, market, liquidity, or ALM?
    - Is any external risk a priority? Like bankruptcies, supply chains, or socioeconomic risks?
    - What kind of metrics/methods is the organization looking to develop? Are data resources enough to measure what is looked for by the organization?
- Clarify if a problem is about corporate or divisional performance evaluation:
  - What are the performance and risk indicators the organization would like to connect?

  - What is the organization looking to analyze in the market? Prediction, simulation, or segmentation?
- Identify practical considerations:
  - Which groups in the bank are most open to working on data analytics?
  - Which data marts or sections of the data warehouse are best equipped in data, historical information, variables, and possible different data sources?
  - What is the organization looking for as deliverables? Software, models, prototypes, documents, or presentations?

The roadmap can be summarized as follows (Figure 3.4):

- Define or identify the key Business Objectives: To help the organization develop the offer with high profitability.
- Identify the value chain: To help the Organization generate revenue.
- Identify the level of analytics needed and the direction: Strategic, managerial, operational, or customer oriented.

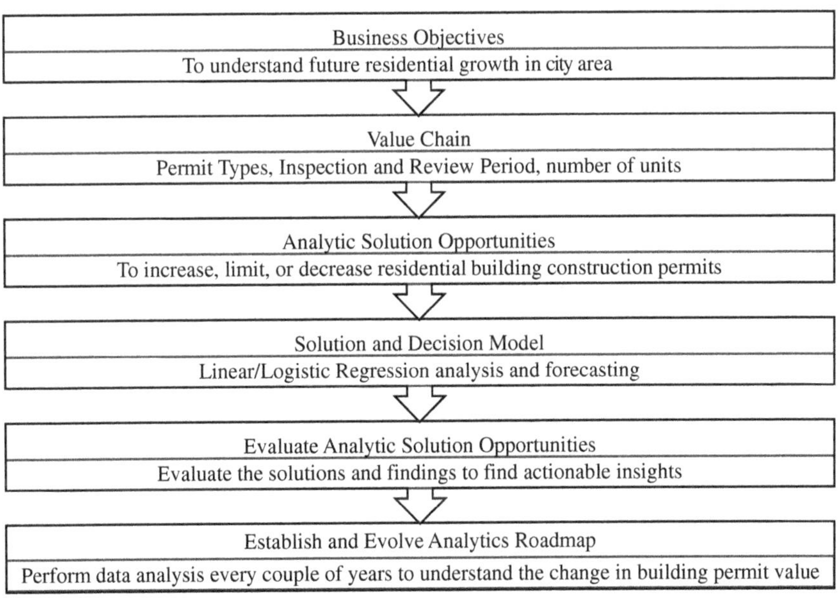

Figure 3.4. Presenting the data analytics process in value generation sequence for a city planning.

- Describe and Clarify Analytic Solution Opportunities: To reduce standard rooms and increase suites, and as a result increase average daily rate.
- Review potential Solutions: Using forecasting, NPV, and histogram/scatter plots.
- Create Analytics Decision Models or Predictive Model: Simulation models can include Monte Carlo, regression, or seasonal factors.
- Review, Evaluation, and Improvement of Models must be calibrated according to the flow of data and monitoring changes of factors affecting the models.
- Evolve Analytical Roadmap: This is the general feedback loop.

A roadmap requires a specific review of the following aspects in the planning, development, and implementation of solutions:

1. *Defined Business area*: How can we apply analytics to a new business area or problem?
2. *Quality and effort to get data*: What are the data sources? What data can the organization require to enrich the analytical insights creation?
3. Approaches to identify and discover new patterns and value.
4. *Precision*: What are the steps and levels of accuracy, adaptation of solutions, levels of understanding, and levels of use of results? Models and their results are evolving and enhancing according to problems and the factors of understanding.
5. *Algorithms*: Development of mathematical, computational capabilities that can be assets for the organization. Documentation and ways to build the more complex solutions step by step.
6. *Inserting*: Embedding analytics into operations, business processes, workflow, and operational information systems.
7. Capacity to operate faster and create faster according to learning of the data analytics process and roadmap development.

The following aspects are interrelated to the delivery of the data analytics project that is under implementation:

1. *Clear delivery of business value and impact*: Build and continuously evolve analytics for high-value business impact. Ensure that the data analytics process is working.

2. *Focus on the last mile*: The deployment capacity is when the project will be alive, generating proof of concept, prototypes, and clarifying how the enhancements and calibrations will be.
3. *Leverage Kaizen*: Simplify the process and concentrate on understanding the problem and possible application of solutions, evaluate what is required, what is needed, and what is not through multiple experiments. This is part of all the required steps.
4. *Develop and accelerate learning and execution*: Learn by doing, adapting, and repeating. Act quickly. Automate or somehow speed up data preparation and mining.
5. Think in the valuation generation is on human–machine interaction to differentiate and having new capabilities to compete and succeed in a market.
6. Design an architecture of the technological and human interaction capacity that is relevant, current and with future in mind, clarifying how the changes can affect certain areas of the technology structure, languages vs. algorithms, models vs. coding, multitype data storage vs. only one type, combining skills in managing access and possibilities to feed models. It is fundamental to work with open software, integration, virtualization, cloud, computational capacity, etc., that can be external but keeping the intelligence inside the organization.
7. *Build on human factors*: Foster and develop talent interaction and creative thinking for problem resolutions. Work in multidisciplinary and diverse teams and projects. It is fundamental to develop individual and collective intelligence, combining humans and machines.
8. Grow the capacity to be closer not only to customers but also suppliers and create the capacity to maintain network value.

Another set of steps to create a roadmap was proposed by Lin (2015): problem definition, data identification, review of analytical techniques, including the analytics process in a value chain through model assessment, testing, learning, deployment process, integration, optimization, and connection to the strategic and operational implementation of the organization's plans.

3.1.1 *Data mining as a component of the data analytics process*

The analytics process is developed using techniques of data mining. Data mining leads to identifying variable relationships, correlations, patterns, trends, behaviors, and randomness. Data mining is a set of techniques with a condition of looking at what is possible to identify in the data that are available. In the data analytics process, the first question is about the problem and how to gather the appropriate data to deal with the problem. The data mining development or search for solutions/conclusions is inductive of specific cases where there is a search for the possibility to generalize or infer results. The danger is when analysts use the data under the belief that the data represent populations, and they can follow generalizations just because the data exist and the volume is big. Data are stored in multiple types of data repositories, databases, data warehouses, data marts, data lakes, and in clouds and are oriented to use big data tools in parallel computing. At the same time, data mining and models for creating knowledge use techniques that are related to different types of learning and problems as indicated in previous chapters.

There are methodologies for data mining such as CRISP and SEMMA (see Exhibits 3.1–3.3). On the one hand, a framework like the CRISP Methodology (Chapman *et al.*, 2000) or cross-industry standard process for data mining is about the following steps:

- Understanding the business.
- Identification of objectives of the business and criteria for success.
- Evaluation of the present situation.
- Determining goals of mining the data and criteria for success.
- Producing a project plan.
- Data understanding is partly identifying and defining possible problems, but in data mining, the search for patterns is of primary importance and it is possible to formulate hypotheses to test. The first model starts with exploratory data analysis (EDA) and Visualization.
- Results of data analyses will be connected to goals and objectives in the organization.
- Data Preparation, cleaning data, and organizing data to work on.
- Modeling and developing a conceptual model to describe the ideal solution and the blocks that are required to get that solution. Identifying the blueprint to build the solution by blocks.
- Evaluation deployment.

On the other hand, SEMMA from SAS starts with the concept of Sampling and moves to Exploring and describing data, Modifying according to the needs and quality of data, Modeling, and Assessing (SEMMA)

Summary guideline steps integrating analytics process — CRISP–SEMMA	Expected results in the analytics process
Identify an organization and describe current conditions of said organization. Examples: How is the business doing? What are the goals in the near future? What are the main performance indicators used? What are the factors affecting the achievement of the performance indicators? Where is the organization doing well and where is it doing poorly? How is the behavior of the key performance indicators in the industry? The answers to these questions should be a mixture of qualitative and quantitative responses. Clarify what data are currently available about the organization and what data the organization would like to have? Does the organization have all the required data, or is something missing? Is it possible to have historical data? Are the data useful? Organize data that the organization can have access to, from internal and external sources. It is possible to use sources like EBSCO's list, APIs, qualitative and quantitative, scraping methods for the web, etc.	Produce a summary based on your business review: • The problem definition • Where is the problem located in the value chain? • What are the business questions associated with this problem? • What are the required data and what is the quality of the data? • What type of knowledge does the organization require to create? What are areas involved in the knowledge creation? • How could the organization review if what they want to use/do is appropriate and if it is feasible? • What are the things that an organization needs for implementing a solution? • What is the link between what the organization wants to do and the metrics of performance evaluation?
Based on the data and the answers in the first stage, a next step is to prepare a summary explaining various aspects of the organization that can be derived from the data. What are the questions that the organization would like to answer from customers, operations, finance? What kind of data can be used? Are there different types of methods to use for data analysis? Are there trends? Are there specific issues indicated in the data?	Organize and summarize based on a problem review: How are the data regarding the Vs in big data? Are they regular data? Can they be converted into a big data problem? What are the types of data that the organization expects to use? Review all possibilities. Remember to start from what you want to achieve or keep the end goal in mind. Data in this case are related to all dimensions of a strategy that are related to the organization's problem to solve.

Exhibit 3.1. How to organize a data analytics project part 1.

Summary guideline steps integrating analytics process — CRISP–SEMMA	**Expected results in the analytics process**
Is there any expected result in some areas/items/business of the organization? How can the organization find out if their expectations are good or not? Does the organization need to review the variation of the key performance indicators? How can the variation analysis be organized? Are data available to variation analysis, identifying possible causes?	Is the organization using sensor/streaming data? Unstructured data? Describe how. Are the data syndicated data? Describe how. What are the formats of the data that the organization is using? Is the data structured, unstructured, a mix? What can you say about the databases that the organization would like to have access to, to use, or to build? Are they following ACID (Atomicity, Consistency, Isolation, and Durability) compliance for data storage? What are the attributes of these data structures?

Exhibit 3.1. (*Continued*)

Present a way to gather and organize the data that the organization needs to answer the strategic plan control questions. Answer how the organization would manage integration, quality, security, governance, preparation and the manipulation of data into this plan. Identify sources of errors, barriers, and possible solutions. Look for metrics to control data quality.	Organize and summarize a data review answering the following: If the organization is using data from different sources, how is it integrating data? Is it possible? What is the level of data quality that the organization has? Is there any gap of data in time? Outliers? Is the data the organization is using open, accessible, proprietary, private? How can the organization assure that the data will be organized? How will the organization keep the data in good shape? In data preparation, what is the cleaning process that the organization needs to perform? What are the attributes of the organization's data? Are the data categorical, nominal, with ratios, attributes? Explain. Do the data need to be normalized? Partitioned? Resampled? How can one fill data holes? What is the organization using to overcome data issues? Explain the details to visualize and explore organizational data? What are the observations/variables/values that the organization has with regard to the problem to solve?

Exhibit 3.2. How to organize a data analytics project part 2.

Identify, justify, and explain which tools to use (to build what?). Think in this order: What does the organization want to perform? Understand what data are needed, and the organization needs to find the way to identify the tools to build what they need. Explain the options the organization has, including pros and cons, limitations, and model assumptions.	Present based on your first data understanding review: What kind of tables, graphs/charts are possible to use for the organization's problem analysis? What kind of cross tables would the organization like to use? Are reports dynamic, shareable, interactive? Provide examples. What are the organization's preferences in terms of the problem and data for using analytics tools? Explain. Is the organization using dependent/independent variables? What are their definitions? Is the organization using newly created variables? What new variables is the organization creating? How is the organization going to use these newly created variables? Can the data possibly be split in groups for training a model? Is the organization using models that are unsupervised? Is the organization dealing with classifications, grouping? Explain. Start creating the workflow. What are the first organizational conclusions of pros and cons of the possible tools to use for solutions of the organization's problem in accordance with data availability?
Prepare a conceptual model about the steps that the organization needs to follow in the business analytics process. Explain all the steps according to the selected problem to study, the problem that the organization wants to solve, the data that the organization is using, and the tools that it is able to use.	Now, based on what you have done, the organization needs to put it all together! Is the organization using CRISP/Methodology? SEMMA? The design of analytics process workflow is crucial. In that regard, KNIME is a tool to use. Clarify steps and components of the analytics process. Is the organization able to create a first full prototype? What are the first conclusions? What are the potential issues to sharing the organization's knowledge, implementing changes, promoting new ideas, innovating? All this is based on what the organization has gotten from your analysis. What are the groups/teams that the organization needs to involve in the project? Does the organization need to develop any special group?

Exhibit 3.2. (*Continued*)

	How could the organization recognize the resources to work in the implementation of the new knowledge? How is the organization going to keep alive the dynamic of the technical aspects management and the practice of implementing changes in the business process? Explain.

Exhibit 3.2. (*Continued*)

Select two business processes and follow the steps for the business analytics process in each one. Identify the "pain points" of the business processes. Connect the analytics business process with the two business processes. How are they related, and how does the organization need to build models to analyze and improve the processes?	How does the organization connect work done in analytics with businesses processes? What is the way to show value of analytics work for business processes? How can one embed your analytics work in operational systems? Could the analytics process be connected with management control systems? Explain. How can analytics work demonstrate value to manage organization performance by creating actions, metrics, for achieving the goals, for following up the metrics?
Create reports, prototypes, and indicate results that are possible to implement in the information systems	Can the organization connect all the points of the analytics project to get conclusions? What would the organization like to know more about? What is it not possible to know now? What would you like to have access to/use for in improving the organization's analysis? Explain. Review and summarize the full project, and complement the approach/use of methods with the tools like KNIME that you consider important (Do not worry about possible prototypes, models, etc.) At the end, you need to define what are the best points to report. Again, remember that the organization is justifying analytics projects based on value added.

Exhibit 3.3. How to organize a data analytics project part 3.

data with the purpose of discovering patterns that could help organizations make decisions and solve problems for better performance. Data mining is not limited to functional areas or certain data types or problems. It is applicable in the whole organization to disclose possible clues for customer knowledge, issues in production, opportunities in segments, etc. The meaning of the SEMMA components is as follows:

- Sampling to identify the input to use in the analysis and the characteristics of the unit of analysis.
- Exploration of data, looking for what the data indicate about the current and past situation using exploratory data analysis and techniques for data visualization.
- Modification of data is about raw data, new variables creation, cleaning, transforming, partitioning, and data management according to types of data.
- Modeling the data using statistical and machine learning tools.
- Assessing the data and results of the models, outcome value, and impact.

In summary, an analytics process is highly valuable if there is support from top management and area owners of problems and data. Support involves finding the way to overcome barriers, identifying possibilities to achieve reasonable goals, providing time windows for development, and maintaining an engaged analytics process as a piece of strategic development of the organizations to mitigate strategic risk and possibly prepare for a complete digital transformation. As mentioned earlier, digitalization is going to be an outcome of the analytics AI process and the analog–manual processes have to operate properly. The highest risk is to adopt technologies or new management paradigms without answering the following basic questions: What is a data analytics–AI process for? What are the goals to achieve when using these analytics steps and how are they going to be used? Are expectations according to the understanding of what analytics processes represent in organizations? Exhibit 3.4 illustrations of past issues of a lack of good results with regard to changes in organizations and several cases where the main failure is about lack of management clarity. The next section indicates how digital transformation and analytics process implementation are linked. Assuming that data are generated and possible to use, the question is how to use them.

Wallace Co. won the prestigious Baldrige award (1990) for its success in adapting Japanese management methods. While the company was gaining recognition from the award, it was losing $300,000 a month, according to a consultant brought in to turn the company around (January 31, 1992 *Washington Post*). Armstrong World Industries, Inc., whose Building Products Operations was a 1995 award recipient in the manufacturing category, filed for Chapter 11 reorganization in December 2000 to enable the company to continue its full service to customers and its employee pay and benefit programs while resolving asbestos liability issues. In March 2006, Dana Corporation — the parent company of two Baldrige Award recipients (Dana Corporation–Spicer Driveshaft Division, manufacturing category, 2000; and Dana Commercial Credit Corporation [DCC], service category, 1996) — filed for Chapter 11 reorganization. Dana reorganized and subsequently emerged from bankruptcy in January 2008 as Dana Holding Corporation, which includes the driveshaft operations and several other core businesses. The assets of Dana's former DCC leasing operation have been divested (https://www.nist.gov/baldrige/baldrige-faqs-baldrige-award-recipients).	Bankruptcies Re-engineering and no adaptation: • Compaq computers • Kodak • Radio Shack • Circuit City • Enron • Blockbuster • PanAm • Tower Records • Polaroid • Pets.com • WorldCom • Lehman Brothers After bankruptcy, the business survived: • Texaco, • Sbarro • Marvel Entertainment • Chrysler • General Motors • Apple

Exhibit 3.4. Adoption of technologies with purpose. One of them is to avoid destroying the business.

Digitalization generates data and data generate answers to develop digitalization. This is a bidirectional relationship.

Data analytics should lead to the creation of actionable knowledge. According to that capacity of having knowledge and intelligence, digital transformation is moving ahead to improve the organization's performance.

3.2. Data Analytics Integration to Digital Transformation

This section is dedicated to understanding that digital transformation is an outcome of a data analytics process. The creation of knowledge from data to develop strategic intelligence is supported by solutions like digital transformations. At the end of the section, an example is presented on using digitalization steps with regard to a data analytics product. A document, for example, a data analytics report, is an artifact to digitalize and to use in a digital manner. The example illustrates concepts of digitalization that are beneficial and provides opportunities for implementing data analytics and digitalization to improve business processes inside organizations. In this case, the fundamental business process in strategic intelligence development is knowledge transfer. Digital transformation is a set of actions in the strategy of organizations to develop adaptive sustainable competitive advantages that represent improving the organization level to succeed in a market. Exhibit 3.5 classifies a sequence of steps from identification of data, models, solutions, and implementations to the manner to translate to machines and automated systems what for example, a prediction, classification solutions, clustering, simulation or visualization can be. Looking for answering the organizations' needs to sustain and enhance competitiveness and explore attractiveness of markets. All these adaptation stages have the final purpose of mitigating the strategic risks that the organization is exposed to.

To find the connection of data analytics and digital transformations, the European Commission Digital Strategy stated the main principles which indicate that data, models, computational capacity, results, security,

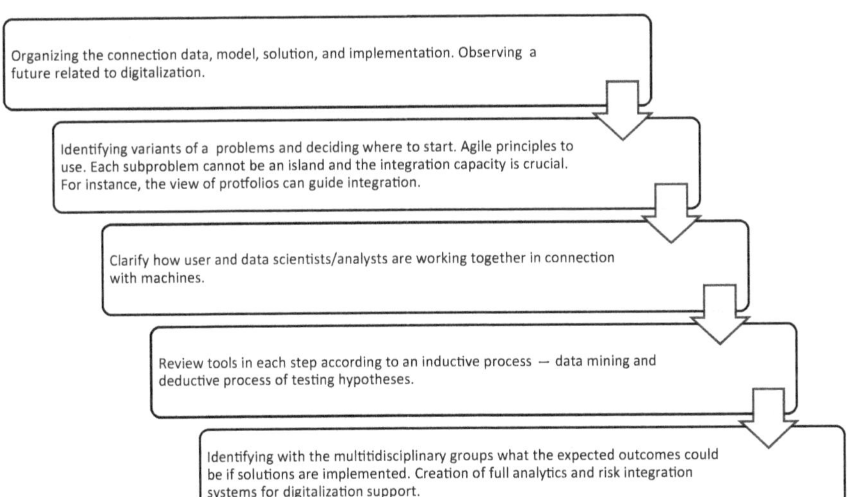

Exhibit 3.5. Organizing the human support of the data analytics projects.

etc., are components for implementation of flexible solutions with the capacity to overcome the following barriers:

- Digital workplace: Digital tools to work, any place, any time.
- Digital solutions: Support administration and policies.
- Reusable solutions platforms: For experts, ready-made and reusable IT solutions.
- Data ecosystem: Sharing and reusing data repositories.
- Digital infrastructure: Corporate, hybrid cloud services.
- All oriented to maintain Innovation and support Cybersecurity and IT governance.

Digitalization principles need to be linked to how processes of digital transformation should be developing organizations' capabilities. With regard to the way to think in terms of capabilities (Exhibit 3.6) that can guide digital transformations, Brown (2022) pointed out the following:

> The journey to digital transformation starts with the customer and operation actions to improve efficiency, effectiveness, and satisfaction. There is evidence that companies with digital transformation have better results in revenue than those that have not yet transformed. The following capabilities have been identified:

An example for achieving the goal of connecting data analytics and digital transformation is related to the creation of data products to

Customer capabilities	• Portfolio of products in a multichannel environment. • A value promise from organizations that is not concentrated only on profit creation for shareholders, but also on improving performance in other KPIs and KRIs of a BSC.
Operational capabilities	• Flexibility of products and services to adapt to customers' needs. • Use technology to provide customer opportunities and to control costs in the organization.
Ecosystems capabilities	• Develop ties with organizations to amplify customer options. • Provide opportunities to customers to use partnerships.
Foundational capabilities	• Deal as the main assets, data, talent, models, creation of intelligence through learning.

Exhibit 3.6. Capabilities to build in each strategic dimension.

permeate data analytics results into an organization's processes. The following paragraphs explain how a reporting process converted into a digital product modifies several activities and methods to perceive and use artifacts in a digital organization. A document is an entity that is alive; it is a means to transform implicit knowledge into explicit knowledge, that is, it is not static anymore but a dynamic instrument, where users co-create it and use it by mixing multiple sources of data. Documents are digital entities that people are able to share while working and updating content. Digital transformation with products and services is moving in equivalent directions. In Exhibit 3.7, the content's structure for a document represents what a digital product will require to be created. It is necessary to define the purpose: What is the product going to do or say? What are the methods and technique used? How will the results be used to obtain a final real outcome that benefits the organizations? What is additionally

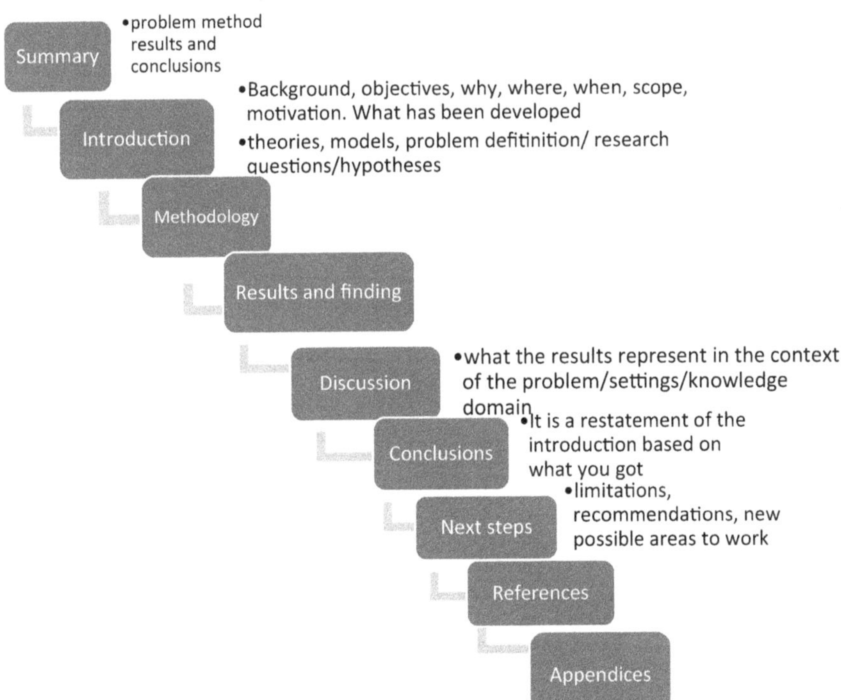

Exhibit 3.7. Creating the reports to maintain three pillars: possibility to share, dynamic, and interactive.

important is that, given the digital attributes, a continuous updating process will flow through the information systems and users.

As an illustration of using technology in the creation of the digital product, basics of R Markdown are indicated in this section. The goal is for people create a professional report that includes all components of results, explanations of results, methodologies, and the code used in the same document. It is possible to generate a paper copy using PDF conversion in cases where that is required. See Exhibits 3.9 to 3.17 to generate pieces of data products-reports-presentations. A reference for further analysis of the digitalization process along with examples and guidelines can be found at https://bookdown.org/yihui/rmarkdown/basics.html.

R Markdown: The Definitive Guide, 2019, Yihui Xie, J. J. Allaire, Garrett Grolemund. Exhibit 3.8 indicates several suggestions to guide the creation of a digital data analytics product:

The previous presentation of what digitalization can be in the practice of a data analytics process opens the review in the following subsection to the evolution of risk analytics as a way of dealing with strategic risk and creating strategic intelligence using data analytics. In a general approach, the first step in understanding and working on problems is to describe it, explore the current situation, then question and evaluate the models. The use of models will be related to data types and converting regular and big data into smart data. The conversion process starts with appropriate data management and basic EDA exploratory data analysis.

Start installing available tools and according to the analysis of the needs of document generation, updating, and use	Install the required tools R, RStudio, R Markdown, shiny packages, and additional packages for Latex documents as needed in the business context.
	# Install from CRAN
	install.packages('rmarkdown')
	# Or if you want to test the development version,
	# install from GitHub
	if (!requireNamespace("devtools"))
	install.packages('devtools')
	devtools::install_github('rstudio/rmarkdown')
	If you want to generate PDF output, you will need to install LaTeX. For R Markdown users who have not installed LaTeX before, we recommend that you install TinyTeX. (https://yihui.name/tinytex/):
	install.packages("tinytex")
	tinytex::install_tinytex() # install TinyTeX that is good LaTex distribution

Start using the tools	Some tips for using R Markdown and shiny The main purpose of R Markdown, documents, and presentations including code, that can be documents as PDF (static documents) or HTML (ongoing updates for the document) files. Keep the presentation updated using HTML, RMarkdown, and Shiny. The markdown capacity includes Layout Text with Headings and Subheadings. Format Text with italics, bold, and bullet points. Link to Content. It is possible to use R Markdown templates from RStudio. Steps for generating documents: • create a new project. • make a new directory.

Exhibit 3.8. Starting to create digital documents as data products.

	• Make an empty project. • Save it on to the desktop. • Add an R Markdown file to this. • Go to file, new file, and R Markdown.
Work with specialized packages, e.g., RMarkdown and Shiny	• Install the libraries that RStudio is asking for. • Select templates. • Fill the slides. • Press Knit HTML and the R Markdown file will generate an HTML file and then save it to get the compiled file. • Create/use code in the R Markdown presentation using code pieces and press the Insert Code Chunk button, or with the keyboard shortcut Cmd+Shift+I. Code pieces begin with ```{r}. • Give names to code lines. • Press Knit HTML in order to knit the presentation with an HTML document. • Shiny is used to create interactive applications, in particular, interactive visualization and running models. See Exhibits 3.9–3.17.

Exhibit 3.8. *(Continued)*

Using flexdashboard

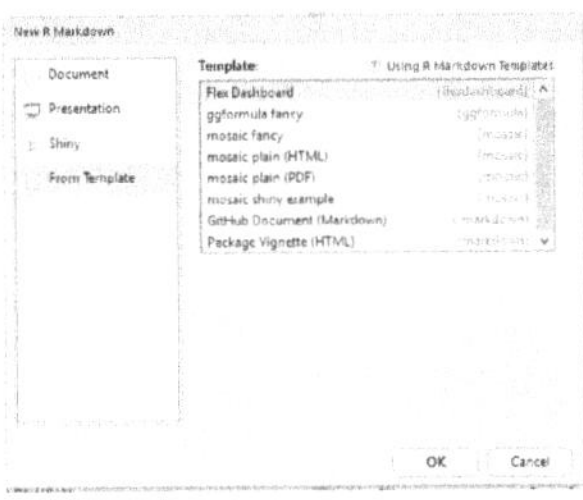

- It is possible to have the summary static or dynamic
- It is allowed to select multiples layouts
- There are options to use components such as gauges. The idea is to get htmlwidgets framework that can be used in the format

Exhibit 3.9. Starting with flex dashboard.

Different layouts

```
title: "Single Column (Fill)"
output: flexdashboard::flex_dashboard:
vertical_layout: fill
---### Chart 1
  ```{r}
```
Chart 2
```{r}
```
```

```
---
title: "Multiple Columns"output:
flexdashboard::flex_dashboard
---
Column {data-width=600}
------------------------------
 ### Chart 1
```{r}
```
 Column {data-width=400}

 ### Chart 2
```{r}
```
Chart 3
```{r}
```
```

Exhibit 3.10. Guides of R code to use in flexdashboard.

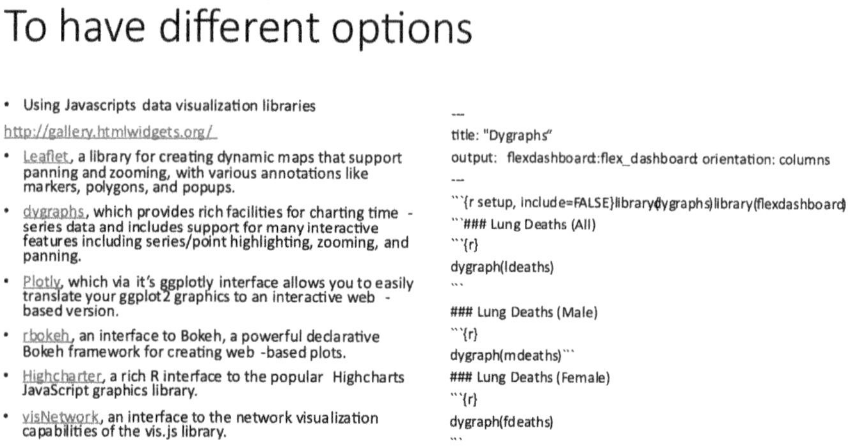

Exhibit 3.11. Possible R packages to enhance presentations and reports.

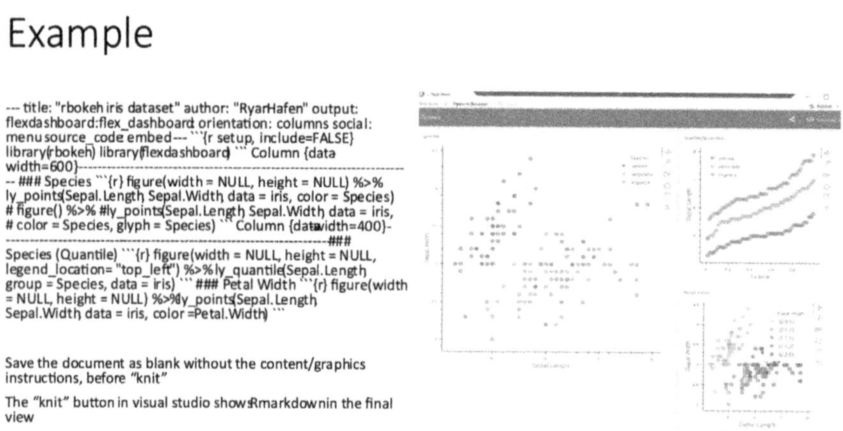

Exhibit 3.12. Creating meaning from data.

Example

````
-- title: "Dygraphs Linked Time Series" output:
flexdashboard::flex_dashboard: orientation: columns social: menu
source_code: embed
---
```{r setup, include=FALSE}
library(dygraphs)
library(quantmod)
library(flexdashboard)
getSymbols(c("MSFT", "HPQ", "INTC"), from = "201401-01",
auto.assign=TRUE)
``` ### Microsoft
```{r} dygraph(MSFT[,2:4], group = "stocks") %>%
dySeries(c("MSFT.Low", "MSFT.Close", "MSFT.High"), label = "MSFT")
``` ### HP
```{r} dygraph(HPQ[,2:4], group = "stocks") %>%
dySeries(c("HPQ.Low", "HPQ.Clos
e", "HPQ.High"), label = "HPQ")
``` ### Intel
```{r} dygraph(INTC[,2:4], group = "stocks") %>%
dySeries(c("INTC.Low", "INTC.Close", "INTC.High"), label = "INTC")
```
````

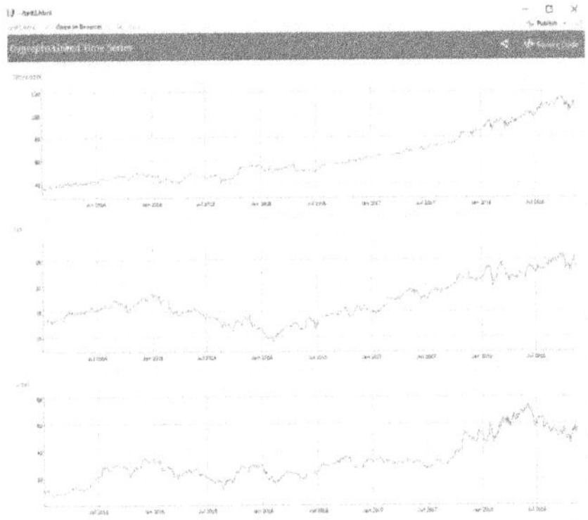

Exhibit 3.13. Comparing descriptive representation of data and model's outcomes.

Flexdashboard, shiny and shinydashboard

- Creating interactive document
- Deployed to a shiny server

````
---title: "Old Faithful Eruptions"
output: flexdashboard::flex_dashboard
runtime: shiny
---
```{r global, include=FALSE}
# load data in 'global' chunk so it can be shared by all users of the dashboard
library(datasets)
data(faithful)
```Column {.sidebar}
-----------------------------------------------------------------------
Waiting time between eruptions and the duration of the eruption for theOld
Faithful geyser in Yellowstone National Park, Wyoming, USA.
```{r}
selectInput("n_breaks", label = "Number of bins:", choices = c(10, 20, 35,
50), selected = 20)sliderInput("bw_adjust", label = "Bandwidth adjustment:",
min = 0.2, max = 2, value = 1, step = 0.2)
```
Column-----------------------------------------------------------------------
### Geyser Eruption Duration```{r}
renderPlot({ hist( faithful$eruptions, probability = TRUE, breaks =
as.numeric(input$n_breaks),     xlab = "Duration (minutes)", main = "Geyser
Eruption Duration")
 dens <- density(faithful$eruptions, adjust = input$bw_adjust) lines(dens, col =
"blue")})
``
````

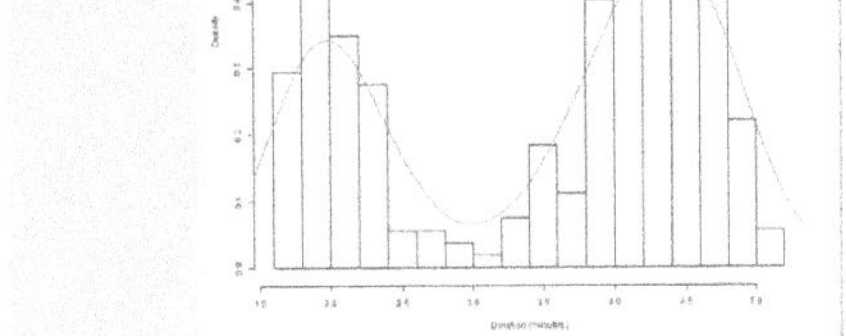

Exhibit 3.14. The family includes shiny, flexdashboard, shinydashboard, rmarkdown.

Shinydashboard structure

- library(shiny)
- library(shinydashboard)
- server<-function(input,output){
- }
- UI<-dashboardPage(
- dashboardHeader(),
- dashboardSidebar(),
- dashboardBody()
-)
- shinyApp(UI,server)

Exhibit 3.15. Using shinydashboard.

Shinydashboard outputs

```
ui <- dashboardPage(
 dashboardHeader(title = "Basic dashboard"),
 dashboardSidebar(sidebarMenu(
   menuItem("Dashboard", tabName = "dashboard", icon = icon("dashboard")),
   menuItem("Widgets", tabName = "widgets", icon = icon("th"))
 )
 ),
 dashboardBody(
   tabItems(
    # First tab content
    tabItem(tabName = "dashboard",
          fluidRow(
            box(plotOutput("plot1", height = 250)),
            box(
             title = "Controls",
             sliderInput("slider", "Number of observations:", 1, 100, 50)
            )
          )
    ),
        # Second tab content
    tabItem(tabName = "widgets",
          h2("Widgets tab content")
    )
   )
 )
)
```

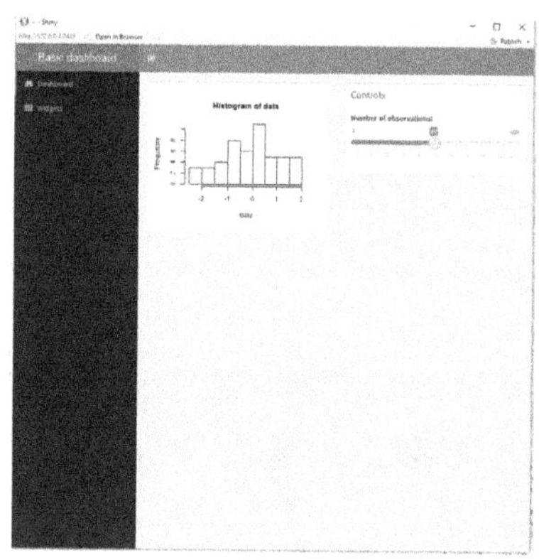

Exhibit 3.16. Code structure shinydashboard.

Shinydashboard outputs

```
server <- function(input, output) {
  set.seed(122)
  histdata <- rnorm(500)

  output$plot1 <- renderPlot({
   data <- histdata[seq_len(input$slider)]
   hist(data)
  })
 }

 shinyApp(ui, server)
```

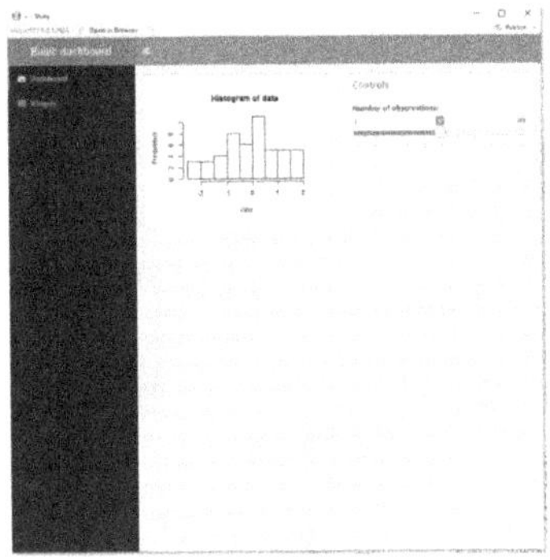

Exhibit 3.17. Shinydashboard UI and Server components.

3.2.1 *Evolution of risk analytics*

The Risk Analytics process is based on the incorporation of analytics approaches/methods/techniques to deal with risk-related data, in particular, structured and unstructured financial and non-financial data that can affect risk management practice. This book concentrates on the principles of applying analytics techniques that can be improved by new emerging algorithms, mathematical/statistical and computational capacity. Structure and techniques are in continuous development. New models and techniques are continuously discovered, and organization of data and the process to work with it will be continuously evolving and based on the risk analytics knowledge acquired by organizations' employees.

Topics related to the use of data analytics have been part of the practice in risk-related areas for many years; techniques have been used in several cases for many years as well. In the current socio-economic environment, there is more computational capacity, data are less expensive, and there are approaches through machine learning to supplement statistical methods that are leading research in AI and data science use. The speed of advances in data science is high and the acceleration of knowledge creation is not well understood. A reflection about the advances can be done based on what was observed some decades ago and what is happening now. Currently, the speed of knowledge creation is at a different rate than what it was in its infancy. The capacity for solving problems, working in real time, and using software capabilities is very robust

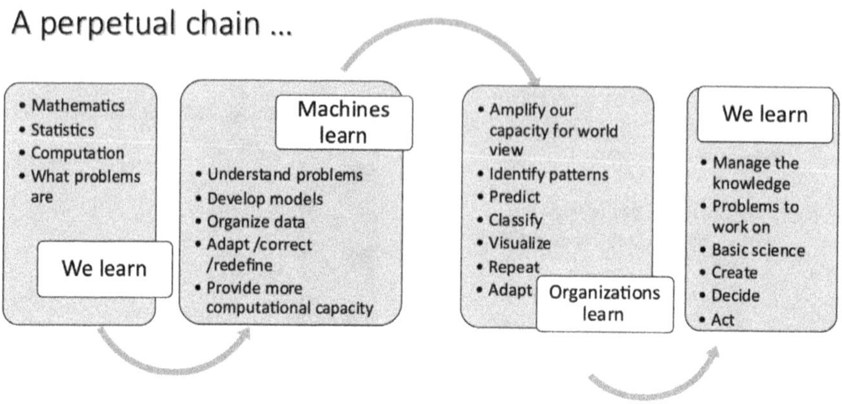

Figure 3.5. Illustration of the continuous chain of learning from data. People in organizations and machines.

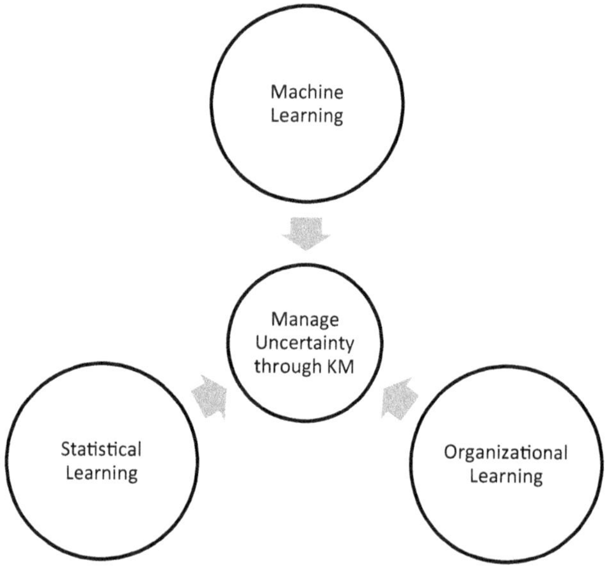

Figure 3.6. Creation of the Risk Analytics bases through the Analytics Knowledge Processes.

and accessible. Organizations and professionals have access to more opportunities to use analytics capabilities. For example, currently, there is a high possibility of people using several algorithms and methods of solving problems that were developed years ago, because of the

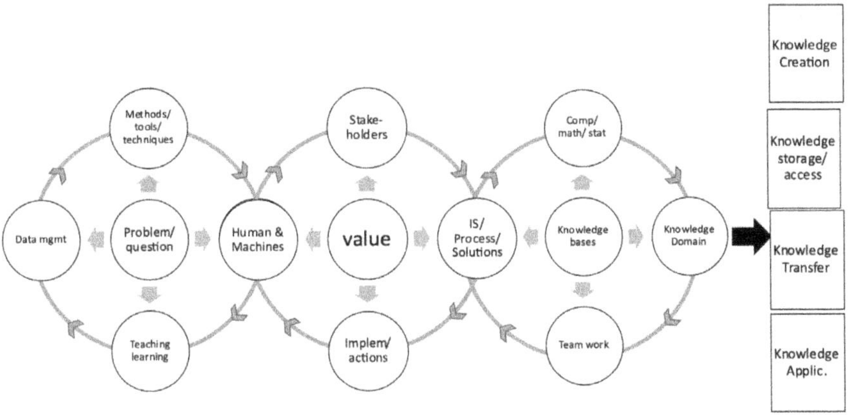

Figure 3.7. The learning molecule model indicating cycles that are connected to creating value.

improvement of computing capacity, handy algorithm implementations, and greater education and consciousness of the value of data analytics in organizations.

Historically, analytics capabilities have evolved and consolidated the pillars of what is currently data analytics and what is possible to use in the future:

- Open source tools that are used in solutions, automation, and creation of AI.
- Computational capacity that can be used in a schema of pay as you go.
- Interest of organizations in data analytics solutions and attraction of new talent through new hires or upskilling employees.
- Learning processes of using models in multiple contexts, conditions, constraints, and types of data.
- Improvement of means to involve multidiscipline solutions, in many cases generating better communication bridges.
- High knowledge about new techniques, solutions using new methods, and approaches has enriched the analytics process.
- Creation of better frameworks and roadmaps to take people from the beginning to the end in a data analytics process.
- Data analytics is accessible to many organizations, not only big organizations; in most cases, what is required is talent to push the data analytics use.

- Data analytics has been identified as a mitigant of risks and a way to formulate and control strategy implementation.
- Organizations work with better understanding of managing data to convert it into a productive asset.

At this point, the combination of business learning, statistical learning, and machine learning is connected to creating more intelligent organizations (Figures 3.5–3.7), which means more strategic intelligent organizations. Strategic intelligence is the joint creation of value through business intelligence, competitive intelligence, and artificial intelligence and in terms of learning, it is the perpetual chain of human and machine learning, using techniques of statistical learning, machine learning, and organizational learning.

Learning through the accumulation of knowledge is a tool to manage uncertainty and it emerges (Figure 3.6) when risk is considered a variation of results and knowledge as a means to reduce uncertainty. When analytical knowledge is oriented to deal with the variation of organizations' results is when data analytics is transforming into a risk analytics setting. The Risk Analytics work is based on the analytics knowledge management processes: analytics knowledge creation, analytics knowledge storage, analytics knowledge access, analytics knowledge transfer, and analytics knowledge application.

The molecule conceptual model (Figure 3.7) illustrates the connection of three different types of learning that are converging in an organization to create value in an uncertain business environment. The atoms of the "chemical bond" are technology–machines and human capabilities. Each atom of learning includes the proper activities of the learning process in machine learning, in business learning, and statistical learning.

In summary, this subsection shows a view of data analytics from the perspective of access and possibility to build capabilities of data analytics and integrate learning processes that involve humans and machines in continued risk mitigation. This section ends with a quote from Frees (2020) who indicated the connection of concepts around analytics and risk in the book Actuarial Community Loss Data Analytics: "In any data-driven industry, analytics is a key to deriving and extracting information from data. But what is analytics? Making data-driven business decisions has been described as business analytics, business intelligence, and data science. These terms, among others, are sometimes used interchangeably and sometimes refer to distinct applications. Business intelligence may focus on processes of collecting data, often through databases and data warehouses, whereas business analytics utilizes tools and methods for statistical analyses of data. In contrast to these two terms that emphasize business applications, the term data science can encompass broader data related applications in many scientific domains. For our purposes, we use the term analytics to refer to the process of using data to make decisions. This process involves gathering data, understanding concepts and models of uncertainty, making general inferences, and communicating results" (Loss Data Analytics (ewfrees.github.io)).

3.2.2 *Risk analytics crucial concept in the risk management processes*

The concepts used in risk analytics comprise discrete and continuous variables, which are the same as deterministic and stochastic variables, methods, and techniques, for finding means to deal with risk in organizations. In 1996, Stultz (2022) wrote, "This paper presents a theory of risk management that attempts to go beyond the "variance minimization" model that dominates most academic discussions of corporate risk management. I argue that the primary goal of risk management is to eliminate the probability of costly lower-tail outcomes — those that would cause financial distress or make a company unable to carry out its investment strategy. (In this sense, risk management can be viewed as the purchase of well-out-of-the-money put options designed to limit downside risk.)" This means that variation of results is part of the problem to solve in Risk Analytics and the impact of events is a component of the problem to solve in sustaining continuity in the business. It is not only about prediction of adverse events, valuation of the adverse event, or variation of results; it is additionally about the capacity to deal with post events and to continue operating and having good performance.

After the financial crisis of 2008–2010, people asked about the possibility of measuring risk. The value of risk management is in providing insights to prepare organizations to deal with uncertain events and circumstances that can modify the bottom line of the organization. The analytics arsenal is supporting the creation of those insights to provide orientation to certain decisions based on what the data are showing. It does not mean that the results of the risk analytics process will be 100% certain (in that case, we could convert the world into a deterministic world), but the better the risk classification, risk assessment, risk monitoring, and estimation, the better the awareness and orientation of the efforts of the organization to compete. Knowledge is a risk mitigant and analytics is a knowledge creation process. Risk analytics knowledge management through risk knowledge creation, transfer, storage, access, and application provides structure to the organization's management. Fraud detection, identification of factors influencing defaults, identifying opportunities of investments, etc., are risk management endeavors that analytics can handle and help manage to make decisions and solve problems. Hubbard (2009) states, "The ultimate common mode failure would be a failure of risk management itself. A weak risk management approach is effectively the biggest risk in the organization." In his presentation of how to fix risk management, he pointed out, "Most of the key problems with risk management are focused primarily on the problems with risk analysis." In his terms, the process of risk analysis should concentrate on enhancing the simulation capabilities, managing the quality of the risk management process itself, managing the model risk as a part of the control method, and improving the risk management knowledge and practice of the members of teams across the organization.

As in the analytics process, the rational and intuitive approaches act together to develop decision-making and control systems. Artificial Intelligence based on the analytics process can liberate human resources to study events and possible adverse conditions with special attributes (possible outliers of patterns) that can modify the course of actions of the organizations and that are not part of the identifiable patterns of event realizations. Risk analytics in this book comprises the following: first, understanding the risk analytics process including the interaction of risk and business concepts; second, the basic concepts of risk analytics used for risk modeling; third, the use of analytic methods to support risk modeling and creation of solutions to improve risk management processes; and fourth, the steps of implementation with the review of barriers and opportunities to implement risk analytics.

Risk analytics has multiple dimensions that require various quantitative and qualitative methods to discover and implement solutions. These methods include the use of statistical and machine learning, and optimization tools with an appropriate understanding of data analytics management. In particular, risk analytics involves a review of the governance of needs in usable data creation, reporting, portfolio overview, analytics support, and a review of risk management strategies. The concepts of descriptive analytics, predictive analytics, and prescriptive analytics are covered in this book and presented in a general perspective of analytics through managerial and strategic responsibilities.

In risk analytics, it is crucial to identify not only the steps for the analytics process but also the type of methods, techniques, and models that are used. Risk analytics reviews the construction of models with different structures such as the following:

- Logic and conceptual models that allow the description and visualization of the relationships of the variables and steps for the risk analysis.
- Models in spreadsheets which provide structures of relationships among variables through the definition of formulas using data and mathematical/statistical models to determine outcomes. In the following link, you can find examples of good and bad practices in spreadsheet modeling: http://www.eusprig.org/about.htm.
- Mathematical models refer to the mathematical representation of the variable relationships describing phenomena.
- Statistical models refer to the structure of the model; for example, a multiple regression model can be used in many analyses and several different evaluations of relationships among variables. However, the final model is when the parameters are estimated and the variables to use are selected.
- Machine learning models that represent, through computational algorithms, the solution to risk management problems such as classification.

Another important aspect in the development of risk analytics is that the "model risk" is real and there are several aspects that are needed to maintain the standards of development and implementation of the risk model design and policy creation based on constructed models. One of the aspects that was mentioned earlier was risk knowledge transfer. Rodriguez and Edwards (2019) identified several issues in creation of value: the impact in the organization of a lack of understanding of the outcomes of risk analysis and the issues in the implementation and deployment of risk systems.

Individual risk studies involve the practice and separation of risk by activities. The main issue in general is the organization of a system where any component influences the performance of the system as a whole. This means that risk management by individual risk is the start, but the goal is get a holistic view of risk across the organization, understand it, and then go back to the individual risk analysis. The challenge is immense mainly in identifying relationships, correlations, joint distributions, and models that can be used and the structure to understand these relationships and cause and effect (Causal Inference).

A risk analytics process starts with questions to answer and assessment of the inventory of data to use. Once data are organized for review, the first step is to use Exploratory Data Analysis (EDA) that comprises concepts related to visualization and descriptive statistics. The EDA approach mainly includes graphical data visualization techniques and descriptive statistics. EDA is based on the principle of exploring the easiest means to present data in a way in which people can infer general points of behavior, identifying patterns, and with the combination of tables to present variable relationships. In a study, the focus can be on representing two-dimensional data: organization and metric-data value. The reason is to generate comparisons among the organizations/areas/actions included in the study.

Risk analytics is an integration of learning and acting. Leoni *et al.* (2022) indicated that KM and AI integration in manufacturing indicates the positive effects of AI in KM processes, manufacturing processes, and supply chain resilience, which is similar to the positive effect of knowledge management on manufacturing processes and supply chain resilience. The concepts of using data analytics and AI to create knowledge, plus sharing and transferring that knowledge, will have positive effects on the production processes. The use of data analytics is not the same as creating knowledge and transferring knowledge; however, the use of the techniques, methods, and technologies will be potentialized by the data analytics–AI processes. Digital transformation steps are involved in the use of data analytics. For instance, knowledge transfer is implemented using collaboration means. SLACK is an example that is combined with Learning Systems, or other collaboration systems and support projects development.

The reflection here is about the time and value that are required to think about technologies and about the appropriate use of outcomes and operation improvement through a good knowledge diffusion and application strategy. It is a means of connecting and supporting the HOW of doing things to answer customer requests and deal with the constraints represented by internal aspects like the budget or external aspects like access to resources. Management in digital transformation will continue with the basic pillars of good implementation of strategies such as, effective communication, fostering the use of new resources and techniques to solve problems, and providing bridges for people to be closer to new possibilities to perform well. The mystery is, as in most of the cases, about the spectrum of what cultural change is. Each organization will adapt to new ways to work to control the challenges that develop on the road to changes. The goal is to strengthen what is the differential, unique, and clear driver of the organization. Technology in terms of physical devices or artifacts does not differentiate; technology can be converted into a commodity in an industry but what will be different is how the organization will deal with the creation of value using a strong human–machine development that is going to create the advantages. It is about dealing with the use of outcomes of machines and the agility of humans in supporting the strategic implementation. At the end, the issue to solve is how AI and digitalization create intelligent organizations because the business processes, people, customer experience, and financials are improving to order to achieve the goal of sustaining the organization under good performance.

3.3. Models, Prototypes, and Solutions

In the previous section, there was an introduction of risk analytics as a common component of the risk management processes. Risk analytics and in particular the risk modeling knowledge process are associated with interdisciplinary work and interdepartmental work, controlling the whole process from problem definition to solution evaluation. Davenport and Harris (2005) said that there is a need to align the organization to the age of the automated decision systems, applying codified knowledge and providing decisions plus a knowledge sharing environment. Human intervention is identified as a means to confirm decisions and to analyze particular cases, which means the use of knowledge for a risk solution. An organization needs to develop the capacity to solve problems and to provide support for the modeling process under the following premises (Mladenic *et al.*, 2003):

- Decisions come from humans and machines. Machines include decision systems and humans use some theory frameworks and decision support systems.
- Management is about knowledge and knowledge management is about people, processes, technology, and organizational structure.

- Old computing is about what computers can do and new computing is about what people can do. New computing is about intelligence creation, reliability, comprehensibility, universality, and harmony with human needs.
- The power is not in having knowledge. The power is in sharing knowledge and using it to add value and to create a sustainable competitive advantage, going beyond analyzing business processes and information systems.
- Technology is more than software or hardware and is the answer to HOW to solve something. For example, modeling process capacity is a competitive capacity (Davenport, 2006).

Raiffa (1968) introduced the decision analysis, and he identified the value of the outcome of the models based on the relevance in a real-world problem. He said "In these lectures I have indicated how a decision maker's preferences for consequences, attitudes towards risk, and judgments about uncertain events can be scaled in terms of subjective utilities and probabilities and how these can be incorporated into formal analysis. By these means it may be possible in some circumstances to reduce the judgmental gap and to bring the output of the model closer to the demands of the real-world problem; the model will then have more a chance to pass the test of relevance." Moreover, Leonard's model (Leonard & Sensiper, 1998) called "knowledge creating and diffusing activities," considers a cycle where core capabilities for shared problem-solving in organizations are connected to implementing and integrating, experimenting and prototyping, and importing and absorbing knowledge. The core capabilities have to reduce the core rigidity that is coming from skills and knowledge, managerial systems, physical systems, and values. Subprocesses in risk modeling processes are looking for better knowledge development in order to use knowledge to tackle different problems.

Through the comparison of what is performed in risk modeling, it is possible to identify communalities of the risk analytics process (Exhibit 3.18). The examples are typical in risk analytics: use of the compound Poisson for loss distribution modeling and risk classification modeling, and use of the Markov process for credit risk evaluation and credit behavior prediction. From the review of modeling examples, it is possible to identify four main components in a risk modeling process: information management, mathematical work, experimenting and prototyping, and communicating. These four components of the modeling process go from data gathering up to application of the theoretical concepts to different kinds of problems.

Process	Risk analysis — classification
Problem Definition	
Problem definition: understanding the phenomenon	Meaning of customer classification, attributes available, timing, groups, etc.
Search for general models/ theoretical support/mathematics	New theory for parameter estimation, testing new model decision trees, regression trees, neural networks, GLM
Moving from data to modeling	
Reducing the core rigidity: People coordination/project development	Expert identification, blueprint, maps, plans. Blocks & Steps definition, capacity and roles identification
Data gathering	Data experience, profile variables, default definition, claims data, exposure set definition, clustering for outliers
Data store	Data mart creation/access, record selection, variables/fields selection
Data selection/preparation	Learning set, out of time, out of sample
Data for control	Selection of the samples, out of time, and out of sample
Programming/specialized software	Testing assumptions, normality, modeling, categorization, regression process, model identification, model preparation

Exhibit 3.18. Example of steps in solving problem process and the meaning in risk management classification process — part 1.

Exhibit 3.19 shows subprocesses from problem definition up to data manipulation. The process comparison presents the way to move from discovering relationships and modeling initiation to getting the solution applicable to other kinds of problems. This means application of risk knowledge gained to get new solutions, possibly with different data and variable relationships.

Another way of representing relationships among variables that was indicated in the introduction is creating maps where variables identify conditions or results for potential use. In a risk heat map (Exhibit 3.20), each box is the component of the BSC and inside each box there is a map of Likelihood vs. Impact of the objectives. The risk heat map is about defining priorities in developing solutions according to the factors in the results calculations. A prototype is a good instrument to move toward problems and possible ways to tackle the solutions.

Process	Risk analysis — classification
Prototyping	
Prototyping: Model/program Testing definition of structure and relationships/model structure selection	Input data to different models
Parameters estimation and solutions of relationships/equations	Testing different methods
Model performance evaluation	ROC, classification tests, Kolmogorov–Smirnov
Model improvements	Identification of different set of variables, parsimonious metrics, testing more variables
Reporting	Problem solved, scope, model specifications, results, interpretation, new challenges, and priorities
Reducing the judgment gap	
Reducing the judgment gap: Result interpretation	Meaning of classification
Communication	Presentations to different groups, taking feedback
Search of the statistical law	
Search for a statistical law: New generalizations/weak assumptions	Look for panel data, time series indicators
New applications/input new models	Developing variance metrics, identification of new significant variables, benchmarking, development of segmented models (economic sectors, by different clusters)

Note: Many steps have common knowledge that needs to be aligned to produce capacity for risk modeling, for instance, describing group (groups can be defined as sets of customers according to the due date, delinquency level) clustering, selecting variables from linear approach, and classification process profile of payment quality. There is a basis for the loss distribution for other applications such as calculating maximum loss probability. The groups of debt quality can be organized in a different way, producing a sequence of the credit process from selection to control of credit portfolio.

Exhibit 3.19. Example of steps in solving problem process and the meaning of risk management classification process — part 2.

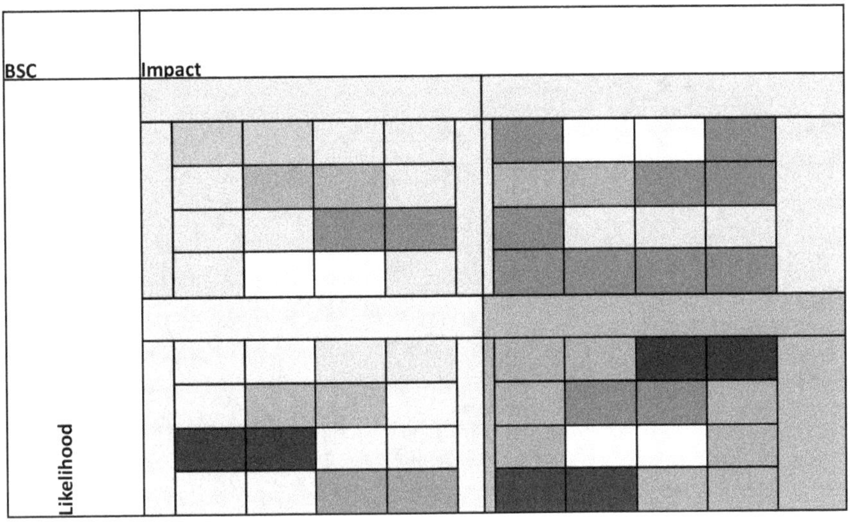

Exhibit 3.20. Creating color heat maps to represent the level of likelihood and impact of risk.

In general, for an approach to the sequence models, prototypes and solutions in risk management-analytics follow the illustrated centricity of Figure 3.8 and set of steps as shown in Exhibit 3.21. The focus moves from risk tolerance to achieving risk targets and goals (Figure 3.8).

Steps from risk appetite to goals are translated in the sequence of strategy to creation of system structures for risk analytics (Exhibit 3.21).

In the context of strategic risk analytics, the purpose is to examine what the measurement system for strategic risk management could be. Measurement is related to the definition of the metrics and the way to obtain and use these metrics. The analytics process starts with definition of metrics according to the strategy needs. A process of metrics creation requires a review if data is available or potentially available. We cannot develop a measurement system if data cannot be used. The measurement system needs to be related to the goals of the organization and we need to develop the dimensions of the metrics according to the needs of the stakeholders. These dimensions can be related to time, units, users, etc. Given the immense size of the control process, it is necessary to define which risk assessment alternatives are suitable. A mature organization in data management can be optimally supported by statistical methods. An organization for which data are still something to manage properly

Figure 3.8. The targets/goal are the end and beginning of the definition of what is acceptable in risk control, tolerance, and appetite.

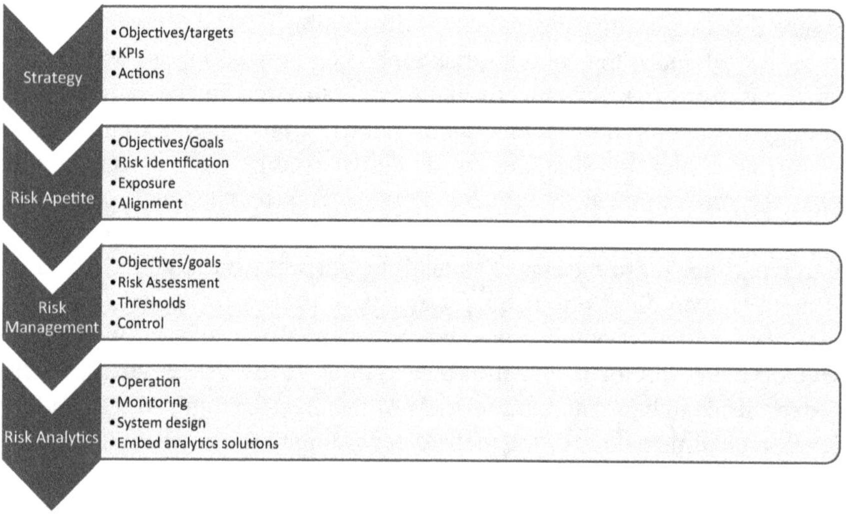

Exhibit 3.21. Risk analytics is the way to develop answers to support strategic risk policies and strategy implementation.

requires the improvement of methods and the incursion of some methods of knowledge. It should be noted that the evaluation process will be successful if there is no transition to the configuration of better objective methods, which implies a better culture of data and statistics.

3.4. Case Studies of Strategic Risks

Figures 3.9 and 3.10 help to understand case studies in the process of strategic risk analysis. The exhibits ahead illustrate a variety of strategic risks that organizations have dealt with and that have influenced the performance of organizations and societies. The approach of reviewing the

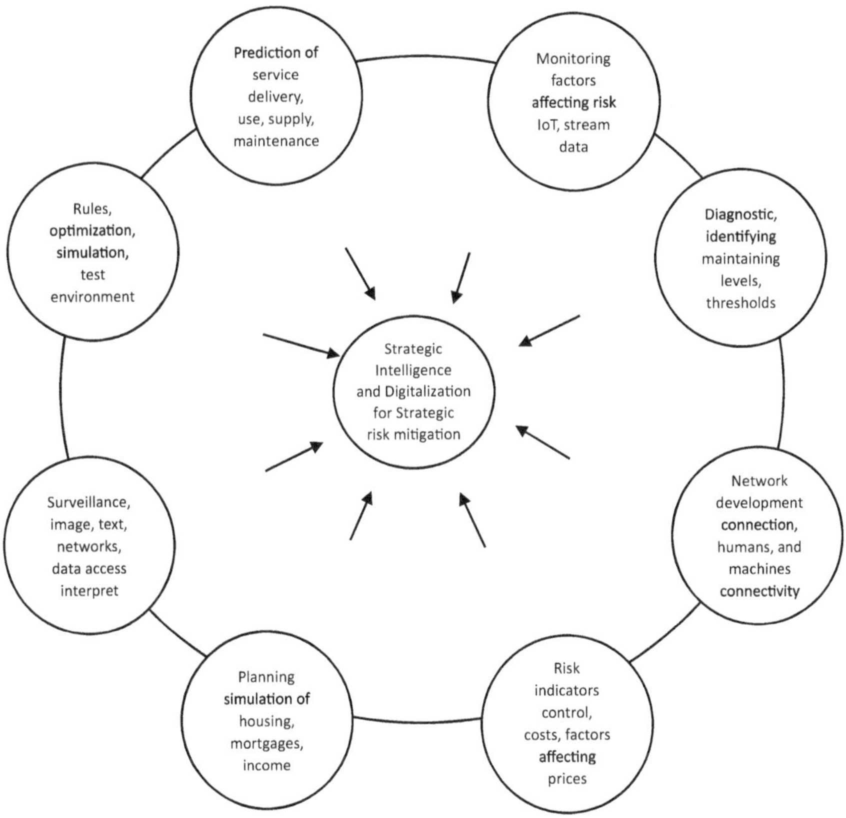

Figure 3.9. Middle components to connect external factors Exhibit 3.5 and strategic intelligence.

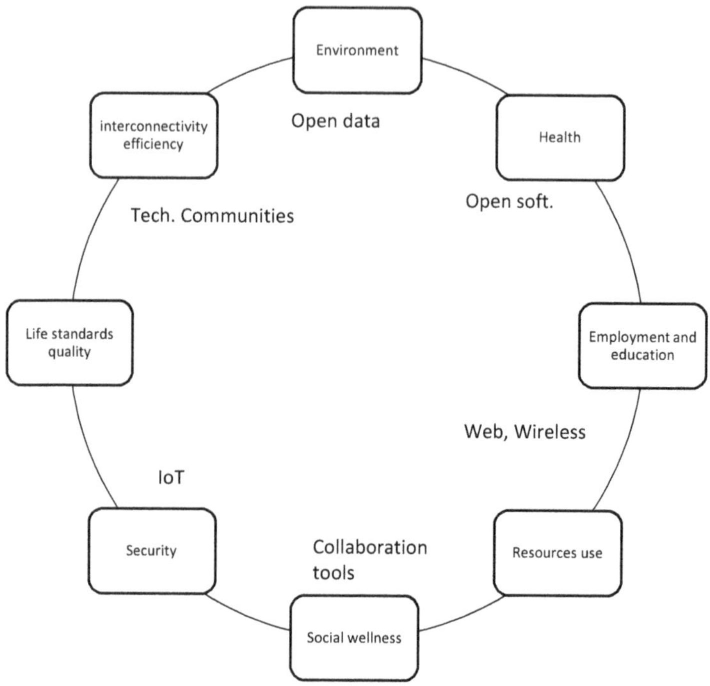

Figure 3.10. Example of external factors in strategic intelligence related to strategic risk observation.

aspects in Figures 3.9 and 3.10 helps to create the monitoring systems and build the risk analytics tool and means to analyze data.

The examples can be reviewed using Exhibit 3.22. This exhibit indicates the principles of strategic risk management that can support strategic intelligence development. The exhibit includes important concepts for understanding risk analysis and the development of a measurement system. Exhibits 3.23–3.27 are a good reference for questions that appear in multiple circumstances in organizations and society regarding strategic risk. In the following chapters, more case studies will be presented.

In summary, in this chapter there is a review of what an analytics process means, and the difference between data mining methodologies and the observation of how the data analytics process can be used in certain problems of organizations. A general way to see the transition from data analytics and data transformation to strategic risk mitigation is more

Some principles of Strategic Risk Management:	**Three main concepts:**
• Not only for negative outcomes. • Preparation to improve to compete. • The risk of being good without a clear understanding of WHY. • One thing is strategy formulation and another is implementation.	1. Strategic risk is linked to the management information systems. 2. The management information systems are the vehicles to provide value from the measurement systems in the organization. 3. The priority is to create the measurement system or at least align/ define metrics, data, analytics.
The required system and Measurement Process: • Start from the goals of the organization. • Review the business processes and the way that they are related to the goals. • Make it part of the management control systems. • Key is to keep understanding the organization. • Maintain data alignment/availability. • Review business process steps with partial results that contribute to the final result. • Organize final values of metrics as part of the cause–effect and relationships of business process steps.	**The required system and metrics relationships:** Metrics are based on goals and they have dimensions. • This means a metric cannot be just a number; it is a piece of business knowledge. • Dimension means that we can measure sales but how often? Every second, every year. • The same goal can have different metrics. • Metrics, planning and reporting are connected. • Search for expressing the same kind of event/activity/phenomenon in different and equivalent ways. For example, a ratio can have income as the numerator and you can express income in many ways keeping the same denominator. • Split metrics into pieces/factors/terms. • Information and knowledge management systems start from what we want to measure. • Metrics can be very good but not feasible or understandable. • Metrics can have assumptions that are key to understand correctly, e.g., VAR. • Metrics could be considered in groups: deterministic current and facts, forecasts, and at random (In any case it is required to review-calibrate metrics through time.).

Exhibit 3.22. Aspects to start a case of strategic risk.

Case strategic risk	Process stage	Projects and processes to create strategic intelligence
Housing affordability in a society	Problem definition	Questions to answer (all the answers are related to the Strategic risks of citizens living a low-quality life): What are the factors affecting prices? What are the barriers for families to afford houses? What are price behaviors? What are the relationships among prices, mortgages, and household income? Is there a critical limitation for people to buy houses? To high prices? Ratio mortgage to income is not possible to sustain by families? Cox and Pavletich (2018) pointed out that the rule of 3:1 between household income and house mortgage equivalent is a metric to identify when a house is affordable or not.
	Managing data	Use of open data in a city which will be a mix of data types: Identifiers, geographical location, permit attributes, number of units to build, dates, organization that received the approval, type of use of the building permit, and external data that can be used as, for example, surveys of needs, services and infrastructure for families to live, commuting times, industry location, age of houses, taxes, etc.
	Managing models — knowledge creation	Several questions can be tackled using forecasting techniques, regressions for identifying factors affecting affordability, classification of groups of families, identification of groups of projects, supply chain, etc.
	Understanding, meaning, intelligence	Metrics and their interpretation according to the variables to use: For instance, to answer questions just with EDA or using outcomes of models, statistical testing of hypotheses, etc., the process is to build metrics and their interpretation, such as calculations based on constant dollars (ratios under constant dollars provide a more accurate measurement for relationships) of income to mortgage, services index for families, crime index, factors affecting prices, expectation of interest rate, city special programs for building affordable housing project (trends of budgets), how many shelter beds are in use in the city, how rental conditions are in the city market, how the waitlist for affordable houses is growing, and so on.

Exhibit 3.23. A case to generate strategic intelligence in a community — Housing affordability.

Case Strategic Risk	Process Stage	Projects and processes to create Strategic Intelligence
	Knowledge sharing/ transfer	Dissemination of outcomes across governmental agencies, financial services, developers, families, etc. The value of the outcomes is related to how several services are related to prices and quality of life of citizens.
	Application, business process	Smart and intelligent cities use integrated views of the problem. Connecting the stakeholders and managing possible links of cause and effect in the affordability of housing. The factors affecting housing prices, the value of living or having assets of a high price, and ratios of income and benefits of quality of life.
	Analytics and digital transformation opportunities	Digitalization starts with open data as is; the important aspects at this level of development of analytics are related to identifying what variables are crucial to answer questions. Digitalization helps with the data access and visualization and description of data but the opportunities to connect variables, identify relationships from multiple sources of data are when a more complete solution can emerge. Simulations of multiple types of conditions and variables affecting the capacity to obtain houses are a wonderful help to support decision-making processes.

Exhibit 3.23. (*Continued*)

Case Strategic Risk	Process Stage	Projects and processes
Infant mortality in a society	Problem definition	Strategic risks related to the capacity to keep a society healthy, effects of family's wellness on the infant's health, multiple lives affected because of infant's health, costs of infant's programs and resources used for infant survival, maintenance of children's health, capacity to develop intelligence and study-learning, etc. The groups of infants require different types of care, groups of infants of less than one years, 1–2 years, etc. One of the complex problems to solve is the limited knowledge of medical system for assessment and treatments because of the lack of history of medical conditions given that the infants are without medical records. A way to start with data analytics and AI is analyze what data are available for understanding trends, frequencies, cases, types of illnesses, etc., all based on what the current data of cases are.
	Managing data	Using data that are about cases and not about medical treatments or conditions when infants are born. Data can be related to actual and past infant mortality rates, in dimensions like locations, aggregation by ethnicity, physiological attributes, regions, ages, etc. The ratios can be comparable with scales that are per thousands of births or any other according to the study. Data are open and there are different sources (WHO, World Bank, OECD, and UNICEF). One value of data concerns causes of mortality. The number of categories of causes can create levels of data points with small numbers, affecting the data analytics possibilities for models to learn. That is part of what can be required for the level of aggregation of a study.
	Managing models — knowledge creation	Depending on the problems and available data, models can be related to time series — prediction forecasting, identification of groups. If the time is combined with records such as country and regions, the studies can be more on longitudinal with multiple factors. The first analysis completed on the data was a time series analysis. Steps of modeling will start with EDA and review categories and factors that can be used for finding relationships among variables. Target variables can be defined such as the causes of mortality or new categorical variables' construction such as having growth in the rates above certain thresholds or not. Models to work on can be the available in the times.

Exhibit 3.24. A case to generate strategic intelligence in a community — Infant mortality.

Case Strategic Risk	Process Stage	Projects and processes
		series arsenal with the evaluation of parameters per model and accuracy, reduction of error, for instance, a Double Exponential Smoothing model, when there is a trend and no seasonality. The optimize option was selected in order to set the alpha and beta weights. Time series can be evaluated according to categories such as age range, gender, time windows for data, and for predictions. Fundamentally, the search is for error reduction, identification of confidence intervals, and deviations regarding certain metric of interest. Comparison of results by groups will lead to use statistical methods for comparing means, proportions, variances, etc. Correlation evaluations will help to assess possible factors relating one to another and can help to reduce the number of variables and possibly groups of causes.
	Understanding, meaning, intelligence	Given limitations in obtaining knowledge from data before births for a complete analysis, there are several intelligence opportunities with cases in terms of prediction and simulation. Prediction not only helps to discovery when to assess change from one stage to another (low risk to high complexity cases) because of illness factors but also helps as a classification problem can guide one to collaborate with more vulnerable groups in societies, and will provide input to centers for public health control and follow-up of adverse events that can affect society.
	Knowledge sharing/ transfer	Centers of data and created indicators and evaluation of conditions of newborn or mothers in a joint communication means provide opportunities to support public health and families to activate alarms and to know how to react or to prevent adverse events affecting babies and mothers.
	Application, business process	Early warning systems, follow-up systems, communication centers for instruction, telemedicine, centers of prescription/medicaments for delivery and stock of product control, monitoring case evolution, and treatments.
	Analytics and digital transformation opportunities	Digitalization around mobile applications and interaction with medical suppliers using the web channel provide a huge opportunity to modify habits, hygiene, food intake, etc., and control factors that have incidence in mortality.

Exhibit 3.24. (*Continued*)

Case	Process Stage	Projects and processes
Starbucks and market: supply and demand	Problem definition	Risks related to organization's market value, profit, and revenue sustainability under coffee futures — supply management, trading, customer habits, and the reactions of the commodity prices and prices of coffee in the shop, how organizations can obtain buffers of cost control, logistic infrastructure, supply chain support, and so on.
	Managing data	Company Performance and Data from market, financials, stock market, industry. Data types such as company data, consumer data, sensor data, and syndicated data. A critical data input in the analytics process is related to the prices of the raw material of the business production; in this case, the grain of coffee trade-off for buying futures or paying spot prices. This business requires data integration from multiple sources with data about suppliers that can have levels of granularity different from the customers. In the case of the suppliers, data can come from supply registration, market value of the coffee prices, and in the case of the customers, it can come directly from the purchases or from the suppliers of payment services. Transaction dates are crucial to have alignment between demand and supply for coffee bean negotiation/investment. Furthermore, data quality is different from the sources given the characteristics of public company information in contrast with supplier data that can be incomplete. Data security and governance have different levels of interest; while security could not be high risk, governance is a priority including data preparation for analysis, updating data, dealing with time definition of transactions, and production.
	Managing models — knowledge creation	Data visualization, time series analysis, ratio analysis, correlation analysis, review of prices, and bottom-line results using simulation. Review the NPV of the revenues considering the randomness of several factors in the revenue through time. There is a need to identify how copulas can describe the multivariate correlations that have an effect on the joint probability distribution of NPV.
	Understanding, meaning, intelligence	Learning emerges from identifying factors affecting the stock price, net income, and market conditions in dealing with supply chain. Prices are going to be in confidence intervals that can help the decision toward future trading and identify how the revenue management should proceed. Revenue management will act as a hedge means to connect what is expected revenue and the contribution of a cup of coffee and other elements of the offer in a shop.

Exhibit 3.25. A case to generate strategic intelligence in a community — Starbucks.

Case	Process Stage	Projects and processes
	Knowledge sharing/ transfer	Collaboration is about multiple shops' branches and suppliers. Use of understanding of how markets behave is a valuable help for suppliers, for production, and for dealing with customers. Techniques and technologies development to improve supply ties through knowledge oriented actions. In this regard, the company as global organization has a lot of customer knowledge because of seasons and changes in customer behaviors in local markets that can help employees around the world, support licensors and countries, as well and where franchises are possible (outside USA and Canada).
	Application, business process	Budgeting, marketing, operations, training, supply chain management, value creation customer experience
	Analytics and digital transformation opportunities	Promotion, service follow-up, orders management, additional services — entertainment, meetings, and groups. From the point of view of managing futures and supply chain risk, the opportunities are coming from monitoring market conditions of prices, volumes, conditions of crops production or development in countries, and so on. Going to the customers: In Startbucks using Wi-Fi services to connect with customers was not with enough attention from management and the process had a low organizational adoption. Support in adoption of technologies by employees is associated with human factors, technology that is related to the past, and volume of changes — innovation — re-organizations — no cases to buy by employees. Fitzgerald *et al.* (2013) suggested that digital technologies the most common barrier for adoption is lack of urgency. Deloitte (2022) presented the quadrants for organizations according to strategic index and operative index: high-high offers flexible and operational cost advantages, high-low is creating an innovative portfolio with work on operation improvement, Low-Low needs to link initiatives and improve skills to use digitization to enhance efficiency, Low-High concentrates on digitalizing what is fundamental in value creation, providing innovative and flexible solutions.

Exhibit 3.25. *(Continued)*

Cases	Process Stage	Projects and processes
Veterinary clinic	Problem definition	Two possible problems in the strategic risk arena are business profits and reputation of the clinic operation and care. Profits are related to revenue development, a possible low level of growth in revenue creates issues in the clinic operation. Questions about strategies to change the revenue current and outlook are a priority to compensate for changes in operational costs. The questions are about promotion and business attraction which lead to answers about targets and a combination of revenue sources.
	Managing data	Using internal sources, industry-aggregated data (using specialized veterinary software) and data the clinic has available consisted of thousands of records, representing customer transactions. Every transaction was recorded. The data consists of three types: client, patient, and transaction data. Client data included names, addresses, client numbers, clinic join date, and number of pets. Patient data consisted of the patient's name, breed, age, and gender. Transaction data consisted of service charge amounts, treatment type, service date, and time. Data preparation includes outlier identification, sorting, gaps of data, wrong data, and formatting according to the data type.
	Managing models — knowledge creation	Descriptive models based on dates, last appointments, time of service, follow-up, location, and so on. Definition of tables for description scatter plots showing breeds and requirement of services, time of recovery, and slicing and icing data tables to discover possible patterns. Moving to levels of type of animal species, several types of demographic data are organized and aggregated with metrics around age, charges, pet type: for example, breeds of dog, cat, or another type of animal. All those cross tables with define sets where the metrics will be compared using general statistical methods for proportion, mean, variance comparisons. In terms of operations, metrics can be the sum of revenues by days, by hour, frequencies of treatment by day, by treatments such as dental and general surgery.

Exhibit 3.26. A case to generate strategic intelligence in a community — Veterinary clinic.

Cases	Process Stage	Projects and processes
		Should a related study continue further to the scope of this specific project, the observers, in conjunction with the clinic owner and key employees, will be engaged in the deployment of marketing materials. Meetings will be created to explain the modeling process to key staff members and explain any clinic action that may be needed. Any required training will ensue.
	Understanding, meaning, intelligence	Data visualization and geographic and time analysis help to identify potential behavior of customers or needs of distribution in terms of distance to the clinic. Several aspects of the analytics applications are related to the appropriate use of staff, allocation of resources, scheduling with variation of service requests. Identification of sources of revenues, for example, because of type of animal and services, will help to deal with the balance and assignment of tasks in the clinic, such as additional services offer, vaccination control, outreach, and customers support.
	Knowledge sharing/ transfer	At least three components to connect: veterinarian staff, owners, and services for pets. The key part is to concentrate on the same animal and its care with regard to aligned treatment and support to owners and animals.
	Application, business process	Operation of the clinic is going to obtain value of data analytics, AI support in monitoring pets, controlling the workflow, providing guidance to owners, keeping the control of treatments, and remote monitoring.
	Analytics and digital transformation opportunities	Remote follow-up of treatments, observation of behavior, through cameras, recording for diagnostic and follow-up, recommendations and communication with owners, sharing experiences and practice of similar pets owners, monitoring conditions using devices/ sensors, and hygiene orientation.

Exhibit 3.26. (*Continued*)

Cases	Process Stage	Projects and processes
Crime in a community	Problem definition	Mitigation of strategic risk of crime in an intelligent community and government is a leading objective. The high complexity of crime analysis is tackled by small pieces and sectorized by types of crimes. The goal is to identify how crime is related to organizations and their criminal members, what the modus operandi could be (seasonality), areas and how social intervention programs could produce more effective and efficient results (education, managing time of young people, shelter programs, etc.).
	Managing data	Selection and grouping variables according to problem definition requirement; for example, the cases can be studied with analytics targets in mind. A target could be associated with fatalities, levels of economic damage, etc. Some types of crime are arson, assault, breaking and entering, counterfeit, dangerous operation of a motor vehicle, deprivation of freedom, driving suspensions, drugs/substances, escaping lawful custody, etc. Different types of factors and people and assets can be affected. The use of the data by targets of the study is a decision to make for the review of datasets. Data have multiple sources: community open data bank, unemployment rate from statistics, police budget and police staff, from the community reports. Data preparation comprises identifying the incorrect, incomplete, inaccurate, irrelevant, or missing part of the data and then modifying or deleting them according to the necessity.
	Managing models — knowledge creation	Regression analysis and correlation analysis of administrative police enforcement variables and variables associated with type of crime. Possibly as a guide to allocate resources. Seasonality is a crucial factor to understand correctly crime behaviour to support scheduling, resource allocation, creation of multi-crime groups, etc., can help for concentration and orientation of resources use. Social factors affect criminal behavior such as unemployment, population composition, location in city areas, etc. Classification and clustering methods help to identify areas of intervention and resource allocation; some areas can be mapped depending on frequencies, severity of crime vents in combination to other factors affecting crime. Moreover, forecasting is a way to indicate how trends could be and how the confidence intervals of certain goals-policies of the city can be defined.

Exhibit 3.27. A case to generate strategic intelligence in a community — Crime in a community.

Cases	Process Stage	Projects and processes
	Understanding, meaning, intelligence	Effective and efficient utilization of resources; metrics of crime as a combination of factors is oriented to a more precise evaluation of what is happening in a city, how policy implementation is achieving goals, and how goals are determined. In an intelligent approach, prediction of events, warning systems, and orientation to levels of resource use in supporting the community can be simulated and observed under metrics combination, indices development, and connecting police and other member of the community aligned with similar goals under the assumptions, to be tested, of cause and effect. For instance, occupation of population and effects in criminal behavior.
	Knowledge sharing/ transfer	Among members of different groups of police, groups of social workers, groups in the agencies that are associated with good citizen conduct. The systems will support alignment of plans, their implementation, and communication in multiple areas regarding specific community objectives.
	Application, business process	Clustering methodology to identify groups of crimes, communities, or factors affecting crime. Exploration of criminal behavior and socio-environmental-economic factors. Simulation and optimization analysis under assumptions of predictions for resource allocation and orientation of efforts to mitigate risk. It is fundamental to improve the education, reinsertion into the society, and enable behavior changes in the members of the community, with and without crime records.
	Analytics and digital transformation opportunities	Interactive crime maps, interactive models affecting factors to simulate what the effect could be in metrics that lead to actions, defining threshold for risk level orientation of actions, surveillance, monitoring location of people under the support of networks, communication devices, orientation of actions in cases of events. Coordination with IoT devices, drones, communication devices, points of control, sensors for policing use in mobiles and fixing locations.

Exhibit 3.27. (*Continued*)

about a transformation mindset to deal with strategic risk generating actionable knowledge which will be translated into digital solutions in several cases. A data analytics process involves creation of solutions and value identification through applications and development of strategies based on digitalization starts and is supported by stages of implementation from conceptual models to actions in real settings. Thus, the first activity is to get answers to the following questions: What resources does the organization need? What does the organization want? What does the organization measure? What is the impact? What has been the experience? What are the errors? Where is the failure based on lack of knowledge management? This component of the risk management process is based on the needs of the stakeholders, their value definition, and the strategy planning process. The risk management, data analytics, and digitalization processes are in agreement with "design approach to planning" as introduced by Ackoff (1981) following his five proposed phases: formulating the systems of problems, identifying ideals, definition of objectives and goals, planning resources/means, and design of implementation and control. In summary, a strategic risk management process starts with the recognition of the strategic context and contribution that it will make to the strategic process and the components for intervention — mitigation using data analytics and digitalization processes.

The second activity refers to the creation of enablers of strategic risk analytics knowledge use through the development of data analytics and digitalization required to overcome barriers or traps in the decision-making process (Hammond *et al.,* 2006). If the data analytics process is not complete and maintains the dynamic of ongoing feedback, it is possible to be caught up in decision-making traps:

- "The mind gives disproportionate weight to the first information it receives."
- "Decision makers display, for example, a strong bias toward alternatives that perpetuate the status quo."
- "...is to make choices in a way that justifies past choices..."
- "The bias leads us to seek out information that supports our existing instinct or point of view while avoiding information that contradicts it."
- "The way a problem is framed can profoundly influence the choices you make."
- "While managers continually make such estimates and forecasts, they rarely get clear feedback about their accuracy."

It is necessary to clarify whether the models will be used for decision automation or for getting insights into problem-solving only. For example, the automation of quantitative solutions in a trading operation can produce issues in a market if everyone is using the same strategy. As Avery (2007) commented, "The report suggests that many of the quantitative portfolio construction techniques are based on the same historical data, such as value premium, size premium, earnings surprise, etc., and that there is a widespread use of standardized factor risk models that would explain why quant funds act in unison." Additionally, the risk modeling process can be affected by a lack of knowledge transfer, thereby producing risky exposure. Some examples of the financial practice show the influence of lack of knowledge transfer in the creation of losses:

- *Expansion*: Growth affected the operations at American Express. Expansion was faster than growth capacity. The knowledge support was minimal (Simons, 1999).
- *Culture*: The Banker Trust expansion reduced the quality of the product to the clients. The reason was cultural pressure. There was a lack of information flow and the products were not well understood. The culture of avoiding bad news reduced the possibility of finding solutions to errors (Simons, 1999).
- *Controls*: Barings Bank's failure is related to the creation of early warning systems and the relationship to a work environment of rewards and recognition. A short-term performance view and internal competition contributed to the bad results (Simons, 1999).
- Lack of understanding of what is happening, the complexity increment, transaction creation, lack of control, information management, and cost as the only important factor to manage reduce the capability to react in difficult and opportune times. This complexity and the cost of knowledge show the need to manage the understanding and use of information rather than information itself (Sutcliffe & Weber, 2003).
- Lack of communication of business values in an understandable way which people can embrace. The identification of off-limits actions was possibly not clear (Simons, 1999).
- Reduced stimulation of a learning system in order to review processes and to discuss the results and adequate diagnostic control systems (Simons, 1999).

Moreover, there are additional factors to take into consideration to supplement the previous list: new workers' mentality, openness to technology, and different communication means, in some cases a silo culture, living at the same time with a larger desire to understand and search for solutions to doubts; new problems with higher complexity and demanding transformation of organization to solve problems that require enterprise-wide answers with appropriate technological support.

The third activity of the process relates to the understanding of flows of data to produce risk knowledge and how to use these flows in risk management. Strategic risk requires a collaboration schema of using knowledge from different sources and disciplines. In practice, there are techniques and tasks to develop in building risk knowledge:

- Application of prediction and classification models (Burnstein *et al.*, 2002) such as financial service technology and knowledge development of the organization.
- Data mining practice as a means to support the customer focus, risk classification, and loss estimation (Hormozi, 2004; Dzinkowski, 2002). The emphasis is on cost of integrating risk analyses, control, and risk policy creation, deployment, and application (Cumming & Hirtle, 2001).
- The emphasis on acquiring knowledge and problem-solving capabilities or on increasing the orientation to people and processes (Edwards *et al.*, 2002).
- Search of a solution for sliced risk management data (McKibben, 2004) and the development of solutions to control risk exposure, data structures to share them with different areas in the problem-solving process.
- Orientation to new technology for data and information management, and for the modeling process (Shaw, 2005).

Limited use of data analytics in strategic risk mitigation is a potential factor to modify the possible adoption and use of solutions based on AI and digitalization. Goovaerts *et al.* (1984) pointed out that an expert in risk analysis is one who decides what data, techniques-/models to use and has the potential to create actions in business process through digitalization and its management evaluation.

Chapter 4

Strategy and Data Analytics Techniques and Technologies

In the three previous chapters, the sequence of creating knowledge and intelligence using data analytics has been presented to mitigate risk and deal with strategic risk using digital transformation. The common idea in these chapters has been to identify how a data analytics process moves step by step to achieve intelligence creation that is integrated to digital transformation in organizations. In this chapter, the emphasis is on how to create actions with regard to the tools used and support the adoption of technologies, to successfully compete in the world.

4.1. Knowledge, Learning, and Acting

Section 3.2.1 presented how the learning system can be developed using the learning molecule model. The aim of this section is to review how to use the means to develop data analytics and to create solutions to improve organizations' intelligence and provide means to act for better strategic risk mitigation and control. The section includes a brief review of cases to explain sequence knowledge, learning, and acting. Figure 4.1 is a summary of how data analytics and AI creation of knowledge will move through organizations in terms of learning and creation of solutions to foster and support actions.

The development path for moving from knowledge creation to learning and acting needs a review of confusing jargon and labels used for

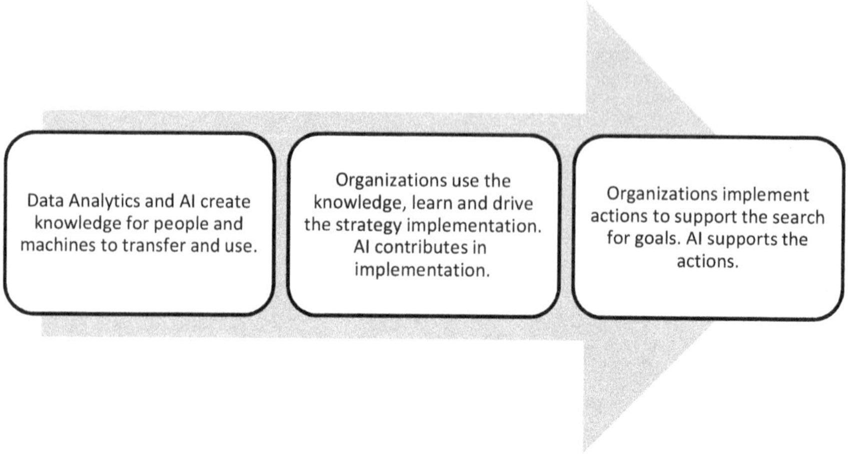

Figure 4.1. Leading the AI support to organizations' actions.

scientific processes, tools, techniques, and technologies. In several cases, there is a problem where people are talking about the same concept, but require time to align their work and focus on the problem. In Exhibit 4.1, there is a sample of issues in identifying the task, tool, and means to use to solve a problem. The value of the analytics work is the solution that is possible to implement, which provides opportunities to organizations to consolidate capabilities and capacity. In some cases, many methods can be used to find relationships among variables if organizations want to evaluate a variation of goals or KPIs or evaluate risks. The confusion is when the selection of methods and techniques is part of the complexity of finding a solution, because it is a major distraction as it will only be adjusted to statistical learning techniques, machine learning techniques, or a mix. The issue is that when assuming a way to solve a problem at a certain acceptable level of accuracy, reliability, and validity, one needs to know what is going to be the next step, what to do with results, if the significant variables to explain variability are going to be the variables that define priority, or if it will be just technical exercise.

To move from knowledge creation to learning, one requires a system as indicated in Section 3.2.1; at this level, one can revisit Ackoff's system definition (Ackoff, 1981): "A system is a set of two or more elements that satisfies the following conditions: The behaviour of each element has an effect on the behaviour of the whole. The behaviour of the elements and their effect on the whole are interdependent. All possible subgroups of

<table>
<tr>
<td>Example: Issues with language used to describe the same concept in machine learning and statistics language.
In statistics:
• Inference
• Estimation
• Discriminant analysis
• Mathematics based / parametric
• Limited data/invent samples
• Variable
In machine learning:
• Induction
• Learning
• Classification/patterns
• Non-parametric/empirical
• All data
• Attribute</td>
<td>Example: Everyone wants to predict, and the possibilities of using models and approaches is extensive, mainly because of overlap of the following:
• Computer science
• Statistics
• Machine learning and data mining
• Operations research
• Business intelligence
• Predictive modeling
• Industrial statistics
• Mathematical optimization
• Actuarial sciences
• HPC. High performance computing
• Operations research
• Six sigma
• Quants in risk management
• Artificial intelligence
• Econometrics
• Data engineering
• Business intelligence
• Data analysis
• Business analytics</td>
</tr>
<tr>
<td>Revising the principles of using analytics learning:
With ideas of learning system requirements/ use, it is possible to integrate principles:
• Appropriate machine learning paradigms use
• A well-posed solution
• Observations from the roots not only tips of icebergs
• Clarity on what society does in science
• Meaning of intelligent in the following sense:
  o To be more intelligent is to deal with constraints
  o To be more intelligent is to make better decisions
• Understanding more some realities like Ackoff
• Ongoing work on defining more problems to solve</td>
<td>Reviewing and following the appropriate paradigms (Carbonell, 1990):
• Inductive paradigm
• Analytic paradigm
• Genetic paradigm
• Connectionist paradigm
Cross-paradigmatic observations possibly fit better for the Learning system in intelligence development:
• Signal–symbol mapping
• Continuous and discrete pattern recognition
• Acquiring new concept descriptions
• Acquiring rules for expert systems
• Enhancing the efficiency of rule-based systems
• Instruction and symbiotic reasoning
• Integrate reasoning architectures</td>
</tr>
</table>

Exhibit 4.1. Possible aspects that create difficulties to integrate knowledge to produce actions when analytics is used.

elements also have the first two properties." Learning is a process with a system that starts with knowledge discovery/creation moving to innovation and actions to intervene in the creation of reality. It is more than adaptation; it is about building reality. Silos of knowledge should be part of the past, and integration and holistic view could be the norm for developing learning systems.

The learning systems in organizations have been explored for many years. Machine learning, statistical learning, and organizational learning emerge from various scientific roots. Each one has a specific jargon, methods, tools, and conceptualization process. However, the purpose is the same: understanding the learning process and how to create valuable knowledge from the learning process. Organizations need to improve computational capacity and discover methods to solve more complex problems to be more intelligent. Organizations need to find the way to use the huge arsenal of methods to strengthen people's action to add value to their work. Learning systems have opportunities and limitations according to the development of statistical, machine, and organizational learning as separated fields. This section concentrates on value creation through knowledge, meaning development, and understanding of improvement to support problem-solving and decision-making processes in organizations.

A dialogue that is now common to human minds and machine "minds" is "I am trying to learn" or "I want to learn": what problem to solve, what framework to use, what method to use to approach a solution, what I have to observe/review, what I need to understand/interpret, and what I could say to complement other solutions and generate actions. There are issues in organizations to connect analytics work and learning. An organization can claim that it learnt what it could not use because of organizational limited view; for example, an organization can use certain scoring methods for risk classification based on parametric approaches while there could potentially be great opportunities to obtain solutions using machine learning that have not been explored. In some cases, regulators do not accept certain calculations because of not using the traditional methods in risk analytics. Another situation is when models and machines are learning but it is not clear if the organization's members are learning. Similarly, one needs to learn what difficulties apply in using, explaining, and accepting a model, for instance, a Markov Chains vs. "Brute Force," to understand changes of status in a credit risk management problem. Moreover, organizations need to be focused on learning;

they cannot learn everything at the same time and they cannot learn from only one point of view.

Dyagilev and Saria (2016) commented, "We propose a novel ranking-based framework for disease severity score learning (DSSL). DSSL exploits the following key observation: while it is challenging for experts to quantify the disease severity at any given time, it is often easy to compare the disease severity at two different times. Extending existing ranking algorithms, DSSL learns a function that maps a vector of patient's measurements to a scalar severity score subject to two constraints." This is an example of an analytics process of creating knowledge through a learning process in a healthcare problem. There two aspects of learning from data: one is about learning in a model and the other is about learning to use methods to provide clues to act in a way that was not possible or known earlier. Another example is what Ustun and Rudin (2016) pointed out: "Scoring systems are linear classification models that only require users to add, subtract and multiply a few small numbers in order to make a prediction. These models are in widespread use by the medical community but are difficult to learn from data because they need to be accurate and sparse, have coprime integer coefficients, and satisfy multiple operational constraints." This comment represents another part of learning to review the creation of actions. The field or knowledge domain can use methods; methods are used in other knowledge domains; and the issues in learning are not about models but about the data to use and the management preparation to be used. Organizational learning starts connecting what is learnt in stages of knowledge creation which will lead to effective and efficiently used actions in solving problems. Ramli *et al.* (2015) pointed out that it is not about a technique, data, or knowledge domain but about a combination of methods that are interdisciplinary, or a combination of intuition and reason, and in particular a combination of techniques, as proposed in this book. "The combined classifiers are support vector machine with k-nearest neighbor, logistic regression with k-nearest neighbor and finally LADTree with k nearest neighbor. These three combined classifiers are tested on 13 chosen macroeconomic indicators which the data is taken from first quarter 1980 to third quarter 2012. The results of this experiment showed that these three different combined classifiers averagely have same higher accuracy and quite comparable. Our proposed method, nearest neighbor tree has the highest area under ROC curve number among these three combined classifiers although in terms of computational time it took longer running times than the others."

There are two approaches to defining learning in order to understand strategic risk. One approach is learning in humans and the other is learning in machines. UNESCO defines learning as follows: "Learning is defined as a process that brings together personal and environmental experiences and influences for acquiring, enriching or modifying one's knowledge, skills, values, attitudes, behaviour and world views. Learning theories develop hypotheses that describe how this process takes place. The scientific study of learning started in earnest at the dawn of the 20th century. The major concepts and theories of learning include behaviorist theories, cognitive psychology, constructivism, social constructivism, experiential learning, multiple intelligence, and situated learning theory and community of practice." The omission of machine learning weakens that definition because, as Mitchell (1997) indicated, learning is about the current situation in society: "A computer program is said to learn from experience E with respect to some class of tasks *T* and performance measure *P*, if its performance at tasks in *T*, as measured by *P*, improves with the experience *E*."

Furthermore, a concept of learning and a learning system look for integration of learning in machines and organizations, using statistical tools (Exhibit 4.2). Any learning process requires a problem definition with good standing, shape, scope, etc. Another aspect is that in the evaluation of models, the technique of learning can have communalities such as evaluation. This evaluation can based on metrics of good classified observations or the way of managing methods to obtain the quality of the fit of models (error measurement). The definition of a learning system is a chain of steps and actions related to the problem, users' needs, solutions, knowledge management process, or the interaction of individuals' learnings (organizational, statistical, and machines).

An outcome of the learning process and action creation is innovation. Innovation is identified as an output of a learning process in this book. Exhibits 4.3 and 4.4 exemplify how in the case of manufacturing innovation is related to the analytics process. Innovation is about products and different types of components of the organization system. It can be in products and at the same time in processes. In particular, in a data analytics process, innovation is about development of new algorithms or mathematical methods to tackle problems; similarly, innovation can be in the way that a technique is used. In any approach of innovation, the purpose can be solving a problem, enhancing previous solutions, and/or creating value. In operations, to be ready for innovation, the demand of aligned

Organizational Learning (Argote, 2013): • "Although learning occurs at different levels of analysis in organizations, the knowledge acquired from learning must be embedded in an organizational repository in order for organizational learning to occur. Learning generally occurs through individuals in organizations." • Argyris (1994) wrote, "Single-loop learning asks a one-dimensional question to elicit a one-dimensional answer… Double loop learning takes an additional step or,… it turns the question back on the questioner."	Von Neumann and Morgenstern (1944) wrote, "There is no point in using exact methods where there is no clarity in the concepts and issues to which they are to be applied." Norbert Wiener (1961) wrote, "The theory of linear prediction and of non-linear prediction both involve some criteria of the goodness of the fit of the prediction. The simplest criterion, although by no means the only usable one, is that of minimizing the mean square of the error. This is used in a particular form in connection with the functionals of the Brownian motion which I employ for the construction of non-linear apparatus,…" Brownian Motion describes by Brown (1827) used by Einstein (1905), Wiener (1961) and Black and Scholes (1973).
Machine Learning (Mitchell, 1997): "The field of machine learning is concerned with the question of how to construct computer programs that automatically improve with experience." "How can we build computer systems that automatically improve with experience, and what are the fundamental laws that govern all learning processes?"	To build the learning system requires one to work on the following: (1) Alignment around the core = problem to solve. The mission is the solution of the problem and its associated problems: technical computational/modeling and steps in the processes of learning, possibly better solution if there is alignment of machine, statistical, organizational learning around the problem. (2) Understand users/use of solutions. There is no evidence that people who make things happen will be interested in the method behind the scenes but there is high interest from the person using the method to interpret/understand what the method is doing. (3) Open the view for searching solutions/to learn. It seems that we could use a lot of knowledge from different sources without waiting for too much time to reinvent solutions. Avoid being prisoners of our paradigms/literature. (4) Enhance the learning chain. Learning process for organizations cannot stop at the machine, statistical, or organizational learning processes in isolation. The construction of a chain of the three learnings is the priority.

Exhibit 4.2. Organizational, machine, and statistical learning.

Statistical learning (James *et al.*, 2013): "Statistical learning refers to a set of tools for modeling and understanding complex datasets. It is a recently developed area in statistics and blends with parallel developments in computer science and, in particular, machine learning. The field encompasses many methods such as the lasso and sparse regression, classification and regression trees, and boosting and support vector machines."	(5) To learn and move through the KM processes, a design of AI and knowledge management systems is required. (6) More and more interdisciplinary people are working in problem-solving, but it is important to talk about the same in equivalent "languages." Possibly, we need to take the time to review and reflect on the three disciplines (machine, statistical, and organizational learning) and their interaction. We need to learn about the "learning process" and how each component connects to the mainstream of creating knowledge.

Exhibit 4.2. (*Continued*)

pieces that need a clear evaluation. For example it can from the definition of quality to the maintenance of reliable and stable business process. Sight Machine (https://sightmachine.com/resources/building-your-foundation-for-digital-transformation/) proposed a process to get digital transformation: "...Apply predictive analysis to deliver advanced notification of impending downtime or defects, and use advanced statistical techniques (such as multivariate regression, factor analysis, decision trees, and clustering) to identify root causes of persistent problems. Potential benefits include increased production, reduced cycle times, and lower scrap rates." In general, a digital transformation like sight machines involve three components of manufacturing transformation: technology infrastructure that includes capacity in analytics, aggregation, connectivity; plant productivity in the sense of defining the new KPIs; and dealing with the value chain internally, observing benchmarks, validating data, and working with factories as part of the portfolio. One component is related to data science, where AI and BI are integrated, from good data to creation of AI models and management of data assets.

As indicated in Exhibit 4.3, digital transformation acts as a strategic risk mitigation strategy in manufacturing. Digitalization captures and manages data with good quality. A wave that hits manufacturing is that data drives

<table>
<tr>
<td>Innovation as a process:
Bruce Posner and Martha E. Mangelsdorf, 12 Essential Innovation Insights MIT Sloan Management Review, Magazine: Fall 2017 Issue Vol 59 No. 1:
• Innovation is not necessarily about new things; it is about new value.
• Challenge competitors by playing a different game.
• Focus on identifying and resolving uncertainties in innovation projects.
• Remember that being first to market is no guarantee of success.
• Let your customers develop your next product.
• Invention is a process of creating new combinations of elements — with results that have a highly skewed distribution.</td>
<td>Bruce Posner and Martha E. Mangelsdorf, 12 Essential Innovation Insights MIT Sloan Management Review, Magazine: Fall 2017 Issue Vol 59 No. 1:
• Understand your options for working with external innovators.
• Create systems and structures that support ongoing innovation.
• Connect the people in your organization who identify new ideas with those who can commercialize them.
• Innovation does not have to entail major breakthroughs; it can also involve making new product development faster and cheaper.
• Make customer communities your allies.
• Do not antagonize your creative people.</td>
</tr>
<tr>
<td>Analytics for innovation in manufacturing:
• Design of goods and services
• Managing quality
• Process and capacity strategy
• Location strategy
• Layout strategy
• Human resources and job design
• Supply chain management
• Inventory management
• Scheduling
• Maintenance

Heizer, Render, Munson, Operations Management, Pearson, 12th Edition, 2016</td>
<td>Defines what is required of operations:
• Product design determines quality, sustainability, and human resources
• Determine the customer's quality expectations
• Establish policies and procedures to identify and achieve that quality
• How is a good or service produced?
• Commit management to specific technology, quality, resources, and investment
• Nearness to customers, suppliers, and talent
• Consider costs, infrastructure, logistics, and government
• Integrate capacity needs, personnel levels, technology, and inventory
• Determine the efficient flow of materials, people, and information</td>
</tr>
</table>

Exhibit 4.3. Analytics for manufacturing and its innovation process.

<table>
<tr><td></td><td>• Recruit, motivate, and retain personnel with the required talent and skills
• Pinpoint the integral and expensive part of the total system design
• Integrate supply chain into the firm's strategy
• Determine what is to be purchased, from whom, and under what conditions
• Inventory ordering and holding decisions
• Optimize considering customer satisfaction, supplier capability, and production schedules
• Determine and implement intermediate- and short-term schedules
• Utilize personnel and facilities while meeting customer demands
• Consider facility capacity, production demands, and personnel
• Maintain a reliable and stable processes</td></tr>
<tr><td>Analytics for innovation in manufacturing
Sight machine as the data foundation for manufacturing indicates the following:
• "…data and analytics can help tremendously in improving operational efficiencies and business processes, and in transforming business models."
• "…they're realizing that as manufacturing becomes more networked and takes on the characteristics of a system, just like in the virtual world, the key to making the system effective and being strategic about it is the data that is generated in the system."
How Big Data and Analytics Can Transform Manufacturing September 21 2017 Knowledge @ Wharton</td><td>"Many companies are trying to build do-it-yourself solutions, ... The major industrial companies such as GE and Siemens have invested, literally, billions of dollars in this opportunity. And then, the largest software companies, the cloud companies, the business process software companies, they're all funding and developing initiatives to provide insight."
"Previously, if you wanted to understand how the same machine is performing in two different plants …small percentage gains in efficiency can be huge dollars at scale."
"Today, we can put up a screen that shows the actual performance and the reasons for variation. In some cases, operators might be doing things differently. In other cases, aspects of the process itself are different."
How Big Data and Analytics Can Transform Manufacturing, September 21 2017 Knowledge @ Wharton</td></tr>
</table>

Exhibit 4.3. (*Continued*)

what the plant is going to be, how predictions will be used, optimization and how all indicators will be controlled under a continue observation to reduce variability of targets. The process for digital transformation creates the need for redefinition/recreation of products and modification of business models, including data products, such as the reports presented in Section 3.3. There

Analytics for innovation in manufacturing Vijay Govindarajan and Jeffrey R. Immelt, The Only Way Manufacturers Can Survive, MIT Sloan Management School, Spring 2019 Issue Opinion & Analysis March 12, 2019: "Digital transformation is no longer optional for industrial companies. The problem is it's really, really hard." "We're both convinced that executing a digital transformation is not only the most complex but also the most critical challenge that any manufacturer faces today." "A digital transformation entails reimagining products and services as digitally enabled assets; generating new value from the interconnection of physical and digital assets through data; and creating ecosystems to make that possible." "The CIO, whose knowledge base is inward-focused, must concentrate on increasing productivity inside the company. The CDO, who focuses on external markets, should worry about customer productivity. Keeping those two roles separate is critical for success; combining them will ensure that one of the two roles becomes ineffective."	Govindarajan and Immelt indicated sensors to collect and analyze user data continuously and periodically. Analyzing data helps in "improving the performance and reliability of machines in real time, as well as the efficiency of the systems that link them, offering the opportunity to continually boost customers' productivity." Organizations providing AI - digital transformation support to manufacturing: **Uptake, Oracle-Opower, Tendril Networks, Onzo, Aclara Technologies, and Flutura** "Three ideas for success: Business models eat technology for breakfast - A digital transformation is about changing business models — create and capture new value Digital operations should be distinct but linked CEOs must not be scared to lead." "First, they can go the software-as-a-service route and sell subscriptions and licenses for the software products they develop in order to analyze the data from and refine the performance of their machines." "Second, digital-industrial companies can offer "success as a service" through guaranteed customer outcomes — safety, speed, fuel efficiency, zero operator errors, no unscheduled downtime."

Exhibit 4.4. Reality and dreams in the use of analytics do not match.

Dreams Everything is • Automated • Data driven • IoT related • At minimum cost • With less people • With more control • With more profits • …	**Reality** • No clear path for data-driven organizations • No everyone is a data scientist/a lot of cleaners/cleansers and reporters • The work does not finish with good models • The complexity grows very fast; thousands of packages in R and Python • Use of data / jumping to conclusions just because of volume • No contextualization/understanding • Reduced/limited problem-solving capacity/ not having the end in mind
From dreams to reality Companies Are Failing in Their Efforts to Become Data-Driven, Randy Bean, Thomas H. Davenport February 5 2019: • 72% of survey participants report that they have yet to forge a data culture. • 69% report that they have not created a data-driven organization. • 53% state that they are not yet treating data as a business asset. • 52% admit that they are not competing on data and analytics. • Further, the percentage of firms identifying themselves as being data-driven has declined in each of the past 3 years – from 37.1% in 2017 to 32.4% in 2018 to 31.0% in 2019.	Demystify Analytics To Think About • Analytics is for a company of any size • Analytics is for any business • Analytics is about analytics thinking, analytics reasoning, and analytics applications But analytics is not • Only crunching numbers • Only modeling • Pushing buttons • Unplanned • A force • A static process • A process that finishes • About professionals only

Exhibit 4.4. (*Continued*)

are plenty of opportunities and possibilities; however, dreams and reality do not necessarily match. Organizations show year by year the gaps between what they achieved versus what they wanted. In some cases, it is a problem of expectations, in others, it is that the data available are not usable and require a lot of prior work. An example is the transition of data in accounting ledgers and information systems to be used as statistical data for forecasting of certain variables. Accounting data need to be transformed as labels that are well defined and ranges of values like sales cannot be

<table>
<tr>
<td>From IoT to AoT
• Perform analytics on IoT
• Barriers to overcome:
o Define priorities/problems and value
o Gathering data sensors
o Managing data — from quality to security
o Identify and implement the analytics process
o Maintenance and improvement</td>
<td>Bias in decision-making
• Overconfidence
• Emotion risk
• Loss aversion
• Confirmation Bias
• Indecisions or avoidance
• Counterintuitive recommendations

Bias from analytics
• Establish a data-driven decision culture
• Review the decision models
• Enforce presentation guidelines
• Decision-making guidelines
• Establish a learning by doing culture</td>
</tr>
<tr>
<td>"If the analysis is window-dressing, do not waste your time on improving it. If your brother has already chosen the woman he will marry, your analysis of the match may not be valuable. If your analysis does not support a call to action (which includes a "stay the course" action), think again about why you produced it." Saxena and Srinivasan, Business Analytics, page 77.</td>
<td>Big Data Analytics for Smart Manufacturing: Case Studies in Semiconductor Manufacturing James Moyne and Jimmy Iskandar, MDPI, Processes:
• Integration with the supply chain network
• Improved use of cyber–physical systems (CPS)
• Incorporating the simulation space and the concepts of virtual factory and digital twin
• Leveraging big data architecture infrastructures
• Leveraging advanced analytics
• Reliance on a knowledge network Classification
• Next-generation fault detection and classification
• Predictive maintenance (PdM)</td>
</tr>
<tr>
<td colspan="2">• Factories of the future
European Commission summarized the following:
"The Hyperconnected Factories pathway: towards networked enterprises in complex, dynamic supply chains and value networks."
• "Autonomous Smart Factories pathway: towards optimized and sustainable manufacturing including advanced human-in-the-loop workspaces."
• "Collaborative Product-Service Factories pathway: towards data-driven product-service engineering in knowledge intensive factories."</td>
</tr>
</table>

Exhibit 4.5. Analytics without actions does not create value.

negative; in terms of accounting, it could a net value, real sales, and returns, but statistically speaking both real sales and returns are needed in a time series analysis. In general, the question of what analytics is and what it is not appears and several resources will be involved (see Exhibit 4.5).

Cases to review: Jeffrey D. Camm, Prescriptive analysis in manufacturing to boost profitability, March 3, 2019 in Manufacturing: "Is everything in your operations as connected as it could be? How would investing in sensors and/or smart tags in various stages of your operations provide data that could be leveraged to take advantage of prescriptive analytics?" "Is it possible to make your product smarter to create new offer/service? John Deere and aircraft engine manufacturer GE Aviation sensors for helping customers better manage their equipment." "Sensors and AI could be used for predicting and then scheduling preventive maintenance of the machinery…adjustment to the machine in real time based on quality control data."	Dave Oswil, Autonomous Systems: Big data in your products, services and operations, Published Online: Analytics (2018): "One of the first steps in the development of an automated system is to select a scalable tool that can easily provide access to a wide variety of systems and formats used to store and manage big data sets." "After the data is collected and aggregated, data scientists and engineers must interpret and transform that data into some form of actionable insight."
Corporate profile: Data science at Monsanto Shrikant Jarugumilli, Published Online: Analytics (2018): "We have applied machine-learning algorithms to transform our plant breeding pipeline by leveraging 15 years of data from a corn R&D pipeline to move early product testing from the field to the lab, which is helping our researchers more precisely predict how thousands of seeds will perform in the field." "Monsanto's Internet of Things (IoT) platform collects data from sensors deployed in fields, on various equipment, and on machinery within processing facilities to provide a high volume and variety of data."	Network Design Decisions: Strengthening global supply chains Chris Gordon Published Online: Analytics (2018): "Research carried out by Supply Chain Insights and commissioned by AIMMS shows that 72 percent of companies have a network design process in place, with 35 percent of them using in-house technologies. However, only 19 percent of these respondents rate their process as very effective, and 65 percent of them are using spreadsheets to sustain the process." "As a best practice, supply chain teams should look for tools that: • include prescriptive analytics capabilities which allow them to model their network, quickly and easily evaluate scenarios, and make contingency plans when things change or go wrong;

Exhibit 4.6. Cases of data transformation in manufacturing.

"Monsanto leverages a variety of optimization and simulation techniques to increase the efficiency of operational activities and drive innovations and inventions throughout the company. These applications can be classified into two categories: planning for our facilities and planning for our field operations." "Strong support from leadership and cross-functional collaboration among domain experts from business units, data scientists and IT teams are enabling these successful outcomes across the company."	• provide access to the model logic, so they can understand what's behind the answers; • allow for data clarity and data sharing for other supply chain needs; • do not require the constant intervention of specialists to run; and provide a realistic path to train and self-enable end (business) users."
Matt Sias Greg Noble Pooja Singh, Advanced analytics at Kroger, Published Online: Analytics (2018): "Kroger has the largest deployment of the ZigBee protocol mesh network throughout its stores with more than 50,000 access points, and Kroger continues to develop new sensors and integration points that allow its associates to be more customer-centric, focusing their time on more value-added tasks." "Temperature monitoring R&D was able to design a temperature monitoring tag that allowed Kroger to autonomously measure every cold bin in the store every 15 minutes with a higher degree of accuracy." "Kroger's loyalty program has been an industry leader for more than a decade and highlights the largest source of highly advanced analytical talent in the company, which is wholly-owned subsidiary 84.51°."	OpenText, 6 advantages of using analytics in manufacturing. Capitalize on Industry 4.0: • Improve new product development • Enhance customer experience • Improve operations to boost profitability • Extend existing product lines • Automate repetitive human processes • Volume, business custom metrics

Exhibit 4.6. *(Continued)*

In digital transformation and transition of innovation in manufacturing, IoT is a resource to use. What is required in the transformation is to obtain Analytics of Thing (AoT); this means gathering data but making the data say something that guides the organization. It is part of AoT creation to

Organizations in manufacturing need to embed the analytics system in the operational information systems and decision management systems.
You cannot do everything at the same time — Build by blocks.
"All models are wrong but some are useful" (Box, 1976) — The process.
"The only source of Knowledge is Experience" Albert Einstein — The Learning and Knowledge application process.
"I have not failed. I've just found 10,000 ways that won't work" Thomas Edison — Documentation, adaptation and adoption.
"If you torture the data long enough, it will confess" Ronald H. Coase, Essays on Economics and Economists, 1994. Work with a clear analytics mind.
"Another brick in the wall" — Pink Floyd, 1979. Be committed to digital transformation

Exhibit 4.7. A brief of what is in the transition from data analytics to actions.

avoid bias or confusion, for example, thinking that analytics is only for big companies and investments of a high degree. Nevertheless, barriers to overcome appear to implement smart manufacturing visions such as priorities definition and bias in decision-making that can come from analytics.

Manufacturing innovation, in the direction of digital transformation, is used in diverse fields. According to Rodriguez (2017), there are examples of using the analytics process in small organizations in Latin America and emergent economies. Human resource areas in organizations need to move through a data analytics process, leading digital transformation; however, one common issue in other transformation framework implementations is the crucial involvement and support of management; without it, the barriers to overcome grow and limit possibilities. Exhibit 4.6 shows examples from Monsanto, Kroger, OpenText, CE, and John Deere.

Exhibit 4.7 suggests a systematic approach to digital transformation, defining what to look for and try reviewing results in each step, following the data analytics process with care, knowing that bad data will produce anything that is likely not good.

The next section presents techniques, technologies, and their connection with problems and questions to solve and answer. As mentioned in Chapter 3, the analytics process is under ongoing feedback, with back-and-forth steps that need to provide appropriate models to answer questions according to data availability, the capacity to implement, and cost.

4.2. Statistical and Machine Learning Strategies to Convert Data into Valuable Actions

This section describes concepts of the integration among data analytics, artificial intelligence, and risk management. This section covers general concepts about modeling and its potential use, and for more details on the models, refer to Risk Analytics by Rodriguez (2023). The analytics process applied to reinforce risk management development is a means of supporting current and future smart organizations to deal with uncertainty and to create dynamic sustainable and competitive advantages in the market. In general, risk management is a matter for all types of organizations. Risk is inherent in any business. Risk is the name of the game. All businesses are taking risks and organizations are always exposed to risks, as any activity creates exposure. This means risk is part of the definition of business; it is part of the operation of any organization because at the end any organization has to prepare to deal with possible outcomes that can be as expected or not.

This section has six subsections to understand how techniques of statistical and machine learning plus basic performance models can be used to build intelligence: first, descriptive analytics; second, descriptions including time; third, tools for evaluation, financial, scenarios, simulation, and optimization; fourth, creating intelligence through data analytics; fifth, cases in education; and sixth, managing models. These concepts are framed by risk analytics. Risk analytics as a way to use statistical and machine learning to convert data into actionable knowledge that mitigates risk is not only for financial organizations but also for other organizations. The lack of an integral view reduces the possibilities of using or reusing knowledge that has been created. Nowadays, organizations are measuring multiple dimensions of the business, including acting like good citizens in society. This measurement is related to strategic risk assessment, and evaluation of reputation is part of the analytics process. Examples involve gathering data and keeping indicators to evaluate changes in the perception of the brand name in the market. Based on the previous fundamental points, the next paragraphs will describe models that are used in risk analytics to create knowledge. The explanations start with descriptive statistics (Exhibits 4.8–4.10) as a way to understand what happened and is happening in the present according to the problem.

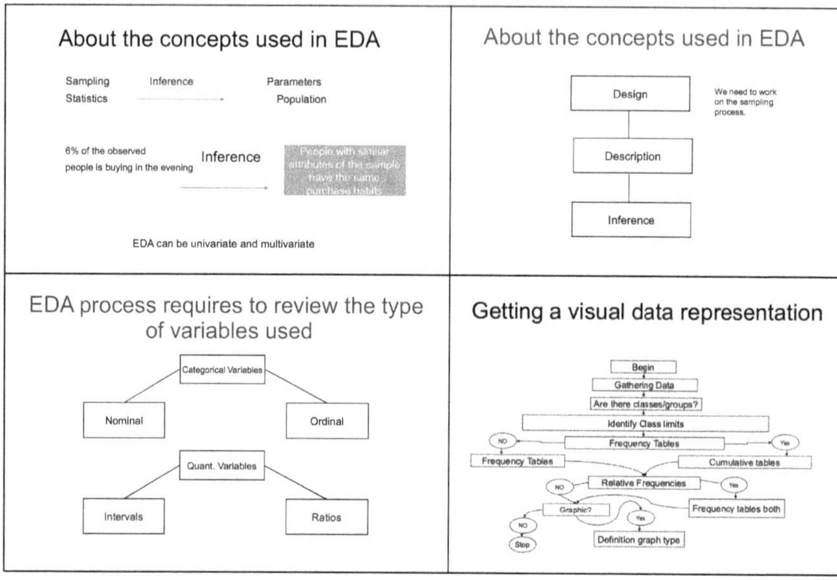

Exhibit 4.8. Type of data and descriptive ideas to support inference.

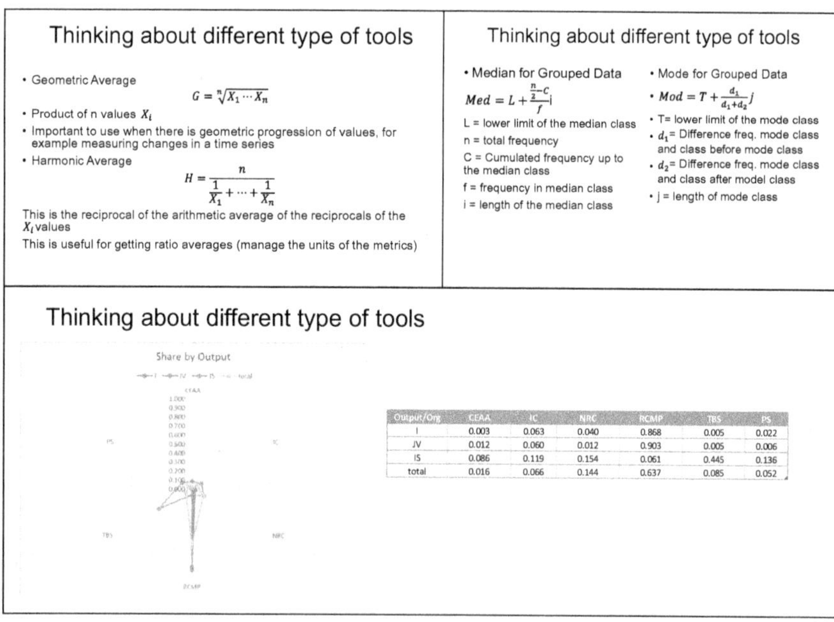

Exhibit 4.9. Examples of descriptions with metrics and graphics.

Different tools describing data Measures of Central Tendency? • Representation of values for an analytics study. • Big questions that appear are related to comparing means from different groups. • Another point is to find dimensions/units as explained in the metrics section. • Important: We have special averages in situations where data are studied. For example, it is a common error to see people calculating arithmetic average of growth rates instead of geometrical average. Another case is the Harmonic average for ratios or reciprocal values.	Some points to keep in mind: outliers, metrics, etc.: • Outlier is only one piece of the problems when we work with data. What about blanks, zeros, etc.? • When are mean, mode, and media equal? • It is important to remember that variance can be relative to any measure of mean, median, and mode. • It is important to see the effect on the histogram. • This is a very common issue to solve in analytics. • Many models are based on the assumption of normality and we need to test it.
Some points to keep in mind: outliers, metrics, etc.: • An error that is observed very often is about comparison of metrics. Two groups can be dissimilar even if the difference in the means is small. The tests have to be performed. It is important to remember the concept of significance. The same as the differentiation to make in statistics when studying "things" related to the mean or to proportions (Sampling for example). • A big issue and cause for concern is that cause–effect is a totally different problem. This is a hot topic in analytics. Models can be affected by outliers, and the definition of outlier is not clear. Most of the cases are a process involving two steps: the quantitative identification of outlier candidates and a qualitative review of the characteristic of the point considered outlier.	Need for more statistics-related tools: • Time series needs special treatment; there are many different indicators of behavior. • Another point is that one needs to be very careful with the kind of data that are compared. Does this mean, for example, that dollars are affected by inflation?

Exhibit 4.10. Describing data, centers, and dispersion.

4.2.1 *Starting with descriptive analytics*

As mentioned in Chapter 3, risk indicators can be created just by observation of variations in the targets of organizations' plans and strategies. However, a better practice is when organizations create indicators that are not only univariate but also multivariate, mainly in strategic risk. The reason is that variations of KPIs or any metric could be caused by several types of factors that act together to produce changes in the expected results of the metrics. Analytics methods can support the creation of better risk indicators through a measurement system that combines data, technology, models, and people. Models are representations of reality, and the outcomes of those models are part of the proposed insights/knowledge used to define actions in organizations. Risk models produce risk indicators and risk indicators can be studied by risk models as well, as it is the case of time series. As mentioned earlier, the analytics process starts with a descriptive process that studies data samples and looks for inference or generalizations, and those descriptions discover important observations that can be converted into metrics, evaluations, goals, etc., after an analytics process. Working in descriptions will depend on types of variables and types of data, i.e., quantitative, qualitative, continuous, and discrete. Description of data will support inference (Exhibit 4.8).

The EDA guides the search of metrics from samples by evaluating if there is a center of data represented by an average, mode, or median or all of them. EDA will guide to imaging the type distribution of data variables and to guide its understanding about skewness or any other statistical moment. What is important to keep in mind is to clarify which metrics are applicable to certain type of problems. For example, a geometric average can be better for geometric series like interest rate calculations, or depending how data have been obtained, i.e., grouped or ungrouped. The same graphics can be just a representation of the raw data variable by variable or something that includes relationships among variables or how several variables can be compared (Exhibit 4.9). Moreover, a selection of visual components and how they can be represented will be part of the understanding of type of data.

The construction of metrics in statistics begins with a search for a value that can represent a variable, for example, the center and how dispersed the values that the variables take can be. At the same time, one needs to identify what potential values are not possible for a variable to take and then figure out how to add techniques to gain better understanding of the results

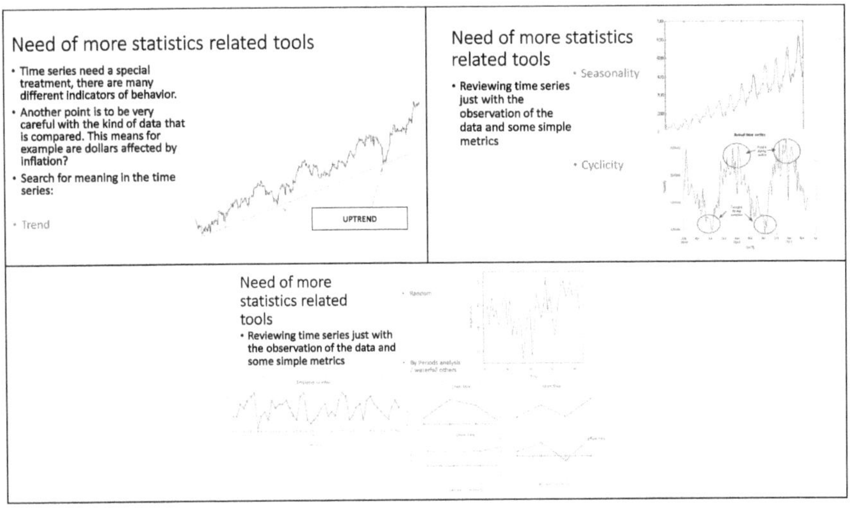

Exhibit 4.11. Thinking involved in studying data, metrics, and results through time.

of the exploration and description of data (Exhibit 4.10). The process of analyzing a variable starts with locating a center, mean, median, mode, and evaluating dispersion, with variance, standard deviation, or interquartile ranges. The measurement can be simplified to have a high probability of falling in the narrowest interval where the parameter of interest (metric target) estimation belongs. Outliers can be values outside the three standard deviations, but the analyst cannot delete them from the original data; they are needed to review if data belong to other populations, if they are errors, or if the value is showing another group in the population.

4.2.2 *Descriptions including time*

Additionally, simple metrics measured many times are converted in a time series that need to be studied using the time series techniques. In data analytics, individual results obtained during multiple periods are new data for time series analysis.

Time is involved in the description of data (Exhibit 4.11); time is a way to include an index in data that is going to be used in the analysis and will be a means to involve stochastic processes or several random variables in the same analytics process. Prediction is something that organizations would like to do very well based on the assumption that the identification of patterns from the past can identify what could happen in the future. In risk management, the main purpose is to find a way to build the organization based on the results of the assessment. Organizations are looking to provide the best assessment of what will happen in the future. The purpose is to produce new insights that will be converted into better actions. Time series analysis can help in this purpose.

Systems modeling for econometric data is done in three parts: econometric modeling, simulation, and forecasting. Often, these tasks are performed sequentially. A model is fitted to the data, then simulated with historical data, and finally used for forecasting. Models for estimation can consist of a single equation or a system of equations; they can be linear, nonlinear, or ordinary differential equations; they can require restrictions on parameters. Time series are any univariate or multivariate data collected over time. Risk analysts can estimate relationships and produce forecasts that make use of information in past values, independent or explanatory variables, and indicator or dummy variables. In addition, the use of model and prediction through models considers levels of variance close to the time of observation. It is the case of the autoregressive conditional heteroskedastic (ARCH) model or its generalizations (GARCH). Additional tools provide regression analysis for linear models with distributed lags and time series cross-sectional regression analysis for panel data. Analysts can perform multiple regressions in the presence of serially correlated error terms, fit models that allow for an error term generated by an autoregressive integrated moving-average (ARIMA) process, or use spectral analysis to decompose a series into cyclical components or perform frequency domain tests.

A panel procedure analyzes a class of linear econometric models that commonly arise when time series and cross-sectional data are combined. The panel procedure analyzes panel datasets that consist of multiple time series observations on each of several individuals or cross-sectional units. The performance of any estimation procedure for the model regression parameters depends on the statistical characteristics of the error components in the model. The panel procedure estimates the regression parameters in the preceding model under several common error structures, including one- and two-way fixed and random effects. The following is a summary of an analysis of generated metrics for forecast and time series understanding:

- A crucial task is to develop metrics and its follow up.
- It is essential to move basic variance analyses of the indicators to their prediction.

- On metrics, results are kept and organized as new data.
- It follows the same time as other data.
- With regard to interpretation, in many cases it will be related to variability.
- Variability is a way to express risk.

Longitudinal and panel data provide the capacity to study data in many cases under time constraints with one observation of all data points (units of analysis/subjects) or with multiple ones. Methods and tools involving time are key in the strategic risk management analysis. A crucial task is to define risk analysis based on the historical results of the key performance and risk indicators. It is important to review if the results/changes are related to changes in factors/strategies through time. In general, "Longitudinal data analysis represents a marriage of regression and time series analysis. As with many regression data sets, longitudinal data are composed of a cross-section of subjects. Unlike regression data, with longitudinal data we observe subjects over time. Unlike time series data, with longitudinal data we observe many subjects" (Frees, 2004, Longitudinal and Panel Data: Analysis and Applications for the Social Science, Cambridge University Press).

As an illustration of how to create panel analysis means, the following statements (Exhibit 4.12) use the cost function data from Greene (1990) to estimate the variance components model. The variable PRODUCTION is the log of output in millions of kilowatt-hours and COST is the log of cost in millions of dollars. Refer to Greene (1990) for details; Exhibit 4.12 is an example in SAS.

4.2.3 *Tools for evaluation, financial, scenarios, simulation, and optimization*

Another type of model used in strategic risk that will provide answers in the measurement process is one that combines deterministic and stochastic interest theory. Nominal interest rate: the growth rate of the money (R) Real interest rate: growth rate of the purchasing power (r) i is the inflation rate

$$1+r=\frac{1+R}{1+i}$$

Expected rate of return is the probability weighted average of the rates of return in all scenarios.

C_{it} = Intercept + $P_{it} + v_i + e_t + \varepsilon_{it}$ $\quad i = \text{I}, \ldots, N; t = \text{I}, \ldots, T$

```
data greene;
input firm year production cost @@; datalines;

1 1955  5.36598  1.14867  1 1960  6.03787  1.45185
1 1965  6.37673  1.52257  1 1970  6.93245  1.76627
2 1955  6.54535  1.35041  2 1960  6.69827  1.71109
2 1965  7.40245  2.09519  2 1970  7.82644  2.39480
```

where C_{it} and P_{it} represent the cost and production, and v_i, e_t, and ε_{it} and are the cross-sectional, time series, and error variance components, respectively. If it is assumed that the time and cross-sectional effects are random, the analyst is left with four possible estimators for the variance components. And selecting Fuller-Battese. Using SAS, the following statements fit a model:

```
proc sort data=greene;
by firm year;
run;
proc panel data=greene;
model cost = production/rantwo vcomp = fb; id firm year;
run;
```

Exhibit 4.12. Example of longitudinal analysis.

$E(r) = \Sigma_n p(k)r(k)$, k represents the scenario index and there are considerations of rates to use and to compare as the case of risk-free rate is a rate that is possible to gain in free risk assets T-Bills. A Risk Premium is the difference between the holding period return (HPR) on an index stock fund and the risk-free rate.

A point to bring to the analysis of strategic risk and learning process is that risk management needs to consider the positive and negative aspects of the organization's performance. This means the construction of risk metrics/indicators should keep a positive outlook of the organization as well. Metrics can be related to fitting loss distributions, probability distributions of the items that are measured, identifying order statistics, and percentiles: sampled values in order minimum, maximum, first quartile, median, etc., working with percentiles of the loss distribution VAR, CVAR, and other Moments of a loss distribution. Andersen (2008) explained that risk management has been focused on identifying and managing negative component risk events and it should be combined with the search for new business opportunities in order to build solid competitive advantages. Andersen's (2008) conclusion is, "Based on a large cross-sectional sample, the study demonstrates that the ability of integrative risk management capabilities to reduce earnings variability in the face of diverse economic, operational and strategic risks is associated with superior economic performance. The positive performance relationships of such a holistic approach to risk management are more pronounced among firms operating in knowledge-intensive industries and companies emphasizing investment in research and development. Hence, the evidence is consistent with the proposition that effective risk management encourages valuable firm-specific investment by essential stakeholders and allows the firm to exploit opportunities as well as guard against downside exposures."

As an example of metrics used on portfolios in organizations is VAR and CVAR. Best (1998) pointed out "value at risk is the maximum amount of money that may be lost on a portfolio over a given period of time, with a given level of confidence. VAR is typically calculated for one day tie period — known as the holding period — and is often calculated with 95% confidence. 95% confidence means that there is (on average) a 95% chance of the loss on the portfolio being lower than the VAR calculated." Sarykalin *et al.* (2008) state, "Conditional value-at-risk (CVaR), introduced by Rockafellar and Uryasev (2000), is a popular tool for managing risk. CVaR approximately (or exactly, under certain conditions) equals the average of some percentage of the worst-case loss scenarios. CVaR risk measure is similar to the value-at-risk (VaR) risk measure, which is a percentile of a loss distribution … For random variables with continuous distribution functions, CVaRα(X) equals the conditional expectation of X subject to $X \geq$ VaRα(X)."

In terms of reviewing possible cash flow results, a rule is that present values and future values are different because of the way that money costs in time and how the use of resources and generation of revenues can depend on time as well. In that search of describing future cash flows, a concept of **expected monetary value** is used as an evaluation system and it assumes that the possible payments that can be obtained by following a decision are known, and so are the probabilities of the different states in which it can be incurred and over which the decision cannot have control, for example, whether or not a market is favorable. For each of the alternatives, the possible payments are weighted by the probability of occurrence of the states of nature or events that may occur, and all partial results are summed to obtain a final result for each alternative. The expression is the weighting of payments by the probability of the occurrence of each of the alternatives:

$$\text{VME} = \sum_{i=1}^{n} A_i P_i$$

i: It is the number of payments.

A_i: It is the value of the payment. P_i: It is the probability of payment that is calculated for each alternative.

A similar approach is the expected value with perfect information where the best alternative is chosen in each event and multiplied by probability. Of the event occurrence,

$$\text{VEIP} = \sum_{i=1}^{k} M_i P_i$$

M_i: It is the best alternative in each state or event. P_i: It is the probability of events.

In the case of no perfect information, the adjustment is VESIP = VEIP − Maximum VME. In any case, a way to maximize the expected monetary value is to minimize the expected opportunity loss. The minimum opportunity loss value is found when the opportunity loss table is constructed, and the expected value is calculated. An opportunity loss table is build using the opportunity cost of not choosing the best alternative of the states, and the value of the expected loss is calculated by making the product of the loss values in each state by its corresponding probability and then performing the sum of the those products by each of the alternatives. Another approach is to use sensitivity analysis by using parameter change and identification of possible outcomes. Moreover, decision theory and decision trees are used following a structure of the problem in terms of decision nodes and event nodes that are connected by arches, representing the options that go into the decision. This gives a tree representation. Then, expected monetary values are calculated, starting from the terminal nodes inward, from the right of the tree to the root node, choosing the branch with the best expected monetary value, which is the least. In the case of projects in which conditions are assumed to be deterministic and there are no changes in expected flows, the net present value is used. This is the discount of future flows at the opportunity interest rate and the sum of these values, after taking the sign into account. Here, the flows are assumed to be true and the number of periods is known:

$$\text{VPN}(i) = \sum_{k=0}^{n} \frac{A_k}{(1+i)^k}$$

where i is the opportunity interest rate. $k = 0, \ldots, n$ periods if assumed to include the initial value. A_k = value of inflows and outflows. A decision is given by the highest net present value (NPV). Another metric is the internal rate of return, that is, the value of the rate that makes it possible for the VPN to be equal to zero. It has the possibility of having several values depending on the polynomial and must focus on deciding which value makes sense:

Value of i such that VPN(i) = 0, this is:

$$\sum_{k=0}^{n} \frac{A_k}{(1+i)^k} = 0$$

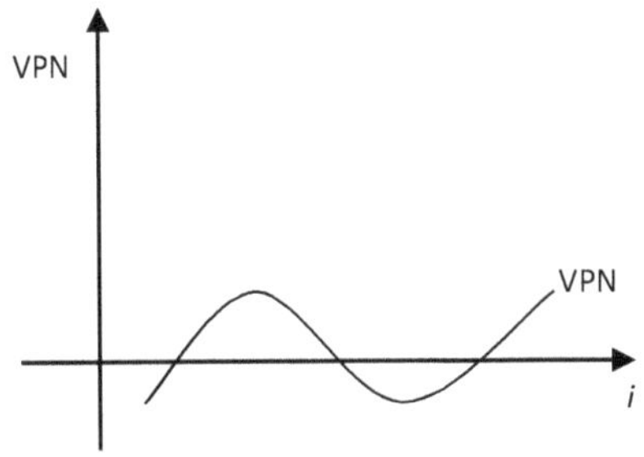

If there is only one i^*, the decision is given by the one that exceeds the opportunity interest rate.

If there are several *i's* that meet this equation, it is necessary to define a flow of an input and an output and study the true profitability of the project. The net present value at the opportunity interest rate should also be studied to decide. True profitability is calculated as the result of the internal rate of return analysis of a simplified flow after leaving only the initial value and the other movements put in the future value at the end of the analysis period, using the opportunity interest rate.

As a mix of the abovementioned issue, the metric generated by the annual equivalent cost appears that is to convert the net present value (NPV) into an annuity, an annuity that equalizes cash flows in time:

$$\text{EAC}(i) = \text{VPN}(i) \times \left[\frac{i(1+i)^n}{(1+i)^n - 1} \right]$$

The decision is given in the order in which the *EAC* is smaller compared to the indicator in each of the projects. Another approach is incremental analysis, used in the case in which the sort of project is required with increasing amounts of investment by analyzing the additional values required in each case. The differences are taken; if the projects are *A*, *B*, and *C*, the differences will be (*B* – *A*), (*C* – *A*), and (*B* – *C*), with the one with the highest internal profitability indicating where it will be better to invest, because if the rate of (*B* – *A*) is higher than the opportunity interest rate, *B* will be preferable to *A*. If it is necessary to analyze another project that requires greater investment, a comparison will be given with the one that is left as best when making each choice. For example, if *B* was better than *A*, a project requiring additional investment will be compared to *B*. They will be sorted according to differences.

In the case where the cash flows are random, the concept of probable present value is established when the future flows of the project or the values that are expected to be received are considered random variables and each one has a distribution that defines its possible outcome. If it were a single payment, the probable present value would be the value that would be expected in the future, discounted at the interest rate that is assumed appropriate, multiplied by the probability that the payment event will occur. If there are several flows that are generated and the analyst requires a net value, the probable discount will be made and all those flows that have taken place during the analyzed period will be added. If the type of behavior that a payment has in a period were discovered, its probability of occurrence could be obtained. The weighted and discounted flow differs from the previous ones in the concept of considering the discount with a predefined interest rate. Of course, the number of payments that are contemplated in the analysis of a project or the time in which the payment is made can also be presented as random. In the case of credit, the situation of the present value of a flow of money that is expected to be received for the payments that the client makes has to be considered in this category since the possibility of payment, or not, must be contemplated.

In case the interest rate is considered stochastic, the main approach is to study the VPN distribution and to work with its moments to make decisions. This means considering interest rate as a random variable for which the discount is modified according to the stochastic behavior of the interest rate. Rates can be considered independent or time dependent. From these conditions, the treatment will be different. A case is when the term used for discount $(1 + i_t)$ follows a lognormal distribution. If interest rates are assumed to be independent, t is an indicator of periods ($t = 1, 2, 3, \ldots,$ n), where $E(i_t) = i$ expected value of the discount rates i_t and variance $\text{var}(i_t) = s^2$. It is possible to find the expected values of the cumulative value of a monetary unit at the end of n periods, where i_t are identically distributed with mean i. It turns out that the expected value of the accumulated value is equivalent to the accumulated value at the expected interest rate:

$$E\left[(1+i_1)+(1+i_2)\ldots(1+i_n)\right]=\prod_{t=1}^{n}E(1+i_t)=(1+i)^n$$

Also, the variance is

$\text{var}\,[(1 + i_1)(1 + i_2), \ldots, (1 + i_n)] = (1 + 2i + i^2 + s^2)^n - (1 + i)^{2n}$ with i equal to an average.

That is, i is different from the one used before, since the probability distribution of $(1 + i_t)$ is lognormal and

$$E(1+i_t)=e^{\mu+\sigma^2/2}$$

Risk measurements involve different statistical methodologies that operate appropriately both to assess variations and identify the maximum and minimum levels associated with these changes. Likewise, risk factors can be studied around the level of exposure that an entity has in a portfolio. The study of the portfolio, whatever it may be, can be helped by models such as value at risk (VAR) as well, which requires in different cases the knowledge of the prices of the assets studied. In the case of credit, a particular situation arises, because although the portfolio presents variables such as destination, term, and amounts, which are usually fully identified and are different, the price ends up being equivalent under each modality, just as the market maintains similar prices. This affects the use of VAR in the credit portfolio; however, deregulation and the competitive level and the condition of segmentation closest to each client can vary the horizon and begin with the development of pricing policies that express differentiation in the portfolio.

Another important factor is measured by considering history, which can lead to the development of prospective working models. Market conditions can be simulated and elements that may affect the future development of the portfolio can be established. You can also use graphical representation methodologies that express classification, such as regression and classification trees. In the particular case of financial asset portfolio risk, the identification of risk is around the following variables:

- Market.
- Variation — Volatility.
- Liquidity.
- Reinvestment.
- Performance indicators.
- Operation.
- Legislation.
- Counterpart.
- Decision — Information.

These represent the conditions in which the portfolio will behave. Obviously, when indexes or measurements are generated, the structuring of indicators appears over time, which leads to the study of the variation of the indicators themselves.

A. *Duration:* $R_1, \ldots, R_n$ are payments at times 1, 2, … , *n*, and the duration calculation is a weighted.

$$D = \frac{\sum_{t=1}^{n} t v^t R_t}{\sum_{t=1}^{n} v^t R_t}$$

average of the payment times where the weights are the present values of each of the payments.

B. *Volatility*: *is the negative ratio between* the first derivative of the present value of future cash flows R_t to the present value of those cash flows. The interest rate can be in a first stage of analysis considering determinants and then considering random variable to study the distributions of the metrics. $VP(i) = \sum_{t=1}^{n} v^t R_t$ where $\text{Volatility} = -\frac{VP'(i)}{VP(i)}$, interpreting VP′($i$) as the instantaneous rate of change of the present values. Another aspect to review is when there are changes in the interest rates leading to variation duration metrics.

- *Modified duration*: Also refers to volatility.
- *Macaulay duration*: Also refers to the concept expressed before duration.

$$C = \frac{\frac{d^2}{di^2} VP(i)}{VP(i)}$$

$$\frac{d}{di} \frac{\sum_{t=1}^{n} t v^t R_t}{\sum_{t=1}^{n} v^t R_t} = -v\sigma^2$$

- *Convexity*: Second derivative of *VP*(i) *over VP*(i)

where σ^2 is the variance of the distribution where D, the duration, is the mean.

Immunization: When there is a complete set of transactions, it is designed as a technique to structure assets and liabilities in such a way that inflows by assets and outflows by liabilities are balanced. If equilibrium does not exist, it is possible to have adverse effects created by changes in interest rates. The immunization strategy seeks to do the following: The present value of cash inflows generated by assets is equal to the present value of outflows generated by assets. The volatility of assets and liabilities is equal. The convexity of assets is higher than that of liabilities. This system has some difficulties to overcome to achieve a good result: What is the interest rate to use? What happens if the changes of i are large? Does the effective rate curve have to be considered? Are cash flows known? What about maturation and interest rate movements? The half-life is a measure of the average maturation time of the title depending on future flows and profitability.

In addition to reviewing these abovementioned relationships, it is possible to consider the randomness of inputs to those indicators. In that case, there is a need to generate sample points, and understand outcomes that can appear under variation of inputs to the analysis of scenarios and simulation. Understanding is required not only in scenario management but also for the capacity to develop Monte Carlo simulations that present the distribution of the outcomes when some decisions are made. The Monte Carlo simulation generates a random set of values, one for each observation and each equation, and computes one set of changes in parameters. These new parameter values, along with the additive error terms, are then used to compute a new forecast that satisfies this new simultaneous system. Then, a new set of additive error values and parameter perturbations is computed, and the process is repeated the requested number of times. Monte Carlo approach supports data understanding and experiment designs, the same as filling the gaps of understanding in places where mathematical models cannot be obtained. An empirical alternative like Monte Carlo simulation and technology capacity will lead to simulate sampling from populations through a repetition of simulated samples that help to explain the events of interest. Simulation is a very broad term that is applied across many fields and industries. In its most general sense, simulation is the process of building or designing a model that mimics the behavior of a particular real-life system. These models can be either physical or logical. Examples of physical models include flight simulators, wind tunnels, and earthquake simulators. This document focuses on logical models, which can usually be represented by computer programs.

A Monte Carlo simulation method has the following steps:

(1) A probability distribution is established for the important variables.
(2) The cumulative distribution function for these variables is constructed.
(3) An interval is set for random numbers for each variable.
(4) Random numbers are generated.
(5) Several tests are simulated.

Simulation and econometric models of complementary process and example of time series and simulation

Monte Carlo simulation and scenarios support decision-making in the following circumstances (see Exhibit 4.13):

```
proc model data=toast; parms a1 a2 -15 a3 1.5 a4-a7 ; parms b1-b4 ;
tsales = a1 * lag(tsales) + a2 * tprice**a3 + a4 * nwed + a5 * gnp + a6 * ad_cost + a7
   * fs_sales;
fs_sales= b1*lag(fs_sales) - fs_price**b2 + b3 * gnp + b4 * tsales;
fit tsales fs_sales/ fiml hessian=fda outest=t_est outs=s outcov;
run;
solve tsales fs_sales / data=forecast estdata=t_est sdata=s random=150 seed=123
   out=monte;
id month;
range month 51; run;
```

Exhibit 4.13. Time series analysis using SAS.

(1) *Deterministic Scenarios*: Events are supposed to occur with certainty.
(2) *Risk Scenarios*: It is assumed that there is knowledge of the distribution of events.
(3) *Uncertainty Scenarios*: The probability distribution of events is not known but it is known that there is chance for their occurrence.

Furthermore, for measurement time series, analysis is based on behavior of the past. Use of time-based models and research operation models helps to connect the best of both worlds because, according to forecasting of the variables used, this could allocate resources. The *risk–return* ratio points in the same direction; if one grows, the other does as well, but the return grows linearly and the risk exponentially. The only thing that can be certain is the past; a good knowledge of the past is not a guarantee of a good present or a better future, but it is essential to learn from previous mistakes or adequate results. Modeling on the knowledge of previous experiences, identifying risk profiles, and grouping and classifying are indispensable in the way of forecasting. The problem of risk is to decide; decisions without actions are nothing and the actions at the time of becoming such cease to belong to each individual and involve the entire organization. Controlling certain risks shows that others increase or generally change the response with matrix scenarios, which describe the possibility of identifying and organizing the risk analysis. The environment changes and in the face of changes in the environment, risk management must be modified, being proactive and not reactive; however, in some circumstances, there is a reaction, and no action is taken to prevent risk events.

In practice, models that are used in risk management often contain components of several applications listed as follows:

- Product mix problems require the mix of products that generates the largest return when there are several products competing for limited resources.
- Blending problems require the mix of ingredients to be used in a product so that it meets minimum standards at minimum cost.
- Time-staged problems are models whose structure repeats as a function of time. Production and inventory models are classic examples of time-staged problems. In each period, production plus inventory minus current demand equals inventory carried to the next period.

- Scheduling problems assign people to times, places, or tasks so as to optimize people's preferences or performance while satisfying the demands of the schedule.
- Multiple objective problems have multiple, possibly conflicting, objectives. Typically, the objectives are prioritized and the problems are solved sequentially in a priority order.
- Capital budgeting and project selection problems ask for the project or set of projects that will yield the greatest return.
- Location problems seek the set of locations that meets the distribution needs at minimum cost.
- Cutting stock problems find the partition of raw material that minimizes waste and fulfills demand.

It is essential to start with risk prevention analysis in decision-making, as contemplating it from the beginning poses a frame of reference that will allow better decisions to be made in the future. The development of service operations, capacity, means to face risk are decisions that affect the current company. These decisions must be within the possibility of analysis and control. The conditions of the problems have also been supported by multiple operational investigation tools.

The basic optimization problem is that of minimizing or maximizing an objective function, subject to constraints imposed on the variables of that function. The objective function and constraints can be linear or nonlinear; the constraints can be bound constraints, equality, or inequality constraints, or integer constraints. Traditionally, optimization problems are divided into linear programming (LP; all functions and constraints are linear) and nonlinear programming (NLP). Data describing the model are supplied to an optimizer (such as one of the procedures described in this book). An optimizing algorithm is used to determine the optimal values for the decision variables so the objective is either maximized or minimized; the optimal values assigned to decision variables are on or between allowable bounds, and under the constraints (Exhibit 4.14). The linear programming model looks for max or min, maximizing or minimizing a linear function, subject to linear constraints where coefficients will be contributions of resources and x_i will be quantities such as products or units in the set portfolio studied:

$$\text{Max}Z = a_1x_1 + a_2x_2 + \cdots + a_k x_k$$

Subject to:

$$b_{11}x_1 + b_{12}x_2 + \cdots + b_{1k}x_k \leq c_1$$
$$b_{11}x_1 + b_{22}x_2 + \cdots + b_{2k}x_k \leq c_2$$
$$\cdot$$
$$\cdot$$
$$\cdot$$
$$b_{r1}x_1 + b_{r2}x_2 + \cdots + b_{rk}x_k \leq c_r$$
$$x_i \geq 0$$

The integer programming model is equal in structure to the linear programming model with an additional constraint of making the X_i greater than zero but with integers.

The quadratic programming model is a special case of nonlinear programming in which the objective function is quadratic and the constraints are linear.

Minimize: $C^t X + 1/2\, X^t HX$

Subject to: $AX = b$ where A is an array $m*n$ of rank m.

$X \geq 0$ H is positive definition over $\{X: AX = 0\}$
C is the matrix of coefficients of the objective function

Dynamic Programming Model: stages n and $n - 1$ and the model can be described as a model seeking to solve big problems by breaking them down into smaller parts. All relative information and previous decisions are transported to stage n by state X_n. The state X_n determines the $D(X_n)$ decisions that are available. Decision Z_n *is* chosen. The state X_n, the decision Z_n determine the effect of step n on the objective function $R(X_n, Z_n)$. The state X_n and the decision Z_n determine the state of the next stage X_{n-1}, $T(X_n, Z_n)$ transfer function. This can be expressed by the following saying: The problem is divided into subproblems or levels, with a decision required at each level. Each level has one or more associated states. The decision that is made at each level transforms the current state into a state associated with the next level.

Given the current state, an optimal policy for subsequent levels is independent of the policy adopted at any previous level. The solution starts with the most future period. There are two ways to analyze dynamic programming — Deterministic: The state of the next stage is fully determined by the state and the current decision rule. In stage n, the process is in the state e_n and with the decision x_n you pass to e_{n+1} in the stage $(n + 1)$. The value of the objective function is given by $f^*_n(e_n)$ = max or min over the e n of the set of $f_n(e_n, x_n)$ where f_n is the objective function of the stages n to the last. Probabilistic: There is a probability distribution function to establish the state in the next stage. For example, if P_i is considered the probability of change to state i, a possible function to be optimized would be the expected

$$f_n(e_n, x_n) = \sum_{i=1}^{N} P_i\left(c_i + f_n^*(i)\right)$$

sum of the contributions of the individual stages.

With N = Number from n (i = 1, 2, 3, …, N), c_i = Contribution of Stage i to the Target Function

$$f_{n+1}^* = \max_{x_{n+1}} f_{n+1}\left(i, x_{n+1}\right)$$

To use dynamic programming requires the definition of the appropriate recursive relationship for each individual problem.

Network Analysis: Two main problems: maximum flow and shortest route. They can be represented by the general linear programming (PL) model and solved by its algorithm or specific algorithms developed for these problems. The difference mentioned in the literature on the two concepts is that in the situation under risk the consequences of an action depend on the occurrence of a random event with or without knowledge of the probability distribution of the event. In the case in which we speak of decisions under uncertainty, it is considered that the probability distributions of the events are unknown, and that decision-making is simply made without knowing absolutely anything about the possible events or results to be obtained. In this second case, sensitivity analysis and scenario management could be considered. However, in this text and in the concepts that are worked on, it is assumed that the purpose of the analyst is to identify with greater certainty what are the conditions of uncertainty that affect a project, which would place him in front of the condition of decision-making under risk.

It is possible to find a mix of forecasts and optimization in the analysis of portfolios: portfolios of products, promotion portfolios, investments in non-financial assets, etc. "Operations Research tools are directed toward the solution of resource management and planning problems." Models in operations research are representations of the structure of a physical object or a conceptual or business process. Using the tools of operations research involves the following: defining a structural model of the system under investigation, collecting the data for the model, and analyzing the model. A Markowitz portfolio analysis (Exhibit 4.14) in investment support strategy where portfolios are used with in the search of minimizing variance under constraints of expected returns. Optimization of the best mix of the portfolio components is part of the planning process. Definition of the constraints based on resources, objectives/goals, and market conditions is part of the strategic risk management process. The Markowitz model is a particular model based on constraints related to variance of returns. *R* represents the return of the full portfolio, x_i is the proportion of

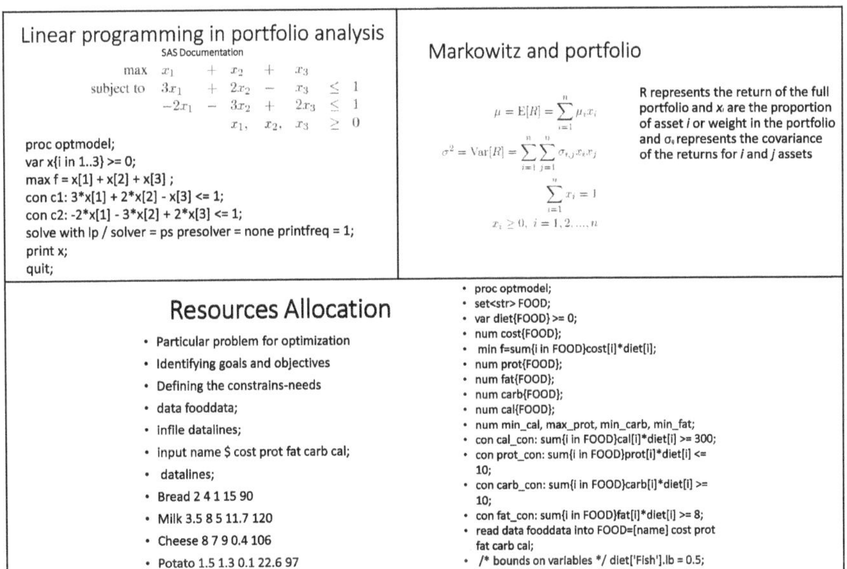

Exhibit 4.14. Use of mathematical programming: Linear and quadratic optimization for problems in portfolios and resource allocation.

asset *i* or weight in the portfolio, and σ_{ij} represents the covariance of the returns for *i* and *j* assets.

An illustration regarding efficiency improvement uses optimization to explain how productivity can be analyzed in terms of understanding strategic risk created because of low productivity/efficiency and at the same time identify what the value will be when digitalization is introduced in the organization. A car manufacturer wants to evaluate the efficiencies of different garages which have received a franchise to sell its cars. The method to be used is Data Envelopment Analysis (DEA). Each garage has a certain number of measurable "inputs." These are taken to be Staff, Showroom Space, Catchment Population in different economic categories, and annual Enquiries for different brands of car. Each garage also has a certain number of measurable "outputs." We need the inputs and outputs for each of the 28 franchised garages.

A central assumption of DEA (although modified models can be built to alter this assumption) is that constant returns to scale are possible, i.e., doubling a garage's inputs should lead to a doubling of all its outputs. A garage is deemed to be efficient if it is not possible to find a mixture of proportions of other garages whose combined inputs do not exceed those of the garage being considered, but whose outputs are equal to, or exceed, those of the garage. Should this not be possible, then the garage is deemed to be inefficient, and the best garages can be identified.

Another example is practicing sensitivity analysis when a manager needs to evaluate how sensitive the solution is to changing assumptions. The LP procedure provides several tools that are useful for "what if," or sensitivity, analysis. One tool studies the effects of changes in the objective coefficients, for example, to change prices and obtain a new solution for the range where the prices can be in order to maintain the optimum. In SAS, for example, "PROC LP has the ability to solve a series of linear programs, each with a new objective function. These objective functions are ordered by priority. The first step is to solve a linear program with the highest priority objective function constrained only by the formal constraints in the model. Then, the problem with the next highest priority objective function is solved, constrained by the formal constraints in the model and by the value that the highest priority objective function realized. That is, the second problem optimizes the second highest priority objective function among the alternate optimal solutions to the first optimization problem. The process continues until a linear program is solved for each of the objectives. This technique is useful for differentiating among alternate optimal solutions to a linear program. It also fits into the formal paradigm presented in goal programming. In goal programming, the objective functions typically take on the role of driving a linear function of the structural variables to meet a target level as closely as possible. The details of this can be found in many books on the subject, including Ignizio (1976)."

Moreover, the search for managing goals and objectives requires controls that are related to actions, results, and people (Merchant, 2012). Analytics is a means to connect all these three components in order to improve performance. In this section, we indicate how to use goal programming to develop a better plan and implementation process based on the use of the organizational limitations and prioritization of the objectives. In addition to scenario analysis, one can perform goal seeking. Goal seeking enables one to specify a target value for the forecast measure, and then determine the values of the underlying factors that would be required to achieve the target value. For example, if one forecasts the profit of a company, and material cost is an underlying factor, then one might use goal seeking to determine what value for material cost would be required to achieve a 10% increase in profit.

Statistical fitting of data distributions: Using SAS (see Exhibits 4.15 and 4.16), the simplest way to use PROC HPSEVERITY is to fit all the predefined distributions to a set of values and let the procedure identify the best fitting distribution.

The PROC HPSEVERITY statement specifies the input dataset along with the model selection criterion, the LOSS statement specifies the variable to be modeled, and the DIST statement with the _PREDEFINED_ keyword specifies that all the predefined distribution models be fitted.

```
Goal Programming
/*Two types of products prod1, prod2. In production, the company uses
10 prog-hours of labor to produce 100
hours of prod1 service and 15 prog-hours of labor to produce 100 hours of prod2
   service.
Without hiring outside help or requiring overtime, the company has 40 hours of
labor available each week. Furthermore, each product generates a
profit at the rate
of $1.00 per hour. The company has the following objectives listed in
decreasing priority: avoid the use of overtime
achieve a weekly profit of $1000
```

Exhibit 4.15. SAS Goal programming example.

```
data test_sev1(keep=y label='Simple Lognormal Sample'); call streaminit(45678);
label y='Response Variable'; Mu = 1.5;
Sigma = 0.25;
do n = 1 to 100;
y = exp(Mu) * rand('LOGNORMAL')**Sigma; output;
end; run;
The following statements fit all the predefined distribution models to the values of Y
   and identify the best distribution according to the corrected Akaike's information
   criterion (AICC):
proc hpseverity data=test_sev1 crit=aicc; loss y;dist _predefined_; run;
```

Exhibit 4.16. Fitting probability distributions.

In the following paragraphs, the types of problems and how those problems are related to techniques that can support solutions and design of systems are provided. The explanation follows a structure of using the theoretical principles of techniques and how problems can be related to those techniques. Techniques and some observations from the literature are indicated in the exhibits.

4.2.4 *Types of problems, learning, and techniques*

The complexity (Exhibit 4.17) of organizing the analytics process and the use of tools appears because of the combination of problems to solve, specific questions to answer (Exhibit 4.18), algorithms to use, type of data that are going to be used, the level of the processes and knowledge domains to apply, problem types to solve, and the sustainability of implementation leading to review the organization of data analytics in multiple steps and identification of how the relationships appear among the previous factors. Exhibit 4.17 summarizes that the basis of all data analytics is mathematics through linear algebra, probability and statistical models, optimization, and related topics in stochastic processes. The pillars will be the workflow to build solutions from the beginning of data organizations to communicate what is discovered and embedded in a system. The construction of the solutions are in a building that is based on all actions in data organization, up to prototypes, model calibration, linking metrics, and generating understanding.

Questions to answer and problems to solve are emerging every time, some of them related to a strategic view and some tactic, but all related to

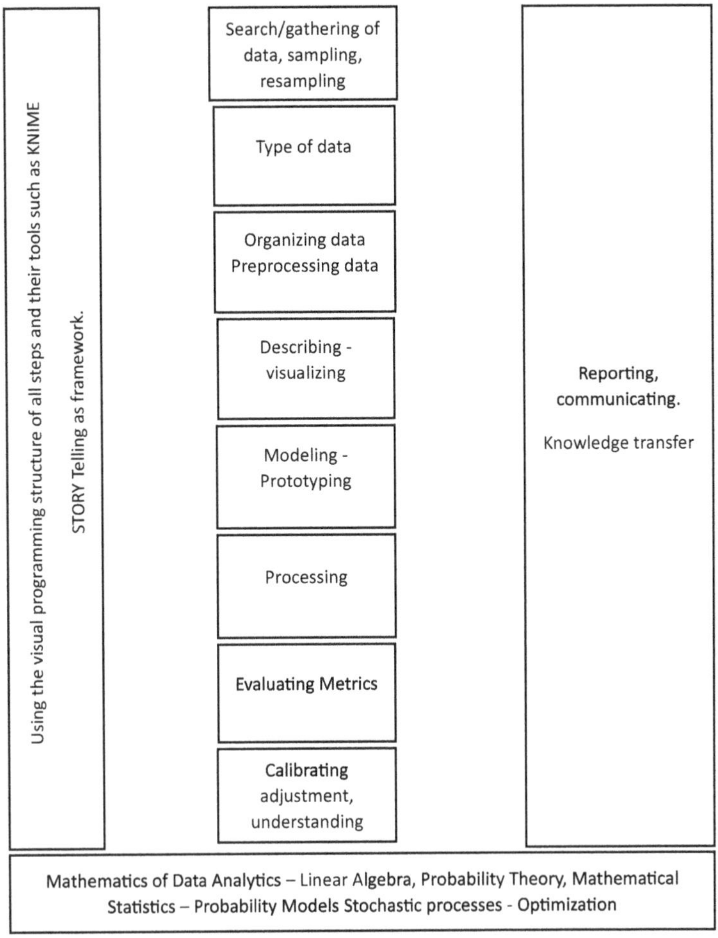

Exhibit 4.17. Sequence to use techniques for data analytics based on the fundamental mathematics.

achieving the goals of the organization. In Exhibit 4.18, there are some questions to answer according to theoretical context or socio-economic sectors. The examples in Exhibit 4.18 includes the general topics in data analytics that require to be addressed and how in healthcare, security, marketing, energy, and finance problems can be opportunities to use data analytics, AI, and digital transformation.

General topics of the theory that should be addressed	• Analyzing productivity shifts in meetings • Temporal feature selection for noisy speech recognition • Simulating naming latency effects • Assessing the sentiment of general tweets • Real-time sentiment-based anomaly detection in twitter data streams • Abstractive meeting summarization as a Markov decision process • Rule extraction from random forest • A density-penalized distance measure for clustering • Learning paired-associate images with an unsupervised deep learning architecture • Incremental cluster updating using Gaussian mixture • Emotional affect estimation using video in deep neural networks • Active learning with clustering and unsupervised feature learning
Healthcare analytics	• A novel model for predicting future health risk and cost stratification at a member level • A novel predictive model for identifying members at high risk of falling • Application of survival model in the health insurance sector to predict member lapses • Health insurance review and assessment service HIRA's big data utilization and disclosure • Risk adjustment analytics: measuring illness burden to optimize health plan payments • The spatio-temporal impact of urgent care centers on physician and ER use • Visual analytics in healthcare to promote accountable care • Sentiment transitions in online medical forums
Security analytics	• Cybersecurity • Police operation • Fraud Similar type of problems to solve • Classification of events/fatalities/severity • Probability of occurrence • Changes in risk/performance indicators • Factors affecting the patterns • Validation with knowledge domain • Simulating the events and the results • Simulating the bottom line of police operation • Security intelligent security-solutions for enterprises in 21st century

Exhibit 4.18. Possible questions to answer according to knowledge and practice domains using statistical and machine learning to create strategic intelligence and mitigate strategic risks.

Marketing analytics	• Consumer analytics faster, higher, stronger: the consumer DNA factory • Social media the base for new business models in digital enterprises • Taking mobile solutions seriously: development, securing, application, adaption • Cloud success stories of the cloud • Big data and analytics: building the analytics platform for the real-time enterprise • Social: The base for new business models in digital enterprises • Big Data and analytics: A new way to work: Insight and business analytics and Hadoop in the enterprise • Network analysis for business applications • The journey to multi-model environment: From creation to measurement • Weather forecasts: Deterministic, probabilistic or both? • What Is Relevant? The key question when working with big data • The growing role of m-learning in the analytics revolution: Application to management education
Energy/Oil industries	• Seismic attribute analysis • Reservoir characterization and simulation • Drilling and completion optimization • Reservoir management • Production forecasting • Production optimization • Multivariate geostatistics
Finance	• ATM Cash Optimization through an inflexible supply chain • CRM: Balancing the speed, relevance, and frequency of your customer conversation • Improving behavior scoring models by using ensemble methods • Model Risk: Evaluating the performance of GARCH-based VaR models through back testing • Modernizing analytics to enhance business efficiency • The 'supremacy' econometrics deliver when modeling the purest form of losses on retail credit risk: start to finish • Using big data to enhance risk measurement

Exhibit 4.18. *(Continued)*

These examples of potential application of data analytics/ AI to solve problems have in common (Exhibit 4.19) multiple steps in data mining that are connected to specific applications in text mining or web mining, and they are oriented to answering questions of generalization, inference, prediction, etc. The reference framework of the project management

Exhibit 4.19. Common components in data analytics projects.

Types of problems to solve	Types of data	Type of subproblems	Possible techniques
Data development	All type of data collection and organization / management, regular and big structured and unstructured data and combinations, in sets or groups.	Sampling Resampling Imputation Storage Acquisition Type of feed	Monte Carlo Simulation Experiment Design techniques
Description — exploration —	Exploratory data analysis, visualization before models, during models and after models, for representing graphics or for images	Graphics Languages and scripts: ggplot2 in R, Tableau, PowerBI, Javascripts, scientific visualization-images	Bi- and three-dimensional graphics, correspondence analysis, evaluation model graphics (ROC, LIFT, Trees)
Prediction	All data require transformations for being used in any of the techniques, text converted into matrices of structured data, structured data defining the appropriate variables	Classification (Supervised Learning) Regression (Supervised Learning) Forecasting (Supervised Learning) Next item/object (Supervised Learning)	Ensembles, classification and regression tress, different types of regression, e.g., logistic regression, ANN, SVM, Rough Ste, Genetic Algorithm

Exhibit 4.20. Problems to solve, data to work on, subproblems, and techniques.

Association	Data in the way that transactions or realization of variables-data	Networks and link analysis (Unsupervised Learning)	Graphs analysis, a priori algorithms, expectation maximization, network analysis
		Sequence Analysis (Unsupervised Learning)	
Grouping	Data that are structured and transformed from unstructured data, possibly require the changes in measurement of similarity	Clustering of data points, variables, time (Unsupervised Learning)	*k*-means, *k*-medoids, hierarchical algorithms,
		Outliers (Unsupervised Learning)	
Processes and rules	Creation of data and answers by mathematical formulation, simulation, inputting outcomes in new tools	Mathematical programming (Unsupervised Learning)	Linear, integer, dynamic programming, optimization methods, Monte Carlo simulation, discrete process simulation
		Resampling methods (Unsupervised Learning)	
		Simulation continuous and discrete (Unsupervised Learning)	
Causality	Organizing data according to the variable's interaction in processes/ procedures	Econometric and non-econometrics models, non-parametric models	Causal inference, econometric methods (Structural Equations), causal qualitative models in combination with regressions

Exhibit 4.20. (*Continued*)

approach helps to obtain the results in an appropriate time to control, operate, strategize, and deal with risk management needs.

With those common means of action in the data analytics process, the difference will appear depending on the problems (Exhibit 4.20). Each problem can use certain types of data and have subproblems to solve using techniques that can be created only for the specific type of problems. A good example is when actuarial science models were used for operational risk understanding. Knowledge of actuarial science is applied to understanding assets and liabilities in organizations that are defined in a financial setting. The possibility to obtain answers regarding operational risk requires the same techniques/models as used for understanding potential losses in machines, systems, fraud, and operations.

The use of techniques for solution of problems and answers to specific questions does not imply learning in the organization. Learning as was mentioned in Chapter 1 appears with the systematic approach of managing knowledge created from data. A way to start is to identify different types of learning: supervised, unsupervised, reinforcement, active, deep learning, and the combination/hybrid with inference methods coming from statistics and mathematics in terms of deduction, induction, and e combinations appearing in steps to obtains solutions for tasks/steps involving human interaction to solve doubts, streaming, or continuous input to deal with the flow of data, and need for updated answers.

Supervised learning uses data to train models that will be used for producing what an organization needs; models are tested with real results and evaluated for effectiveness of the models for use in actions. Unsupervised learning does not need the training of a model; it is about understanding data through a model using the whole set of available data in each iteration of a model to provide accurate results. Segmentation questions can be solved using clustering algorithms; the number of clusters plus performance of the models will help to obtain the result according to the metrics used for defining a good or bad model. Reinforcement learning is based on feedback, active learning is based on the practice, and deep learning is a component of neural networks in in machine learning.

Figure 4.2 is a representation of five components of a modeling process with any learning system. All models will start by clarifying data that will be used as discrete, continuous, streaming, how it is possible to deal with processes that will transform the data, deal with a clear and efficient storage, how members of the organization will have access to data, and how data will be used. In the same direction, data will be used by multiple

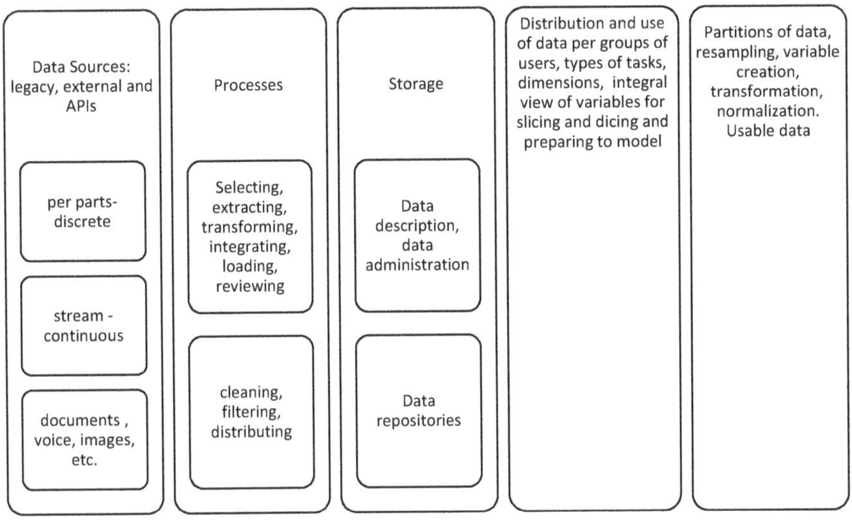

Figure 4.2. Data use and organization from gathering to put in use in modeling with and without learning steps.

groups in the organizations, and data partitions, resampling, normalization, and more actions will be required to obtain the final usable data.

Once data that are usable are ready, a required answer is available if the organization is supporting the whole process: Is the organization understanding what the process is or will be, the level of involvement to create actions that provide value to the data analytics efforts, and the possibility of using the data analytics projects integrated into the business? The learnings from the data analytics projects are going to be useful to reduce risks in operations and new development in various areas across the organization. It is not necessary to reinvent the wheel every time as illustrated in Figure 4.3.

A good example of how to solve problems in the data analytics process is going through a review of tools that can be used in each subproblem (Figure 4.3). In the case R, several packages exist and are appropriate to solve specific issues in the data analytics process. Exhibit 4.21 indicates a basic inventory of packages that are highly useful for tasks that are required in the data analytics process, such as visualization, descriptions, data mining, and data preparation up to packages that are specialized according to the knowledge domain as in risk management, actuarial packages, simulation, and optimization.

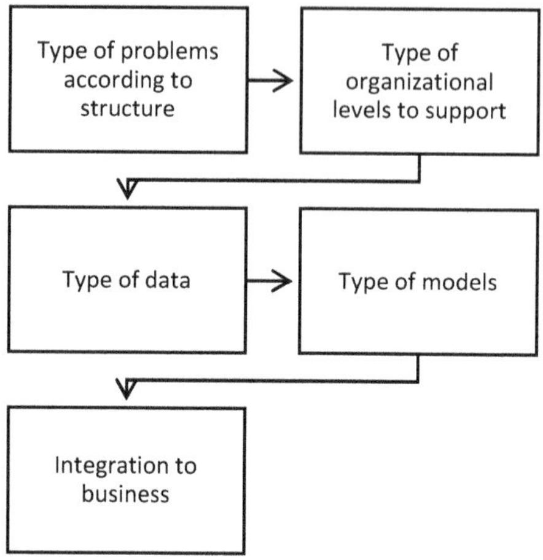

Figure 4.3. Moving from a problem to integration of solution and business.

Problem	**R related package**
General purpose, data mining, machine learning	Rcmdr, Rattle BlueSky, caret, mlr
Organization of data and cleaning	Dplyer, RODBC, tidyr, tidyverse
Description of data and summary statistics	Stats, MASS, broom, Data Explorer
Visualization	ggplot2, GGally, ggmosaic, plotly, shiny, R Markdown, ggforce, html tools html widgets, sf, shiny dashboard
Clustering	Cluster, fastcluster, ClusterR, flexclust
Classification	CARAT, E1071, rpart
Networks, link analysis and text	iGraph, Worldcloud2, tm, network
Neural Networks and Deep learning	Nnet
Big data	sparklyr
Bootstrapping — ensembles	Hmisc, Randomforest
Time series	Ts, TSA, forecast, smooth, xts, tseries, MTS, Time series, fGarch
Simulation	Monte Carlo, Sim helpers, parSim, purr, simulator, simmer (discrete simulation)
Optimization	Mboost, Optimx, ompr, Deoptim
Finance — risk	Quantmod, Portfolio Analytics, actuar, actuary

Exhibit 4.21. R packages by type of tasks in data analytics.

These types of packages can have specific syntaxis and the way to use them will include means to read and retrieve data up to obtain results with models. Exhibit 4.22 summarizes what data analytics is doing for organizing the data sources up to the point of having a feedback of the full process where data use will be a structure and sample to continue using it. Information systems will feed the data analytics structure to operationalize the process.

Another set of tools is related to sources of data from the web (Exhibit 4.23); scrapping and obtaining results through web mining of gathering data is a very powerful process. In the process of gathering data from the web, there are many points to consider such as type of data, individual, aggregated, text, numeric, continuous, and discrete. This illustrates that the source can be the same in terms of the possibility of accessing data but each dataset required can come in multiple formats, structured and unstructured, and all data analytics processes will start by translating what is available to tables that are usable. An example is Excel that has an AI tool for recognizing characters obtained from pictures of tables on the web or other sources, e.g., printed tables, to be input directly into the Excel spreadsheet. A data analyst requires the time for reviewing what is needed to accept or reject the value of the data to use for modeling.

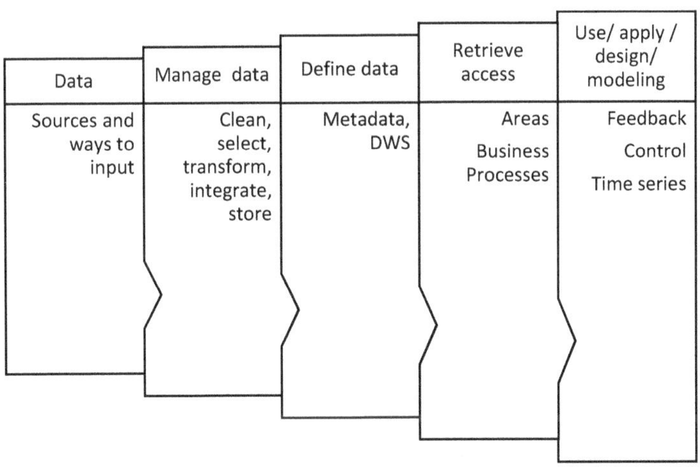

Exhibit 4.22. Pieced in the sequence of data usability.

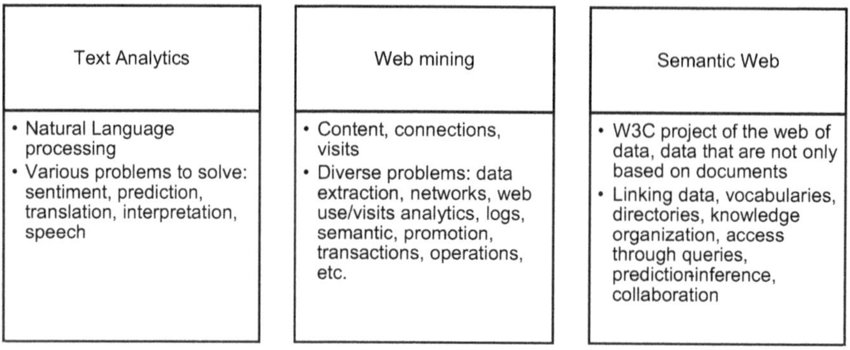

Exhibit 4.23. Obtaining knowledge from unstructured data and interrelated data.

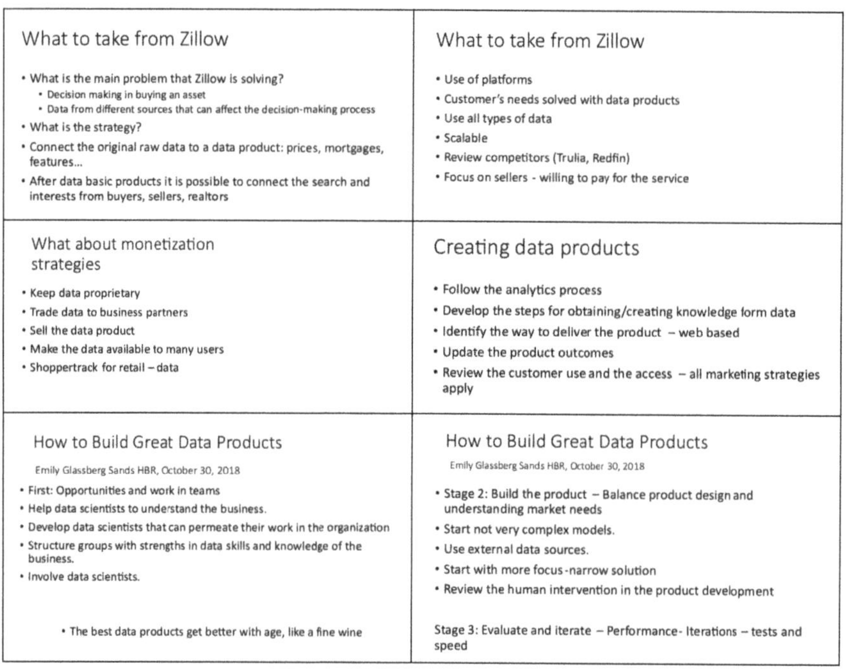

Exhibit 4.24. Data products are outcomes converted into reality for users to work on.

The aspect of having ways to use techniques create knowledge from data is converging to the creation of outcomes that are not only just simple answers but also alive reports and digital products. The knowledge creation evolves according to the flow of data that is feeding models and data analytics structures. Exhibit 4.24 shows some examples of using regressions to provide extra value to users. The problem solved connects factors to the price of an asset, that is, with the same idea of the applications used to match people according to known profiles. The message here is that the final step of having results through a model can be converted and, in some cases, monetized by generating actionable knowledge that the user can work with.

All those tools and techniques to solve multiple problems require one to have a proper understanding. A basic guide to the technologies and tools is offered in the next subsection.

4.2.5 *Technologies and tools*

With the previous paragraphs indicating how the data analytics process is connected to the selection of means to deal with data, it is required to identify certain type of problems to solve that can be more on the optimization side or on the prediction needs. In most cases, the means to use data requires an understanding of computational capacity and the sequence of questions, i.e., problem-data-model-data-problem, that means that according to the first problem definition the final shape or scope in the projects will depend on how the data and models needs are satisfied and how to find possibilities to embed solutions in operations. This subsection and the following ones present exhibits with descriptions and examples of technologies associated with data analytics/AI and digitalization to create intelligence. Exhibit 4.25 shows a review of all steps for supporting intelligence creation which requires the integration of techniques, technologies, and capabilities in organizations to solve problems. The integration is advanced through digitalization and ways to connect dots of designs of AI and operational information systems.

Technologies are required to evolve as well, not only in the internal technology growth and enhancement but also in terms of infrastructure that is changing/evolving as is the case of the Internet that comprises at least IoT, Internet of documents, internet of data, connected to what humans and machines will be required to operate, think, and develop (Exhibit 4.25). The same happens with techniques and technologies to obtain data and to analyze data from surveys, to trace transactions, where they are coming from and how they are going to feed networks of speech, graphics, images, text, etc. All the connections are made with the support of knowledge, learning, developing intelligence, and solutions and actions as is illustrated in Figure 4.4.

Data repository	"MongoDB is a document database. It stores data in a type of JSON format called BSON. If you are unfamiliar with JSON, check out our JSON tutorial. A record in MongoDB is a document, which is a data structure composed of key value pairs similar to the structure of JSON objects." "Records in a MongoDB database are called documents, and the field values may include numbers, strings, booleans, arrays, or even nested documents." From https://www.w3schools.com/mongodb/ The use depends on the type of business/problem and they coexist. SQL: schema, all records same fields NoSQL: no schema, can be different fields in records, more like documents. Kubernettes Cassandra Delta lake

Big Data Analytics, deep learning	• Hadoop is an open-source framework for storing and analyzing massive amounts of distributed, unstructured data.
	• Originally created by Doug Cutting at Yahoo!.
	• Hadoop clusters run on inexpensive commodity hardware so projects can scale out inexpensively.
	• Hadoop is now part of Apache Software Foundation.
	• Open source — hundreds of contributors continuously improve the core technology.
	• MapReduce + Hadoop = Big Data core technology.
	• MapReduce distributes the processing of very large multi-structured data files across a large cluster of ordinary machines/processors.
	• Goal — achieving high performance with "simple" computers.
	• Developed and popularized by Google.
	• Good at processing and analyzing large volumes of multi-structured data in a timely manner.
	• Example tasks: indexing the Web for search, graph analysis, text analysis, machine learning, etc.
	• How Does Hadoop Work?
	    ○ Access unstructured and semi-structured data (e.g., log files, social media feeds, other data sources).
	    ○ Break the data into "parts," which are then loaded into a file system made up of multiple nodes running on commodity hardware using HDFS.

Exhibit 4.25. Summary of certain technologies used in data analytics and digital transformation.

	◦ Each "part" is replicated multiple times and loaded into the file system for replication and failsafe processing. ◦ A node acts as the Facilitator and another as Job Tracker. ◦ Jobs are distributed to the clients, and once completed the results are collected and aggregated using MapReduce. • Hadoop Technical Components ◦ Hadoop Distributed File System (HDFS) ◦ Name Node (primary facilitator) ◦ Secondary Node (backup to Name Node) ◦ Job Tracker ◦ Slave Nodes (the grunts of any Hadoop cluster) ◦ Additionally, Hadoop ecosystem is made up of a number of complementary subprojects: NoSQL (Cassandra, Hbase), DW (Hive), etc. NoSQL = not only SQL • Hadoop consists of multiple products. • Hadoop is open source but available from vendors, too. • Hadoop is an ecosystem, not a single product. • HDFS is a file system, not a DBMS. • Hive resembles SQL but is not standard SQL. • Hadoop and MapReduce are related but not the same. • MapReduce provides control for analytics, not analytics. • Hadoop is about data diversity, not just data volume. • Hadoop complements a DW; it is rarely a replacement. • Hadoop enables many types of analytics, not just Web analytics. "Apache Spark™ is a multi-language engine for executing data engineering, data science, and machine learning on single-node machines or clusters." Works with batch and streaming data, SQL, EDA, and machine learning. Interfaces for R and Python. TensorFlow is defined as a full machine platform from preparing data, build ML models, deploy models, and put in production the models. Models include deep learning and with the capability of using the models through the cloud and Pytorch the same aim as TensorFlow using the libraries from Scikit-learn, Captum and Pytorch geometric
Blockchain	"Blockchain is a shared, immutable ledger that facilitates the process of recording transactions and tracking assets in a business network. An asset can be tangible (a house, car, cash, land) or intangible (intellectual property, patents, copyrights, branding). Virtually anything of value can be tracked and traded on a blockchain network, reducing risk and cutting costs for all involved." https://www.ibm.com/topics/what-is-blockchain

Exhibit 4.25. (*Continued*)

	"Blockchain technology is an advanced database mechanism that allows transparent information sharing within a business network. A blockchain database stores data in blocks that are linked together in a chain. The data is chronologically consistent because you cannot delete or modify the chain without consensus from the network. As a result, you can use blockchain technology to create an unalterable or immutable ledger for tracking orders, payments, accounts, and other transactions. The system has built-in mechanisms that prevent unauthorized transaction entries and create consistency in the shared view of these transactions." https://aws.amazon.com/what-is/blockchain/
Internet and analytics of things	"The Internet of Things (IoT) describes the network of physical objects — "things" — that are embedded with sensors, software, and other technologies for the purpose of connecting and exchanging data with other devices and systems over the internet. These devices range from ordinary household objects to sophisticated industrial tools. With more than 7 billion connected IoT devices today, experts are expecting this number to grow to 10 billion by 2020 and 22 billion by 2025. Oracle has a network of device partners." https://www.oracle.com/internet-of-things/what-is-iot/ "The Internet of Things (IoT) is the network of physical objects that contain embedded technology to communicate and sense or interact with their internal states or the external environment." https://www.gartner.com/en/information-technology/glossary/internet-of-things "NIST understands the importance of the Internet of Things (IoT) and how it impacts our everyday lives in a big way. The IoT could revolutionize the American economy by enabling a fully connected world with on-demand access to data, systems, and each other. Since an IoT product might be defined as including an IoT device and any other product components that are necessary to using the IoT device beyond basic operational features, there are risks that come along with this level of connectivity — especially among so many devices across the globe. We must be able to trust the privacy, security, authenticity, and reliability of these devices, as well as the advanced networks that support them." https://www.nist.gov/internet-things-iot

Exhibit 4.25. (*Continued*)

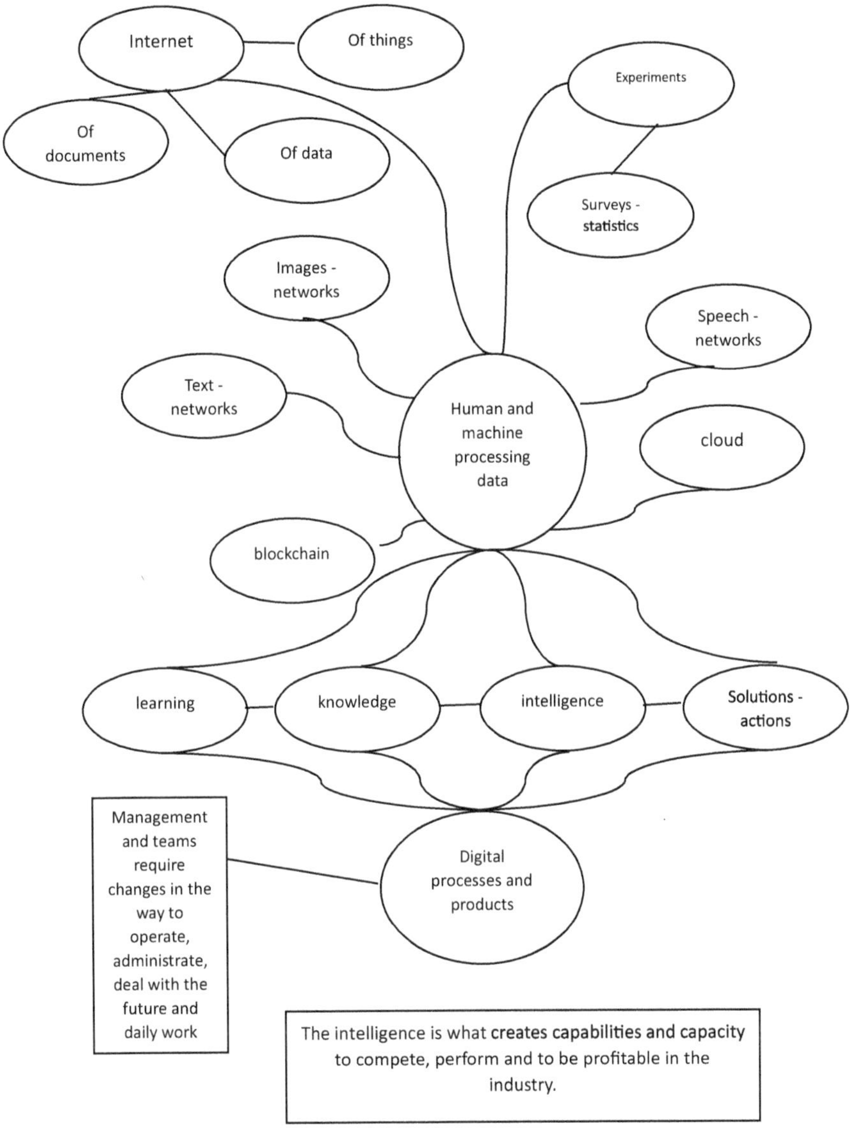

Figure 4.4. Connection of all that is required in the analytics process for the evolution of technology to remain relevant and maintain intelligent organizations.

<table>
<tr><td>The nine macro forces: analytics, cloud, digital experience, core systems, risk, business of technology, cognitive systems, blockchain, and digital reality (Deloitte Insights, 2019).</td><td>"...Ant Financial uses artificial intelligence and data from Alipay—its core mobile-payments platform—to run an extraordinary variety of businesses, including consumer lending, money market funds, wealth management, health insurance, credit-rating services, and even an online game that encourages people to reduce their carbon footprint." Marco Iansiti M. and Karim R. Lakhani K.R. In the AGE of AI How machine intelligence changes the rules of business HBR Jan-Feb 2020.</td></tr>
<tr><td>"The greatest impact of intelligent technologies won't be from eliminating jobs but from changing what people do and driving innovation deeper into the business." By MIT Sloan Senén Barro And Thomas H. Davenport 2019.</td><td>• Assisted Intelligence
• Augmented Intelligence
• Autonomous intelligence</td></tr>
<tr><td>• Parallel computing: divide tasks in small units to perform in parallel
• Multithread computing
• Distributed computing
• Freestanding analytics
• Partially integrated analytics
• In database analytics
• In Hadoop analytics</td><td></td></tr>
</table>

Exhibit 4.26. AI technologies are advancing to support organizational advancement.

In the evolutionary process, there are forces that are influencing the way that organizations are working and performing. A common condition in data analytics/AI is about the set of technologies and the collaboration to develop innovation and ways to move from a complete operation in house to supplementing capabilities (Exhibit 4.26). In China, a good example is that since a credit record of most of the population does not exist, there are AI tools from independent organizations and other countries that can help provide clues to credit organizations to assess risk; similarly, one should keep in mind that the purpose of AI is to support humans and not to do more with the capabilities in terms of creation.

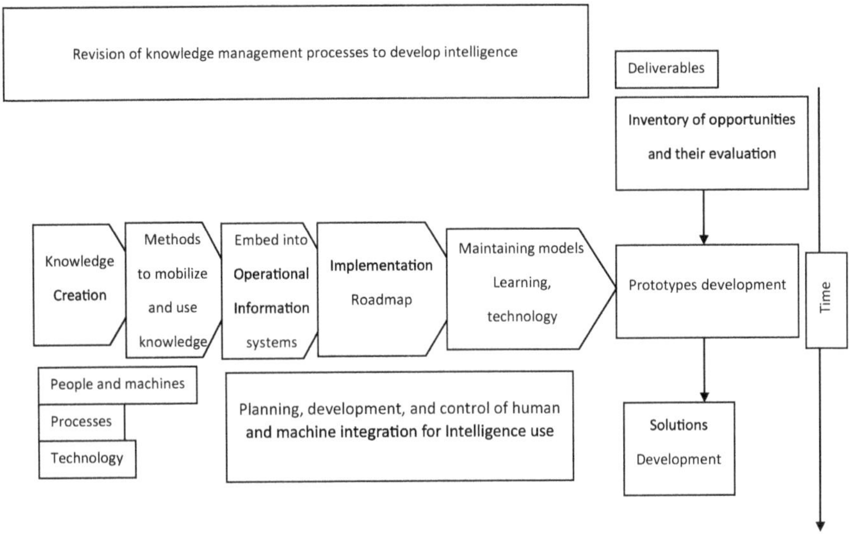

Figure 4.5. Moving knowledge to create intelligence through time.

An organization's use of technology to create knowledge follows the knowledge management process, and the way that knowledge creates intelligence through improvement is by moving ahead to achieve required competitive levels and relevance (Figure 4.5). The stages of the process use humans and machines with process enhancement and technology. The final solutions will be internal and external, i.e., in the form of digital and traditional products that are offered in the market.

The transition of knowledge to final solutions is full of distractive aspects to avoid or control, mainly to maintain the direction of the search for mitigating risk (Exhibit 4.27). The point is that isolated concepts are part of the purpose of using knowledge in an appropriate way. Knowledge as a means to mitigate risk will provide what organizations need and will help to avoid confusing issues, for example, having large volumes of data in order to have good data analytics. The issue is that to achieve the use of data analytics and AI to build robust and intelligent organizations, one has to be part of leading organizations and societies. This is why strategic intelligence is knowledge and risk management: what could happen, what happened, and what is possible after events.

<table>
<tr>
<td>How to connect these isolated concepts?
• Knowledge (analytics, measure, estimate, predict, describe) helps to be smarter.
• Knowledge (analytics) is a risk mitigator.
• To be smarter is to adapt better to the environment, control risk.
• Sustainability and competitiveness
• Risk management is for learning, improving, developing competitive capability.</td>
<td>• Improve the decision-making process under risk.
• Avoid falling into decision and strategy traps.
• Evolve the way problems are solved.
• Develop capacity to integrate data, technology, people, processes (reason and intuition).
• Intellectual capital (data, relationships, minds).
• Doing more with what you have (scope, economies).
• No more technology and great methods if people do not have the capabilities to use them.
• It is an opportunity to have access to the resources at a moderate cost.</td>
</tr>
<tr>
<td>• The problem is not big data; the problem is to create knowledge of data to use the actions we have access to. Big Data are an information systems problem and meaning generation is an analytics problem. Having only marketing intelligence or competitive intelligence is a valuable thing.
• Move to the next level: Strategic intelligence based on knowledge and risk management.
• Create knowledge from data, be able to transfer it, accumulate it, access it, and apply it.
• It is necessary to measure the variation of the expected results.</td>
<td>(1) Wine.com, one-to-one mail
(2) Yahoo, segmentation, email retention
(3) Evaluation of clients and their life
(4) Online campaigns
(5) Income prediction
(6) Ask.com search engines for interactive marketing
These are examples of using technology and techniques to increase capacity and capabilities in organizations.</td>
</tr>
</table>

Exhibit 4.27. How to connect isolated concepts that at the end are related to use of knowledge in an effective way.

The use of created knowledge, the tools to create it, and putting the knowledge in practice are exemplified in government and public health applications (Exhibit 4.28).

This capacity to develop data and convert them into knowledge requires administration of data repositories and reports in areas of ERM;

Government related	Public Health related
• Use knowledge of populations, groups • Better use of experts • Better use of technology • Better data management • Developing the education system • Using algorithms to process low-quality data on many computers • Develop the use of computers to do more with them • Multimodal transport is an example that requires a lot of data, shipments, procedures, transport by different means, companies, etc. How to control this dispersion? • Problems to solve: Costs, accidents, connectivity, service, etc. • Security Data vs. Privacy. Everything cannot be shared • Problems crossing data from different repositories • Include metadata from other areas where they are used • Grouping small databases	• Monitoring the health of individuals, predicting heart attacks — connection with cell phone • Patterns in previous records • Infection analysis • Manage having different data in different formats • Time management is part of the categories of being (Ontology) • Using special dictionaries such as SNOMED CT • Establishment of early warning systems • Continuous process monitoring • Documentation and difficulty understanding what is written by doctors and nurses

Exhibit 4.28. Examples of what public health and government are doing to be more effective in using emerging knowledge.

fundamentally, the organization requires clarity that data are values of variables that describe research questions and research questions are the discrimination of the specific aspects that are researched in the data analytics process. In the case of risk models related to classification, there variables that can be a combination of financial and non-financial indicators but that can provide profiles of the risk units to organize risk assessment and control. Outcomes in each step can be new inputs to the following steps that are required to solve the problem; for example, outputs regarding types of issues with data lead the decision of what data to use or clusters of risk units that can be the classification categories required to the risk management analysis. In the same way, the implementation of solutions to generate intelligence for operations will help improve clarity to give priority to the search of results based on impact, groups of interest, types of issues, feasibility to get solutions, etc. Exhibit 4.29

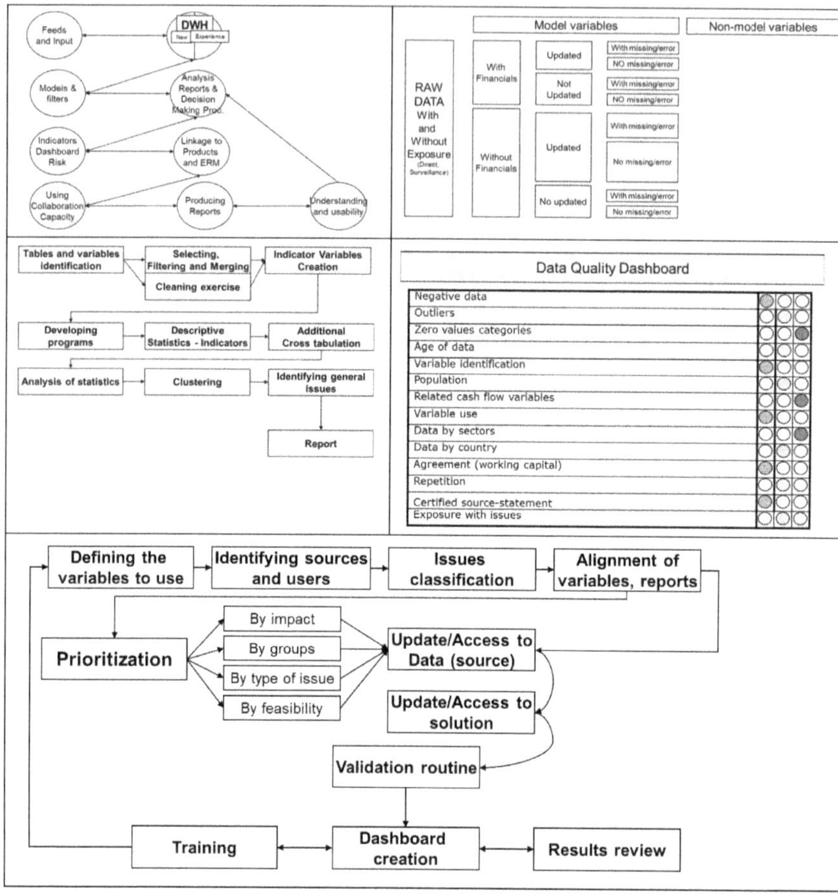

Exhibit 4.29. Moving through a chain of knowledge creation and final results where partial results feed steps in the data analytics/AI process.

illustrates how all these chains of steps are interconnected, including learning, training and development of users, knowledge creators, and machines.

It is interesting to review what China has been developing in the last decade: big data centers with specific purpose were created. At the beginning, data were not attractive to use because of a lot issues. However, with the development of multiple projects or organizations that are working to use data analytics and AI to solve problems of education, security, transportation, etc., data resources have improved, open data have emerged, and more people can use data. Digital organizations offer a wide variety of services, transforming social media such as WeChat into something more: as the means to do transactions, to have communication and coordination among operators (delivery and suppliers/users of the logistic chain), provide access to resources, move goods and services from places which was complex to do before such as rural areas to cities, and complete integration of services. This means digital transformation has its own transformation. Evolution of digital services continues to move levels closer to the daily life of people (Exhibit 4.30).

A way to connect the previous points is through the use of statistical and machine learning based on the VIBO model. V's are about the values of big data, I's are about the important connections to the generation of Impact, B's mean business connection, and O's are everything related to operations (Exhibit 4.31). In the case of big data analytics, the v's are numerous but fundamentally in creation of intelligence the attention is on generation of value. Value is meant to be the potential impact that work in data analytics will provide to the organizations. Impact is associated with adaptation of organizations to the new circumstances of market evolution. In terms of opening opportunities for using data analytics, one needs to keep in mind the I's of big data (Exhibit 4.31) that represent impact attributes.

The VIBO model is a means to indicate the set of conceptual components required in data analytics work. An example of where these pieces of data analytics work can be used is the education field. Development of strategic intelligence in education (Exhibit 4.32) is a task of huge value. The traditional business model of education is more than 800 years old. New circumstances pressed the education system to be more effective and efficient in terms of providing students and educators with possibilities to receive and deliver education. The process of improvement and transition on the operational part cannot be isolated without understanding the valuable data that educational institutions provide. Understanding what students are thinking, doing, or could do, how these thoughts can be related to performance, interaction with professors, and improvement of the teaching–learning process are all questions that can be tackled step by step using data analytics and AI. Discovering how students can predict their own final outcomes of performance according to time of study, use of library resources, interaction with professors, search for sources to answer assignments or exams, etc., can allow one to understand what the learning profession is about and how one can help students succeed.

China's view of Big Data: Promote economic restructuring and development of new power. Reshape national competitive advantage. Build governance capabilities. Guide ideology, resource allocation, government credibility, public service enterprise development. Promote the development and application in the next 5–10 years with objectives related to governance, multilateral; collaboration, smooth operation. Promote open data resources and the 2018 national open data platform.

"Certainly the hope of the Communist Party is that the system of social controls with which they're most comfortable can be brought into the modern economy with only a few compromises for economic scale and growth," said Anne Stevenson-Yang, director of research at J Capital Research.

"In a sense, the arrival of the digital dangan was inevitable. Preparations for the 2008 Summer Olympics had already armed the government with vast capabilities to track vehicles and people through facial and fingerprint recognition technology at ports of entry. The advent of virtual money paved the way for the potential to collect and usefully analyze more personal data. The government has attempted to create credit bureaus before, but credit cards until recently were limited in use, and banks preferred to build their own database to check borrowers' collateral, dispensing with and ultimately sidelining the prototypical credit bureaus."

The term dangan translates to "social credit system." The government, must "strengthen the establishment of a national population-based information repository and improve the social credit system" to "improve the mechanism for crisis intervention."

"The outcome of Beijing's massive social experiment could still range anywhere between mostly benign to highly intrusive. This is a country, after all, where public expectation already is clear that the state can control even the most intimate activities of its people. But the potential powers it hands an already pervasive authority pose questions for privacy, as well as a fact: Bigger Brother is heading for China." 5:20 am HKT, Nov 6, 2015 ECONOMY & BUSINESS

China Wants to Tap Big Data To Build A Bigger Brother http://blogs.wsj.com/chinarealtime/2015/11/06/china-wants-to-tap-big-data-to-build-a-bigger-brother/, accessed on November 13, 2015. For example:

- Tsinghua University's Center for Statistical Science has set up a Medical Big Data Center
- Range International Information Group Langfang
- China Broadband Capital Partners LP Shenzhen
- Data Center Guizhou Guiyang City

"Companies who have already built data centres in China include Amazon, IBM and Microsoft — although in December it was reported that cloud computing providers in the Asian country were to be tested for their 'trustworthiness', potentially meaning bad news for foreign CSPs."

Exhibit 4.30. Example of China's development of big data centers creating opportunities to develop services for citizens.

"Only companies that get full security clearance from the government will be allowed to join Smart City and various other government-funded projects, said Zuo Xiaodong, vice-president of the China Information Security Research Institute, an industry think-tank." Trust rating for cloud firms on cards. Updated: 2014-12-20 08:10 By Gao Yuan(China

"Pacnet's Business Solutions in China ("PBS") was recently awarded an Internet Data Center (IDC) license by the Ministry of Industry and Information Technology (MIIT) to provide data center network services in Chongqing, China." Chongqing: The Big Data Star of China Posted on October 31, 2013 http://datacenterdiscovery.com/

"The Chongqing Data Center is part of a strategic cooperation agreement for cloud between the Chongqing Municipal Government and Tencent." Tencent plans $1bn Midwest China data center April 14, 2015 By Laura Luo http://www.datacenter dynamics.com/

Inventec's development plan reveals that the company will launch five data centers in five cities, including Chongqing and Shanghai by 2017. "The research center will construct itself as a solution support center to provide the comprehensive IT solutions to small and mid-sized enterprises in western and central China," said Cong Yulin, vice manager of the Inventec Cloud Service Center." Inventec launches big data research center in Liangjiang Updated: 2015-10-22 By Ge Jieru, chinadaily. com.cn

"China and the UK are enhancing their cooperation on big data research. Chinese President Xi Jinping visited the Data Science Institute of the Imperial College London Wednesday."

Exhibit 4.30. (*Continued*)

Strategic intelligence is developed through analytics, analytics generates knowledge, knowledge helps control risk and better risk control supports appropriate performance. Being able to define goals more precisely helps reduce frustration, disorientation, and wrong strategy. The idea is to create the equivalent of target areas (confidence intervals) and measure the chances of failing. Analytics is not only about the modeling step, i.e., to go from data to actions immersed in business processes, but also about the integration of areas and knowledge.

Another practical case to review is of banks which use the following analytics tools:

- Development from simple models to sophisticated models for transactions, risk assessment, prediction, etc.
- Techniques are related to guiding business decisions in risk and capital management and to support the continuous operation in lending, trading, underwriting, funding, investment, and operational development.

<table>
<tr>
<td>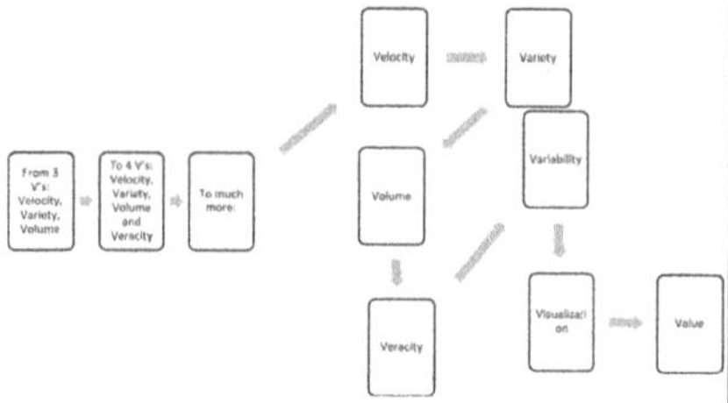
</td>
<td>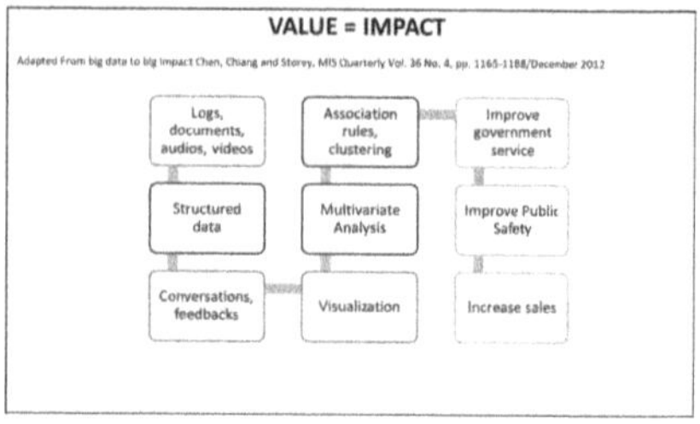
</td>
</tr>
<tr>
<td>• Identification/Management of scale/ Problem definition
• Intelligence/Formal research process/ Risk Control
• Interpretation/Context and application
• Importance/Bias analysis/good sampling
• Interest/Expected value
• Integrity/Data cleaning-organization
• Integration/Accommodate data or people properly
• Improvement/Ensuring continued results
• Inherent/Guided by organizational processes/Risk Control
• Impact/Application and usability</td>
<td>• Business: All work in analytics and big data need a link with the organization's business/Risk Control.
• Benefit: In search of benefit, not necessarily profits/economic but clear purpose.
• Barriers: Clearly defining limitations.
• Boundaries: There is a problem of scope. Working/building by blocks.
• Background: Developing and building based on previous understanding/ feedback.
• Bridging: Creating the spaces for connecting areas and disciplines in order to provide better solutions.
• Building: Generating actions with the knowledge of what model outcome is and a permanent review of the results.
• Benchmark: Keep the process up to date with the best of the resources available.
• Boards of directors: The hope is everyone is connected and understanding.
• Behavior: Managing the learning/ teaching process, reviewing the way to gain good attitude/willingness to solve the problem in a good/correct way.</td>
</tr>
<tr>
<td colspan="2">• Organization's Systems
• Operations
• Opportunities</td>
</tr>
</table>

Exhibit 4.31. Definition and structure of VIBO model for Big Data Analytics: V's of Big data, I's of Impact, B's of Business, and O's of Operations.

- Quantitative tools support the definition of assumptions and limitations of models, and control the stages of solution development, validation, implementation, and different types of models.
- Models require a combination of qualitative review, judgment and follow-up, calibration, and awareness of operational changes that can modify the model's definitions.

Intelligent Education Organizations	
Around the world, there are issues of bankruptcy of higher education institutions, churn, lower graduation rate, and lower employment after graduation. It is not only the impact of COVID-19 pandemic, "Even before the global pandemic caused craters in the economy, some institutions were facing financial hardship after years of deep cuts in state funding for higher education." Jessica Dickler, CNBC M 27, 2020. "Covid-19 crisis could bankrupt a dozen UK universities, IFS warns: Overall, the sector is well placed to deal with the fallout, but those who entered pandemic in weak financial health could be at risk." Simon Baker July 6, 2020.	In China, there is a phenomenon of bankruptcy in private higher education institutions (Guoping & Zuoxu, 2007). In 2018, "The total number of students enrolled in private higher education in China increased from 5.3 million in 2012 to 6.3 million in 2016 and is expected to further increase to eight million in 2021. Currently, about 22% of students in higher education are studying at private institutions" (University World News Oct 2018). The issues go beyond the good scores in "rankings." They are not only about bankruptcy but also about the balance of educational quality and possibilities to sustain students' success (academic and careers).

Institution	RankT	RankQS	totalscore	No. of FTE Students	No. of students per staff	Internat. Students	Citations	Industry Income	Internat. Outlook	Research	Teaching	Academic Reputation	Citations/ Faculty	Employer Reputation	Faculty Student	Internat. Faculty	Strategic Group
University of Washington	17	61	157.1	44945	11.4	0.16	99.3	50.3	56.7	83.9	81	92.3	98.8	56.7	28	57	1
Tsinghua University	20	25	167.7	42089	13.7	0.09	79.7	89.6	25.2	91.5	87.9	99.2	75.3	99.6	87	42	1
University of Illinois at Urbana-Champaig	21	69	152.3	43402	22.8	0.23	98.1	40.8	51.4	82.7	81	95.1	93.5	59.8	72	20	1
University of Toronto	22	31	165.5	69427	18.7	0.17	99.6	37.5	75	80.5	74.6	99.7	50	95.6	75	97	1
Peking University	25	38	160.5	42136	8.9	0.16	79	99.8	37.5	84.6	82.7	99.8	61.7	99.9	67	53	1
University of Texas at Austin	26	67	146.3	48561	17.1	0.1	99.9	48.3	31	78.5	66.5	97.6	95.7	82.1	72	74	1
University of British Columbia	28	51	152.7	51889	18.1	0.29	94.2	38.7	85.8	70.7	64.4	99.1	63.7	95.5	38	92	1
RWTH Aachen University	37	141	125.1	43721	57.7	0.18	74	88.4	41	74.4	64.3	71.3	42.1	98.4	72	33	1
University of Melbourne	39	41	148	42116	26.6	0.4	88	49.6	88.8	55.3	58.8	99.8	77.2	99.5	26	95	1
Zhejiang University	45	87	132.3	58051	14.1	0.06	60.4	79.4	24.4	76.9	65.8	74	80.2	87.1	37	54	1
KU Leuven	50	71	133.3	44412	37.1	0.15	90.9	88.5	47.1	53.7	49.4	88.1	88.9	78	73	95	1
University of Montreal	58	130	119.3	41017	21.9	0.22	83.8	50.5	86.8	61.6	36.7	67.2	49.9	73.5	72	91	1
National University of Singapore	13	15	176.5	30602	17	0.3	88.5	42.8	95.9	90.4	84.1	100	66.2	99.9	89	100	2
Technical University of Munich	16	64	156.7	38689	54.4	0.23	90.3	94.1	54	90.9	79.5	86.3	26.6	98.7	86	53	2
UCL	18	7	136.7	30304	10.5	0.49	94.7	42.3	95.7	80.8	78.4	99.7	74.7	99.5	99	97	2
University of California, San Diego	24	38	161.8	29633	12.8	0.17	99.4	88.4	41.6	85.3	68.5	96	90.3	61.3	59	65	2
University of Wisconsin-Madison	27	55	151	38960	10.7	0.12	99.3	48.7	57.8	77.8	60.1	94	54.2	62.1	84	53	2
University of Southern California	30	132	131.2	38380	12.8	0.23	96.4	43.7	66.4	78.5	54	64.8	70.4	55	28	45	2
University of Maryland, College Park	32	129	131.9	31772	16.5	0.1	94.9	41.9	31.6	79.5	64.6	63.8	75.8	33.2	55	26	2
University of Waterloo	33	152	126.3	32000	26.1	0.17	90.1	45.1	76.4	73.8	59.1	48.8	80.9	82.4	72	78	2
LMU Munich	47	66	137	36091	15.6	0.15	82.8	50.4	49.7	67.7	56.4	95.8	55.1	88.2	39	55	2
University of California, Irvine	49	164	116.1	30419	17	0.21	95.6	39.6	65	46.5	56.1	54	89.2	0	72	51	2
National Taiwan University	53	76	131.5	31758	11.5	0.08	45.1	84.6	26.9	73.9	72.2	95.6	74.1	74.2	33	74	2

Exhibit 4.32. Understanding how to use data analytics in education.

Answer questions: Are professors performing better in the second year of appointment? Are students performing consistently in all subjects? Are students and professors following similar patterns of performance? Very controversial — doubts about Measurement Systems — Algorithms — Variables — Data, in general about the analytics process, possibly with a wrong design. See the example of the scatter plot where 13000 teachers' 2008–2009 score on the *x*-axis and their 2009–2010 score on the *y*-axis. Posted on February 26, 2012 by Gary Rubinstein New York Times data and concerns about value-added models (VAMs). https://garyrubinstein.wordpress.com/2012/02/26/analyzing-released-nyc-value-added-data-part-1/ "Based on a series of consultations with senior managers from 83 different higher education institutions in 24 European countries, we observe that LA is primarily perceived as a tool to enhance teaching and institutional management" (Tsai *et al.*, 2020). The challenge is to create a system that "links the concepts of academic analytics, data mining in higher education, and course management system audits and suggests how these techniques and the data they produce might be useful to those who practice the scholarship of teaching and learning" (Baepler & Murdoch, 2010).	To combine variables and define measurement systems that can provide accurate support to improve the learning and teaching process, more than profiling. Assumptions of linearity for learning! EDS or Educational Data Science is a general approach that enclosed the Learning Analytics Concepts. Google Trends shows the numbers from October 2019–September 2020 Learning Analytics:
Think not only about evaluations, there are many factors to review and even though if the problem is or not wrongly defined. Use of tracking issues of academic integrity, repositories of work/projects, analytics, tools, support what is not possible with other means. Use predictive analytics to identify a person of interest. Improve the communication and knowledge sharing/search engines. Create One-stop shops for software, algorithms, data. Understand use of networks at the university.	This perspective is related to how to teach and learn analytics. Some variables to deal with: • Leveraging analytics in the direction of AI: supervised, unsupervised, reinforcement learning. • Applying analytics by knowledge domain: Healthcare analytics, financial analytics, etc. • Creating analytics knowledge/ application of analytics knowledge. • Adapting and adopting of analytics knowledge.

Exhibit 4.32. (*Continued*)

	• Moving from data to understanding/meaning and intelligence development. • Creating capabilities for strategic, managerial, operational, scientific analytics. • Connecting the dots of descriptive (visual) analytics, predictive analytics, prescriptive analytics.
Interaction and joint enhancement/improvement of solutions between humans and machines in many settings. Concentration on areas: languages, tools, models, data, etc. Generalization capacity of results/overfitting awareness/responsibility/accountability. Practice and Ethics of using the Weapons of Mass Confusion (ER), Weapons of Math Destruction(Kathy O'Neil), Weapons of Mass Destruction (P. Bush). Adoption: know what, know how, know why… Analytics in practice (Rodriguez *et al.*, 2019).	This is the creation of means to support research across the institution to develop more high-quality quantitative research. • The emphasis is on using the research methods that are based on data mining, machine learning, simulation, population data (no samples), continuous data, and so on. • Create analytics support which promotes a culture and environment across the campus to improve work and do research across disciplines. • Design experiments, surveys, and other studies that produce statistically meaningful results. • Select proper statistical methods for analyzing data and interpreting results. • Collaborate with industries doing research and identify clear research questions that can be answered quantitatively. • Establish a sampling or experimental plan that will provide enough power to support or reject research hypotheses. Develop additional research questions that can be addressed through analytics.

Exhibit 4.32. (*Continued*)

	• Perform statistical analyses and interpret results. • Assist in presentation of quantitative findings (Data products — dynamic and interactive). • Pursue research opportunities generated from unresolved issues brought forward. • Monitor intermediate stages of long-term projects. • Contact an expert in the particular area of statistics or mathematics to share knowledge and experience.
• Creation of service across disciplines research, learning by doing, and all schools gaining data analytics skills. • Collaboration: internal and external. • One-stop shop for data, technology, interaction, community of practice (networked capable). • Possibly of using the Consilience Concept (Wilson, 1998) as an analytics application principle. Alpaydin E, 2014, Introduction to Machine Learning, Third Edition by The MIT Press ©. "Almost all of science is fitting models to data. Scientists design experiments and make observations and collect data. They then try to extract knowledge by finding out simple models that explain the data they observed. This is called induction and is the process of extracting general rules from a set of particular cases. We are now at a point that such analysis of data can no longer be done by people, both because the amount of data is huge and because people who can do such analysis are rare and manual analysis is costly. There is thus a growing interest in computer models that can analyze data and extract information automatically from them, that is, learn."	• Alignment around the core problem: The mission is the solution of the problem and its associated problems: technical computational/modeling and steps in the processes of learning. Possibly better solution if there is alignment of machine, statistical, organizational learning around the problem. • Understand users/use of solutions: There is no evidence that people who make things happen will be interested in the method behind the scenes but there is high interest from the person using the method to interpret/understand what the method is doing. • Open a view of learning and searching for solutions: It seems that we could use a lot of knowledge from different sources without wasting too much time to reinvent solutions. Avoid being prisoners of our paradigms/literature.

Exhibit 4.32. (*Continued*)

	• Enhance the learning chain: Learning process for organizations cannot stop in the machine, statistical, or organizational learning processes in isolation. The construction of a chain of the three learnings is the priority. • Learn and move forward through the KM processes and design a KMS. • Foster more and more interdisciplinary work on solutions. Everything is about talking with the same and equivalent "languages."

Exhibit 4.32. (*Continued*)

- The key aspect is to consider is that the models are models and do not exist in reality. This means models guide and help to disclosure possible states of nature, their probabilities, multivariate relationships, possible results, and estimation of required parameters, but models are not reality.
- A model can be good, and model risk also arises from the potential for misuse of models or model output. This framework sets out an end-to-end approach for model risk governance across the model life cycle and helps to ensure that model risk remains within the limits of the bank's risk appetite.
- Dealing with model risk includes identification of model risk management principles that require detailed risk management processes with roles and responsibilities of the multiple areas/groups involved in modeling. There are three main levels to deal with model development and its risks: first model owners, developers, and users; second modelers; and third auditing groups. The modeling team develops the model, is compliant with internal and external directives of frameworks, retains the complete knowledge of organization/control/support of the variety of models that is available, the conditions to use them, and the connection to risk knowledge sharing.

- The modeling team requires permanent monitoring, meetings, review of results related to model development, calibration, simulation, outcome analysis, back-testing, variation analysis, error/loss analysis, time series and metrics evaluation, identification of confidence intervals of metrics, validation, parameter estimation methods and improvement, model selection, performance analysis, etc.

The search for solutions starts, as always, with a good problem definition; for example, in the classification problem, the definition of the classes is a crucial step. As mentioned in previous chapters, a crucial step is to shape the problem, give scope, and clarify the target. It is fundamental to understand the metrics, which is not the same as a default rate defined, for example, as the number of accidents per year with a denominator given by number of cars in a year and the number of accidents per year with denominator given by number of miles on the road by cars per year. In credit risk, the definition of what bad credit could be is different based on time, institutions, policies, strategies, etc. This means the class definition will be part of the problem definition and on the contrary the problem definition will be about classes definition. The problem definition is related to the scope of work, the shape of the problem itself, and the expected results. A way to define the problem is to define the questions to answer, define the variables related to those questions, and start reviewing what is known, what is unknown, and what information the project needs to know. The level of knowledge is key; there are different steps regarding, for example, the definition of a classification problem with binary classes or a level of granularity (more than two risk levels) such as the risk categories in a credit agency.

In a risk analytics process, the identification of groups of risk units or type of risk is an important task. A sampling is crucial even though there is big data access or full work with population data as it is necessary to clarify the experiment data to use. In the process of data selection, special attention is required in the search of structures of similarity to identify groups. Once the groups/classes are identified, a problem is to define how certain profile can be classified. The classification process will have an impact on operation and strategy, on decisions, and final models and implementation evaluation. There are several models for classification and, in this chapter, there is a brief description of models used in classification, relationship definition, and variable distribution analysis.

4.2.6 *Managing models*

Strategic risk and creation of intelligence in organizations use models. This subsection supplements the previous one with the introduction of techniques of statistical and machine learning practice. The presentation starts with the concept of distance measurement and continues by connecting distance, metrics, and methods to create groups and classify units of analysis in risk analytics processes. The risk analytics professional has to keep in mind that the creation of models is under the principle of simplicity (parsimony) and better understanding as opposed to creating extremely complex solutions with procedures that are not easy to digest. Testing assumptions opens the gate for testing of modeling, revising the risk model, prototyping, delivery of partial and results in each step, validation, and feedback of results. Permanent feedback from each step is needed. This is a back-and-forth process to get appropriate models for the problem solution, the data available, and constraints related not only to the operation but also to the understanding of outcomes and possibilities of implementation / deployment. The agile approach is highly recommended in the risk analytics process. Keep in mind that in the process of modeling the creation of time series of developed metrics (not only a one-time NPV calculation but simulation of the distribution of the NPVs) is important in order to perform further analysis when the same experiment/business solution is repeated.

Specific terms used in this section are as follows:

- **Classification:** It consists of examining attributes of new objects and assigning them to a set of classes predefined.
- **Estimation:** It works with results and continuous evaluation. Example: Neuronal Networks. Given a dataset to estimate means to find a possible value(s) to describe the behavior of variables and their relationships.
- **Prediction:** The records are classified according to a predicted or possible future behavior or future value.
- **Affinity groups:** Activity to establish the groups of similar attributes.
- **Group/clusters:** Segmentation, organization in homogenous groups.
- **Description:** Identification of patterns.

The variety of models is based on the problems to solve, forecasting, classification, grouping-clustering, optimization, visualization, etc.

As mentioned earlier, clustering is for identifying possible groups of observations in a population. In other words, cluster analysis identifies a set of groups that will minimize within-group variation and maximize between-group variation. Cluster analysis is very useful when trying to reduce the number of variables in a dataset and to discover similarities in the information available. Factor analysis reduces the dimensionality of a dataset and illustrates the structure of a set of variables. Factor analysis converts many variables into a smaller number of factors. The original variables have the highest correlations with the factors. These factors are orthogonal and uncorrelated and thus solve a multicollinearity problem in the data. Principal component analysis (PCA) is a form of factor analysis that analyzes total variance that is commonly used. PCA finds a linear combination of variables such that the maximum variance is extracted from the variables. This variance is removed, and a second linear combination is calculated; this second combination explains a large fraction of the remaining variance and so forth. All principal components are orthogonal.

The possibility of working with data to approach reality involves the creation of methods that support their suitable use and give sense to the models. For example, the expected value of a phenomenon described from the general model is known, but the probability distribution to describe this type of phenomenon is unknown, or the relationships among variables that are associated with the phenomenon. In the conceptual design of the model, variables that have already been established as predictive of failure/default in relevant literature would be tested and included, if they are significant or not for the study and its explanation capacity of variation. In practice, there are several models already used with multiple variables and significant according to the combination and target definitions such as Altman's models, RMA, Moody's, etc. All of them have been tested and used with sets of variables that have a greater power in predicting financial distress/default. A model would use the available information to select the appropriate variables that reduce issues of multicollinearity, data population of the variable, and cost of obtaining the data, such as bond ratings, financial information, credit information, and possibly macro variables (GDP, Inflation, etc.) that prove to be significant in exploratory analysis.

Measurement has been one of the most important activities in science and technology to support the development of problem-solving processes in societies. In risk analytics, organizations are in a continuous process of creating solutions that are related to the measurement process, definition of metrics, and the way that concepts associated with risk management can be described as a measure among numbers and non-numeric variables. Probability and statistics are measurement means for science and in particular risk analytics. Metrics and indicators start as deterministic and move to stochastic. For example, ratios in financial analysis are deterministic at the beginning and they move to be considered random variables and analyzed trough several models. In risk analytics, measurement of probability can be an indicator of similarity in risk classes or possible events. Different types of variables are comparable using similarity measures. The measure of the distance between two objects with the Euclidean definition using the location of the objects is one common way to work with numerical variables. The situation to represent the distance between categories of variables requires a specific definition of the similarity. Probability distribution of default is a way to define the levels of risk/categories in credit risk. There is a need to define the scale, units, and way to interpret the results. In risk analytics, for example, the measurement of positive–negatives or negative–positives in a classification problem can be a similarity measure among classification techniques.

The general concept to use is the measurement of similarity based on the definition of distance measurement for quantitative and qualitative variables. In the measurement of similarity, the higher the value of the metric, the more it represents similar sets, events, objects, variables, etc. The selection of the similarity measure is crucial in the goodness of the algorithm or technique in risk analytics. In quantitative data, there is a definition of distance as part of L_p-norm definition that will be $p = 2$ for the Euclidean distance or $p = 1$ for the Manhattan distance metrics. A distance function has the following attributes: Distance from A to B, $d[A,B]$ has four properties:

(1) $d[A,B] \geq 0$
(2) $d(A,A) = 0$
(3) $d(A,B) = d(B,A)$
(4) $d(A,B) \leq d(A,C) + d(C,B)$ when C is between A and B

Similarity measures give a statistical distance between two p-dimensional vectors of observations, for instance, $d(x,y)=\sqrt{[(x-y)'\mathbf{A}(x-y)]}$ where $A = S^{-1}$ and S is the sample variance–covariance matrix (See Chapter 1). Other possible norms are the Euclidean, Minkowski, Camberra, and Czekonowski distances [see Johnson & Wichern (1998)].

For instance, $A = (x_1, \ldots, x_k)$ and $B = (y_1, \ldots, y_k)$ and the L_p-norm is given by $(\Sigma_{i=1}^{k} |x_i - y_i|^p)^{\frac{1}{p}}$.

There are factors affecting the use *of* L_p-norm because of the data distribution, the type of attribute that is used to describe the phenomenon, how the values are separated, etc. In certain cases, there are other measures of similarity to use such as the Minkowski distance $(\Sigma_{i=1}^{k} w_i |x_i - y_i|^p)^{\frac{1}{p}}$ that can give a weight (w_i of the attribute *i*) to a parameter that could be more relevant in a problem.

Another example for improving the definition similarities can be related to the variation of the data around points which will determine how correlations can affect the metric. The Mahalanobis distance is defined between two points $A = (x_1, \ldots, x_k)$ and $B = (y_1, \ldots, y_k)$ as $\sqrt{(A-B)\Sigma^{-1}(A-B)^T}$ where Σ^{-1} represents the inverse of *kxk* covariance matrix.

Strengths and weaknesses of the method of using distances in similarity measurement:

The modeling process plan includes several steps from business understanding to deployment and actions. However, there are some filters and guide points to keep in mind for a modeling process:

(1) Once objectives are clear and data are relatively clean and organized as raw data tables, it is required to define new variables if they are needed in the analysis, transforming the fields, techniques, tools to be organized, clarify the research questions, or split the general problem into more specific testable questions to answer which of the questions can be converted into hypotheses to test. Answers will need planning for level of aggregation and groups where the answers can be used. Models for subsets of data are a good practice if that adjustment supports decisions in those groups. In marketing, for example, it can be segmentation and in credit risk the types of loans, groups of customers, or policies because of combination of products, etc.

(2) Build various models that are compatible with data and objectives. At this level, it is important to recognize that a model can be the structural model type and calculate results. The first concept of structural model in this book refers to the models such as regression with

multiple forms of regressions according to the variables used. The second concept of model to use is when the structural model as regression has parameter estimated from data and the estimators in the model will be the source to calculate the values of interest. This means the final model to implement is a structural model (one or many) with specific estimated parameters.

(3) In general, a modeling process is successful not only because of accuracy indicators but also because of the possibility of assessing the model, and the limitations/constraints on operating and developing the models. Availability of data, similar to measurement of outcomes, possible ways for automation and data feeding, is a requirement to support the modeling process.

Models are mainly under supervised and unsupervised learning modeling processes and introduce other ways of learning like reinforcement learning (Figures 4.6 and 4.7). The unsupervised learning models require evaluation and tests based on the selection of the algorithms, similarity measures, data use, and data organization. For example, on the one hand, in the case a model for clustering/creating groups of risk units, the variables values should be in a similar scale, with most of the cases creating normalized data. On the other hand, the test and evaluation of models in supervised learning requires the partition of data: partition in minimum two sets, one for

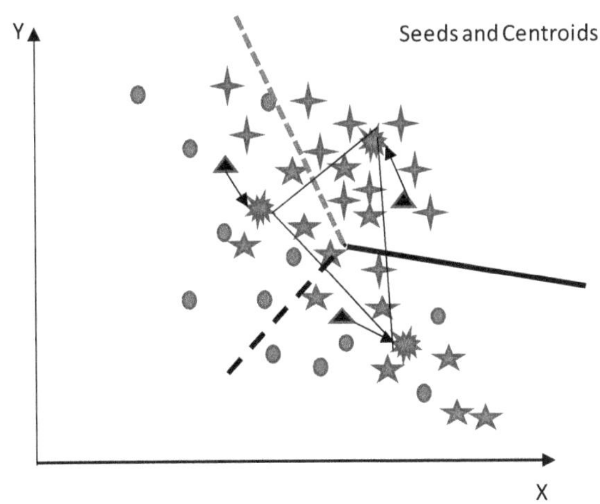

Figure 4.6. Separation of groups based on similarities to centroids.

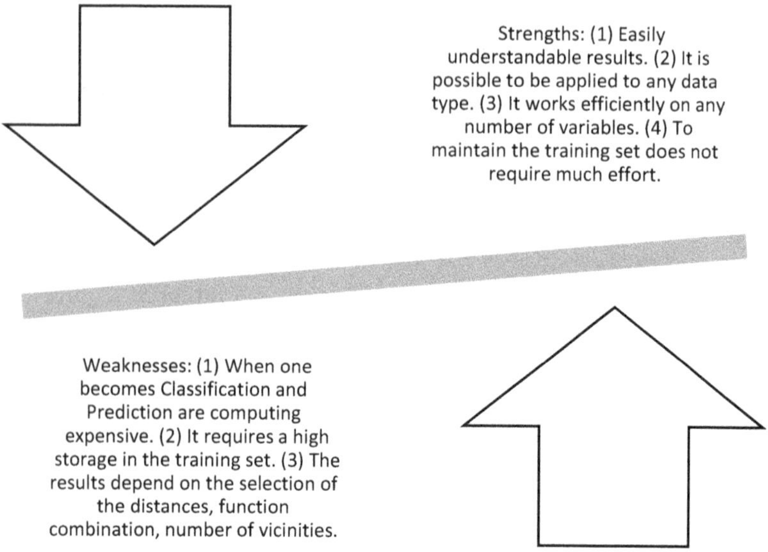

Figure 4.7. Balance use of similarity measurement, variables, and models according to targets.

training the model and another for testing it. Model validation and testing are crucial parts of developing risk analytics systems. If the model is not validated and tested, there is no certainty that the results of the model agree with reality and that it can be generalized. One of the complex aspects can come from overfitting; this means that the model could fit very well to the original data but not to a new dataset. Records can be related to time and in that case the partition will be based on the selection of a set of data points in time for training and another for testing. Models usually use the selection of records in a random way to create a partition of training and testing a model.

Another aspect in risk analytics for the evaluation of the models is sensitivity analysis. In the evaluation, the purpose is to identify how results can change because of changes in parameters and assumptions. Back testing is intimately related to the concept of credit value-at-risk. Back testing assures that actual losses correspond to projected losses. Stress testing consists of analyzing the results of the model output given various extreme scenarios. Model performance measures are necessary to understand how each model represents reality and to be able to compare models among themselves.

In performance evaluation of models, there are methods that help risk analytics processes. ROC curves (receiving operator curves) measure the performance of a model with a categorical outcome (e.g., "bads" and "goods"). It is a graphical representation of the fitting process quality, e.g., how many real "goods" vs. how many false "bads" there are in the predictions (type I and II errors). The area under the ROC curve (AUC) is the measure of performance, where 0.5 indicates random prediction and 1 indicates perfect prediction. Another method is cumulative accuracy profiles (CAPs), which are a special type of ROC. This method uses ordered data points by the scores in the scales of classes from high to low risk and selects a percentage of the total number of risk units as the calculated percentage of the members of the target class (for example, risk units that are performing poorly) that have score equal or lower than the score for the selected fraction of companies. With the CAPs, it is possible to generate what is called ARs (accuracy ratios) that represent how close the CAP is to an ideal CAP according to the dataset being analyzed.

Two Other metrics of model performance: The Kolmogorov Smirnov (KS) D Statistic is an indication of the separation between two datasets, for example, "bads" and "goods". KS does not make any assumptions about the underlying distribution. The Gini criterion for model performance measures the quality of the separation in models, especially in some algorithmic (machine learning) approaches like classification trees, to identify the quality of splitting. It compares the frequency of cases in the branch with the total associated with a parent node. The purpose is to minimize the value of the index. Gini is appropriate when the contribution of the variables to explain the event of interest needs to be identified.

$\text{Gini}(t) = 1 - \Sigma_{j=1}^{n} p(j \mid t)^2$ where the p represents the relative frequency of class j at node t. The Gini coefficient takes a cumulative distribution curve to compare the distribution of a specific variable with the uniform distribution. The greater the deviation of the cumulative distribution from the uniform one, the greater the divergence or separation.

A simplified guide to models according to different questions (as a supplement to what was presented in the Exhibit 4.20) is indicated in Exhibit 4.33:

Grouping is done based on similarities or distances. Common algorithms for sorting objects in groups are similarity measures, hierarchical clustering methods, multidimensional scaling, and correspondence analysis. In clustering, the intention is to find a partition of the data in which the differences among members of a group are diminished (Figure 4.8). All the measures are taken with respect to a centroid and points near the centroids are assigned; the centroids are modified in different iterations

Need/action	Technique/method/tool	General aspects to review
Exploration and visualization	EDA, statistical summaries, distribution variable analysis, scatterplots, correspondence analysis	Appropriate research questions lead to data and model selection. In another level, the type of learning that is required: supervised, unsupervised, reinforcement. Additionally, the concept behind technique selection is about selecting inferential or non-inferential techniques. Identify type of variables and appropriateness of the models or transformations required. Predictors: continuous, discrete, categorical, dummies; targets: continuous, categorical. There are many algorithms for solving problems as mentioned in the left-hand columns.
Data dimension reduction	Factor analysis, principal components analysis	
Optimization	Calculus-based optimization, numerical methods and specific algorithmic optimization, mathematical programming models, DEA	
Prediction classification	Discriminant Analysis, Logistic regression, classification trees, ensemble algorithms, ANN, CNN, deep learning	
Prediction regression	Multiple-linear and multivariate regression, stepwise, ANOVA Generalized linear models Adjusted Regression, Lasso–Ridge Poisson, Tobit, Burr, Weibull regression	
Prediction forecasting	Time series models with or without stationarity data, with and without variance weights: ARMA, ARIMA, GARCH family	
Association	Link analysis Network analysis Sequence analysis	
Clustering	*K*-means, *k*-medoids, *k*-modes, hierarchical, single-complete link, minimum spanning tree, PAM portioning around medoids, or using genetic and NN algorithms for clustering, BIRCH, CURE	
Simulation	Monte Carlo, discrete events simulation	
Cause and effect identification	Econometric approach, structural equations, causal inference	

Exhibit 4.33. A brief of problems and relationships of techniques.

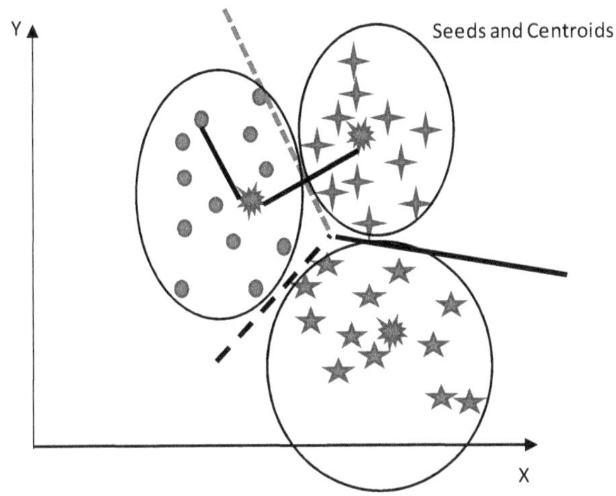

Figure 4.8. Illustration of clustering process.

and the allocation of points is repeated until the centroids do not modify the minimum differences in group members. The algorithm should converge, and the process is affected by the initial selection of the points. The first selection of points is based on the observation of the points where there is high density, and they are separated widely. The centroids are updated depending on the minimization of the squared error or distances among points. Averages or middle points are taken as centroids for groups. The points are allocated by proximity to the centroid. There is a difference in finding the centroid inside the group or outside. The *k*-mode, *k*-medoid, *k*-medians, or *k*-prototypes (the algorithms use the higher frequency or center of distribution *o* a mix) are used with categorical variables inside the group in the center of it. Distance methods for identifying similarities include a concept of vicinity that is a circle around the centroid; it can be an issue to solve in certain data where there are irregular not convex sets or where outliers affect the vicinity definition.

One of the methods to find groups of risk units is the *k*-means algorithm. With *k*-means, the number of groups is predefined by the researcher and the *k* number is tested with different *k* values up to the point the clusters are not improving. There is a method known as the elbow graphic that helps to identify the best *k* to select: elbow method, silhouette method, and gap static method. The idea is to test several *k*'s looking for the total within-cluster variation minimization.

Algorithm *k*-means:

(1) To choose the number of groups that are desired to form.
(2) *K* is the number of seeds to determine the centroids. Each seed is a combination of values by each measurement.
(3) To each record in the data base allocate the point to the groups where the centroid is closer.
(4) The centroids of the new groups are calculated, and the complete process initiates with new centroids taking the role from the seeds. The points can be moved from a group to another one.
(5) Iterate several times.

In summary, the process is the search of separate in groups of certain number of members with the search of *k* minimizing the within-groups sum of squares for all variables.

In *k*-means, the selection of *k* is a problem of identifying the number of clusters that can use the elbow approach that is based on the average distance of the points to the clusters' centroid and observing when the value of the average changes at the speed of reducing the value. Silhouette score can also be used that provides a way to decide the k based on the fact that the higher the value, the better the clusters are defined.

Clusters have important points to keep in mind for implementation:

(1) Standardization: there is a difference between scales and ways to maintain a similarly good evaluation among members of the clusters.
(2) Evaluation of performance using metrics.
(3) Use of numerical and non-numerical variables according to similarity metrics defined in each case.

The silhouette calculation is based on $S_i = (b_i - a_i)/\max\{(a_i, b_i)\}$; for each of the points, a_i, b_i $i = 1, \ldots, n$. The comparison of different clusters is tested to indicate the best number of clusters to use, i.e., the higher the value, the better the separation of the clusters. One can take the value of seven as the elbow rule suggests. Correlations are calculated with the quantitative non-normalized and normalized values (the same correlation value) of the variables. This is to illustrate that the clustering process is different when the clusters is for data points or for variables.

Another clustering method is the hierarchical clustering method which is a linkage method where the smallest distance in a matrix $D = (d_{ik})$ of all the distances between points is found. Merging the corresponding objects, say *U* and *V*, produces cluster *UV*. The distance between (*UV*) and any other cluster *W* is computed by $d_{(UV)W} = \min[d_{UW}, d_{VW}]$, where the distances are between the nearest neighbors of clusters *U* and *W* and clusters *V* and *W*, respectively. The procedure is the hierarchic use of dendrograms or clustering. In summary, clustering methods are selected according to problem and data. For example, in agglomerative clustering, one needs to start with a cluster defined by each observation as the algorithm combines clusters according to similarity (distance), obtaining bigger clusters; the process is repeated to have a root cluster with observations. The graphics of the process are represented by the dendrogram. This uses a proximity matrix and it can be down to top or top to down. Each element is based on similarity measures, or a variable belonging to an individual group is combined with the most similar groups, becoming a division until a group of a single element is left.

The opposite view of the agglomerative method is divisive hierarchical clustering which begins with the root, in which all observations are included in a single cluster and the algorithm looks for a set with the highest dissimilarity. The branch definition can be maximum or complete linkage clustering that looks for the maximum value of the dissimilarities among clusters. Another is minimum or single linkage clustering where the groups are created based on the minimum dissimilarities. The mean or average linkage clustering does not take maximum or minimum but averages of group observations; centroid linkage clustering is based on the definition of a centroid (for example, the mean) of the groups and measuring the dissimilarities using the centroids. Finally, Ward's minimum variance method reduces the variance in the cluster/group to the minimum and has the maximum separation of the groups.

4.2.7 *Models in risk classification, relationships, and predictions*

The development and use of statistical and machine learning require probability and statistics theory. Statistical learning is oriented to inference and discovering variable relationships. The validation of the models is not based on testing datasets as it is in machine learning; it is based on mathematical optimization or mathematical definitions of the model structure. In a classification problem, let $\boldsymbol{X}$ be the set of variables $(X_1, X_2, \ldots, X_p)$ each one takes as a value per risk unit and it produces a vector $\boldsymbol{x} = (x_1, x_2, \ldots, x_p)$ with all the attributes. Let A be the set of all possible answers and this is assumed to be finite. This set represents the sample space or the set of all possible answers. This means two classes. The general problem to solve is to get **x** set G and B where $G \cup B = A$. G can represent the set of good risk profile and B the set of bad risk profile. The definition of bad risk profile for the classification is made according to the business and it can be modified through time. The change will modify the classification results. In general, there are two costs associated with the classification: C_1 if a good risk is wrongly classified and not accepted and C_2 if a bad risk prospect is accepted. P_G and P_B thus refer to the proportion of applicants with a good risk profile and a bad risk profile, respectively. For this set of expressions, the random variable is considered discrete and **x** is a vector.

The error is the classification of wrong profiles. There are expressions in terms of conditional probability that provide the structure of all the conceptualizations. The first step is to define $p(\boldsymbol{x}|G) = \frac{p(x \cap G)}{p(\text{Good})}$ as the probability of a good risk applicant with attributes **x** divided by probability of a good risk profile. And we call $q(G|\mathbf{x})$ the probability that a risk unit is good, given the attributes **x**. $p(\mathbf{x})$ is the probability to have attributes **x**. Then, $q(G|\mathbf{x})p(\mathbf{x}) = P(\mathbf{x}|G)P_G$ or $(G|\boldsymbol{x}) = \frac{P(x|G)P_G}{p(x)}$; thus, the cost of misclassification will be $C_1 \cdot \sum_{x \in B} q(G|\boldsymbol{x})p(\boldsymbol{x}) + C_2 \cdot \sum_{x \in G} q(B|\boldsymbol{x})p(\boldsymbol{x})$.

If the level of acceptance is r, the G has to satisfy $\sum_{x \in G} P(\boldsymbol{x}|G)P_G + \sum_{x \in G} P(\boldsymbol{x}|B)P_B = r$. The problem is converted to minimize $\sum_{x \in G} P(\boldsymbol{x}|B)P_B$ the default rate,

subject to

$$\sum_{x \in G} p(\boldsymbol{x}) = r$$

because

$$\sum_G p(\boldsymbol{x}) = \sum_G P(G|\mathbf{x})p(\boldsymbol{x}) + \sum_G P(B|\mathbf{x})p(\boldsymbol{x})$$

$$\sum_G p(\boldsymbol{x}) = \sum_G (1 - P(B|\mathbf{x}))p(\boldsymbol{x}) + \sum_G P(B|\mathbf{x})p(\boldsymbol{x})$$

The general condition to belong to the good risk profile set has to be addressed by the following set definition where c defines the condition to be considered good risk profile:

$$G = \left\{ x \left| \frac{P(x|B)P_B}{P(x)} \leq c \right. \right\} = \left\{ x \left| \frac{1-c}{c} \leq \frac{q(G|x)}{q(B|x)} \right. \right\}$$

In the continuous case of the random variable, all the previous approaches have to be changed for a probability density and the sums transformed by integrals, but the relationships to be defined are the same. For example, the following is used in the logistic case:

$$\ln\left(\frac{p_i}{1-p_i}\right) = \ln\left(\frac{P_G f(x|G)}{P_B f(x|B)}\right)$$

Risk classification involves different steps with several approaches available at each step:

(1) Collecting the data; in this case, numerical or categorical data can be used. The sampling should be defined, wherever possible, to reflect the characteristics of the data. For example, values of claims or profiles of clients can be used or a mix of both.
(2) Classification of the groups of insured/risk units. Here, we have two different problems: One is the definition of groups and selection of variables; the other is to classify a new client into one of these groups. Discriminant analysis, correspondence analysis, or cluster analysis techniques are used to define the profiles of the groups with numerical data. Logistic regression is also used, especially with categorical data.
(3) Cross-validation of the classification with the current data.
(4) For new data, assign each new insured/risk unit to the classification group with the closest characteristics.
(5) Review the results and perform a misclassification analysis.

In general, the solution of a classification problem requires an identification target with a two-variable model with different categories, or n-variable models with multiple categories. This means using explanatory variables that are numerical or categorical and classification of two or multiple groups. Clustering and classification models have relationships with risk selection of insurance prospects, credit users, customers in organizations, etc. In the following paragraphs, models with qualitative and quantitative variables are considered. Some of the most important characteristics in risk analysis and a few applications are given. An automobile insurance illustration is given. The main problem can be defined as a set of steps from grouping, sampling, and classification up to the price, premium, and revenue calculation.

The risk classification problem is one of the most important subjects in financial services, in marketing, and in particular in insurance and reinsurance, as much for underwriting as for actuarial calculation of premiums, reserves, and ruin problem evaluation. For example, classification methods based on scoring are used in bank loan analysis. The process requires one to identify good or bad prospects, the probabilities of monetary losses on a portfolio, and the survival of loans to maturity. Risk classification and credit analysis have a probability of misclassification, which must be minimized. However, in risk classification, there is a prior problem, i.e., to define the classes or groups used to separate risks. The definitions of what is the target, what is bad or good, and what is success and failure represent the crucial part. From the definition, using the business and theoretical knowledge, the data and models will be organized. Moreover, in industries such as insurance, classification requires one to have some important information:

- Risk can be classified relative to frequency, for example, bad or good drivers, winter season or not. Besides, the intensity of the risk can change and it is possible to have a small number of large claims. The strategy of the company can be given for a mix between number/frequency and intensity/severity. This, in terms of the model, means a different set of the variables for making decisions about the risk in each group.
- Classification methods require complete data. For example, in insurance, sometimes data are missing, as variables important to the claim process may be difficult to find in a file. For example, car parts that are expensive can impact on the claim costs in automobile insurance, but this amount of detail is usually not kept on record.
- Loss distributions are usually heavy tailed, that is, they depart from the normal distribution and in many cases are mixed distributions.

- The effect of time is very important; the risk is good today, but it can change in the future.
- Some of the variables in insurance are categorical and it is necessary to create dummy variables to include them in models.
- Contracts in insurance have different simultaneous risk coverages. It means some groups could be good for one risk but bad for others.
- There is a difference between collective and individual contracts. The analysis of collective contracts is similar to that of a company.
- These are some differences with the analysis done using scoring methods in the banking industry.

Another common and important approach to understand relationships of variables is the use of the Generalized Linear Models, which form the bases of many risk modeling processes. In this section, the possibility to use more options to identify the good relationship between explanatory variables and the dependent variable (target) is included. There is a generalization relative to the assumption of the probability distribution of the events in the population. It is possible to consider different distributions for the errors, random effects (because of risk units), and for the dependent variables, not only normal, for instance, Poisson, Binomial, Normal, Gamma, and Inverse Gaussian (exponential family members). At the same time, different link functions can be used to obtain the linear structure required in the analysis.

The link function gives us the relationship between the mean of the *i*th observation and its linear predictors. $y_i = g_i(\mu_i) = x_i^T \beta$. The link function is a means to transform the dependent variable to use the least squares method. A specific case used in a study is the logistic regression where the assumption of the probability distribution is binomial and the link function is the natural log of the odds. In the same way, the Generalized Linear models offer the possibility to include ANOVA, ANCOVA, and MANOVA analysis, very important in transactional models, because they introduced the risk level as a factor affecting the transaction risk. The approach using generalized linear models has been used in similar problems, for instance, survival modeling and graduation, multiple stage models, risk classification, premium rating, and claim reserving in non-life insurance.

At this level of the search of relationships among variables, it is important to distinguish what is multiple linear regression and multivariate linear regression. In both cases, there are several variables that influence the behavior of one output variable (multiple linear regression) or several output variables (multivariate linear regression). An example of multiple linear regression is risk analytics where there can be interest in describing the severity of a risk event based on the variables related to the risk unit, market environment, or any other set of possible attributes. In the case of multivariate linear regression, an example is when there are demographic variables, product use in an organization, and a marketing campaign with output variables of revenue and volume generated by the marketing strategy. In multiple linear regression, the following takes place:

(1) The dependent variable is continuous.
(2) A set of continuous independent variables is used.
(3) The points of deviation of the line follow a normal distribution.
(4) The residuals are independent of the values that are predicted.
(5) The objective is to construct a linear function of the independent variables that allows one to explain or to predict the value of the dependent variable.

The assumptions in multiple linear regression are as follows:

(1) All the predicting variables must have a linear relationship.
(2) Error distribution is normal. The expected value of the error of the model must be zero.
(3) There must be no autocorrelation of the remainders of the models.
(4) There must be no correlation between the independent error and variables.
(5) Multicollinearity must be absent between the predicting variables.

In the following paragraphs, one will find classification models using various regression-related models. The models will classify risk units as organizations and as transactions. In the first stage, all risk unit-specific variables are considered to predict the risk unit risk. In the second stage, the risk unit model output is used as an input for the transaction model. Subsequently, all other transaction-related variables are used simultaneously with the risk unit model to determine the transaction risk. This two-stage approach was chosen to ensure that no risk unit-specific information is lost in modeling the transaction risk. This way, the level of significance associated with multiple variables will be distributed among the risk unit and transaction-specific variables and not only the transactional variables.

Risk differentiation refers to the ability to classify risk units in groups that are homogeneous within each class and heterogeneous among classes. A good data structure is considered necessary to improve a model's robustness. In particular, a data structure that includes changes over time is preferred (panel/longitudinal data). Many alternative methodologies have been reviewed, but there are two that are worth focusing on. The first one is a traditional logit model using cross-sectional data for a cohort of risk units that includes several years of data. The second one is based on longitudinal data analysis for unbalanced panels. An unbalanced panel is one in which each individual (risk unit) has a different number of observations through time; in other words, the entry and exit points of each buyer are different. The unbalanced panel handles entries due to new exposure added to a portfolio on a risk unit and exits due to withdrawal, exclusion, expired cases, or events of interest submission. Based on this technique, a logit model with fixed or/and random effects would be employed. The second modeling structure is preferred given that the advantages between the explanatory variables and time are combined under a logistic structure. The selection of this model is a fundamental step in the perspective of a modeling dynamic structure. A panel data model allows one to control for heterogeneity and variability caused by the explanatory variables and time for each particular risk unit.

The data use in risk analytics requires the combination of data sources and profile attributes. For example, in this illustrative case, two approaches are tried. The first one consists of building two sub-models: one will rate risk units with available non-financial and financial information, and the other will rate risk units with only non-financial information available. Each sub-model would be calibrated based on each of the subpopulations. The structure of each sub-model would be, in principle, similar and the criteria used to define which variables remain in each sub-model will be given by the significance level or the variables and the sub-models themselves. The outputs of the sub-models would then be amalgamated into a unique score, the model's score. Each particular score level would represent a certain probability of default (or a range of probabilities of default). The second approach is to transform certain variables into categorical variables, where missing information would be considered one special category. One such variable could be the existence or non-existence of financial information; another variable could be age of financial statement if available. This is derived from the fact that missing value can be interpreted and can provide clues related to the event of interest.

There is in a modeling process a special consideration about specific variables, for example, industry and country, which are potential factors affecting the risk unit and transaction models. Three approaches are common ground in real applications. The first approach or the ideal one is to have one model per combination of country and industry. In this case, several models would be fitted to the data for a specific combination of country and industry and the results of each model would then be harmonized in an equivalent scale through the probabilities of default. The second is to fit several models per industry sector or per geographic area. The results would then be combined in a score according to their particular probabilities of default. The third is to introduce categorical variables to account for industry and country-specific variations. These variables would be included in the general model.

In the analysis of having separated models, a point to consider is the number of events of interest that are related to the input data. The number of events of interest can be an issue of unbalanced data for performing an appropriate model. The number should be one that provides capacity to create a model with an appropriate level of robustness (power of the model sampling process). In most of the cases having different models per combination of industry and country cannot not feasible, given the amount of events information that would be needed per sector. Information would be unavailable in many of the combinations or in some cases results would not be robust and thus lack any meaning. The design of models per industry sectors or geographical areas can possibly be explored. This alternative would perhaps be the most efficient, but availability of the event of interest observations is still a factor that can limit the modeling capacity. Introducing a categorical variable is an alternative that will provide knowledge about the significance or not of the sector and region variables in explaining the events of interest to implement in practice.

In the search of variables to include in a risk model, there is one to consider, in particular for default or bankruptcy, that is, the relationship to parents in financial or industrial conglomerates. The organizations that are related because of ownership will be affected by risk events in each

Advantages	Disadvantages
Predicts the probability of failure per risk unit for the period under observation.	Does not account for time variations among individual risk units.
Easy to replicate.	Available data are reduced.
Straightforward.	Resulting probability is related to the chosen period.

Exhibit 4.34. Working with cross-sectional data advantages and disadvantages.

risk unit. The impact of the effect will be associated with the level of equity ties in the organization ownership. There is a higher chance that the parent will take its subsidiary to bankruptcy if the parent itself goes bankrupt.

As mentioned at the beginning of the section, the two possible models are cross-sectional and longitudinal logistic regressions. First, the data selection and modeling process is a cohort of risk units, and their attributes (cross-sectional data, see Exhibit 4.34) at a specific point in time are selected and the events of interests are observed at the end of the chosen period. Once data are prepared, a logistic regression is run on the data to model the probability of the event of interest and to identify those attributes that contribute to explaining the events of interest. This procedure would be repeated by changing the cohorts and performance windows to obtain cumulative probabilities of default for different time periods.

Second, longitudinal (panel data as mentioned in Chapter 3) data refer to cross-sectional observations that are followed over time. An independent variable and a set of explanatory variables are observed at each time, permitting the study of the dynamics of an event, for instance, the claims event. Tracking each risk unit over time has advantages compared to cross-sectional analysis. When using cross-sectional data, individual variation cannot be separately identified. However, by taking repeated observations per risk unit, risk unit-specific variations are identifiable, thus accounting for heterogeneity of the risk units.

There are possible variations in the linear regression model because of the records/risk units evaluated. In a linear regression, the coefficients are considered fixed, but it is possible to think that the coefficient can have random behavior according to the risk units. Evaluation of variables of risk units can be correlated. The simplest case could be through time observations of attributes of one risk unit, e.g., a patient, a driver, etc. The **general mixed model** is defined as $y_{it} = z'_{it}\ \alpha_i + x'_{it}\beta + \varepsilon_{it}$; each risk unit i is observed at each time t_i. y_{it} is the response variable that can take values

0 or 1, if there is an event of interest or not. The explanatory variables are $x_{it} = (x_{it1}, \dots x_{itK})'$ and the parameters are $\beta_{it} = (\beta_1, \dots \beta_K)'$. The model uses an additional set of explanatory variables $z_{it} = (z_{it1}, \dots z_{itq})'$ whose parameters $\alpha_{it} = (\alpha_{it1}, \dots \alpha_{itq})'$ represent the randomness of the variable's coefficients because of the risk units. The α_i are assumed *i.i.d.* N(0, σ_α^2) and ε_{it} are *i.i.d.* In addition, α_i and ε_{it} are independent and not observable.

The fixed-effects logit model is given by prob $(Y_{it} = 1(\text{bad})) = \frac{exp^{\alpha_i + x_{it}'\beta}}{1+exp^{\alpha_i + x_{it}'\beta}}$ where $\alpha_{it} = (\alpha_{it1}, \dots \alpha_{itq})'$ are individual effects that are constant over time and risk unit specific, and $x_{it} = (x_{it1}, \dots x_{itK})'$ are the explanatory variables and whose parameters are $\beta_{it} = (\beta_1, \dots \beta_K)'$.

The **mixed** (fixed- and random-effects) **logit model** is given by $Prob(Y_{it} = 1(bad)) = \frac{exp^{z_{it}'\alpha_i + x_{it}'\beta}}{1+exp^{z_{it}'\alpha_i + x_{it}'\beta}}$ where $\alpha_{it} = (\alpha_{it1}, \dots \alpha_{itq})'$ are risk unit specific and are *i.i.d.* N(0, σ_α^2), $x_{it} = (x_{it1}, \dots x_{itK})'$ are exploratory variables with parameters $\beta_{it} = (\beta_1, \dots \beta_K)'$, and $z_{it} = (z_{it1}, \dots z_{itq})'$ are an additional set of explanatory variables related to the α_i's.

The advantages and disadvantages of using a mixed model are shown in Exhibit 4.35.

The mixed model methodology is recommended to account for heterogeneity of the risk units and to analyze the dynamics of a portfolio as

Advantages	Disadvantages
Allows us to study a change in the response over time in reference to each risk unit.	Difficult interpretation of fixed and/or random effects.
Allows us to separate dynamic relations from static comparisons.	Predictions are not straightforward.
Provides a larger set of observations.	Difficult to program.
Provides more robust estimates and conclusions.	Difficult to estimate.
Allows us to identify factors that are not observable in cross-sectional analysis.	
Allows us to identify changes in performance through an economic cycle.	
Allows us to account for individual variation.	

Exhibit 4.35. Advantages and disadvantages of mixed models.

well as the attributes that explain the probability of the event's interest. Fixed effects are adequate when risk units in a portfolio are unique, e.g., large quoted companies, where the sample is not random. The fixed-effects model applies to cross-sectional observations and all inferences are made with respect to the specific variations within the sample. A random-effects approach is appropriate if the cross-sectional observations are drawn randomly from a population. The random-effects approach makes inferences with respect to the population characteristics. As an example, an unbalanced panel (some observations can have missing values for certain years; this means the time dimension is specific to each individual) of m years of data is used with $t = 1, \ldots, m$ and $i = 1, \ldots, n$, where n = total risk units at each time t. As the dependent variable, the event of interest would be modeled. As independent variables, all relevant variables defining profiles (financial, demographic, macroeconomic, etc.) would be used. This model would be used to measure the probability event of interest at each time t, and would allow one to identify the variables that are related to the event of interest. The model's output would be the probability of a risk unit of indicating the appearance of an event of interest in $1, \ldots, m$ years. The probability output would then be converted into a score to define risk levels. In the actuarial practice for pricing, the general mixed model is the balanced Bühlmann model that is used in the context of the credibility theory to calibrate the pricing of different risk units and risk types. As Frees (2004) pointed out, "Data used for insurance pricing in the credibility rate-making context often fit into this panel data design. For insurance pricing, "subjects" may be individual or group policyholders, rating territories or industries. Explanatory variables, or covariates, help to explain claims differences among subjects and thus provide useful information for pricing different risks. For the panel data design, the critical component is that the claims (the response) and the explanatory variables are tracked over time, for each subject."

Prediction of the risk unit-specific probabilities of default has the following connotations:

- Prediction of a probability of an event for a period of time.
- Prediction with the variables of the expected loss and the portfolio structure.

- Prediction under variance components of the most important effects affecting a portfolio.
- Prediction of changes in the default rates though time and their impact on the risk level distribution.

In general, the effects of the risk unit-specific explanatory variables through time are part of the questions to answer in risk analytics (Frees, 2004). Particularly, the panel data model based on the prediction power is given by a linear mixed-effects model:

$$y_{i,T_i+L} = \boldsymbol{Z}'_{i,T_i+L}\boldsymbol{\alpha}_i + \boldsymbol{x}'_{i,T_i+L}\boldsymbol{\beta} + \varepsilon_{i,T_i+L}$$

where L is a time in the future, and the random effects, variables $\boldsymbol{\alpha}_i$ effects of the i-th specific subject included in the data set, the vectors $\boldsymbol{x}$ of explanatory variables and $\boldsymbol{Z}$ as the risk unit specific are assumed to be known. Then, the forecasts will be given by the use of the covariance matrices and the BLUP (Best Linear Unbiased Estimator) estimation (vector of coefficient estimators for $\boldsymbol{Z}$) for a_{BLUP}.

For example, the forecast for a one-year period would be represented by $\hat{y}_{i,T_i+1} = \boldsymbol{x}'_{i,T_i+1}\boldsymbol{b}_{\text{GLS}} + \boldsymbol{z}'_{i,T_i+1}\boldsymbol{a}_{\text{BLUP}} + r'^{V_i^{-1}}\left(y_i - X_i b_{\text{GLS}}\right)$, where $\boldsymbol{r}$ represents the correlation vector and V is the variance–covariance matrix for the model.

GLS represents the estimation method, in this case generalized least squares, to estimate the β's. And BLUPs represent the best linear unbiased predictors for the random effects. The concept is that given two random variables, for example, following a joint bivariate normal distribution, the estimated mean of one corresponding to a specified value of the other is unknown as a predictor of the particular realization of the random variables.

It is common that a model includes fixed and random effects for the description of the relationship between dependent variables and predictors (independent variables). The estimators and interpretation have to be produced in order to generate the predictions. Prediction power of the models can be identified with a set of assumptions and constraints. The general improvement process for prediction will consider a simulation framework for the portfolio. The results of the distribution modeling and a general set of empirical results are included in the Monte Carlo simulation process, based on the following steps:

- Identify a rule for acceptance of risk units based on the probability of default. The rule has to identify a cut-off; at the beginning, the cut-off is only for classification purposes (acceptable or not).
- Generate observations with the attributes used in the default event analysis.
- Determine which applicants will be granted a credit limit; this step is necessary to calculate the expected default probabilities. Then, the rules for all these who have got an approval are applied and the total credit losses on the portfolio are calculated.
- The process has to be repeated in order to calculate an approximation of the loss distribution, based on the number of cases generated.
- Finally, the process is tested many times to validate results.

In general, in regression, in ordinary least squares, what is solved is to find coefficients that produce this equality $y_i = \beta_0 + \beta_1 x_i + \varepsilon_i$ where the residuals (difference estimation and actual values) are minimized. The y_i are response-dependent variables or targets that depends on x_i that are explanatory-variable-independent variables. A maximum likelihood estimation in regression is applicable from the definition of the logit/probit model where $p(y_i = 1) = F(X_1, \ldots, X_k) = \beta_1 X_1 + \cdots + \beta_k X_k$ looking for the probability of an event such as $y_i = 1$ through a function F, that is, the probability of a category for the response variable. The purpose is to maximize the function that is called likelihood and to obtain the product of of having the value $y_i = 1$ in each observation. Formalization is presented in the following paragraphs. A scoring system can be expressed as a decision rule based on a linear function F where X_i are the relevant variables and β_i are the weights or scores corresponding to variables X_i.

Discriminant analysis (see ahead) is most frequently used to determine the coefficients β_i. However, it imposes the assumption of normally distributed variables X_i, which are violated for categorical variables. Each variable can have different categories. The assumption in the two-response model is that the risk units can be classified as good or bad, depending on the variables X_i. In the binary case, the dependent variables is Bernoulli distributed and in that case the linear regression (linear combination of the independent variables) or mean response is the probability of one of the two values in y and the variance as it is in Bernoulli distribution. The logistic regression model is used under the assumption that the probability of a risk unit (for instance, insured individual risks) being good is dependent on the level of the variable X_i. To formalize the logistic regression model, the function (P) that indicates the relationship of expectation of a response variable and explanatory variables will be given by P_k, and the parameters are estimated using maximum likelihood. This means, the response variable is binary with p explanatory variables. For n cases, the data will then consist of n vectors

$$(y_k, x_{1k}, \ldots, x_{pk})$$

of jointly observed values of the response variable and the explanatory variables. Y_k is equal to 1 with probability P_k and 0 with probability $1 - P_k$, $k = 1, \ldots, n$ and denoted like

$$P_k = P(Y_k = 1 | x_{1k}, \ldots, x_{pk})$$

$$P_k = \frac{\exp(\beta_0 + \Sigma\beta_j x_{jk}^p)}{1 + \exp(\beta_0 + \Sigma\beta_j x_{jk}^p)}$$

$$\ln(P_k / 1 - P_k) = \beta_0 + \sum_{j=1}^{p} \beta_j x_{jk}$$

A model with two response variables could be, for example, bad and good risks. The choice depends on the expected forecasting power. To evaluate the number of risk units in each group, the tests χ^2 and Student-T values are used. Examples of variables and categories are marital status, sex, age, class of tariff, car trademark, driving experience, and profession; bonus categories are Malus class, geographic zone, selected coverage, or type of driving [for more details, see Greenacre (1984), Andersen (1990)].

With this information, the following steps are carried out:

(1) Correspondence analysis.
(2) Choice of axis.
(3) Factorial discriminant analysis, analysis of the results, two-way classification. Definition of the good and bad characteristics.
(4) Validation sample test.
(5) Analysis of a new sample and relation with the results.
(6) Analysis of the cross-classification variables and interaction effects. Here, a reduction of the correlation effect is sought to improve the predictive power of the model.

Loss ratios of claims over premiums in a given period, for example, three years, can be used to identify good and bad risks. The definition of that is part of the complexity of the process. The researcher/analyst will decide the criteria. For example, values greater than 2 claims or at least one claim with corporal damages in one period would be classified as bad. Variables and categories are obtained from the sample. Correspondence analysis is built through a contingency table with the following attributes [see Johnson & Wichern (1998)]:

X is an $I \times J$ two-way table of unscaled frequencies or counts. $I > J$ and X is made up of full column rank J. I is the number of individuals and J is the total number of response categories to the questionnaire. P is called the correspondence matrix. $\tilde{\mathbf{p}}$ is centered by subtracting the product of the row total and the column total from each entry. That is,

$$P = (P_{ij}) = \frac{(X_{ij})}{n} = \frac{1}{n}\mathbf{X},$$

for $i = 1, \ldots, I$ and $j = 1, \ldots, J$. Now,

$$r = \mathbf{P}1$$

$$c = \mathbf{P}'1$$

and hence

$$\tilde{p}_{ij} = p_{ij} - r_i c_j,$$

which gives

$$\tilde{\mathbf{P}} = \mathbf{P} - rc'$$

For diagonal matrices, $D_r = \mathrm{diag}(r_1, r_2, \ldots, r_I)$ and $D_c = \mathrm{diag}(c_1, c_2, \ldots c_J)$ define the scaled matrix

$$\mathbf{P}^* = \mathbf{D}_r^{-1/2}(\tilde{\mathbf{P}})\mathbf{D}_c^{-1/2}$$

The following steps are required to find the coordinates of the points in the graph:

Step 1: Find the singular value decomposition of P^*:

$$\mathbf{P}^* = \mathbf{U} \Lambda \mathbf{V}'$$

with rank(P*) = rank($\tilde{P}$) $\leq J-1$ and $\Lambda = \text{diag}(\lambda_1, \ldots, \lambda_{J-1})$, containing the singular values ordered from largest to smallest.

$$\mathbf{U'U} = \mathbf{V'V} = \mathbf{I}$$

Step 2: Set

$$\tilde{\mathbf{U}} = \mathbf{D}_r^{1/2}\mathbf{U}$$

and

$$\tilde{\mathbf{V}} = \mathbf{D}_c^{1/2}\mathbf{V}$$

The singular value decomposition of $\tilde{P}$ is given by

$$\tilde{\mathbf{P}} = \mathbf{P} - rc' = \tilde{\mathbf{U}}\Lambda\tilde{\mathbf{V}}'$$
$$= \sum_{j=1}^{J-1} \lambda_i \tilde{u}_j \tilde{v}'_j$$

where $\tilde{u}_j, \tilde{v}'_j$ are the j-th column vectors of $\tilde{U}$ and $\tilde{V}$, respectively.

$$\tilde{\mathbf{U}}'\mathbf{D}_r^{-1}\tilde{\mathbf{U}} = \tilde{\mathbf{V}}'\mathbf{D}_c^{-1}\tilde{\mathbf{V}} = \mathrm{I}$$

The columns of $\tilde{U}$ define the coordinate axes for the points (see Exhibit 7.10) representing the column profiles of P and the columns of $\tilde{V}$ define the coordinate axes for the points representing the row profiles of P.

$$\mathbf{Y} = \mathbf{D}_r^{-1}\tilde{\mathbf{U}}\Lambda$$

Step 3: Calculate the coordinates of the row profiles and the coordinates of the column profiles:

$$\mathbf{Z} = \mathbf{D}_c^{-1}\tilde{\mathbf{V}}\Lambda$$

The first two columns of *Y* and *Z* contain the points and column points in the best two-dimensional representations of data.

Step 4: The total inertia (See Exhibit 7.9) is the sum of squares of the non-zero singular values:

$$\text{Total inertia} = \sum_{i=1}^{K} \lambda_i^2$$

where $\lambda_1 \geq \lambda_2 \cdots \geq \lambda_k \geq 0$, $K = \text{rank}(\tilde{P})$, and $\text{rank}(\tilde{P}) = \min(I-1, J-1)$ usually.

The χ^2 statistic measures the degree of association between the row and column variables in a two-way contingency table with I rows and J columns. $O_{ij} = x_{ij}$ is the observed frequency and the E_{ij} is the expected frequency in the (i,j)th cell if the row variable is independent of the column variable. Then,

$$\chi^2 = \sum_{i,j} \frac{(O_{ij} - E_{ij})^2}{E_{ij}}$$

With $E_{ij} = nr_i c_j$, the latter can be rewritten as

$$\chi^2 = n \sum_{i,j} \frac{(p_{ij} - r_i c_j)^2}{r_i c_j}$$

which is seen as a discrepancy between P and rc'. Equivalently, the matrix notation

$$\text{Intertia} = \frac{\chi^2}{n} = \text{trace}(\mathbf{D}_r^{-1}(\mathbf{P} - \text{rc}')D_c^{-1}(\text{P} - rc')') = \sum_{k=1}^{J-1} \lambda_k^2$$

where the inertia is the weighted sum of the square distances of the row profiles (or column profiles) to the centroid. The inertia associated with the row points is the same as the inertia associated with the column points

$$\mathbf{Y}'\mathbf{D}_r\mathbf{Y} = \Lambda^2 = \mathbf{Z}'\mathbf{D}_c\mathbf{Z}$$

The following paragraphs explain about additional multivariate tools. Once groups and variables have been defined, it is possible to assign observations to these groups. This is the following step in the classification process where the problem no longer requires a cluster analysis but a classification analysis. For numerical continuous variables, discriminant analysis is used, while for categorical variables, it is logistic regression presented before any of the machine learning tools that are appropriate for the problems, data, and implementation needs.

In the case of numerical data, the value of claims, for example, in insurance, and the coverage taken by the risk unit are used. These depend on the automobile value in a car insurance problem, the coverage, the premiums paid, the value of deductibles, or franchises. In a case like this, it is possible to use discriminant analysis. The populations are assumed normally distributed. There are cases in the analysis where it is required to reduce the dimensionality of the data and principal components, and factor analysis can help to identify the best combination of variables to use.

The essential concepts and results of an analysis of principal components look to explain the variance–covariance structure of a set of variables by means of the linear combination of these variables. The search is now about a p variable k principal component with n measurements. The principal components are the linear combinations of non-correlated variables with the highest variances as possible. Take p random variables X_1, $X_2, \dots, X_p$, the random vector $\boldsymbol{X}' = [X_1, X_2, \dots, X_p]$ with covariance matrix Σ and with eigenvalues $\lambda_1 \geq \lambda_2, \dots, \geq \lambda_p \geq 0$. The linear combinations are

$$Y_1 = \boldsymbol{a}'_1 \boldsymbol{X}$$
$$Y_2 = \boldsymbol{a}'_2 \boldsymbol{X} \dots$$
$$Y_p = \boldsymbol{a}'_p \boldsymbol{X}$$

The i-th principal component is the linear combination $\boldsymbol{a}'_i \boldsymbol{X}$ that maximize $\mathrm{Var}(\boldsymbol{a}'_i \boldsymbol{X})$ subject to $\boldsymbol{a}'_i \boldsymbol{a}_i = 1$ and $\mathrm{Cov}(\boldsymbol{a}'_i \boldsymbol{X}, \boldsymbol{a}'_k \boldsymbol{X}) = 0$ for $k < i$. The coefficients are the components of the Eigen vectors; this means $Yi = \boldsymbol{e}'_i \boldsymbol{X}$ where $\boldsymbol{e}_i$ are the eigenvectors associated with the eigenvalues l_i of Σ, where

$$\mathrm{var}(Y_i) = a'_i \sum a_i = \lambda_i$$
$$\mathrm{Cov}(Y_i, Y_k) = a'_j \sum a_k = 0$$

where i and k are from *1* to p.

It is possible to define the proportion of the variance generated by the *k-th* principal component as $\lambda_k/\lambda_1 + \lambda_2 + \cdots + \lambda_p$. This is a consequence of having the variances of the principal components as the eigenvalues. The correlation coefficients between Y_i and the variables X_k are given by $\rho_{YiXk} = e_{ik} \lambda^{0.5} / \sigma^{0.5}{}_{kk}$ with $i, k = 1,2, \dots, p$.

Now, a factor analysis is looking for the relations of covariance among many variables in terms of a small group of underlying variables called factors. This is an extension of the analysis of principal components. It can be used in segmentation or classification, identifying the underlying variables in groups of clients. In product research there is a value in determining the products attributes that influence products selection. Also, sensitivity to price of the consumers can be identified. Suppose variables can be grouped by their correlations and the variables in a group are highly correlated, but have low correlation with other variables in a different group. The principal component analysis and factorial analysis are looking to approximate the covariance matrix Σ. The random vector is *X*s with p components, mean $\boldsymbol{\mu}$, and covariance matrix Σ. The model is $\mathbf{X}-\boldsymbol{\mu} = \mathbf{LF}+\boldsymbol{\varepsilon}$ where **L** is the matrix of the weights of the factors with μm_i = mean of variable *i*,

ε_i = *i*-th specific factor
F_j = *j*-th common factor

l_{ij} = weight of *i*-th variable of the *j*-th factor satisfying the following conditions:

E(**F**) = **0**, Cov(**F**) = **I**, E(ε) = **0**, Cov(ε) = **Ψ** where **Ψ** is the diagonal matrix, **F** and **ε** are independent.

There is a difference with regression analysis; in regression, the independent variables are observable, whereas **F** and **ε** are not observable. Now, the variance of *i*-th variable that is determined by the *m* common factors is called *i*-th commune. The specific variance is the part of the variance of $\mathbf{X}_i$ due to a specific factor. The relations are the following ones:

$$\vec{\Sigma} = \lambda_i \vec{e}_1 \vec{e}_1' + \cdots + \lambda_p \vec{e}_p \vec{e}_p' + \vec{\psi}$$

$$\psi_i = \sigma_{ii} - \sum_{j=1}^{m} l_{ij}^2$$

$$\vec{L} = \left[\sqrt{\lambda_1} \vec{e}_1, \ldots, \sqrt{\lambda_m} \vec{e}_m \right]$$

$$\vec{\Sigma} = \vec{L}\vec{L}' + \vec{\psi}$$

where the eigenvalues are ordered and the weights are the correlations.

Fisher's discriminant analysis can be used as a first step to separate groups, discrimination, and classification. It is assumed that the $p \times p$ population covariance matrices are equal and of full rank (Johnson, 1998). Consider the linear combination $Y = a'X$ which has expected value $a'\mu_i$ for population π_i and variance $a'\Sigma a$.

The ratio $\frac{a'B_{\mu}a}{a'\Sigma a}$ measures the variability between the groups of Y-values relative to the common variability within groups. The objective is to select a to maximize the above ratio. Estimation of the values for μ and Σ (the variance–covariance matrix) is, required taking a sample from the populations. Let B be the sample between groups and $\bar{x}$ the estimator for μ. For Σ, the sample within groups matrix $W/(n_1 + \cdots + n_g - g) = S_{\text{pooled}}$. The sample size n_i is from population π_i, $i = 1, \ldots, g$. The x_i are the dataset from population π_i and g is the number of groups.

$$\bar{x} = \frac{\sum_{i=1}^{g} n_i \bar{x}_i}{\sum_{i=1}^{n} n_i} = \frac{\sum_{i=1}^{g} \sum_{j=1}^{n_i} x_{ij}}{\sum_{i=1}^{g} n_i}$$

Let $\hat{\lambda}_1, \ldots, \hat{\lambda}_s > 0$ denote the $s \le \min(g - 1, p)$ non-zero eigenvalues of $W^{-1}B$ and $\hat{e}_1, \ldots, \hat{e}_s$ be the corresponding eigenvectors (scaled so that $\hat{e}' S_{\text{pooled}} \hat{e} = 1$).

Special models with enormous use in AI are Artificial Neural Networks (ANN), Deep Learning, and TensorFlow. An ANN model emulates the brain and the way that communication and results appear in the connected neurons, from an input layer (attributes that can be demographic, transactional, promotion, etc.), the creation of hidden layers, and output layers (classification or prediction result) in a model definition. Modeled basic units are biological neurons with each unit having many inputs that combine in a specific value of result. The units are connected in such a way that the output of one is the input of another. The connections create a network with flow in a direction that can be given (Feed-forward, recurrent, probabilistic, etc.). The model architecture Feed-forward combines a multi-layer perceptron with a backpropagation learning algorithm. Artificial Neural Networks (ANNs) (Figure 4.9) are possible to use not only for prediction but also for clustering. There are different algorithms according to the learning algorithms and the type input: discrete or continuous in a supervised or unsupervised learning process. Moreover, the architecture for supervised learning is recurrent and feedforward, while for unsupervised learning the groups of algorithms are estimator and extractor.

A single neuron is represented by $S = \sum_{i-1}^{n} X_i W_i$ (Combination function) that has a transfer function $f(S)$ to obtain the outcomes $\boldsymbol{Y} = (Y_1, Y_2, \ldots, Y_n)$. The main concept is the activation function that is defined by two parts: a combination/summation function and a transfer function. For several

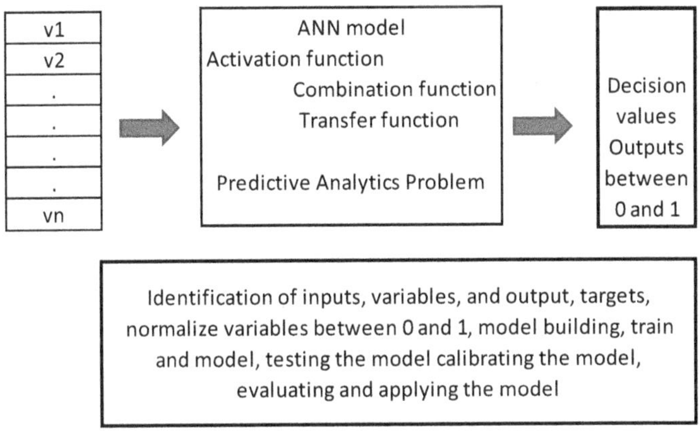

Figure 4.9. Description of ANN model.

neurons, the combination function can take a form such as in the case of two inputs and three outcomes with different inputs for each one:

$$Y_1 = X_1\, W_{11} + X_2\, W_{12}$$

$$Y_2 = X_1\, W_{12} + X_2\, W_{22}$$

$$Y_3 = X_2\, W_{23}$$

A structure of the ANN (Exhibit 4.36) in the case of having only one layer of calculations is $f(w_1x_1 + w_2x_2 + b) = y_1$ where f is the activation function and the linear combination of the inputs x_i has weights w_i, b is called the bias, and y_1 is the target. In case of having several layers of calculations, the functions are composed. Assuming two hidden layers with four variables, the first layer has three neurons and the second layer has two neurons, with two different activation functions by the two layers.

To choose a training set, one can follow the principles of sampling that are applied in the partition of training and evaluation/testing for the models. The set consists of the records whose prediction or classification is already known, and it is the source for the model to identify the variable relationships to support the classification modeling process. The training set includes the values for all the attributes and the number of attributes, including the identification. Decide the network architecture and its organization, indicating the learning algorithm to use. Start the

• Take random values to start the weight assignment and input model parameters. • Organize data input and output definition. • Start the computation of outputs following the layers in the model. • Measure difference between computed and desired outputs. • Modify the weights moving backward using the hidden layers. • Repeat the steps till the weights do not change.	X1, X2, … , Xn W1, W2, … , Wn $S = \sum_{i-1}^{n} X_i W_i$ $f(S)$ and calculate $Y{=}f(S)$ and calculate Y_i and Error measurement $\propto (\boldsymbol{Z}_i - \boldsymbol{Y}_i)$

Exhibit 4.36. Simplified view of the backpropagation algorithm.

parameterization with initial values and to review the weights of a first iteration and validation; continue to create feedback to tune the inputs, weights, and parameters. When the tests show appropriate results, use the ANN to predict. A step that is crucial to start the understanding of the ANN black-box process is the sensitivity analysis. It uses the test dataset to determine sensitivity to the inputs generating and observing changes in the outputs. A possible approach to black-box understanding can be through the use of averages and measuring the results when averages are the inputs. It is the same as the measure of the result of the network when each entrance is modified simultaneously with the maximums and minimums.

Neuronal networks have strengths and weaknesses as models. Understanding the model for implementation in several cases is a priority for analytics deployment, and ANN can be considered a model to support certain solutions. The following strengths of neuronal networks must be mentioned:

(1) Applicable in a wide number of problems. They can be used with nonlinear relationships of the variables. They can be used with numerical and categorical variables through a transformation.
(2) The model still produces good results in complex types of problems.
(3) The model can work with categorical variables continuously and in general with no normality or independence assumptions.

(4) The results in comparison with other models produce better classifications.

The following are certain weaknesses of neuronal networks:

(1) Inputs of ranks 0,1 required.
(2) The explanation of results is not straightforward. They do not present/display explicit rules. It is not clear what input is more important than others.
(3) The model can converge prematurely to an inferior solution (one does not know if the model is the best one for the data). The optimal solution for a considerable number of parameters of the network is not easy to find. The training process for large datasets can require sampling in order to manage the computational effort.

In addition to the brief view of ANN, it is important to understand what a simplified view of deep learning, tensorflow, and time series can be:

(1) What is deep learning? It is a process from data observations to outcomes/results through multiple layers. Layers are transformations of data. The transformations are functions that are differentiable for stochastic gradient descent. There is a calculation of weights for data.
(2) What are tensors? They are multidimensional arrays, that is, scalars, vectors, matrices, matrices of matrices, and matrices of matrices of matrices, meaning for dimensions. This is possible to review in terms of data, that is, pictures and then attributes.
(3) The tensorflow computing library supports machine learning and deep learning. It can use CPU, GPU, TPU (tensor processing unit), and automatic differentiations.
(4) What is a tensorflow? It is a graph of units of computation in nodes that are defined in R, and the data tensors are computed in the nodes, that is, executing functions, models, flowing along the defined graph.

The use of KERAS and Tensorflow through RStudio requires only the installation of the two packages directly from the CRAN repository. KERAS is in Tensorflow. You can use convolutional and recurrent networks as they are time series. The idea is to work in the modeling process using layers from sequential or functional API to layers to organize the data. After it from model to functions such as the loss function to create and evaluate the metrics. After normalization, the training and test files are generated and the KERAS model will define the parameters of layers, the activation function to use to compile the model according to a loss function definition and optimizer method. In KERAS, the components are layers and models.

Another option for using R and deep learning is through Torch. Torch in R was launched in 2020. Torch is originally the pyTorch, now with R native.

Furthermore, the integration with tools like KNIME is powerful and indicates the main nodes to use. In KNIME, the integration with KERAS and Tensorflow is found in the nodes' repository as integration after deep learning and the selecting of KERAS or Tensorflow. Once the node is selected, the definition of the layers of the network will be available.

Another data analytics algorithm is the Genetic algorithm. It has the following properties:

(1) It evolves successive generations of genomes that obtain progressively more and more adjustment. The intention is to maximize the adjustment of the genomes in the population, to create an initial generation of genomes.
(2) It modifies the initial values when applying selection, crossings, and mutations.
(3) It repeats step 2 until they do not obtain more improvements.

A genome is a gene of 5 bits for a parameter. Selection: It takes the measurement from the constant population and increases the fit of the following generation. Crossing: It forms to change 2 genomes. Mutation: It makes random, occasional modifications in the random position of a genome. The algorithm uses a SCHEMA: form, figure, succession of symbols, the first and empty ones of a genome is increased by (*), that agrees with 0 or 1. LENGTH OF THE SCHEMA: distance between the external most positions. ORDER OF THE SCHEMA: number of fixed positions that it has.

Strengths of the genetic approach:

(1) It produces explicable results.
(2) Facility to apply the results.

(3) It can handle an ample rank of data types.
(4) Applicable to optimize.
(5) Possible to integrate with neuronal networks.

Weaknesses of the genetic approach:

(1) Difficulty to codify many problems.
(2) Optimality is not guaranteed.
(3) Computation is expensive.
(4) Limited availability in analytics platforms.

Balance, understandability, and accuracy of a model in terms of complexity are highly appreciated in implementation steps and adoption in organizations. These three aspects are found in analysis based on trees. Tree algorithms are good for visualizing what is happening, in several cases for good classification and understanding. Traditional procedures imply the adjustment of a model (regression or discriminant) according to the behavior of the data. In this subsection, the review is about classification of tree algorithms and ensembles that include the Random Forest approach. A decision tree divides data, successively, based on a criterion that implies relationships between the predicting variables and the objective–target variable. Breiman *et al.* (1984) developed C&RT (Classification and Regression Trees), which performs successive binary separations in the data, guiding them by a criterion, not a statistical test as in the CHAID algorithm. In each node, the predicting variable that improves, plus the criterion, is used to make the following partition. The trees created with this criterion let themselves grow widely and are later pruned: Pruning diminishes the complex cost. The terminal nodes show that groups can have a greater concentration of cases with the desired characteristics. There are advantages in using decision trees in classification: the trees are designed to work with an elevated number of variables; non-parametric methods capture relations that the linear models cannot capture (nonlinear relations and complex interactions); different methods can handle different types of variables; one can use or not use statistical criteria for choosing and dividing variables in branches.

Additional concepts for understanding the use of algorithms are associated with fitting, trimming, and accuracy. One of those concepts is impurity, which is the name of the criterion to grow the tree with a nominal objective variable. Impurity captures the degree in which the cases, within a node, are concentrated in a single category. A pure node is one in which all the cases are in a single category. The greater degree of impurity occurs when all the categories of a predicting variable contain the same number of cases. The impurity is possible to measure according to an impurity criterion that remains, but it is moderate according to the variance of the interior of the node. It captures the degree to which the answers within a node are concentrated around a single value. The impurity of a branch is the weighted average of the variances of the terminal nodes. The Gini metric index guides the evaluation of impurity. The index of Gini is described: If the set T_o has elements of n classes and f_j is the relative frequency of class j in A, then $gin(A) = 1 - \sum_{j=1}^{n} f_j^2$. If T_o in two sets of sizes $|A_1|$ and $|A_2|$ defines the index of Gini like a weighted average, then the Gini minor is the one used in the partition of the branch.

$$Gini(A) = \frac{|A_1|}{|A|} gini(A_1) + \frac{|A_2|}{|A|} gini(A_2)$$

To grow a tree indefinitely almost always reduces the impurity. The measurement of complex cost increases the measurement in which the tree is greater. It is equal to $R(T) + a^*|T|$, where $R(T)$ is the measurement of substitution of risk of the tree or branch, a is the penalty coefficient, and $|T|$ is the number of terminal nodes of the tree or branch. In order to improve the measurement of the cost complex, the component of substitution of risk must diminish more than the penalty. The measurement of complex cost works well if the tree grows and then it is pruned using this criterion. The method consists of pruning branches in a successive way with basis in the Maxima reduction of the measurement of complex cost. Trees are selected, with the smallest tree being one whose risk (probability of classifying erroneously) is within a rank of one standard error of the smaller risk found during the growth of the tree.

The tree partitions for predicting continuous or ordinal follow these steps: Sort data within the nodes by the values of the categories of the predicting variable. Calculate the reduction in impurity for all the possible cut points. The best partition is determined. For nominal predictors (explanatory variables/attributes), all the possible combinations of their categories are evaluated, and the partition is when the greater reduction in impurity is found. This causes the same predicting variable to often appear within a branch. The costs of erroneous classification can be included in C&RT, but not in a totally satisfactory way, because symmetrical costs are created. If these costs are gotten up the growth of the tree, the allocation of cases and the summaries of risk will be influenced. Another way to incorporate the costs is using the probabilities a priori. The nodes show the frequency results in front of a dependent variable and are part of the results of a statistical test.

The CHAID algorithm is used for analysis of categorical variables. CHAID is chi-square automatic interaction detection, which is a method of heuristic search that consists of examining relations between several predicting variables and an objective or dependent variable. The idea is to develop a chain of implications always from the root for A then B, where A and B are the attributes. The algorithms can stop and become leaves of the tree when a node no longer has other element samples. In the case where all the elements belong to the group or defined class, the model is predicting variables that are categorical and acts as the target variable. The objective is to find the relationship or association between the set of the predicting variables and the target, and a report is made in a diagram of an arbol representing the significant difference in the percentages of the dependent variable. The following is a view of the algorithm:

(1) For each predicting variable, x looks for the pair of categories of x whose difference presents/displays the smaller significance with respect to the variable criterion y. The method to calculate the critical level depends on the level of the y measure.
  - If y is continuous, it uses the F test.
  - If y is nominal, it forms a contingency table with the categories of x like rows and categories of y like columns, to use the chi-square test.
  - If y is ordinal, it adjusts the model of association of y, to use the likelihood ratio test.

(2) For the pair of categories of x with the greater critical level, compare the value of the critical level with the pre-specified level alpha.
If the critical value is greater than alpha, join the pair in a single compound category. The result is a new set of categories of x, and the process initiates from step 1 if the value of the critical level is smaller than alpha move to step 3.

(3) Calculate the critical level for the set of the categories of x and the categories of y, by means of the correction of Bonferroni test.

(4) Select the predicting variable x whose corrected critical level is the minimum, to compare its critical level with the pre-established level alpha.
   - If the critical level is smaller or equal to alpha, divide the node according to the set of categories of x.
   - If the critical level is greater than alpha, do not divide the node; it is a terminal node.

(5) Continue until the shutdown rule is fulfilled.

The function of information gain exists to deal with entropy in classification. Having two classes A and B and there is a C that can be in A or B and it can be defined as information (a, b)

$$\text{information}(a,b) = -\frac{a}{a+b}\log_2\frac{a}{a+b} - \frac{b}{a-b}\log_2\frac{a}{a+b}$$

In general, the entropy is defined for k classes as $E = -\sum_{i=1}^{n} p_i \log_2 p_i$.

If an attribute O is taken, a set C can be divided in sets $\{C_1, C_2, \ldots, C_k\}$, each one having a_i elements of A and b_i elements of B. The entropy is the expected value of information O:

$$E(O) = \sum_{i=1}^{k} \frac{a_i + b_i}{a+b} I(a_i, b_i)$$

where a and b are the totals, and the gain by branch is $I(a, b - E(O))$.

Finally, in this classification review, keep the following note in mind. Models for risk classification can be parametric and non-parametric. Some authors indicate that a classification problem cannot be distribution free in the good sense [see Anderson (1994)]. However, there are ML algorithms doing good work through a non-parametric structure. Some models belong to these main categories:

- A good rule is to assume that the distributions are known. The CDF and PDF are replaced by their respective sample estimates.
- Use a well-known test for the non-parametric samples.
- Some *ad-hoc* methods are typical, like minimum distance.

An additional non-parametric model to classify trees is the Nearest Neighbor (K-NN) that proposes a classification rule for the two-population problem based on non-parametric estimates of the PDF. The method of estimating a density f can be described as follows: Let $X_1, \ldots, X_n$ be i.i.d r.v's with a common PDF f which is continuous at x. Let S_n be a sequence of sets in the sample space with corresponding volumes V_n such that $\lim_{n\to\infty} \sup_{y\in S_n} \| x - y \| = 0$ and $\lim_{n\to\infty} nV_n =$. And let K_n be the number of observations that lie in S_n. Then, $\widehat{f}(x) = \frac{k_n}{nV_n} \to f(x)$ in probability when K_n and n go to infinity. From here, it is possible to use the K-NN rule.

Let X be the observation to be classified. Consider the distance function d and order all the values $d(X_{ij}, X)$, where X_{ij} are the random samples from the i-th population. $j = 1, \ldots, n_{i\$}$ and $\$i = 1, \ldots, m$. The rule assigns X to the population π_i.

If $\frac{k_i}{n_i} = \max_j \left(\frac{k_j}{n_j}\right)$ where k_i is the number of observations from π_i in the k observations “nearest” to x.

Another set of models is when the basic models are iterated, and several samples and results are compared to select the best model to describe data. Examples of these models are Ensembles, Bagging, Boosting, and Stacking. The ensemble models provide the support to reduce overfitting and obtain more generalizable models for risk classification. The ensembles take a set of estimators that are better than the individual components. The ensembles are identified as meta-classifiers because of using the set of individual classifiers. Classifiers are the techniques to classify. This can have the analogy of a combination of solutions to get a better solution through the ensemble process using the individual solution. Creation of ensembles can use the same dataset and different algorithms or different samples with the algorithm classifier. A voting system is used for different samples and different algorithms in the ensemble process. Classifiers are used in the ensemble with algorithms such as decision tress, support vector machines, and logistic regression. For the generation of different samples, the bootstrap method is used. In data analytics, Bagging or Bootstrap aggregating has the purpose of reducing the variance of estimators. One example is Random Forest, a technique that creates decision trees using bootstrap samples as training datasets, and random feature selection for the individual tree models that use a majority voting system to select the best prediction of the target. A voting system means that the class for a solution is selected based on the higher number of individual solutions (the mode of the solutions) that show the selected class. In case of a GUI such as Rattle, the results and the possible comparison are through the area under the curve, indicating the variables in the splits, checking the error rate, different number of observations, and different number of variables considered for random sampling in each split.

Moreover, Boosting is an example of the **AdaBoost** technique, that is, adaptive boosting. In general, the boosting method selects random sub-datasets (samples) without replacement for training the models. The first selection trains a model; a percentage (50%) of the wrong classified examples (points) is added to a second subset that is randomly selected without replacement, and with this new dataset, one trains a new model. Then, with the examples that were misclassified by the first and second iterations, join the new random selection to train a new model. In particular, the AdaBoost method uses the whole training dataset to train the models. The training points are with new weights in each iteration for classifiers that learn from the errors of previous iterations with low-performance models. The misclassified points take a higher weight and use them for training models. Every iteration will modify the weights, then train another classifier. After several models with a low performance, the technique uses majority voting to select the model to use. Another example of Boosting is **Gradient Boosting.** The difference from AdaBoost is basically in the application of the weights in points to include in the iterations and how the classifiers are used together to select the best model. In analytics platforms like R and Python, the XGBoost is implemented. Regression techniques are used to train the models. The models produce errors with several iterations for the purpose of achieving the best points that predict the target.

In general, in risk analytics, there is the concept of model risk that is related to the issue of a model not performing as it should, issues with assumptions, the lack of proper testing, etc. There is another risk to consider associated with model risk, that is, the operational risk of implementation. This means the cost of implementations against the cost of new knowledge/solution that is gained. In ensembles, there are improvements, but the computational complexity will be increased in the implementation and in some solutions it could be more expensive to get a better solution without gains that justify the costs of using it. In the Netflix competition, the situation was like that — the ensemble model was the best solution for classifying but the implementation/deployment was so expensive that the company decided not to use it.

Stacking methods are a combination of classifiers and ensembles; for example, a random forest can be combined with a logistic regression.

As a final note in this subsection, additional statistical learning capabilities enhance final actions in risk management, pricing, reserves, forecasting, calibration, etc. Some of the models that support many of those decisions are Analysis of Variance Components, Misclassification, Credibility, Markov Chains, and ruin problems. In pricing, for example, after the classes are identified and the risk classified, the model is used to calculate the premiums. This requires identifying the risk level for each class and defining credibility premiums. One of the problems is to find the effects of distributions of related variables defined in a model for the profiles of the risk units insured, for example the following (Exhibit 4.37):

A divides the population in classes $A_1, \ldots, A_a$ and B divides the population in classes $B_1, \ldots, B_b$.The proportion of the population that is classified as both A_a and B_b is r_{ab}; r_a = the proportion of the population classified as A_a and $r_{.b}$ = the proportion of the population classified as B_b. The components of variance are useful to analyze. Models used to assign premiums to risk are based on components of variance. For example, fixed effects ANOVA can be used to detect the effect of cellular phones on driving ability. Consider 5 groups of people with various cellular phone use habits and 200 observations within each group. The mean and standards deviation are given as follows:

The variances are similar, but the means are different. There are relationships among the various populations. The model response $y_{ij} = \mu_i + e_{ij}$ for member j of group i, where the uncorrelated errors e_{ij} have the same distribution with average zero and variance σ_i^2.

Another example for decomposing variance is considering groups through a review of random effects, for example, in a population of

A/B	B_1	B_2	$\cdots$	B_b	Total
A_1	r_{11}	r_{12}	$\cdots$	r_{1b}	$r_{1.}$
A_2	r_{21}	r_{22}	$\cdots$	r_{2b}	$r_{2.}$
$\vdots$	$\vdots$	$\vdots$	$\vdots$	$\vdots$	$\vdots$
A_a	r_{a1}	r_{a2}	$\cdots$	r_{ab}	$r_{a.}$
Total	$r_{.1}$	$r_{.2}$	$\cdots$	$r_{.b}$	1

Exhibit 4.37. Partitions in classes of possible outcomes and groups of risk units.

Group	Mean	S.D.
Non-users	3.78	0.79
Passive users	3.30	0.77
Light users	3.23	0.78
Medium users	2.73	0.81
Heavy users	2.59	0.82

Exhibit 4.38. Example where numbers of means and standard deviations require comparison.

200 auto insurance policies that had claims. Randomly select 7 policies. Then, for each policy choose a sample of 50 automobiles. An inference conclusion is sought for the whole population. This means μ_i; the individual policy means scores were drawn randomly from a population (see Exhibit 4.38). Mean scores with overall mean μ and variance σ_A^2 made up of the N eligible policies of the company. σ_i^2 represents the within-variance aspect for policy *i* and σ_A^2 represents the between-variance aspect for a population of true means.

The model is $y_{ij} = \mu + a_i + e_{ij}$ where $\mu_i = \mu + a_i$. The two-way model is $y_{ijk} = \mu + a_i + b_j + e_{ijk}$ where a_i described the effect on *y* due to *i*-th level of the first factor and b_j is the effect of *j*-th on the second factor. There two models: one is nested $Y_{ijk} = a_i + b_{ij} + \mu_{ijk}$ and classified with interaction $y_{ijk} = \mu + a_i + b_j + c_{ij} + e_{ijk}$. c_{ij} is the interaction effect of the *i*-th level of the first factor and *j*-th of the second factor. In the case of random effects, a_i, b_j, c_{ij} are random with variances $\sigma_a^2, \sigma_b^2, \sigma_c^2, \sigma_e^2$, which are the variance components.

The insured claim ratio is decomposed in a sum of uncorrelated random variables. Each of these new random variables represents the contribution of a risk factor or the contribution of an interaction between risk factors to the total variance of the insured's claim ratio random variable. This total variance is broken up into variance components. A hierarchical approach is not adequate if there is interaction between the various risk factors. For example, an automobile insurance portfolio would be given a hierarchical classification first by gender of the driver and then by age, where gender and age represent the two qualitative risk factors. However, some young women share risk with young men who themselves share driven characteristics with older men. The parameters give $\Theta_i^{(1)}, \Theta_j^{(2)}, \Theta_k^{(3)}, X_{ijk1}, \ldots, X_{ijkT_{ijk}}$ the description of the risk. *t* goes from 1 to T_{ijk}.

4.3. Using Technologies to Compete

The aim of this section is to review the ways to develop competencies to improve intelligence using digital technologies. Vrontis *et al.* (2022) expressed that "… scholars have not been clear about the contributions of digital technologies such as social media, the Internet of Things (IoT), blockchain, big data analytics, and artificial intelligence (AI) enabled applications towards the growth of start-up SMEs and related entrepreneurial activities. Scholars and practitioners are also uncertain how, when, and under what specific conditions the use of digital technologies could help start-up enterprises sustain their growth continuum." This is reflection about how digital technologies could be adopted to use in a diverse set of organizations. There are two main streams to analyze the general problem of competency improvement associated with the capacity to deal with digital technologies. On the one hand, organizations need to develop the learning process to use (efficiently and effectively) the new digital technologies in the best way to be more intelligent and mitigate strategic risks. On the other hand, organizations need to gain competencies and deal with risks of new technologies to contribute to developing new capabilities inside organizations to adapt and sustain competitive advantages.

Technology is a continuum of discoveries and applications; technology can itself change what it was created for, e.g., ML is creating ways to substitute work done with ML. Strategic intelligence to mitigate strategic risk is required to avoid falling in the trap of thinking that technology will be static. Data scientists as they are currently conceived can disappear; it is similar in several areas where human knowledge is the input to many solutions, and the solution will substitute the original source of knowledge, for example, underwriting in financial/insurance services. Technology is today one means for performing some tasks and tomorrow new technologies will appear to move ahead in enhancing solutions. Nowadays, people learn languages like R, Python, or Scala with the hope of controlling technology development, but new languages and means to create code are already being developed to change what is currently in use. The pillars to support the adaptation to those changes are the improvement to thinking well and to use principles of mathematics, statistics, computing, human cognition understanding (Exhibit 4.39).

In the creation of intelligence, multiple types of technology and purposes appear and organizations are dealing with the complexity of using the best at different levels of the organization (Exhibit 4.40).

When technology creates improvements, substitutions, risk of obsolescence	
Google search engine	ChatGPT, Bard
Machine learning human development	AutoML — cloud autoML

Exhibit 4.39. Technology has a cycle of life that is continuous change.

Related to strategic intelligence	Examples
Through Data Analytics	From prediction for image recognition, voice, or event classifications to the level of self-learning of algorithms to provide solutions
Through Operations	Development of automated process, robotics, and enhanced human–machine capabilities

Exhibit 4.40. Intension of using technology for creating value.

An additional issue/problem to solve in organizations dealing with technologies to compete is to answer how they can develop learning systems to improve the use/adoption of digital technologies. This means how organizations learn and adapt technologies and how they develop support for the new technologies' adoption. To review technology adoption, a conceptual differentiation in the meaning of the concepts is necessary: technology, technique, and method to clarify the use in strategic risk mitigation. Technology is understood in this book as the means to support a group of techniques systematically organized to provide solutions and perform activities: "At the heart of technology lies the ability to recognize a human need, or desire (actual or potential) and then to devise a means — an invention or a new design- to satisfy it economically" (Cardwell, 1994, p. 490). The following example clarifies this way of understanding technology. In the analytics world, the software built for data mining is considered technology, and deal with a group of techniques associated with different problems or knowledge development sources. A technique and a method are used as the process to complete actions, perform tasks using technologies and human competencies. The difference is just in the scope of the steps and the level at which they are used in a work or research setting. In the example of analytics, the technique could be regression analysis and the methods can be associated for dealing with variable interactions, outliers, assumptions, etc.

Dealing with technology requires an understanding of the different types of technologies available and their purposes when they were designed, the same as clarify the proximity of digital technology to humans use. To provide value and to discover how to do things, based on the use and advances of science, organizations require technologies, techniques, and methods. Human capital/talent is at the center of these concepts because data, process, and knowledge will provide value if they are aligned and ready to contribute to the design and the problem resolution process. Technologies are developed from many different sources and fields. There are technologies associated with medical and biological studies, and technologies used in economic problem resolutions. The means answering to human needs using particular digital technologies, which are very involved in the day-to-day life of people in organizations.

Technologies can be developed by evolution of the technology itself, in most of the cases related to enhancements and improvements of something that exits. Moreover, technology can be related to the revolution of solutions, creating disruptive technologies, in which technology cannot meet the needs of users/customers but establishes new ways to do things (Baltzan *et al.*, 2012). People's needs are evolving, and technology is providing solutions to many of these needs. However, not all fields are at the same level of advancement. Digital technologies have advanced at a high speed in the last decades. Users have advanced as well but in some cases the gap between knowing how to use a technology and how to contribute effectively to solutions of problems is growing as the human capital/talent in organizations is not improving competencies for more effective and efficient use of technologies, creation of techniques, or methods.

In some cases, technology access is not possible and users' preparation to take advantage of the technology is limited. One example is that access, but not skill development, occurs in the use of spreadsheets. The original VisiCalc had most of the things that most people use on a day-to-day basis in the work environment. However, there are applications that are many times more powerful than VisiCalc and the use of the new capabilities is very low even though problems exist and there are good techniques to solve them as well, but the solutions in terms of technologies and techniques are ignored by users. Users are capable of dealing with the basics of the spreadsheet software (the level of VisiCalc) but not with the astronomically different new capabilities in the new technologies because they have not been upskilled. Technological tools are a supplement to the human actions involved in managing business processes which need, at

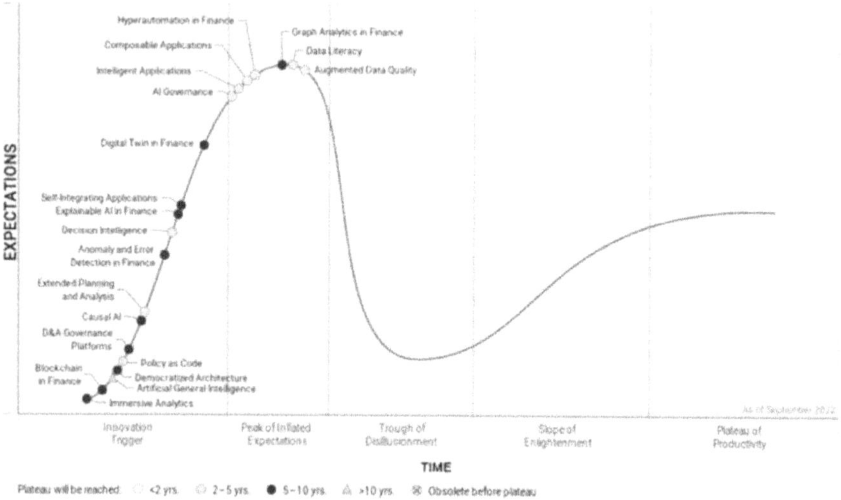

Exhibit 4.41. Gartner life cycle of certain technologies in a digital organizational setting (Source Gartner).

the same time, people's competencies in order to use technology properly. Based on this point, people can have access to technology, but people's correct use will depend on how the organization prepares people to adopt the emergent technologies. Adoption and evolution of technologies have expectations from the people using these technologies to work on developing those solutions with enthusiasm and then connecting those solutions to the reality of use with the possibility of creating value (Exhibits 4.41 and 4.42).

The reduced upskill programs in organizations are an operational and strategic risk for organizations. A good example of not using technologies refers to the sources and settings where knowledge is transferred (Agbatogun, 2013). Agbatogun shows how the faculty in an academic organization can access technological solutions to improve their classes, but the level of use is reduced because of factors related to academic status, academic qualification, gender, motivation, and discouraging effects of the use of digital technologies. However, as Simoes *et al.* (2021) pointed out, "This study investigates how collaborative academia-industry R&D cases accelerated the adoption of digital technologies by manufacturing companies, given the current COVID-19 pandemic situation. Based on multiple case studies, this article reports the challenges and the strategies of three ongoing collaborative industry-academia R&D projects

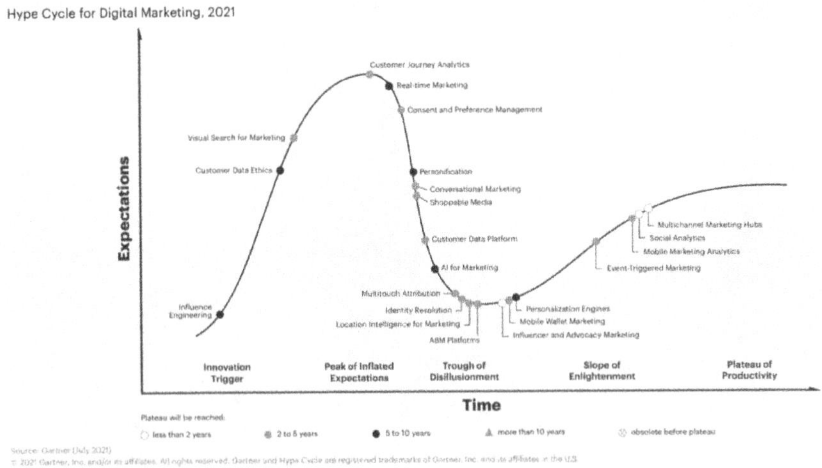

Exhibit 4.42. Example of the expectations through time in data analytics solutions for marketing (Source Gartner).

developed during the COVID pandemic situation." This means events associated with COVID-19 pushed the academic world to experiment with new digital technologies to deliver, control, support, assess, and access knowledge for students around the world. On occasions, the adverse events in strategic risk lead to the use of technologies by certain groups because no better ways of solving the main problems are available in the knowledge domain. Needs of technologies in users and organizations are as in human Maslow scale, it requires to solve the basics and then to move to the highest levels or sophisticated needs. In technology, at the beginning, one needs to have appropriate data and after data, one can move through the creation of systems/models to provide value according to the organization's demand (Exhibit 4.43).

In the following examples, needs are indicated and adoption of technologies and barriers found is illustrated. Dai *et al.* (2012) explain how Video Broadcasting–Second Generation Terrestrial (DVB-T2) was in development to solve more problems of information increment, supporting internet and broadcasting. This is an example of many technologies that can be available for organizations for performance improvement, which are gradually adopted; the risk management of using the technology requires more experience to evaluate the impact of the technology. Tanriverdi and Ruefli (2004) examined the adoption of the technologies

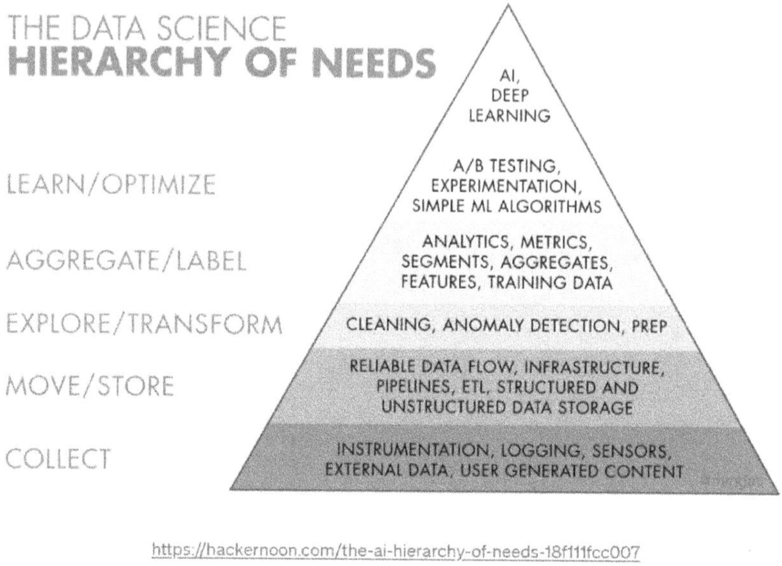

Exhibit 4.43. Hierarchical needs starting with data needs to achieve digital solutions where intelligence is part of the solution.

in organizations and the investment/return analysis: "In particular, we examine the notion that managerial interventions in the form of IT investments and activities can affect the risk/return profile of a firm. Such interventions would have the objective for a give level of return of reducing the chance of loss or the magnitude of loss-or both." The reason for this is that "Risk, as chance and magnitude of loss, captures an aspect of performance that is not captured by return or by cost." The issue is that if there is no adoption of technology, the risks at all levels of the organization will continue without attention.

Scheer (2013) pointed out, "Emerging technologies are underway in a wide array of industrial applications and need fields. When innovating on technologies, one main objective is to improve the management of safety related to their emerging risks." The question is if organizations are prepared for new technology adoption and proper use. This is related to what Hitt and Brynjolfsson (1996) pointed out, saying that IT brings benefits in productivity and consumer surplus but not in profitability. In terms of the practical point of view, technology might not produce a payoff (Devaraj & Kohli, 2003). This can be a cause for the organizations not to incentivize the use of the technology or this might lead to a goal not being achieved because of limited, possibly wrong use, of the acquired/developed technology. Moreover, technology does not have the same effects in all organizations. Zhu *et al.* (2004) indicated that technological readiness is a factor that positively contributes to the e-business value, and the size of the organization is negatively related to the e-business value. In addition, e-business is associated with internal resources, and for launching an e-business the financial resources and government regulations "are more important in developing countries, while technological capabilities are much more important in developed countries."

Another question that emerges in the context of the current business environment is the following: What is the meaning of the new economy regarding the adoption of emerging technologies? The search for the answer to this question is crucial because as Stehr (2002) expressed, "The returns on labour, land, and capital stock are declining .... The traditional forces of production are no longer the motor of economic growth and value-adding activities .... The transformation of the economy as a consequence of the growing importance of knowledge goes far beyond the mere emergence of the 'knowledge company' as discussed in the early 1980s ... the 'knowledge creating firm' discovered and explicated more recently ..., or the firm as a system of knowing activity ..." Thus, supporting knowledge creation is linked to improving learning and innovation vision and a key factor is to provide people trained and ready to use the technology on hand in order to create economic growth and competitive sustainable advantages.

Furthermore, the issue is that it is one thing to use digital technology and another to contribute to the development of the use. Most of new technologies adoption is including the use of digital technologies for their development. At the same time that new changes in business environment are converging and affecting people's adoption of the new technology. Concepts such as knowledge, strategic intelligence development, enterprise social responsibility, social changes, performance evaluation methods, and knowledge management system evolution are key factors in the adoption of technology, its use, and evolution. Different agents can contribute to the dissemination and good use of technology. Universities and many organizations can contribute to new technology adoption. Universities cannot do everything; the updating process in technology is very fast and requires a faster assimilation for stakeholders of organizations. Professional associations, internal learning and development areas, and in general all departments in organizations are required to maintain up-to-date technology use. For Drucker (1968), a "Direct cause of the upgrading of the job is ... the upgrading of the educational level of the entrant into the labour force." To this point, Stehr (2002) identified that "The storage model — schools and universities supply those skills and competencies that can be immediately utilized at work- has to be replaced by a model that couples work, education, and the transmission of key qualifications (that have a degree of context independence) under conditions of uncertainty and agency."

Learning is a way of developing competencies. The upskilling of professors to use technology in a proper way is a good start to motivate students and future professionals to develop capabilities and competencies for the technology. However, Kidd and Murray (2013) said, "We define such technologies as including digital, Web2.0, social media, mobile and information technology tools." They also indicated issues related to the professional development of the teachers: "[s]ome professional development courses essentially focus on developing and auditing the technological competence and skills of teachers. Other types of professional development provision prioritise the adoption of e-learning pedagogies or the deployment of specific types of new technologies in schools, often in superficial ways." This suggests that the application in the teacher's setting can be limited and not extended to other areas. Currently, the needs related to the pandemic situation and the demand for digital solutions accelerated technology adoption, which in the past was not used for the good of all stakeholders.

Not only are universities and teachers players to analyze developing competencies in digital technologies adoption but so are the social changes involved in the learning process. Management of uncertainty and social changes are forces affecting technology adoption. Important changes to take into consideration are related to globalization and global GDP distribution change, population shifts, new composition of demographic profiles, and changes in the demographic of knowledge workers. At the same time, there is an urgent need for new talents and competency development in dealing with supply chain risks, remote work, mobile talent, specialized and independent talent, production everywhere, personalization and personal preferences of the customer's decisions, etc. Changes and challenges in talent are represented by an extreme individualization which is changing and it is highly estimated as a factor that using customized network technologies that provide not only communication and sharing capacity but also economic transactions, collaboration, and much more. Changes in contracts and individualized tools, knowledge, information sources and employment arrangements, are the rules for new work engagements.

If this is the case of changes that will modify work behavior and work environment, the development of competencies has to be based on the expected changes in order to adapt the knowledge management processes to the expected business dynamic. For this step, it is required for one to think about the performance evaluation in organizations to understand what organizations are expecting from the use of their assets. The following are five different views, to consider relating to performance evaluation, and corporate and individual needs:

- What is the value added of technology?
- Missions of the organizations and potential competitive advantages.
- Alignment of the stakeholders.
- Cost-effectiveness of technology intervention.
- The adjustment of technology to industrialization, innovation, and development of learning processes.

Knowledge and learning generate change, and investment in knowledge and learning is transformed into economic, social, and management models. The steps from using technology only to innovation based on technology push and pull technology assimilation and use. The purpose of creating a structure to develop competencies is because a higher investment in IT will be converted into better performance. Alavi and Leidner (2001) pointed out that IT converts knowledge into a sustainable competitive advantage. Tanriverdi and Ruefli (2004) pointed out, "However, findings to date remains mixed: while some studies find a positive relationship between IT investments and firm performance, others fail to find any significant relationships at all." These authors indicate that a firm's performance has two dimensions to analyze: return and risk. The risk dimension has not been analyzed in depth and they said, "By focusing only on the return implications of IT, IS research has implicitly ignored the possibility of a risk/return trade-off." Thus, technology is investment and not only represented in terms of productivity but also in terms of means to manage risk, operational and strategic. Jin and Li (2012) pointed out, "As the emerging Internet and digital technology creates new market opportunities, firms face the problem of balancing the risk of rushing into the new market with high technology investment costs, potential losses from cannibalizing existing business, and the uncertainty occurring in the emerging market."

The possible principles to deal with digital technologies to develop strategic intelligence are associated with technology adoption in terms of innovative business environment development inside the organization. Innovation is a two-way process within any organization. Senior management should review the problems considered strategic and tactical and find solutions through the staff who will be involved in the project. The stages of innovation should not only review the relationship market, customer, company, and industry but also the vision of the business, policies, responses to the market, and the development of responses based on the knowledge of the employees. Vision and strategy are fundamentally the basis of the innovation process and through these, one can measure the impact and requirements of design of the business processes and development of the information inside the organization.

Innovation is directly related to factors that motivate the changes in the organization and a leaning outcome. These changes can be related to product development, usually part of a set or a family of products and brands, and the segments that the organizations want to serve. The outcome of new products does not end the process of innovation; it is essential to understand how new ideas are adopted, how they are introduced to the organization, and the alignment with new technologies. Planning is a multi-stage process that is focused on achieving compliance with organizational policy. Thus, a principle to deal with digital technologies starts with alignment of technology and business objectives, strategy, and governance model. Objectives, such as a certain percentage of the market share or introducing a new product or technology, are related to technology, innovation, change, etc. Strategy is HOW to achieve the objectives, and the governance model represents the responsibilities of the areas and the resulting organizational roles. Implementation of the governance model requires development of tools, coordination, integration, and aggregation of multiple information systems and technologies.

Another aspect in digital technologies to consider is operational risk. The most common definition, first published by the Basel Committee, includes the loss, direct or indirect, that is a result of failure in internal processes, people actions, and system performance. Many of the risks in the operational risk categories can be related to the use of technology, techniques, and methods: internal and external fraud, employee malpractice, safety in the workplace, damage to physical assets, disruption of business and systems failures, and low quality of execution, delivery, and processes management.

An integral view of the cycle involves data, knowledge, and technology as a symbiotic process to solve, knowledge to use, and technological tools to achieve the solution. These capabilities improvement for dealing with new digital technologies is enclosed in a framework of principles of innovation, operational risk and strategy with its governance. To achieve the goal of the capability's improvement, a structure of technology adoption is presented based on the knowledge management processes. Learning and assimilating technology will, at the same time, modify the learning processes and knowledge adoption. Säljö (2010) expressed, "Thus, the technologies do not merely support learning; they transform how we learn and how we come to interpret learning. The metaphors of learning currently emerging as relevant in the new media ecology emphasize the transformational and performative nature of such activities, and of knowing in general."

Moreover, adopting digital technology will include important work on people's mindsets and behaviors. Grudin (2006) indicated, "Despite the considerable sum invested in a technical solution, it failed. Individual consultants did not perceive enough benefit to undertake the considerable training needed to use the system. It is early to say how these technologies will evolve. Top-down structure can serve a purpose. Self-organizing structure, derived by the system from author-generated information, may not be efficient, if it requires too much trial-and-error learning and repair by each user. It is unclear how the trade-offs between bottom-up self-organization and top-down management could play out in different contexts." Thus, in the balance of organizational structure and the knowledge level of the problems and solutions, Earl (2001) indicated that organizations obtain the best results when new systems and technologies arrive. This organizational approach assumes a continuous decision process with an ongoing organizational learning of problems and opportunities where IT can be supportive, keeping permanent and *ad-hoc* managers involved. In the same manner, Lee and Turban (2001) provided an example regarding the adoption of e-commerce in organizations indicating some issues of mistrust, transaction risks, and reduced power to generate change. These three points are similar to the ones that are present in a knowledge market inside the organization and that represent barriers to overcome in technology adoption. To achieve the organizational approach mentioned by Earl (2001), the knowledge management processes are oriented to support a new digital technology adoption. The concept of creating knowledge is observed in at least three ways: one is the use of technology to create knowledge, another is to create knowledge for the development of new technologies, and the third one is knowledge creation for use/adoption of digital emerging technologies in the organization. This process represents the systematization of knowledge of emerging technologies that includes codification or documentation; in this context, documentation of new technologies could be transferred to documents for people to access and use during prototyping and after implementation.

A way to work on the solution of the problem dealing with digital technologies is through adoption of technologies. This is a learning process that is required to apply technology knowledge to solve a problem or different problems. The learning process will be transferred through a variety of means, methodologies, models, metaphors, and concepts related to the technology that people can access maintaining human–machine interactions. A good example of moving in the knowledge creation process is cloud computing capabilities. Once cloud computing was introduced as storage, it transformed a service that includes capacity for processing data, a central repository of software, access to use the software itself, and means to collaborate and develop projects that integrate many different resources. People in organizations and organizations themselves started looking at cloud computing as a new resource and a way to manage some administrative issues in management information systems. The services were defined and developed, and people started to identify them using Infrastructure As A Service (IAAS), Platform As A Service (PAAS), and Software As A Service (SAAS) that are included in cloud computing conceptualization. Cloud computing can be associated with the study of mutual value creation (co-creation) between service systems and organizations. Co-creation and cloud computing are concepts to leverage knowledge management of risk management. Cloud computing is a means of collaborative use of system tools, process capabilities, and knowledge in the organization.

Another example is when organizations realized that they have many information systems and one problem to solve that is related to performance evaluation of the organization not only through financial information but also through business and competitive intelligence developments. Organizations start adopting technology related to ERP, CRM, SCM, etc., to integrate processes. All the steps for integration reduce operational risks and keep a good level of competitiveness. Advanced questions in digital technology adoption are emerging, for example, about potential reduction of technology costs in computing time, computing resources and modeling where the organization gains synergies because of the use of the cloud, speed to access updated technology and with the possibility of using more connected and collaborative functions, management of resources based on pay-as-you-go for applications that are only required for some projects, access to new services for the customers and options in product/service development, reduction of activities related to infrastructure management, potential acceleration of compliance and development of the organization's capacities, extended use of services such as open source and collaborative developments around the world, awareness and early warning systems based on the experiences in different regions of the world, economic sectors, products, and natural phenomena, and data analytics possibilities for dealing with strategy, strategic risk, and digital transformation.

Technology adoption has to overcome issues such as lack of understanding of the technology trends by the executives and other stakeholders, potential threats to the security of data and protection of the digital capital, lack of capacity to organize the enterprises to use the information resources in a different way or the need to answer how to manage the digital capital of the organization, blindness regarding the value of the technology as a solution for the organization, and the balance required for resource allocation in the organization, control, reliability, regulation, and support for the technology. Learning of new digital technologies is part of the knowledge application in organizations. There are areas specialized that will transfer their knowledge to user groups and people related to new technology implementation. There are a means to apply this knowledge to the organizations. Some examples of these routes are based on how organizations and individuals learn:

- Using communities of practice.
- Reviewing the processes/feedback, based on what is the ideal, what is the practice reflection.
- Imitating, following from new people, leaders.

In summary, creation of content using digital technologies (Jin and Li, 2012) is a subject that includes decisions related to new technology investments, strategic changes, operational changes, etc. The most important aspect is to identify that going digital is not just about using the internet as a distribution channel but also about the products and services, people, and operations. Thus, what is indicated is that without a complete view of the impact, the adoption of new technologies is not straightforward. In the decision toward adopting new technologies, it is important to have a clear understanding of competitor costs and in some cases be aware of cannibalization of current products, which is a key point in the decisions. Risks are present in all areas of the organization; it is known, for example, that technological development provides support to an organization but in the same way it is a source of risk (Exhibit 4.44). It is clear that the solution to communication problems or transactional management is achieved through improvement of databases, processing, and other communication elements with the generation of very large benefits compared to the relationship with the client.

However, these improvement activities within the perspective of risk management ignite a wake-up call against the risks associated with implementation, use, and maintenance. The organization must ensure that the means of control and production that reduce risk are obtained. Investments are high and can be lost if it is estimated that easily detected events occur. Damage of multiple records can be catastrophic. As indicated in Exhibit 4.44, technology is not risk free and it is very important to introduce its assessment into the risk program. These risks, for example, are associated with the classifications that were given at the beginning of the chapter; their treatment is special because they would alter the organizational functioning in the technological aspect. Nowadays, procedures associated with processes in companies are not prepared for a rapid replacement of technology, for example, writing a

New technology adoption.	Risks of implementation, failure, time, and obsolescence.	Risk of use, maintenance, and change — adverse events against the benefits that new technology brought.

Exhibit 4.44. New technologies bring new risks.

check with a typewriter or finding errors that occurred in the records without having a means of probing possible incompatibilities — these are two technological extremes that can affect the operation of the entity.

In general, some risks are only identified to the extent that technological tools are used. The reason for this is usually the possibility of understanding the cause–effect relationship that occurs when introducing new developments in the company. Similarly, the development of an information system and its operation structure requires a space to establish at what level of risk the organization is storing data, transactions, generation of reports, etc. This means that risk management will have a very important task in the planning and maintenance of the information system. One crucial set of risks for organizations is innovation and technology risks.

Exhibit 4.45 includes some aspects of innovation risk that require attention toward management design and implementation of strategies:

Innovation risk is associated with creating a model of what to expect and what the return on the investment will be for achieving the organization's goals. The search for innovation implies evaluation of constraints, limitations, user's skill sets, infrastructure preparedness, and a guide on a cognitive level of how creation and implementation will be. A risk that is present in innovation risk analysis is first the possibility of no delivery, no use, misuse, etc.

About the models for innovation (Exhibit 4.46) to review and to learn from past experiences show what the trigger and roadmap are to obtain benefits of innovation (Exhibits 4.47 and 4.48).

Benefits of innovation are associated with success and failures, depending on multiple factors such as business concentration, economic issues in the sectors of concentration or markets, issues in using technologies, and issues in generating wrong solutions. The following section is a presentation of certain cases where digitalization is growing, with challenges along multiple dimensions on digital transformation. The selected case relates to digital banking, P2P banking, and what is happening in the construction industry.

4.4. Strategic Risks and Digitalization Cases

This section is the illustration of how digital transformation is connecting three main areas — services related to banking, construction in potential

<table>
<tr>
<td>2022 PWC Global Risk Survey (Base: 3,584)
"79% report that keeping up with the speed of digital and other transformations is a significant risk management challenge."
"While 75% of organisations report that having technology systems that don't work together is a significant risk management challenge, just 35% of those are addressing that challenge in a formal, enterprise-wide manner."
Bennett et al. (2014)
"Innovation is about changing the way we do things" in any dimension, products, processes, organization, etc.
Risks are present in all possible edges and points of the areas of innovation.
New knowledge creates new risks and at the same time it mitigates risks.
Risk Analytics is needed: "However, such massive and invaluable data from risk analytics may bring new challenges such as data processing, data visualization, data-driven decision models, risk decision support systems, etc., in the era of big data."</td>
<td>Innovation risk requires the following:
• Identification
• Assessment, modeling, analysis
• Mitigation
• Monitoring
• Control
• An ERM (enterprise risk management), priority on strategic risks of organizations and societies
• Avoid innovation failures in design</td>
</tr>
<tr>
<td colspan="2">Joshi et al. (2021)
Hammer in search of a nail: Level of sophistication for possibly simpler tasks.
Unrecognized sources of bias: Model not using all data before and after a classification – credit example.
Right solution, wrong time: changes in priorities, budgets, etc.
Wright tool, wrong user: "Many customers doubted the credibility of recommendations delivered through apps, websites, and emails."
The rocky last mile: difficulties in implementation</td>
</tr>
</table>

Exhibit 4.45. Innovation risks.

bankruptcy, and citizen behavior — which have contributed to modifying strategic risks in a community. This framework develops a measurement system of exposure and default evaluation of the Wenzhou financial organizations. The purpose is to identify exposure factors to control, key risk indicators, and to sketch an exposure measurement system. The risk analysis of this study is concentrated on retail banking organizations. It reviews factors affecting risk exposure based on changes of risk

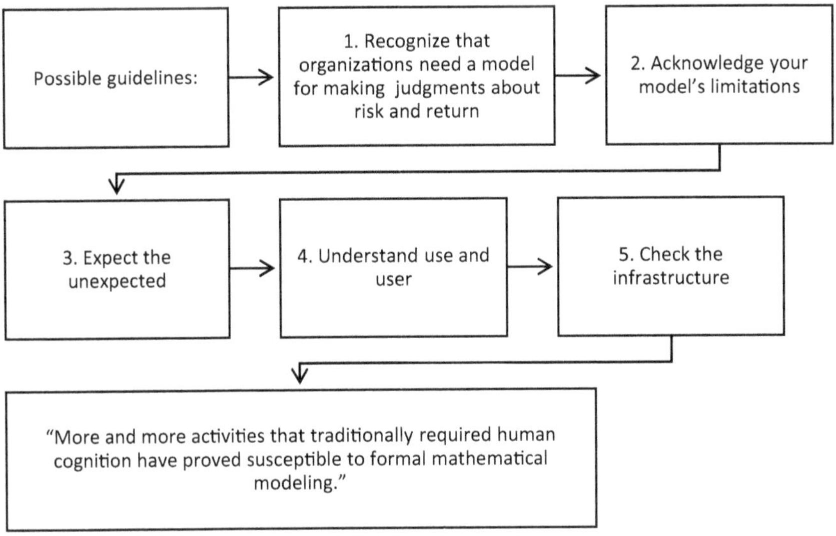

Exhibit 4.46. A model to innovate is required.

Learning from experience, keeping the acquired knowledge BT learning about the importance of human preparedness BT and the introduction of a Social CRM (Orlikowski and Thompson, 2010) provided points to learn from this experience. The search for the benefits happens in many different places but the main one is related to improvement of customer experience, new service and product development with a high friendly touch. The purpose was to find people expressing their concerns and to answer them by creating means to operationalize these answers with the option of follow up and to move from different levels of resolution. The experience put in evidence that the organization has to support a social CRM with the following challenges:	Ross Video is another example of CRM, much simpler to implement: • CRM software enables salespeople to make better decisions more quickly, dramatically improving their ability to satisfy customers and close deals. The introduction of the new system has helped in the following: • Re-engineering each process within its sales chain. • Reducing the duration of its weekly sales conferences by 50 percent. • Improving regional sales managers' effectiveness by 10 percent thanks to live, accurate access to all data for all customers 24/7. • Improving sales coordinators' effectiveness in processing and fulfilling orders by 50 percent.

Exhibit 4.47. Technologies and innovations that provide lessons in the creation of models.

<table>
<tr>
<td>

• Training and changing mindsets and skills of employees. They were required to adapt to a high volume of contacts/ inquires where it was difficult to postpone answers.
• Speed and visibility. Everyone can see what is happening, how the answers are provided, many things can arrive in minutes.
• Difficult to plan the process to provide answer. Many things are arriving in different ways, there are various issues to solve, and the work flow cannot be organized.
• Capability development inside the organization: Find the way to grow and to plan additional levels of use and development.

</td>
<td></td>
</tr>
<tr>
<td>

Mexican Corn Products and improving production

This SME organization found that the problem to solve was related to improving the production capacity. For this purpose, it introduced a new digital technology to support production. Based on this technology introduction, it found that it created new knowledge and people adopted the new technology achieving the following results:

• Develop new means to control production and mainly to measure quality assurance.
• Create new jobs that provided support to the new production level. New people to introduce to the new ways of doing things.
• Production increased the speed and the number of production outcomes increased in very high percentage. These results were in the production and packaging processes.

</td>
<td>

Imprimerie Maxime Inc. more capabilities for printing

This is an example of finding the proper solution for the industry. This is a clear adoption of digital technology because of owners' understanding of the business requirements and a good fit of what was available in the market. The adoption of the technology was faster because of the specific software created for the printing industry. This integral solution was from the quotation process, production, and accounting in the printing industry. The benefits were directly related to the increment in sales, better margins, better productivity, and a faster answer to customers' inquiries. The new technological option gave the opportunity to plan new employee hiring in order to support positive business perspectives.

</td>
</tr>
</table>

Exhibit 4.47. (*Continued*)

New World Technologies introduces ERP
The main point to understand is that the introduction of ERP helped the organization to make better decisions based on a more efficient and effective access to information. The experience with ERP modified the way to do business, bringing the following benefits: • Improvement in productivity. • Improvement and reduction in data entry. Duplication was reduced. • Better service to customers. Faster answers to customers with response time of the next day of the inquiry. • Production time was reduced. Not only were leads supported in a faster way but production costs were also reduced. • Provide the opportunity to change the business model by manufacturing parts in Canada instead of offshore.

Exhibit 4.47. (*Continued*)

Barry Property Services goes digital	Produits de Métal Vulcain Inc.
A landscape business is in many cases not related to digital solutions. However, the needs are numerous because of issues in operation, scheduling, resource management, and business administration. This company installed a package designed as a complete management system, specifically for the lawn maintenance business. The benefits are improvement in sales, cost reduction, administrative workload, production capacity, and customer relationships.	Adopting a numerical laser metrology (a computer-assisted technique to measure large components of frames) introduced a more rapid and accurate way to measure production processes. There is a plan to train people to use this new technology. The company is expecting to increase sales and duplicate the market share. Based on these expectations, the company can get payback in less than three years and maintain one of the bigger contracts that the company has in a good condition. This new technology opened the opportunity to attract new clients that require a more sophisticated production process.

Exhibit 4.48. Technologies and innovations that provide lessons in the creation of models.

Eastern Independent Telecommunications Ltd.	Telco in search of new operation
One of the challenges in organizations is how to plan changes in processes and in structure when they have to continue daily business operations. EIT's strategy gives the firm access to the most advanced technological products and training from global manufacturers, sustaining and creating new high-tech jobs in Canada. Strategically, EIT adds Canadian content to global products by distributing and providing in-country support services.	Changing the business operation adopting a new technology implies several steps. Telco is a telecommunication company, studied by Khanagha *et al.* (2013), involved in the adoption of cloud computing. The organization can have the resources in place and available; however, there are some steps that a company needs to perform to implement cloud technology.
This organization developed a simulation process to test inter-operation between new and existing telecommunication equipment that customers will have. Simulation is a way to save time and money. Other benefits are emerging from this new simulation system and there is a positive expectation to increase productivity in areas such as sales, software configuration, software development, and implementation in optical and fiber-to-home networks.	These steps can be summarized as follows: First, presenting, providing examples and discovering some potential issues like embedding the new technology in traditional areas of the business and potential effects in the business models. The second step was to start an experimentation program to engage people in this new technology project. The main purpose was to create a positive environment of dealing with the new technology. This gave the understanding of issues to solve such as having a common language. Once this experimentation program grew, the decision to make was if the program should be grown or shrunk. The decision was to shrink it as a program and to star pushing the adoption of the technology to the business units and finally to embed it in the organization, because the new technology should be part of the organization's life. This case review indicates the value of having a gradual process to introduce a new technology keeping the assets in the current operation as a complement of the new technology.

Exhibit 4.48. (*Continued*)

USAA (Ross and Beath, 2010)	The US Securities and Exchange Commission (Wixon and Ross, 2012)
This is an example of a financial service organization totally focused on a market and on the technology aspects. The services to the US Army are financial services with the total operations based on the web, telephone, fax, ATMs, and mobile channels. The basic strategy in this organization is to act as a direct marketing company that is in the search of an integrated enterprise. This purpose is highly demanding from innovation in processes and technology. These two areas of business improvements required a well-planned structure to prioritize processes. This structure was based on a project governance schema that was looking for projects where alignment and integration were the core of the new project definition. This is aligned to the strategy and creating value through integration. USAA identified four steps to develop any project: Align, Integrate, Design, and Build. Additionally, the cost efficiency and time to deliver were key points of control of the plan including a satisfied IT group. In the innovation processes, people were involved; they were asked for ideas/answers and the organization identified the project sponsors. Furthermore, everyone was conscious of being part of a permanent learning process with constant identification of barriers to overcome.	Another key piece of the review of new digital technology adoption is the development of a project to work more efficiently and smarter with better evidence of a decision-making process. This project focuses on what is important to answer for the organization, using data and analytical tools, looking for actions to perform. The way that the organization decided to be smarter is based on reviewing the experience with customers' claims and complaints, creating a web-based submission process, creation a market intelligence office to triage what was coming from the web submission, reviewing and documenting the processes, learning and putting in practice solutions and answers. It created an exam process for organizations in terms of compliance as well. All of these points supported by the development of shared data, creation of automated processes with, central data repository and workflow clarification, creation of an organizational structure to develop and support collaboration, transparency and integration of the changes and new actions. For all of these steps, the organization valued the expertise development and leverage of individual skills. The motto was working smarter and with focus. For achieving goals during project implementation, it mixed digital technologies with activities and the solution to the customers' issues, providing the use of technology, analytics tools, and processes, fostering discovery and use of technology.

Exhibit 4.48. *(Continued)*

Delta-Q	Supervalu (Quaadgras *et al.*, 2012)
The firm implemented Design for Failure Mode Effect Analysis (DFMEA), a method used by engineers to document and explore ways in which a product design might fail in real-world use. The final outcome of using this technology is to develop a product with a much lower failure rate than would be possible without DFMEA. It may be several years before a measurable change in the failure rate will be apparent. However, it is already evident that productivity has increased. It is a direct benefit to Delta-Q to have more people with a higher level of design knowledge, and may lead to more innovation, problem-solving, and productivity growth.	In this organization, the main purpose was the search of integrating processes and creating a culture of sharing that includes a process of creating shared tools. Employees learnt how to use the technological means to develop ideas and find solutions to problems in multiple areas. Moreover, the company provided more empowerment to the regional managers in order to achieve the vision of being very close to the neighbors where the stores are located. To get there, Supervalu created a clear profile of the king of regional directors they wanted to have and the willingness to use the shared tools and consolidate a sharing culture.

Exhibit 4.48. (*Continued*)

conditions given new technology involved, changes in the customer behavior, and development of the society. The study also includes a presentation of the mortgage market given the importance and impact that mortgages have on the development of economic conditions in the city of Wenzhou. The aspects related to the city's banking organizations are included in particular the Wenzhou Bank's performance.

According to the thirteenth Five-Year Plan for the Development of Wenzhou's Financial Industry, the contribution of the financial sectors is growing and there is a need to maintain a healthy and well-developed financial system. The city's banking deposits and foreign currency loans reached 136.7 billion yuan and 1038.1 billion yuan, respectively, and the default or credit risk loan ratio of the banking sector remains below the provincial average. The number of village and town bank branches is more than 40, and the number of private lending service centers reached more than 12. The number of listed companies in the domestic and foreign stock markets in the city reached more than 40. Insurance premium income is more than 27 billion yuan, insurance depth is more than 4.2%, and insurance density is 3183 yuan/person or more. The city's rural cooperative financial institutions deposit a balance of 230 billion yuan, a loan balance of 160 billion yuan, and agricultural loans of not less than 70%. However, there are strategic risks and important steps to take into consideration in the new approach to the development of financial institutions and the desire of the city to promote digitalization and structure new business opportunities in a more diversified market. One of those is to prepare organizations to the competition force of shadow banking, non-banking lending organizations, fintech approaches Blockchain technology the same as other technologies that can modify the value added by financial institutions (Knowledge@Wharton 2018).

A proposed framework for analysis is provided in Exhibit 4.49, and it is under the premise of creating an ongoing system that is learning based on the new knowledge that is created by risk analytics (qualitative and quantitative) through digital solutions: data analytics and AI. The framework assumes that a financial organization's exposure is related to Wenzhou city's strategy and its implementation. The financial system in this risk analytics approach reflects where resources are allocated and used. In Exhibit 4.49, the first column is associated with the definition of what Wenzhou city wants to do, the and risks involved; the second column is related to what is necessary to deal with risks; and the third column refers to the implementation using the risk analytics methods and techniques. The framework comprises the following:

(1) **Strategic and Tactical Risk Identification Exposure:** This is the business environmental study of the market, selecting what is strategic (diversification of the industry and digitalization in Wenzhou) and what is tactical (construction building non-infrastructure development and sales, loan and deposit concentration) for the city.
(2) **Strategic and Tactic Risks Monitoring:** Monitoring is about the construction of the risk management information system that supports the creation and maintenance of risk measurement. The monitoring system identifies not only possible risks and effects but also the risk control and mitigation actions.
(3) **Strategic and Tactic Risk Control:** Identification of control actions that can support risk mitigation and provide strategic competitive

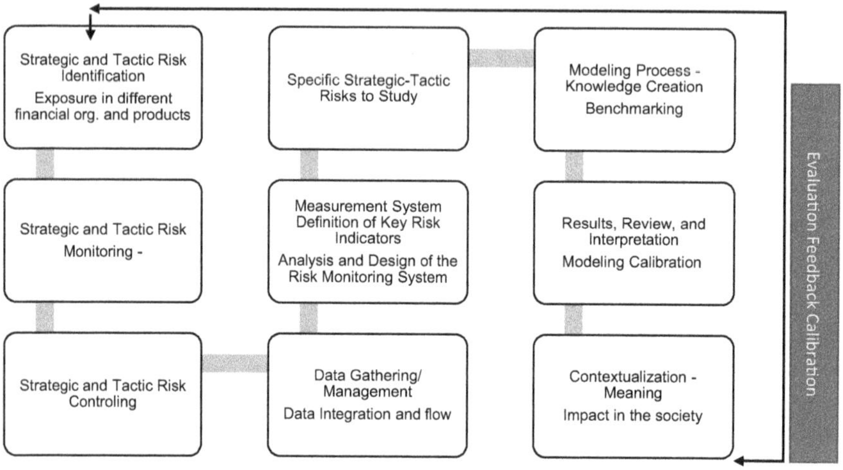

Exhibit 4.49. (Source Author's Creation) Basic framework to monitor exposure in the financial sector.

advantage to the city (How location is appropriate in industry diversification, digitalization, etc.)

(4) **Specific Strategic–Tactical Risk to Study:** Concentration of a chain of risks of strategic goals and tactics, for instance, digitalization as strategy and the risk related to the lack of human talent. Discover actions to foster new generations to develop mindsets for digital societies to deal with intelligent service systems in the society such as transportation and financial systems.

(5) **Measurement System/Key Risk Indicators:** To develop once the selection of risk to concentrate on and the chain to follow the information system associated with risk indicators and control is required. The system is built under the constraints of the data available (Data integration flow from national, provincial, and city levels; the same as aggregation levels and historical data availability).

(6) **Data Gathering:** Data reside in several repositories. The level of aggregation and historical availability are not standard in several sources. The information system requires two main stages of data: (i) data that are raw and represent transactions, values of the variables of the financial system; and (ii) data that are created based on the outputs of the risk analytics work.

(7) **Modeling Process/Knowledge Creation:** Risk analytics creates knowledge based on the data processing using models that learn. Modeling is a process to follow step by step to improve accuracy and scope. The purpose is to illustrate using mortgages analysis an outlook of variables affecting mortgages, sales of real estate, etc., which is a means to maintain value of the family investments.
(8) **Contextualization/Meaning:** Modeling outcomes are not meaningful if they are not under a context or they are not in the direction of leading actions.
(9) **Evaluation, Feedback, and Calibration:** The full system is in a continuous improvement process that can digest more risk. It assesses the accuracy, scope, and capabilities to understand what is happening in financial organizations, Wenzhou city, and the possible impacts in society presently and in the future.

Andersen and Sax (2020) indicated that risk has been a part of management analysis based on understanding exposures and the internal and external socio-economic conditions that can affect organizations' performance. The knowledge of strategic risk management as a way of concentrating on the management of strategic risk takes principles from ERM and the multiple fields involved in the understanding of risk. In a community or a city, strategic risk is related to the possible events/circumstances that can affect the society's development and the standards of living of stakeholders. The risk events can come from changes in business, financial risks, natural risks, etc. Risk exposure analysis requires an understanding of the nature of which risks can be insured or transferred, and risks that are present and require mitigation, but cannot be insured or transferred. Mortgage development is associated with the capacity of the society to invest, acquire a house, allocation of financial institution resources, competition, use of non-banking systems of financing, etc. As mortgages are associated with the Wenzhou urban and rural district development, there is an important concentration of resources in the construction sector, and at the same time it is important to maintain ongoing surveillance of real estate bubbles, differences between square meters built and square meters sold, etc. Changes in business, digitalization, competition, etc., are possible factors affecting the mortgage market, changes in the consumption habits, and migration from rural to cities and from cities to rural areas.

The society/community as an organization can be affected by risk events. Risk events can affect the flow of resources in a city, the conditions of life, and the possibilities to improve economic conditions. In Miller and Bromiley's (1990) study, they presented evidence that "income stream risk reduces subsequent performance and that this influence exists across industries and performance levels." Additionally, they concluded that the influence of strategic risk varies according to industries and their levels of performance. In a city or community, income stream risk can affect the levels of returns of investment of builders and financial institutions if sales do not meet the expectations and asset turnover is reduced. In this framework, Wenzhou is connected to what Frigo and Anderson (2011) pointed out regarding strategic risk: "Strategic risks are those risks that are most consequential to the organization's ability to execute its strategies and achieve its business objectives." Thus, risk exposure analytics is based on creating a risk exposure analytics information/knowledge system because "Risk Management is frequently not a problem of a lack of information, but rather a lack of knowledge with which to interpret its meaning" (Marshal *et al.*, 1996).

The risk exposure concept is used in financial business in insurance as Bouska (1989) commented: "The business of insurance presumes an exposure to loss: if there is no possibility of a loss, there is no need for insurance. However, if an entity does have an exposure to loss, it is desirable that the cost of transferring that loss to another party be proportional to the expected loss, which is assumed to vary with the size of the exposure base. Thus, the selection of an exposure base, which quantifies and proxies for the exposure, is a fundamental step in the insurance process." Furthermore, the concept of exposure is applicable to any other business or organization in a city. The scope of reviewing risk exposure in a city is very wide and with many variables involved; the concentration is on exposure of mortgage business and real estate return risk (house price volatility and price overestimation). In the banking system, risk exposure comes from all banking activities that are risky and knowledge-based businesses, with risks, for example, considered as the variation of expected results in return for investment in real estate. This risk requires two main views of the builder and the final owner, regarding factors such as high interest rates in lending, reduced sales speed, cash flows, projects of low value, lack of control in project, or community development.

Reviewing the Chinese economy, then the banking system's transformation, Wenzhou's development, and finally the Wenzhou Bank case, the indication of risk factors in the OECD report (2019) pointed out, on the one hand, the flow of consumption and income use: "Households are spending increasingly on items such as e-commerce and shared services. As the labour force has been shrinking for a number of years, reflecting population ageing, labour shortages are keeping wage growth high, particularly in large inland cities." On the other hand, regarding the creation of banking assets, the OECD (2019) report states the following: "Government restrictions on mortgages have contributed to housing prices levelling off in the largest cities and have curtailed real estate investment. Infrastructure investment has also weakened, as local governments' borrowing has been reined in." Besides, the corporate risks are growing "Corporate debt is higher than in other major economies, though urban construction-related debt by local government investment vehicles also belongs here, while in other countries it would show up as government debt." But it is not only on corporations but also in local governments "Infrastructure stimulus could lift growth over the projection horizon, but it could lead to a further build-up of imbalances and capital misallocation, and thereby weaker growth in the medium term. Some local governments are heavily indebted. The debt quotas therefore need to consider repaying ability of the issuing local government."

The early warning system in risk monitoring can be linked to specific events as the OECD (2019) suggests: "A collapse in housing prices would hurt some sectors of the economy including real estate, construction, furbishing, home appliances and other related industries, but the impact of a steep fall in house prices would be mitigated by stringent prudential regulations governing household mortgage borrowing and the prohibition of withdrawing housing equity." Moreover, considering the Chinese economic outlook, the Chinese banking system has been under reform since 2015. The Chinese banking system has been evolving very fast in fintech areas and in tackling issues generated by non-regulated lending systems. In 2020, PwC published a Chinese Banking System survey, indicating aspects that concern exposure management in financial institutions. These aspects provide a guide to proceed with the framework indicated earlier:

(1) Information about local government's debts, looking for unifying and organizing debt statistics.
(2) The liberalization of interest rate can contribute to the "loan prime rate (LPR) pricing mechanism."

(3) The bank is promoting differentiation, intelligent banking, and actions in integrated operations.
(4) The man market to focus on involves small and micro enterprises, growing and promoting retail business growth by diversifying banks' business risk under a social responsibility assumption.
(5) The sectors that are supported by loans are mainly urban infrastructure, loans to small and micro enterprises.
(6) Personal housing and mortgage loans represent close 40% of answers of the bankers surveyed.
(7) Credit risk management is a priority, in particular the development of pricing methods (analytics of pricing and interest risk management), the technology, and risk analytics capability development.
(8) Development of management control systems. This is an aspect related to the above point 7 where risk analytics plays an important in capability development.
(9) Development of Fintech capacity using internal capabilities, and implementing and improving cooperation with Fintech companies.
(10) Based on the increment of interest in Fintech, new risk appears related to safety, disintermediation, risk analysis capacity, measurement, regulation, and control of the fintech. However, the risks are not a limitation, but a way "to ensure profitability growth in the future" as almost 60% of the bankers surveyed stated.

Furthermore, OECD (2019) indicated risk aspects that are aligned to the previous list and supplement the risk outlook from a macroeconomic perspective as follows:

(1) Potential corporate big defaults can reduce the speed of growth and increase financing costs. This can create a circle of increasing costs that affect the corporation's bottom line, putting them more at risk.
(2) Possible housing price fall can affect several sectors associated with construction industry, financial organizations, and household investment.
(3) In a transition to a new economy based on digitalization, the business processes and operations need to be stable, with a landscape for internal and international trading that supports business transformation. Currently, there are some possible constraints in trading that can affect enterprise risk of certain industries.

In both of real estate and mortgage markets, a fact that deserves careful surveillance is Peer-to-Peer lending, because of the costs and risky practices associated with sources of funds, cost and pricing of services/loans, guarantees, etc. Ding *et al.* (2021) expressed that "Chinese P2P lending has expanded by a factor of 60 over the 4 years from 2013 to 2017." The term P2P used by Ding *et al.* (2021) means "P2P lending refers to the technology-based platforms that allow investors to participate as investors in loan assets, with a direct claim on payment of interest and repayments of principal." The growth of P2P lending has been substantial. The issues is lack of regulation, and with these issues multiple risks are in place as well, because it is not only about the number of transactions or providers (number of providers close to 2500 in 2018) but also the lending volume, which in 2018 reached more than 208 billion dollars. The risk of bad P2P operation and loans involved grew fast and new regulation appeared in 2018, reducing the growth of the number of platforms and outstanding loans. P2P became like banks asking for guarantees but with weaker regulation. Now, platforms are transitioning to convert into micro lender companies with capital and operation requirements; however, P2P conversion is not mandatory.

Zhao *et al.* (2020) indicate that, on the one hand, the mortgages are adjustable rate mortgages (ARMs) that are potentially affected by monetary policies. On the other hand, a reduction in mortgage payment increases the consumption of non-durable good; however, in this segment, the payment to income ratio is higher with a lower level of consumption. One of the concepts of risk exposure is the "index of land expansion" (ratio between population growth and growth of land available to use). This index is growing just like houses prices and the mortgages which have not been repaid yet. Moreover, the user of mortgage products does not have incentives to repay the loan because of penalties or no financial attraction as the return level in other investments can be better.

The findings require monitoring of what has been presented in previous studies that opened areas and opportunities of monitoring and controlling risk. One of these studies was conducted by Koss and Xinrui (2018), which indicated the conditions of China's Housing Market, opening the question of what is happening now and will happen in the future. Koss and Shi (2018) were looking for the possible causes and effects of the housing bubble bursting in China. They indicated that the Chinese analysis is different from what can be performed in other countries because of differences in high-value cities (Tier 1 cities) and ghost cities. In addition, this article explained the differences between the Chinese market and other markets in the world to evaluate possible bubbles: from the land supply perspective. The state is the owner of the land, decides how to use it and its conditions, variations in the government intervention through time, and the identification of local policies to manage cities development. From the demand point of view, there is high attraction to move for rural and small cities to big cities, reduced options of investment in real estate as an important alternative, the influence of foreign changes in the house markets is limited, and differences between the tier 1 cities and others are stark. Besides, exposure analysis requires one to clarify if, presently and in the future, the level of prices in Chinese cities will be high, similar to other important cities in the world but with a huge difference in income to access houses.

In the same line of analysis, identifying possible risks affecting the real estate market and opening the current investigation, Fang *et al.* (2016) demystified the Chinese housing boom. Their study with data from 2003–2013 indicated that a price-to-income ratio is a potential issue of the housing market if an economic slowdown takes place. According to Fang *et al.* (2016), there are risks related to income growth based on lower GDP growth rates. Another aspect to consider is the demographic conditions that can affect the housing market, mainly because of the aging changes that can modify the distribution of families in rural and urban areas, big and small cities, land available, and cost for housing development.

Finally, another aspect to consider in the present and future risk analysis is what Kuang and Liu (2012) discovered when studied the prepayment behavior of the borrowers. They concluded that there is a difference among segments and regions and suggested a different practice of underwriting mortgages among segments because of risk tolerance differences.

According to OEDC (2021 China Outlook), there is an expected post-pandemic recovery in GDP growth (Exhibit 4.50). Moving to 8.5% growth in 2021 and 5.8% for 2022, the current outlook for 2021 shows that shadow banking does not have high reduction, and the growth is not and will not be expected to be positive.

What happened before 2013 in Wenzhou as a tier-2 city is indicated in Exhibit 4.51.

Source of data and graphics	
OECD ECONOMIC OUTLOOK, VOLUME 2021 ISSUE 1: PRELIMINARY VERSION © OECD 2021	

China	2017	2018	2019	2020	2021	2022
	Current prices CNY trillion	Percentage changes, volume (2015 prices)				
GDP at market prices	83.2	6.7	6.0	2.3	8.5	5.8
Total domestic demand	81.7	7.3	5.9	1.9	7.0	5.6
Exports of goods and services	16.4	3.7	1.5	1.6	11.3	8.2
Imports of goods and services	15.0	8.3	0.5	-0.9	3.1	4.9
Net exports[1]	1.5	-0.4	0.2	0.5	1.7	0.5

GDP Outlook. Source OECD 2021

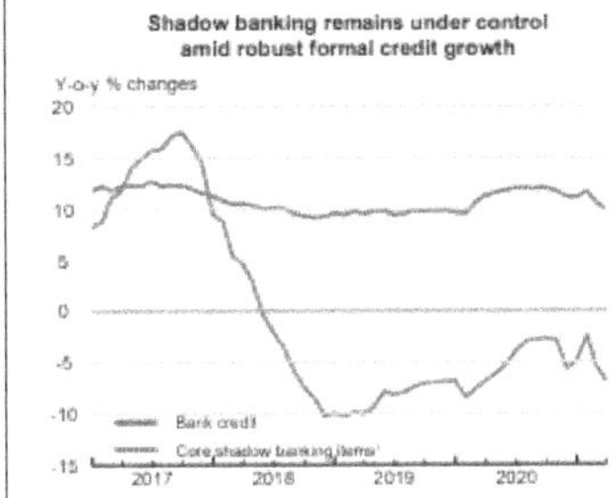

Shadow banking growth Source OECD 2021

Exhibit 4.50. Statistics showing GDP and shadow banking.

Fang, H., Gu, Q., Xiong, W., and Zhou, L.-A. (2016). Demystifying the Chinese housing boom. *NBER Macroeconomics Annual*, 30(1), 105–166.	
Wenzhou is a tier-2 city and its (sq meters) residential space divided by population in 2012 is between tier-1 cities (Beijing, Shanghai) and tier-3 cities. The ratio is around 1; the highest ratio after 2008 is in the tier-3 group of cities.	The price index in 2012–2013 was around 4 and GRP (measures the per capital value of output in the whole city) around 3.5.

Exhibit 4.51. Wenzhou as a tier-2 city.

Regarding the China Economic survey 2019, aspects to review related to risk exposure that supplement Fang *et al.*'s (2016) observations are as follows:

Digital banking (see Exhibits 4.52 and 4.53) has been limited and China has four banks; P2P and shadow banking are reined in and the mitigation of systemic risk is expected with the advances of banking regulation. Digital banks in the province have shown results that attract digitalization as a potential area of growing profits and efficiency for the banking system. A potential risk with effects on the internal and external landscape is the bankruptcy of developer/construction companies.

For the purpose of reviewing what can affect the risk exposure at the financial institution level, the data from Bank of Wenzhou are used to

Source OECD China Economic Survey 2019	
In 2019, the tier-2 housing price change Y-o-y was around 10% below tier-3 and tier-4 and above tier-1 cities.	The new long-term household loan growth collapsed; it was close to zero coming from negative values in 2018, and the weighted average interest rates for long-term household loans was close to 6%. "Informal lending rates at end-2018 have been as high as 17–18%, according to the surveys in Wenzhou city in Zhejiang Province, the "capital" of informal lending."
Deleveraging in the economy has been growing.	Mortgages have the lowest NPL, around 0.3%, locating below all the other lines of credit.
The P2P lending platform is divided into two classes: (i) normally operated that passed from around 3500 in 2016 to 1000 at the end of 2019; and (ii) failing platforms that move in the same period from close to 2000 to more than 5000 at the end of 2019.	The saving rate continues to be high in households, around 25%. "Moreover, the shrinking of the saving-investment balance since the Global Financial Crisis is attributable more to the drop in the investment rate than to a fall in the saving rate."

Exhibit 4.52. Socio-economic conditions that can affect exposure management.

	Profitability (%)	2018	2019	2020
	Digital Banks			
Zhejiang E-Commerce Bank Co., Ltd.	Return on Assets	0.77	1.07	0.57
	Return on Equity	13.36	15.81	10.49
	Return on Common Equity	13.36	15.81	10.49
WeBank Co., Ltd.	Return on Assets	1.64	1.55	1.56
	Return on Equity	24.41	28.15	26.69
	Return on Common Equity	24.41	28.15	26.69
Sichuan Xw Bank Corp.,Ltd	Return on Assets		2.82	1.67
	Return on Equity		30.31	15.16
	Return on Common Equity		30.31	15.16
Kincheng Bank Of Tianjin Co., Ltd.	Return on Assets	0.76	0.65	0.15
	Return on Equity	4.58	4.95	1.24
	Return on Common Equity	4.58	4.95	1.24
	Non- Digital Banks			
Bank of Hangzhou Co., Ltd.	ROAA	0.63	0.69	0.66
	ROAE	9.92	10.98	9.44
	Return on Avg Ordinary Equity	10.97	12.12	11.12
	Return on Average Tangible Ordinary Equity	11.11	12.5	11.43
	Return on Avg Risk-weighted Assets	1.01	1.06	1.01
	Pre-impairment Operating Profit/ Avg Assets	1.37	1.57	1.67
Bank of Wenzhou Co	ROAA	0.24	0.31	0.07
	ROAE	3.84	4.97	1.1
	Return on Avg Ordinary Equity	3.84	4.97	1.1
	Return on Average Tangible Ordinary Equity	3.94	5.08	1.19
	Return on Avg Risk-weighted Assets	0.33	0.44	0.1
	Pre-impairment Operating Profit/ Avg Assets	0.89	1.08	1

Exhibit 4.53. Digital banks compared to regular banks.

Loans Classification	End of the reporting period		Beginning of the reporting period	
	Amount	Proportion (%)	Amount	Proportion (%)
Real estate	13,242,639	17.53	13,896,468	25.92
Building	15,141,276	20.04	10,041,144	18.73
Short-term loan	17,746,126	23.49	13,660,901	25.49
Middle- and long-term loans	45,543,185	60.28	32,552,855	60.74
First-hand housing mortgage	1,333,842	2.87	1,582,529	3.03
Second-hand housing mortgage	1,543,932	3.33	1,868,105	3.57
Loan on collateral securities	61,601,883	50.51	45,860,504	43.31
Loan with mortgages	45,526,175		35,429,308	

Exhibit 4.54. Mortgage share in the structure of loan portfolio.

illustrate what banks are doing based on the perception of risk and exposure management in the market. Mortgages are around 6% of the portfolio for first- and second-hand houses; however, medium- and long-term loans represent 60% of the portfolio, and loans related to real estate and building are more than 37% of the portfolio. Loans with mortgages grew in 2019 to more than 28% (Exhibit 4.54).

Additional aspects to review in exposure analysis are related to aspects such as concentration of customers, concentration of products, the impact of changes in financial technology use, and market condition expectations. The Bank of Wenzhou has taken the actions to strengthen the measures to extend credits, surveillance, and monitoring of the customers. Concentration of customers has two aspects in risk management. On the one hand, the bank can have concentration in sectors and customers to acquire better knowledge of the business; on the other hand, the concentration level for the bank can pull the bank to similar direction as the companies that are with negative outlook and will put the bank at risk. The bank is moving in the direction of "According to the Measures for the Administration of the Large Exposures of Commercial Banks, the credit concentration management of group customers should be further strengthened, the economically dependent customers meeting the requirements for large-sum risk exposure should be included in the management of the group, and the regulations for administration of large-sum risk exposure should be implemented" (Bank of Wenzhou Report, 2019).

The exposure system requires analysis and design of the information systems through regular data or an internal source. The monitoring and risk control system requires the use of structure and unstructured data from internal and external sources. This requires capabilities that include analytics for multiple types of data. The Bank of Wenzhou is working in the direction of risk data enhancement. A key point to review is that even big data are important for risk management; however, they are not enough for the risk monitoring system to go further, because the issues to analyze are not only related to big data but also about what to do with data, analytics capabilities, measurement systems to build, type of variables to control, what predictions to generate, and what rules to review to improve performance. Thus, the risk monitoring system required by the Bank of Wenzhou needs to concentrate on so many aspects in addition to big data capacity: "The Company promoted the construction of big data risk control platform, optimized and improved the internal system, realized the visualization of correlation relationship map, improved the risk monitoring of big-sum assets and the risk control of concentration degree, and prevented the credit risk of group customers" (Bank of Wenzhou Report, 2019).

Besides capacity generation for analytics, the actions related to risk control require risk analytics input to determine priorities and support tactics in reporting, NPL, structure of levels of loans in the portfolio, probabilities of changing status, control of changes in markets affecting business, and surveillance identification.

Currently, shadow banking, P2P, the use of online/social network payment systems, and the increment of fintech including the use of blockchain are in the risk monitoring and control system radar. The effects of concentration can have different outcomes according to the supply chain connections with bank substitutes. The strategic risk in this regard is high and requires a completed review mainly in local commercial banks. These effects of business changes are not clear according to the Basel regulation or the Chinese banking system. As the executives in the J.P. Morgan commented at the beginning of 2021, "If over time an asset class develops that is going to be used by different asset managers and investors, we will have to be involved," referring to blockchain applications such as bitcoins.

In particular, the risk exposure analysis of Wenzhou requires differentiation among districts. The variables used are (Exhibit 4.55): House Hold deposits (hhd suffix); Loans (L suffix); Real estate development (rsd suffix); and Deposits (d suffix). By studying the data from 2001 to 2019, the correlation among variables by Urban and districts shows a high value

2019	hhdep	loans	rsd	dep
Urban	34,459,667	61,484,198	5,777,505	69,696,894
Rui'an	11,734,907	13,518,318	1,896,763	17,225,294
Yueqing	11,033,757	13,847,715	1,560,757	16,345,063
Yongjia	5,278,008	7,159,645	1,010,118	8,061,733
Pingyang	4,567,360	6,425,388	526,778	6,590,295
Cangnan	5,008,848	9,641,872	1,070,179	7,751,275
Wencheng	2,394,677	1,707,508	57,545	3,441,146
Taishun	1,541,095	1,510,900	98,885	2,452,699

Notes:
hhdep = household deposits

Loans = total loans

rsd = real estate development

dep = total deposits

Unit: ten thousand yuan

Exhibit 4.55. Wenzhou Urban and districts.

correlation above .95 for almost all variables except rsdPingyang, rsdWencheng, rsdTaishun, and the variables representing the urban, cities, and counties.

- House Hold deposits: hhdepUrban hhdepRui'an hhdepYueqing hhdepYongjia hhdepPingyang hhdepCangnan hhdepWencheng hhdepTaishun
- Loans: LUrban LRui'an LYueqing LYongjia LPingyang LCangnan LWencheng LTaishun
- Real estate development: rsdUrban rsdRui'an rsdYueqing rsdYongjia rsdPingyang rsdCangnan rsdWencheng rsdTaishun
- Deposits: depUrban

The data state that real estate development in Pingyang, Wencheng, and Taishun are weaker correlated to household deposits, loans, and real estate development in all urban, cities, and counties of Wenzhou (Exhibits 4.56 and 4.57). This is an indication that not all cities and counties follow the same patterns of development and growth as clarified in the identification of clusters of district-cities. Using the data for 2019, it is possible to identify the groups of districts that maintain similarities, which is a guide

Cluster	Number of districts
Cluster 1	1
Cluster 2	2
Cluster 3	3
Cluster 4	2

Exhibit 4.56. Clusters of districts.

District	Cluster
Urban	1
Wencheng	2
Taishun	2
Yongjia	3
Pingyang	3
Cangnan	3
Rui'an	4
Yueqing	4

Exhibit 4.57. District distribution by clusters.

to differentiate and prioritize risk monitoring and actions in each of the markets:

Marchetti (2012) pointed out, "Companies that assess risk, set risk thresholds, and actively monitor and manage their risk exposure within those thresholds are better able to predict future performance more accurately. They are also more likely to achieve higher performance and/or meet financial expectations because they are better able to potentially avoid large fluctuations in business and avoid the negative consequences of unmitigated risk events." This illustration of monitoring risk in local financial institutions starts with the review of what is happening from the world level to country, city, and type of product in a market. The creation of exposure measurement systems includes many steps that start with the classification of strategic and tactical risks, their exposure evaluation, expected losses, and definition of threshold levels that can activate various means of intervention by management and authorities.

Chapter 5

Management in the New Working Environment

This chapter is fundamentally a review of how humans and machines coexist and create value. The main points to cover are as follows:

(1) The purpose of digital transformation and AI is to support and create benefit for humans.
(2) Use and adoption of technologies to mitigate strategic risks possibly creates more risks or increases the severity of existing ones.
(3) Human and machine interaction can occur only under ethical conditions, respecting and managing diversity, and modifying misuse and threats in society.

This chapter has five sections: the first one presents interactions between humans and machines, the second section is about challenges in evaluating talent and machines, the third one is related to the ethical issues, the fourth section is on how to deal with operational risk in a world of strategic risks, and the last section presents study cases of what happened in organizations when they dealt with strategic risks, increasing intelligence, and digital capabilities.

5.1. Interaction of Humans and Machines

This book reviews human and machine interactions in three ways: first, related to the use of information and definition of cybernetics; second, the possibility of people using what is beneficial through capable machines to solve problems and support decision-making processes; and third, the way that machines and humans operate in the same processes but with different and complementary roles and responsibilities. In all cases, creating strategic intelligence is about doing more with the available resources to add value, developing technology, and supporting business process enhancement. The premise is that technology by itself is not of value to the organization, but it is a means to create value; all organizations can sooner or later use similar technologies, so the differentiation is what humans can do with these technologies. Humans and their talent are what will create the differentiation and strategies to enhance value. Another aspect is that AI is being developed to support humans to perform better but not to create layers of complexity with humans because of no control, or to create competition that reduces the energy of what will be the resource to be better in an industry.

First, in relation to the use of information and definition of cybernetics, Wiener (1961) stated that "the science of control and communications in the animal and machine," where the components of the system include a controller, monitor, or feedback or information from the monitor to the controller. The controller will provide actions or answers. Based on data analytics, the development of prediction and generation of rules after algorithms help the computer learn and perform actions that are potentially intelligent in their capacity to solve a variety of problems. From this point of view, intelligence is a result of what machines and humans can do to make a decision; the specific instruments can be models fed by data that produce outcomes leading to problem-solving, movement, classification, prediction, etc.

Kolmogorov (Shiryayev, 1993) worked on the analysis of information and promoted the information theory and computer science study, commenting that "Cybernetics according to Wiener must include the entire mathematical apparatus of the theory of controlling devices of discrete and continuous action. This means that cybernetics according to Wiener includes an important part of the theory of stability for systems of differential equations, classical control theory, the theory of random processes with their extrapolation and filtration, the theory of information, game theory with applications to operations research, the technical aspects of logic algebra, the theory of programming and many other topics." The definition of cybernetics according to Kolmogorov is, "In its more general form, cybernetics studies control processes, and a rational system of control necessitates the definition of information, its obtention, storage, transmission along channels of communication and its processing."

Second, there is a possibility of developing people to use what is beneficial through capable machines to solve problems and support decision-making processes. Exhibit 5.1 shows a mix of concepts about data science, the possibilities of using talent human and machine to create knowledge, solve problems and deal with the time use of employees in organizations. Talent development is about an integral view of the cycle of data, knowledge, and technology as a symbiotic process among a problem, the knowledge to solve it, and the talent and technological tools to achieve the solution. Currently, there are new digital technologies in the organizations to deal with problems, but there is also an increasing volume of data and a limitation of organizational capabilities to obtain knowledge from the data, use the knowledge to solve problems, and support complex decisions. This limitation is possibly because of a lack of understanding of capabilities, reduced development of capabilities, lack of understanding of analytical tools, low use of the technological tools, and low communication capabilities in the organizations. In many cases, the gaps between new technology and analytical knowledge reduce the search for solutions to support multidisciplinary and interdepartmental views of problem-solving approaches.

Third, it is important to recognize the way that machines and humans operate in the same processes but with different and complementary roles and responsibilities. De Cremer and Kasparov (2021) expressed, "AI should Augment Human Intelligence, Not Replace It." They indicated that AI in some tasks is able to perform better than humans and that the AI role is not the correct one because machines should supplement humans, and humans should supplement machines (Exhibit 5.2). Humans are not only rational but also have many other attributes relating to senses, intuition, and emotions that are required for a balance of any problem resolution and decision-making process. The authors mentioned that the new norm of working environment is to create teams of humans and non-humans that require management to produce results or add value.

The previous points are possible to apply to the concept of strategic risk in the sense of trying to create digital transformation. Priorities are to work on areas that can support the creation of sustainable competitive advantages. Exhibit 5.3 summarizes the transition from identifying courses of actions to the use of intelligence based on AI and digital transformation. As illustrated, the steps include the process for creating knowledge and supporting the learning process. When machines and humans act together, both are learning and contributing to the creation of knowledge.

<table>
<tr><td colspan="2">Talent in data science</td></tr>
<tr><td>Supporting the organization to reduce risk: "Most people fail to bring the right information into their conscious awareness at the right time." Bazerman and Chugh, HBR Jan 2006.
Reducing the organization's handicaps: "People with high levels of personal mastery … cannot afford to choose between reason and intuition, or head and heart, any more than they would choose to walk on one leg or see with one eye."
Peter Senge The Fifth Discipline (1990)</td><td>Finding How:
Discovering/Creating, Storing, Providing access, Transferring and applying knowledge. From gathering any kind of data to promoting/developing actions (strategic and tactical).
Following the analogy of a medical doctor and the healthcare supply chain.
This means creating the lab, the measurement system, gathering the data, lab analysis and medical doctor analysis, providing diagnostics, and participating in the control of treatment. After that, inputting new data to learn to better the system.</td></tr>
<tr><td>To get the answers and to support the problem-solving process:
(Making Advanced Analytics Work For You Barton and Court HBR October 2012)
• Choosing the right data.
• Sourcing data creatively.
• Building models that predict and optimize business outcomes.
• Transforming the company's capabilities.
• Developing business-relevant analytics that can be put to use.
• Embedding analytics into simple tools for the front lines.</td><td>Dealing with hyperspecialization
"The promise: … offers both workers and companies much more flexibility than traditional employment arrangements do."
"The perils:
A cloud looming over the future of hyperspecialization is the possibility that it will facilitate … "digital sweatshops," where workers are exploited for very low wages. These wages result in part from labor market arbitrage."
"Another concern is that dividing work into minuscule fragments allows the unscrupulous to conceal the goals toward which workers' efforts are directed."
"Two other potential problems are: the growing amount of work done on spec (that is, with no guarantee of payment) and the increased surveillance of electronically connected workers."
The Big Idea: The Age of Hyperspecialization
by Thomas W. Malone, Robert J. Laubacher, and Tammy Johns HBR April 2011.</td></tr>
</table>

Exhibit 5.1. Thinking about what talent is in the setting of data analytics and AI for producing intelligence.

Dealing with Turnover and Job Satisfaction: "Talented people are going independent because they can choose what to work on and with whom to work." "They leave behind the endless internal meetings and corporate politics …" The Rise of the Supertemp by Jody Greenstone Miller and Matt Miller HBR May 2012	

Exhibit 5.1. (*Continued*)

Humans and machines study attractiveness in market industry, trends, future of industries, conditions of markets.	Rethink the value of analytics	What is search for the organization? Performance with a combination of revenues, profits, use of resources, growth, sustainability, etc.	Rethink the value of actions	What are the risks? Strategic risks, temporary technological advantages, doing the same, not everyone is required to be digitally transformed.

Exhibit 5.2. From market attraction to digital transformation.

What are the organizations doing? Analytics, IoT, AI, Innovation–R&D, robotics, contracts, transactions, etc.	Focus on discovering possible courses of actions	Where are the issues to work on? Big decisions, less analytics possibilities, more complexity in selecting the best solutions	Organize the way to tackle learning and knowledge development

Exhibit 5.3. Courses of actions and AI for digital evolution.

It is fundamental to consider that technology should be the means to achieve the answer for the why and where to use or not use certain types of technologies.

The human–machine interaction is under a socio-technical knowledge–information system design that looks to put together components that are technical and people related. One component is data architecture which includes data in multiple ways, structured and non-structured. Data are required as a means of action and application in a business environment. Another component deals with knowledge attributes of the KM processes that are based on the KM processes defined by Alavi and Leidner (2001) and the KMS components identified by Lehaney *et al.* (2004). An attribute is a dimension along with which different instances of the KM process can vary (adapted from Holsapple, 2003). Thus, the system components (Lehaney *et al.*, 2004; Davemport & Prusak, 1998; Malhotra, 1999; Edwards *et al.*, 2005) can be summarized as follows: People and machine interactions: KM and knowledge acquisition are subject to perceptions and agreement. These human interactions require two subsystems: technology acting as support and the way to enable the KM function, and organizational structures.

In a setting of strategic risk analysis, human and machine interaction occurs in all stages and forms identification for assessment and control. Prediction of vents can be supported by predictive analytics techniques; once events are identified, the assessment of risk is again conducted using models where more machine interaction will appear. Automation and digitalization will assist in decisions and areas to monitor when dealing with strategic risk (Exhibit 5.4). New skills will be required or updating of skills will occur. Several opportunities for human–machine interaction will appear from, for example, the beginning of a transaction to the level of customer satisfaction.

Hence, a proposed means to deal with the adoption of new digital technologies and create human–machine interaction is the design and implementation of a system that takes into consideration the individual bases of knowledge (Von Krogh & Roos, 1995) and their relationships in order to create knowledge using data and technologies. A way to lead the design of the system is based on maintaining the relationships among experts, users, tools, and knowledge artifacts (documents, algorithms, code, models, networks, etc.). These relationships and means to keep those relationships alive are part of the concept of developing human capital in order to be better prepared to adopt new digital

Strategic risk	Customer risk loyalty and churn	What are the data analytics/AI tools and solutions that can be good to control risk? Now, all strategic risks are going to have the same needs, and not all are going to use the same tools. Credit expertise can be common to suppliers and customers, with different perspectives and possibly different implementations, e.g., customers can be with local conditions and credit with suppliers can be with international transactions and rights, the models can be similar but the application to the variables can provide multiple new outcomes to the application. The maturity level of each credit review can need different skills and human–machine contact.
	Credit–distribution channels	
	Credit suppliers	
	Brand equity changes	
	Competitive positions changes	
	Bankruptcy and disruption	
	Supply chain	
	Operation — delivery	

Exhibit 5.4. Strategic risk examples where solutions are through human–machine interaction.

technologies. A digital transformation process includes a vision that joins and engages the members of the organization. To achieve that cohesion, it is proposed to build blocks that include documentation management, governance, and measurement means to support the adoption of new technology. For instance, Mukora *et al.* (2009) pointed out, "Future sources of energy are less economically competitive than conventional technologies but have potential to reduce costs through innovation and learning. Tools for modelling technological change are therefore important for assessing the potential of early-stage technologies." Their study combined learning curves with "engineering assessment and parametric models for improved methods of assessing and managing innovation for emerging energy technologies." The proposed blocks are an answer to overcome the barriers of adopting new technologies and create a positive human–machine interaction. The emphasis is on building a way to keep alive a system that introduces a new technology supported by continuous improvement of relationships between experts and users.

Block 1: Define the following problem: What is the organization trying to solve? This is the beginning of technology adoption. This is the knowledge creation process and at the same time it will begin to define the scope of the projects. This is the way to identify if the new technology has meaning and potential value inside the organization. To get an answer to what solve in the organization is possible to answer questions such as:

- What is the root cause of the problem?
- Provide a description of what is happening.
- How big (size or magnitude) is the problem?
- Provide the metric used to describe it.
- How does the organization know there is a problem?
- What are the indicators?
- Where is the problem occurring?
- Provide the process name and location/team where the problem is happening.
- Who is involved in this process?
- State the key stakeholder.
- When did the problem become an issue?
- Since when has the problem been felt (even if not initially noticed)?
- How is this affecting the users?
  - o Clear roles and responsibilities.
  - o Clear ownership and accountabilities for reference documents and contacts.
  - o Authorization process for new document, contacts, and subsequent updates.
  - o A review process of the actions and updates, including review frequency.
  - o A communication standard, for example, naming convention and document properties required under the new technology.

In addition, the problem has to be clearly identified through a feedback process to enable continuous improvement. Damodaran (2001) stated, "Documented reports of underperformance of ICT systems over several decades reveal that a major factor contributing to the disappointing outcome is the inadequate understanding of the user requirements and thus failure to design new technologies to meet those requirements. To address this problem, it is important early in the innovation cycle to identify and predict human needs and wants. An extensive capability has developed over more than three decades to understand better the requirements of potential users in order to develop user-centred design specifications."

The following issues are related to measuring the impact of the new technology (Fitzgerald *et al.*, 2013):

- Defining the right Key Performance Indicators
- Changing the culture
- Lack of management skills
- Limitations of IT systems
- Data integrity concerns
- Not enough data
- Too much data

Block 2: Knowledge creation and knowledge transfer are related to the new technology and implementation of the human and machine interaction. Gather the system's basic data for analysis and design. Identify the bases of the new technology. Identify what this technology can do and what it cannot do. This mix of knowledge has to be transferred. The vehicle for transferring can be from the use of networks, intranets, extranets, or in general portals to support conferencing, chats, storytelling, and coordination of social activities from social networking inside organizations. This is to create a kind of social CRM for internal customers or in general for all stakeholders.

Some strategies to develop this process are as follows: First, find meaning and common language. The basic strategies are supported by the data gathering process and the way in which people/users start talking the same language related to the new technology. The following are some points to consider:

- Understanding the technical terms
- Knowledge requirements
- Related problems to solve
- Opportunities to improve

Regarding the demographic of the new technology market inside the organization, the following variables are key to frame the current settings of the application, potential applications, and opportunities:

- Teams involved
- Number of employees

- Relationships with other teams
- Principal outputs
- Principal reports affected by the new technology
- Complexity of the work — special skills
- Knowledge considered the most important, how to use it for others
- Opportunities for improvement/use of the technology

In the end all the data can be gathered by the following:

- Internal participation in a data analytics project
- General survey applied to stakeholders
- Interviews for leaders and analysts, core areas of knowledge
- Group interviews
- External stakeholders' implications
- Additional data from other experiences
- Results of the current knowledge practices
- Documents about knowledge considerations
- Consulting companies

Second, develop means to spread this knowledge and understanding:

- Create blogs or workspaces using the technology for internal communication to start contact and interaction with potential users and stakeholders.
- Gather information from different teams and stakeholders.
- Initiate an educational program about the concepts used.
- Introduce some people in the benchmarking process.
- Develop a pilot on a tool already used (it can also be new).
- Position influence for using the new technology.
- Provide examples or cases of solutions to some problems/issues similar to the new technology.
- Technology is currently used and solutions have potential for use.

In summary, a system structure can be developed using various sources of data; however, an important component for human–machine interaction is the capacity to build the bridge between knowledge workers, knowledge, and applications of the new technologies in the process of adoption.

Block 3: Revisit the stakeholders' needs and, with the new technology in mind, identify the pain points that will be reduced with the new technology. This is to assess stakeholders' new technology knowledge, needs, and possible solutions. Use the experimentation process for discovering use and misuse of the new technology. Develop a test using a prototype for the creation of an environment for the users of the new technology and the systems related to it. All these are based on the analysis made from the user's view, information gathered from multiple groups, and the potential use of the updated/cleaned content within the scope of this project.

The work in this block is clearly expressed by Delacruz (2009): "Little did I realize then how time consuming and all-encompassing learning, studying, and adapting technology to teaching would become." Technology can be used for teaching and for improving learning–teaching processes. However in several cases teachers are not prepared to adopt new technologies. Therefore, supplementing block 2 to obtain a clear understanding of the following points is crucial in the adoption of emerging technologies:

- Obtain a clear voice of the internal customer — this is a tool that can be used to gather feedback on the pain points experienced by the new technology audience.
- Benchmarking against other groups in the organization — what have other teams done with respect to their responsibilities and technologies in use, what applies to the task owners and where can new technology leverage work performance?

Block 4: Knowledge transfer, knowledge storage, and access are important. Given the issue of dealing with tacit knowledge, in new technology adoption, there is a need to develop a documentation or communication using reports and judgment outcomes from humans and machines to transform tacit knowledge to explicit knowledge and to manage explicit knowledge. Explicit knowledge transformation can give people access to knowledge using storage means in the cloud or any data repository and a possibility to use it in actions in the team's mandates. The question here is what can possibly be documented and what cannot. For things that can be documented related to the new technology, the following guides support the process to better explain it to the users:

- Provide a detailed inventory of all related technology/product information that is available on various sources.

- Identify what documents need to be broken down in pieces to match the standard process classification and users' questions.
- Consolidate all information in each and every related piece, i.e., all relevant product information that should be in the Key Features section to be merged together in a document.
- In using the standard template, the information should be updated, reduced to point forms, and also as much as possible, put into tables.
- Each piece of content needs to have an owner, date of update, and review date. Develop a governance means for the documentation process.
- Because documents have been broken down into bite-sized pieces, each section or page can be tagged with an owner and a set of metadata describing the content. This tagging will facilitate the maintenance and searching processes. Specifications of the processes and types of documents involved by are according to the following:
    - Products
    - Process step comprehensive level
    - Process step detailed level
    - Categories
    - Review date
    - Owner
- Discuss solutions and recommendations in dealing with the issues, controversies, or problems presented in the preceding section.

A documentation process requires proper treatment of a sub-process of document classification. This classification process comprises the understanding of how explicit knowledge will be presented to the users, options to classify, and potential relationships among documents and actions. It has to be structured the way the users are thinking, in terms of accessing the information; it has to be meaningful for the users and the categories have to be broad enough to allow flexibility. In general, a good practice is to classify documents based on the steps/groups of activities in the processes where a technology and system will be involved.

Block 5: Governance framework refers to the keeping the documentation process alive and updated and at the same time the system that support the adoption of the new technology. The following points are the structural ones:

- Accountability (clear ownership, clear process, clear roles, and responsibilities).

- Consistent creation, update, and review of content (formal documented process and timelines).
- Fostering collaboration (built-in validation process, cross-team participation, broader engagement, alignment).
- Sustaining integrity of the content (acceptance and adherence to the governance process).
- Developing a consultation group.
- Ownership of pieces of content and activities, update date, and review date.
- Revision schedule of actions and documents.
- Discussion times in meetings and review of planning steps to improve the technology adoption.

Negroponte (1995) pointed out, "One way to look at the future of being digital is to ask if the quality of one medium can be transposed to another." This is one of the reflections related to the digital introduction of almost everything where a human is involved. The point is that not everything is possible to manage in the same way and under the same standards when digital technologies are in place. In some cases, there are threats related to the digital incursion in the society. "The information superhighway may be mostly hype today, but it is an understatement about tomorrow. It will exist beyond people's wildest predictions."

Block 6: New technology knowledge metrics means measuring the effectiveness of the knowledge management system's implementation and the benefits derived from it. The metrics to choose should relate back to the problem statement, goals, and objectives and are key to determining the success of the implementation. The metrics are also a way to know where the implementation and its sustainability may have fallen slightly off track. The "control" phase and the metrics that come along with it will allow any adjustments to the framework to ensure the project continues to answer the needs of the users/audience. Because it is so important to measure the "right" things, project leaders should develop these metrics in partnership with subject matter experts and leadership. Charam (2007) explained, "In my observation, people who create organic growth that is profitable and sustainable connect the dots sooner and are on the offensive." Mougayar (1998) presents the concept of Cybermaturity. The author indicates that executive education and awareness topics are key to the development of the services based on the web. These points include aspects such as understanding buyer/seller models, drivers, transactions, and relationships to the strategic planning process. This is a development of the learning process and potential assessment of the understanding of what the business can win of using new technologies.

Block 7: Implementation and change plans follow the strategy pointed out by Dutton *et al.* (2006): "The term 'emerging' in the workshop's title was frequently contrasted with the concept of 'emergence', developed through interdisciplinary studies of complexity in natural and artificial systems. Such complexity sciences view emergent outcomes as being unpredictable results flowing from the interplay and coevolution at a micro level of numerous interactions involving a vast number of interrelated entities and variables. Internet exemplifies an emergent social technology that has co-evolved through the contributions of many individuals, groups and institutions ..."

These are the areas to strengthen in the introduction and implementation of the new technology and developing human–machine interaction in a fluid way:

- Fostering understanding and conviction.
- Formal mechanisms of participation mixed with informal ones.
- Talent and skill development for solving new problems/questions.
- Role identification and adjustment to new environment.

In the book by Weill and Broadbent (1998), there is a clear presentation of the purpose of investing in new technologies. New technologies in an organization are related to value added. Investment in technology is similar to investing in other assets. The first point to review is aligning the business strategy with the information technology requirements and solutions. These requirements and solutions are associated with specific objectives such as increased control, provision of better information, creating more collaboration, increasing sales, increment in productivity, reducing costs, and business integration. If technologies are at the boundaries of the organization, they will not be adopted if no clear value is observed. In general, organizations are looking to improve not only operational infrastructure but also management, risk management, and people capabilities. If technology is offering answers to these questions, the process will start in the proper manner.

Block 8: In a review of the lessons learned, Diaz (2010) provided an example in the educational setting showing how many steps in the process of adoption of a new technology are related to lessons learned: "in Online

Learning many faculty members correctly assert that while today's students enter institutions having had some exposure to Web 2.0 tools such as Facebook, they lack an awareness of how those tools can be used for learning." He continued, "Faculty members may also have noticed that entering students have a heightened comfort level with the type of digital environment that has the potential to be connected to learning. For instance, students tend to have a greater tolerance for figuring out, troubleshooting, or experimenting with technology. They can deal with a trial-and-error approach to tool use and change in general and often have had a broad exposure to a variety of different Web-based software and hardware tools."

Naisbitt *et al.* (1999) indicated that technology cannot exist without a context, as technology is in everywhere and touches daily life. Socialization and adequate use of technology are important to avoid issues of blinding the organization. Carroll and Broadhead (2001) presented examples in which the adoption of certain digital technologies did not the expected produce. For instance, using emails cannot be inversely correlated to the use of papers. In many cases, users, companies, and suppliers recognize the increment of paper after introducing emails. Additionally, they presented the myths of introducing e-business including implementation, costs, customer behavior, and speed of development. These are points to keep in mind in the adoption of any new technology as the main purpose has to be continuously evaluated and followed up.

Block 9: Connecting analytics capabilities and proper use of intellectual capital is important. Digital technologies are included in many different structures and purposes. One common point in adoption is the search for technologies that contribute to the growth of organizational performance. However, new technologies are not only for operational process support but also for strategic processes inside the organization. Thus, currently, not only there are new technologies in the organizations but there are also volumes of data and limitations of organizational capabilities to obtain knowledge from data, use the knowledge to solve problems, and support complex decisions. This is because of a lack of understanding of capabilities, reduced development of capabilities, a lack of understanding of analytical tools, low use of the technological tools, and low communication capabilities in the organizations. In many cases, the gaps between new technology and analytics knowledge reduce the search for solutions to support multidisciplinary and interdepartmental views of problem-solving approaches.

In their book, Tapscott and Caston (1993) mentioned a twenty-item list, that is currently valid, of business applications and areas where a need exists inside the organizations. This is similar to the four points of alignment required that are applicable to the emerging digital technologies adopted. The points are valid in our current setting. These alignment points focus on the IS function: rebuild the image, vision, and scope of the contribution; it is an ongoing process in information departments. It indicates a continuous review of the shape of the information systems area. The main point nowadays is to have more users doing more with available computing resources. For this purpose, more involvement between users and owners of the technological advances is required.

Once a human–machine interaction has been examined, a definition of evaluations has to be reviewed. The review requires an observation of the premises of upskilling needs, development of structures to maintain users in an updated capacity, and providing proper knowledge transfer for the new machine–technology capabilities. These are related to what humans and machines can support through adoption of technology and better interaction to solve a wider variety of problems and operationalize those solutions. The next section introduces the vision of evaluating performance of humans and machines. Performance involves what is looked for in enhancing business processes through humans and machines. Performance evaluation in several cases will not follow the same pattern between creators of knowledge, creators of machine capabilities (data scientists), and users. Evaluation requires alternative views of what a development of project of performance evaluation could be under the criterion of those resources of talent are adding value to the organization.

5.2. Evaluating Performance of Humans and Machines

In this book, performance is about capacity to adapt, learn, use new knowledge, and create solutions for problems according to what organizations would like to do. This is about developing intelligence for the organization and using it. Humans and machines interact to create intelligence; humans have several aspects that can be related to the type of work and responsibilities, while machines are about capacity to be accurate and being reliable. When machines and humans interact, it could be a case of the surgical skills of the surgeon and the precision of machines in images or movements in operations. Another aspect to keep in mind is the digital mindset as described by Neeley and Leonardi (2022): "Learning new technological skills is essential for digital transformation. But it is not enough. Employees must be motivated to use their skills to create new opportunities. They need a digital mindset." Mindset is the sense of interiorizing knowledge and acting according to it with motivation and a driving purpose. One way to describe the human aspect is explaining what a data scientist is and what he/she is expected to do (Exhibit 5.5):

As Exhibit 5.5 shows, there are multiple dimensions that are required for data scientists to be productive, aside from the unrealistic expectations that organizations impose on data scientists. Another important aspect is that several tasks of the data scientist are and will be automated and substituted with machines. What is fundamental is to identify how the training and development of these talents can be associated to complement machines such as supporting the creation of solutions of specific problems: logistics/supply chain, healthcare, etc., where the knowledge domain is crucial, and machines require humans to design plans and course of actions.

What a data scientist is:	What a Data Scientist does:
A good blend of good things: • Achiever and thinker • Computer scientist • Applied mathematician • Statistician • High EQ worker • Organizational learner He/she is not a surrealist human, a super human, but a real, great organizational resource.	• Matching what organizations are trying to solve and the Data scientist's methods, technology, knowledge. Supporting the organization to reduce risk: "Most people fail to bring the right information into their conscious awareness at the right time." Bazerman and Chugh, HBR Jan 06. • Reducing the organization's handicaps: "People with high levels of personal mastery … cannot afford to choose between reason and intuition, or head and heart, any more than they would choose to walk on one leg or see with one eye.". Peter Senge The Fifth Discipline (1990).

Exhibit 5.5. To understand how to evaluate performance, it is required to define the human talent used and barriers to overcome for talent to perform well.

<table>
<tr>
<td>What a Data Scientist does:
• Matching what organizations are trying to solve and the Data Scientist's methods, technology, knowledge. Finding How:
• Discovering/creating, storing, and providing access, transferring and applying data analytics knowledge. From gathering any kind of data to promoting/developing actions (strategic and tactical).
• Following the analogy of a medical doctor and the healthcare supply chain.
• This means creating the lab, the measurement system, gathering the data, lab analysis, medical doctor analysis, providing diagnostics, and participating in the control of treatment. After that, inputting new data to improve the system.</td>
<td>What a Data Scientist does:
To get the answers and support the problem-solving process by (Making Advanced Analytics Work For You Barton and Court HBR October 2012)
• Choosing the right data.
• Sourcing data creatively.
• Building models that predict and optimize business outcomes.
• Transforming the company's capabilities.
• Developing business-relevant analytics that can be put to use.
• Embedding analytics into simple tools for the front lines.
• Reducing one of the most aggressive strategic risks = Blindness.</td>
</tr>
<tr>
<td colspan="2">A vision of the Data Scientist's Future and barriers to deal with for development:
• A closer understanding of the system, the problem, and where the problem emerges and acts within the system.
• A better definition of the value of "activities" to foster the DS's passion and motivation for teaching and learning.
Dealing with management needs as The F-Laws (Russel Ackoff) indicated better management understanding of what is the data scientist work "The lower the rank of managers, the more they know about fewer things. The higher the rank of managers, the less they know about many things" or as Dilbert (Scott Adams, 2000) "When did ignorance become a point of view".
Dealing with understanding that the data scientist's work is science and not magic. Balance between speed and scope. "Any fool can know. The point is to understand" — Albert Einstein
Dealing with value added in the sense to value the work behind the scenes, appreciating two responsibilities and improving organizations to avoid frustration. Data Scientists need to be prepared to create real impact.
Dealing with a black hole in management. Gartner's report (2014) indicated that BI does not meet expectations; however, "By 2015, enterprise buyers of BI platforms will predominantly purchase platforms that support both strong and broad business-user-accessible data discovery capabilities and IT-driven enterprise features for data reuse, governance, security and scalability." ROI is about adoption and proper use of technology and techniques, moving from the model outcomes to the creation of actions.</td>
</tr>
</table>

Exhibit 5.5. (*Continued*)

Additional barriers to overcome are because of

- No IT–business partnership
- No link to corporate strategy
- No connection to the processes
- Not enough governance or too much
- No skills

Dealing with Hyperspecialization

"The promise: … offers both workers and companies much more flexibility than traditional employment arrangements do."

"The perils: A cloud looming over the future of hyperspecialization is the possibility that it will facilitate … "digital sweatshops," where workers are exploited for very low wages. These wages result in part from labor market arbitrage."

"Another concern is that dividing work into minuscule fragments allows the unscrupulous to conceal the goals toward which workers' efforts are directed."

"Two other potential problems are: the growing amount of work done on spec (that is, with no guarantee of payment) and the increased surveillance of electronically connected workers."

The Big Idea: The Age of Hyperspecialization
by Thomas W. Malone, Robert J. Laubacher, and Tammy Johns HBR April 2011

Dealing with Turnover and Job Satisfaction

"Talented people are going independent because they can choose what to work on and with whom to work."

"They leave behind the endless internal meetings and corporate politics …"

The Rise of the Supertemp
by Jody Greenstone Miller and Matt Miller HBR May 2012

Exhibit 5.5. (*Continued*)

Exhibit 5.6 explains a point regarding impact: in terms of performance means to start with data and to be able to have and to put in use knowledge to create capabilities and capacity in an organization. What is indicated as well is that the capacity and creation are part of a process for enhanced collaboration in organizations, to avoid reinventing the wheel. In several cases, it is important to go the origin of the knowledge through learning and promote a non-silo behavior but maintain the capacity for long-life learning can have specializations according to areas of work in organizations. Universities are engine of learning and knowledge creation and need to stimulate multidisciplinary work/research and use literature to move further in related fields. Examples about jobs searches in data

<table>
<tr>
<td>Organizations need super organized human collaboration, not super humans!
• Experts who support and share
• Organizations that learn
• Processes that foster collaboration
• Technology that enables collaboration
• Work environments that enable/engage/promote collaboration</td>
<td>Organizations need a different performance evaluation.
Confusion: Can we evaluate a Boxer as a Tennis Player or vice versa?
Both very good independently, but it is not common to have a great tennis player be a heavyweight boxer or a heavyweight boxer be a good tennis player.</td>
</tr>
<tr>
<td>VALUE = IMPACT
Adapted From big data to big impact Chen, Chiang and Storey, MIS Quarterly Vol. 36 No. 4, pp. 1165–1188/December 2012
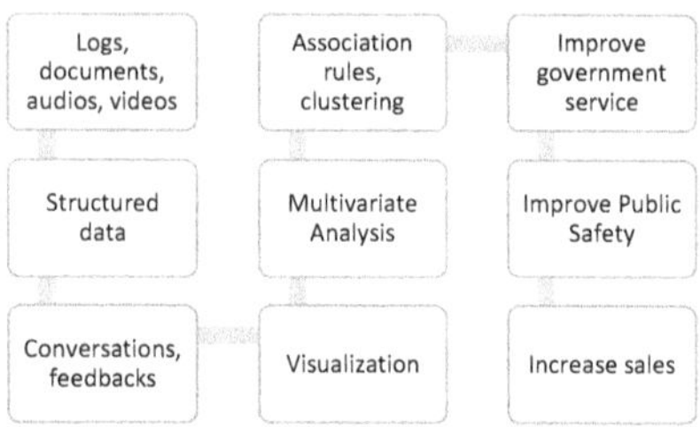
</td>
<td>• Organizations need a different work environment.
• Impact exists when the target is clear.
• Target and Mission definition a must
• About the Job 1(Small org.)
• The Data Science team has developed cutting-edge technologies that accurately link publicly and commercially available data to support a broad range of applications centered on drawing deeper insights about people.

Example of a job search advertisements: “We are a team of scientists with vast expertise in Record Linkage, Natural Language Processing, Entity Resolution, Machine Learning, and Information Retrieval.
We are looking for an experienced data scientist to join the team in our headquarters in Bellevue, WA.
About the Job 2(Huge org.)
Help AAAAA invent the next generation of e-commerce; integrated experiences that leverage the store, the web and mobile, with social identity being the glue. Apply your strong expertise in Java, machine-learning, data mining, and information retrieval to design, prototype, and build the next-generation of AAAAA semantic-based engines and service.</td>
</tr>
</table>

Exhibit 5.6. Reflection about what organizations need to work in areas like data science.

	Be challenged to create applications that will impact over 1.5 billion customers in a true global environment. Build next-generation search and natural language interfaces that apply semantic technology to match user intent and interests with products — learn that this is not just a classic algorithms position! Passion for consumer experience, a willingness to go the last mile, and a desire to take on not-yet solved technical challenges with your superb coding skills. Be excited about making an immediate impact on a global scale"
Qualifications Job 1: (Small org.) "— PhD, dissertation in: Information Retrieval, Recommender Systems, Machine Learning and Natural Language Processing — Experience: online marketing disciplines (Mobile marketing, Display, SEM/SEO, Social Mobile, etc.) large-scale graph algorithms, clustering, page-rank, and community detection with a focus on strong software design skills with massive multiprocessing architectures; proficiency with Hadoop and MapReduce experience in Linux/Unix dev environment with a combination of Java and Python Unix shell scripts with a combination of Hadoop, HDFS, Hive, HBase, MapReduce, NoSQL stores	"Programming: Back-end Programming, Front-end Programming, Systems Administration Stats: Classical Statistics, Data Manipulation, Science, Spatial Statistics, Surveys and Marketing, Temporal Statistics, Visualization Math: Algorithms, Bayesian/Monte Carlo Statistics, Graphical Models, Math, Optimization, Simulation Business: Business, Product Development Machine Learning/Big Data: Big and Distributed Data, Machine Learning, Structured Data, Unstructured Data High EQ: in the sense of adaptation, collaboration … Data Businessperson: Business person, Leader, Entrepreneur Data Creative: Artist, Jack-of-All-Trades, Hacker Data Researcher: Scientist, Researcher, Statistician Data Engineer: Engineer, Developer"

Exhibit 5.6. (*Continued*)

Team player, strong communicator Qualification Job 2: (Huge org.) MS or preferably PhD in computer science or similar field with 2–5 years of related experience Deep knowledge of machine learning, information retrieval, data mining, statistics, NLP or related field Expert level knowledge of one of the scripting languages such as Python or Perl Superior ability to analyze and interpret the results of product experiments Experience working with large data sets and distributed computing tools a plus (Map/Reduce, Hadoop, Hive, Spark, etc. Proven experience working with statistical languages such as R Strong programming skill in one of the following languages, Java, Scala, C/C++ Strong communication skills both written and verbal"	

Exhibit 5.6. (*Continued*)

science show that it is almost impossible to find Leonardo da Vinci in each data scientist. The problem complexity requires teams that equilibrate what are skillsets required for problems resolution.

On the performance of a machine, reliability and accuracy can be concepts that need to be under control. In machine evaluation, the following are analyzed: model evaluation, algorithm evaluation, level of errors (confidence intervals where errors can fall with high probability), performance of services (cloud, parallel computing, processing, storage), possible support, and ergonomic design for human interaction. Exhibit 5.7 indicates examples of metrics that are commonly used for evaluating a machine's performance including multiple possible problems to evaluate, classification, forecasting, testing hypothesis, selection and creation of samples, adjustments of data to models, and risk as variation of expected results.

Confidence interval	The confidence intervals provide the limits where, with a certain level of probability, the estimator of the parameters will be. The search is for high probability of narrower intervals. In general, in data analytics, steps for improvement are oriented to reduce the difference between interval limits under a confidence level that is determined by the analyst/researcher.
Confusion matrix	Problems of classification are evaluated by the combination of the frequencies of cases that are in a model and located in the same categories as they are in the training dataset. The error evaluation is based on the misclassification frequencies. The higher the percentage that is misclassified, the greater the probability of having a less accurate model.
Gain and Lift Chart	They are the representation of results with or without a model. They are used for model performance.
Kolmogorov–Smirnov Chart.	Comparison between models — probability distribution is possible using the KS evaluation, that is not parametric, which measures how similar two distributions will be. This is used for fitting theoretical distributions to what has been observed.
Chi Square.	This is a parametric test that evaluates the difference between distributions.
ROC curve.	This means Receiver Operating Characteristic curve that evaluates the relationship of two variables: the true positive rate (TPR) Sensitivity vs. the false positive rate (FPR) (1-specificity).
Gini Coefficient.	This used the Area Under the ROC Curve (AUC) and it is calculated as Gini = 2*AUC – 1. This is not the same as Gini index or Gini impurity.
Square root mean of the Error.	The calculation in RMSE is the square root of the mean of the error (residuals or difference in each point between actual value and value form the models).
Cross-validation.	Method of changing samples/resamples for partitions of training and test data and evaluating results of the models. The combination of selection of training and test data will provide measures to compare if the results are similar/consistent.

Exhibit 5.7. Traditional methods used to evaluate what a machine is doing according to models and actions generated by data analytics process.

An additional performance evaluation dimension that machine and human interaction requires for critical performance evaluation is the dimension of ethical machine–human development and behavior. The next section takes into account ethical issues that require attention in a human–machine interaction.

5.3. Ethical Issues

This section is about possible circumstances in which data analytics and AI can affect the ethics level of a society with regard to use of technology and innovation. Possibly the best way to say is ethics consequences because of creation more intelligence and how this intelligence is correctly directed to support positively the ethical organization evolution. Exhibit 5.8 contributes with identification of what diversity issues can be and how data analytics/AI can contribute to good or bad practices which will negatively impact society. Diversity appears in multiple facets products, people, etc., in the cases where the concept of diversity is considered some issues can appear because misuse of defining profiles, classifying, labeling components of the society, mainly when people are involved. It is the same with recommendation systems, generating prices, or other data analytics and AI applications. It is fundamental to understand that errors or deviations regarding certain criteria are not intentional and they can be part of the opportunity to enhance and improve performance of machines.

No intentional ethical issues are a risk in the search for algorithms to improve mitigation, define regulation, train organizations, and use them use correctly in processes and in data analytics-AI. Exhibit 5.8 illustrates examples from UNESCO and the European Union on regulation and principles to avoid damage from misuse, misunderstanding, or incorrect orientation of results to make decisions and implementations. Organizations are working to find ethical issues in the use of data analytics/AI and the results of their applications and regulations in countries, and are sharing experiences and defining strategies/plans of AI use.

From the point of view of effects that data analytics/AI can have on society, the volume of opportunities is growing from healthcare to supporting the well-being of societies. However, potential risks of negative effects are present in innovation and technology growth. Figures 5.1 and 5.2 show how areas such as safety, human rights, well-being, and responsibility can be negatively affected by data analytics/AI. The reasons are numerous because in the same way that ethical hacking exists, criminal hacking also exists. The same happens with potential losses of jobs,

Diversity in what: people, products, societies, organizations. The universe is diverse and new knowledge and its applications need to be diverse to be valuable and to generalize results. Promoting diversity Daugherty *et al.* (2018). Using Artificial Intelligence to Promote Diversity, MIT Sloan Management Review • "AI can help us overcome biases instead of perpetuating them, with guidance from the humans who design, train, and refine its systems." • "Some of the worst stories have been about systems that exhibit racial or gender bias in facial recognition applications or in evaluating people for jobs, loans, or other considerations. One program was routinely recommending longer prison sentences for blacks than for whites on the basis of the flawed use of recidivism data."	Possible issues in using data analytics • Profiling • Labeling • Classification • Product definition • Everyone can use • Misuse/wrong use • Misunderstanding of results • Errors treatment • Use control • Management of the new knowledge
Data analytics/ AI in profiling/labeling/ classification of ethical issues (minorities) of wrong data, unbalanced data, bias. Data Analytics/ IA and permeability of knowledge in less privileged society/ education systems and access. Data analytics has been open and is open, not much cost; we need to provide means and control of quality of knowledge, access/ storage/transfer and use (Ethical issues of having great tools and excellent knowledge in bad hands, bad hackers). Data analytics/ AI in the development of entrepreneurs/small economies/-countries, low cost as priority but capacity for creating strong capabilities to go to markets and grow.	Issues in pricing products Bertini and Koenigsberg (2021), The Pitfalls of Pricing Algorithms, Harvard Business Review "Many companies use algorithms to set prices and adjust them in real time so as to maximize profits. But constant price changes can alienate customers, undermine their loyalty, and damage brand reputation."

Exhibit 5.8. Diversity as example of potential ethical issues in data analytics/AI application.

Figure 5.1. Potential effects of data analytics and AI.

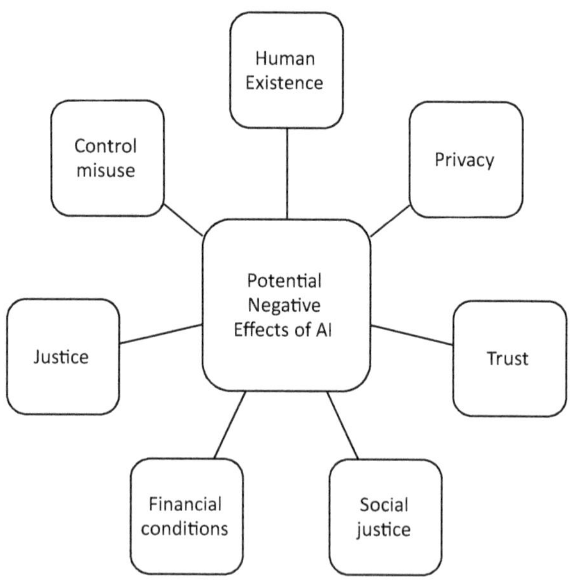

Figure 5.2. Continuation, potential negative effects of data analytics and AI in a society.

threats of lost jobs, and the opportunites to develop methods and practices to reduce the number of hours that people need to work and dedicate to other activities such as family or learning. In various cases the results of the data analytics/AI are contributing to a polarized scale. Accountability, for example, is a field to work through regulation and increasing the maturity level of the ethical use of data analytics/AI in organizations. The threats in certain areas of society are increasing because of potential changes in job possibilities, loss of privacy, reduced social justice, or a fundamental risk about the concentration of data in the hands of a few who can create or control threats toward the many.

This reflection is supported by Exhibits 5.9–5.11 on the possible capacity of data analytics and AI to create or enhance intelligence in organizations, and to identify that a better level of intelligence is not coming without opportunities and possible issues. Data boom is a potential asset in organizations that have the capacity to deal in a proper way with data availability; it could be an issue if the data are concentrated in a small number of hands instead of being used in areas of human development and support for society. There are problems that cannot be confused such as having low independence, being under high surveillance, and having possibilities to maintain security, or acting faster and better in cases of human difficulties. At the same time, it is not the issue of not having regulation to the level that is required yet, but it is clear that are groups of people and government working on ethics committees. The world is full of open technology to use in data analytics and AI. Open technology and data are the pillars of processing big data and developing what AI is able to do for educational purposes to further learning in organizations. These opportunities and positive results are only possible if there are rules to manage transparency, the power involved, and knowledge increment, but users and creator of solutions of possible implications of what technology is creating, and in general the good design of strategic risks mitigators that protect a society from adverse events generated though data analytics-AI use.

Another reflection is to distinguish what is an ethical issue and what errors are part of the learning evolution that can create misconception or concerns leading to potential ethical issues or intentional ethical issues. The issues are related more to the following:

- Wrong questions to answer
- Wrong data to use
- Poor control of assumptions in modeling
- Wrong modeling process

https://en.unesco.org/artificial-intelligence/ethics — November 2021 "Values o Respect, protection and promotion of human rights and fundamental freedoms and human dignity o Environment and ecosystem flourishing o Ensuring diversity and inclusiveness o Living in peaceful, just and interconnected societies Areas of Policy Actions o Ethical Impact Assessment o Ethical Governance and Stewardship o Data Policy o Development of International Cooperation o Environment and ecosystems o Gender o Culture o Education and Research …" There is awareness of issues and people are working hard to tackle these problems.	Organizations are working to solve ethical issues and regulation. Countries are sharing their plans in AI development. General principles for the ethical and values-based design, development, and implementation of autonomous and intelligent systems (as defined by the IEEE's *Ethically Aligned Design* First Edition March 2019). The ethics of artificial intelligence issues and initiatives, European Union 2020 report of the European Union indicates potential benefits on the following: • "Helping people to acquire new skills and training; • Democratizing services; • Designing and delivering faster production times and quicker iteration cycles; • Reducing energy usage; • Providing real-time environmental monitoring for air pollution and quality; • Enhancing cybersecurity defenses; • Boosting national output; • Reducing healthcare inefficiencies; • Creating new kinds of enjoyable experiences and interactions for people; and • Improving real-time translation services to connect people across the globe."

Exhibit 5.9. Organizations and countries are working to limit ethical issues of Data Analytics and AI use.

But

- Many problems are known and many people are working to fix the problems
- More opportunities for diverse societies are open

<table>
<tr>
<td>A very fast pace of knowledge creation leads to work not only on modeling but also increases the need and possibility to do more good things with what we have!
"While great ideas can spring up anywhere, access to data is not evenly distributed. Today, the collective we refer to as Big Tech — Google/Alphabet, Amazon, Facebook/Meta, Apple, and Microsoft — has a far greater capacity to collect data than startups and smaller competitors do. Even large corporations in other sectors often have only limited ability to access relevant data."</td>
<td>Mayer-Schönberger and Ramge (2022), The Data Boom Is Here — It's Just Not Evenly Distributed, MIT Sloan Management School
"For many innovators exploiting digital technologies — especially AI and machine learning — great ideas need to be paired with relevant data to create a viable product. Without mountains of suitable training data, safe and reliable autonomous vehicles will remain a pipe dream."
We need to do more with what is available. There are tons of good data to use for understanding and solving many problems. Not every problem or organization requires the streaming of data, big data (volume terms), etc. That is a BIG Confusion!</td>
</tr>
<tr>
<td>In this new economy, to be rich in the sense of satisfying society's needs is more about pencil, paper, computer, brain, and motivation to solve problems!
• AI and Entrepreneurs, SMEs
• Data analytics for any size organization
• Open tools infrastructure — Hadoop, Spark, etc.
• Open knowledge
• Open code
• Open cases
• Computational; capacity is not expensive
• Regular valuable computation is in common machines
• Experience in several ways is available
• Open data
• Experiences in testing/evaluation</td>
<td>• Finding solutions.
• Creator teams of the models require diversity, e.g., Girls Who Code, AI4ALL Stanford.
• Train the models better, unbalanced data, wrong representation — sampling.
• Conceptual bias, e.g., gender related to medical field — nurses are women and medical doctors are men. Bots and voices according to a variety of transactions/services.</td>
</tr>
</table>

Exhibit 5.10. Needs of society and capacity improvement using data analytics and AI.

<table>
<tr>
<td>Avoid Confusing problems
Chamorro 2020 Can Surveillance AI Make the Workplace Safe? MIT Sloan Management Review
• Pandemic developed employee surveillance.
• “Soon, organizations may also start monitoring employees’ whereabouts and behavior more closely than ever, using surveillance tools such as cellphone apps, office sensors, and algorithms that scrape and analyze the vast amounts of data people produce as they work.”
• “First, “employees should know … what data they are collecting and why.””
• “Second employees to “… have a chance to opt out without fear of penalty or, even better, proactively choose to opt in because they see the value of doing so.””
• “Third, the employees themselves should benefit from sharing their data and having algorithms analyze their activity”</td>
<td>Avoid errors
Blackman (2022), Why You Need an AI Ethics Committee, Harvard Business Review
“In 2019 a study published in the journal Science found that artificial intelligence from Optum, which many health systems were using to spot high-risk patients who should receive follow-up care, was prompting medical professionals to pay more attention to white people than to Black people. Only 18% of the people identified by the AI were Black, while 82% were white. After reviewing data on the patients who were actually the sickest, the researchers calculated that the numbers should have been about 46% and 53%, respectively. The impact was far-reaching: The researchers estimated that the AI had been applied to at least 100 million patients.”</td>
</tr>
<tr>
<td>Ethics Committee
• Ethics Experts
• Lawyers
• Business Strategists
• Bias scouts and subject matter experts
• Technologists</td>
<td>• Three points
• There is a problem that is present all the time.
• The reason is that bias exists from many sources.
• An ethics committee can help to mitigate the risk.
Shocking to see what the MIT article said in 2018 and what in 2019 was reported and presented in 2022:
New knowledge/technology is always bringing new risks and the risk management process starts again and again.</td>
</tr>
</table>

Exhibit 5.11. Ethics initiatives to surveil the use of AI and Digitalization.

- There is a lot of hope in developing more solutions and opportunities for more people with what we have and we can create

A view in the ethical analysis is about the use of data analytics and AI as an engine to detect wrong use or creation of potential issues in organizations and society. This potential capacity is at the same time related to the good definition of an ethical problem and how the goal has been defined (Exhibit 5.12).

Ethical issues are in a process of being disclosed and there are challenges to dig deeper, starting with the definition of AI if it is oriented to optimize under any circumstances what humans can do or support human development with improvements to produce better results for society. The next section reviews aspects related to operational risk, given the need for balance among ethical, strategic risk and operational risk for the good of digitalization/AI adoption.

Goals definition:	AI regulation is in progress:
"In some cases, the problem lies with the goal you've set for your AI — that is, in the decision about what the AI should predict. "Wrong questions, wrong data" … your AI to determine which patients were most likely to use the lungs for the longest amount of time, you would inadvertently discriminate against Black patients. Why? Because life expectancy at birth for the total U.S. population is 77.8 years, according to the Centers for Disease Control and Prevention's National Center for Health Statistics. Life expectancy for the Black population is only 72 years." Blackman (2022), Why You Need an AI Ethics Committee, Harvard Business Review.	Candelon *et al.* (2021), AI regulation is coming, Harvard Business Review "The EU, which is again leading the way (in its 2020 white paper "On Artificial Intelligence — A European Approach to Excellence and Trust" and its 2021 proposal for an AI legal framework), considers regulation to be essential to the development of AI tools that consumers can trust."

Exhibit 5.12. Problem definition in ethics is related to what is or not intentional in data analytics.

<table>
<tr>
<td>What to do:
Unfair outcomes Risk of AI
• Impact of outcomes
• Nature and scope of decisions
• Operational complexity and limits to scale
• Compliance and governance capabilities
Transparency
• Level of explanation required
• Trade-offs involved
Learning and evolving
• Risks and rewards
• Complexity and cost
• Human input</td>
<td>Avoid failures
Joshi et al. (2021), Why So Many Data Science Projects Fail to Deliver, MIT Sloan Management Review
An important part of AI development is the delivery based on tests and ongoing review, calibration of outcomes:

(1) Hammer in search of a nail: using sophisticated things for something known — misapplication of a technique with unclear context.
(2) Unrecognized sources of bias: CAMS were letters used as sources of data "… CAMs were prepared only for loans that had already been prescreened by experienced relationship managers and were very likely to be approved. Data from loan applications rejected at the prescreening stage was not used in the development of the model, which produced a huge selection bias."
(3) Right solution, wrong time: for example, changes in priorities, budgets.
(4) Wright tool: wrong user: "Many customers doubted the credibility of recommendations delivered through apps, websites, and emails."
(5) The rocky last mile: difficulties in implementation.</td>
</tr>
</table>

Exhibit 5.12. (*Continued*)

5.4. Operational Risks and Influence on Strategy

The use of data in operational risk analysis is as necessary as in other risk fields. The difficulty is that in several cases there are no usable data in organizations or the data require quantitative and qualitative components that are not available. Risk management requires multiple processes to develop and one of them is to achieve solid data to support a decision-making process. Qualitative and quantitative data are static and dynamic; data are structured and unstructured, and generally collected to record opinions and evidence of the presence of risk, solutions, and control.

As a case study, a bank description illustrates the main aspects of the operational risk analysis. Bank products have common areas of operation and supply but with an independent complexity that must be understood to standardize risk assessment and its indicators. Although the metrics or factors are not necessarily the same, this is, the indicator can be human hours but in other cases it can be transaction time or value of the operation. It seeks to use in operational risk in a bank the type of failures that can be control by appropriate indicators. The banking business can be described as a union of management risk and operation sophistication. In the banking business (It is applicable in general), the following points are important:

- Have consistency in the definition of what is measured. This means that exposure values, probability of event, and severity of the event have to be very clear as concepts to be measured.
- The review of the operation and the incidence of events at the levels of operation/production (back office), management of support processes (middle office), and the presentation to the client (front office and front line) have different data, ways of affecting risk, and workflows, or different meanings. Metrics have to be associated with meaning.
- The management of organizational culture is one of the most difficult problems to overcome in operational risk management. The question to be answered is what indicators of people's performance are associated with risk, which will make you feel that it is a good work climate with a sound understanding of the solution for problems.
- Place the data in order, define what is possible and what is not, establish how to develop the method of passing from top-down or bottom-up according to what happens in the organization:
  (1) A description of the risk
  (2) Cause and effect where possible to discover
  (3) Factors contributing to risk
  (4) Controls in the place where risk is generated
  (5) Recovery amounts
  (6) Time and duration
  (7) Localization

- Develop the working mechanism for data quality use. When operational data are collected, a number of explicit or implicit assumptions are made that have to be absolutely clear:
  (1) Assumptions and in what context; when can the assumption be modified.
  (2) The effectiveness of controls and their applicability.
  (3) Data that have been captured or created.
  (4) Conditions of operation change (i.e., the change in exposure to a loss incurred five years ago).
- Consider the future, not only the present. One of these elements of analysis in relation to the estimation of future losses introduces the following factors:
  (1) The bank's risk appetite.
  (2) Manage the concept of holding and business integrality.
  (3) The amount of loss data captured.
  (4) How the organization and corresponding data have changed from one year to the next.
  (5) An estimate of the perceived future losses of the entire organization.
  (6) Develop the necessary control and operational dashboard according to specific operational routine and challenges.
  (7) An operational database of the event that is widely available through the organization will assist in capturing this information. Moreover, the database population should be encouraged through incentives and management assistance.

Operational risks are based on the following:

- Develop methodologies for collecting, extracting, using, and maintaining data associated with operational risk based on the use of indicators to be used in the bank's performance evaluation.
- Establish how the information and reporting system will be associated with the data and your organization.
- Establish the orientation of control and management of operational risk according to the bank's performance structure.
- Presentation of prototypes for the simulation of operational risks; also prototype for the development of the risk structure.
- Organization of risk maps that include probability, event value, and exposure indicators.

The benefit of operational risks starts from the highest need of the bank's management, which is to make decisions based on evidence. The construction of the bank's performance evaluation information system should include operational risk management. This means building a chain of data that provide the value required by the executive group in decision making. Additionally, the following tools should be designed consistently:

- Work tools, forms, structure, prototypes.
- Identification of coordination of the different business fronts.
- Definition of the concepts to be developed.
- Introduction of the operational risk system in the general system.

Tools and data for operational risk analysis should be based on Exhibit 5.13.

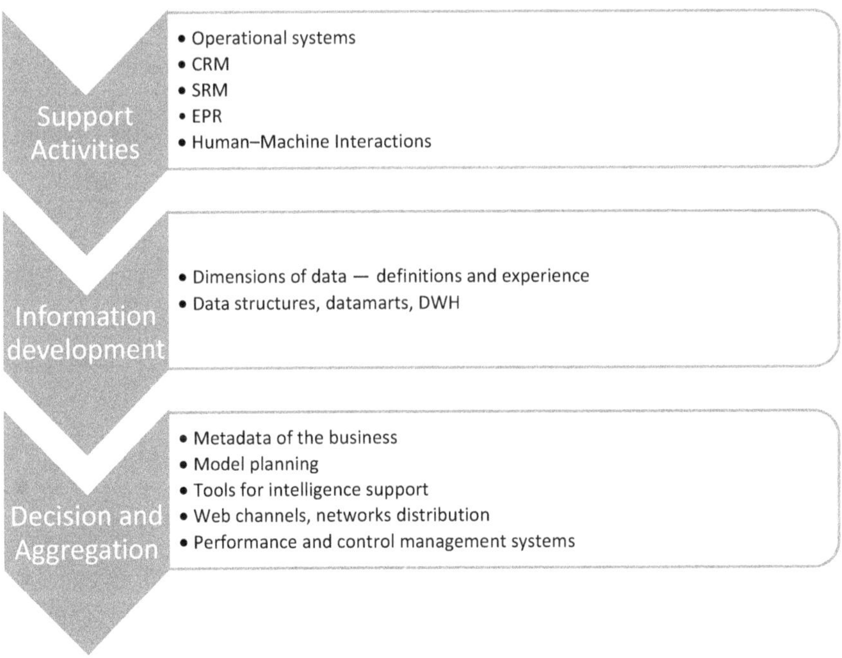

Exhibit 5.13. Form a plan to control based on data and outcomes of models and interpretation of results.

Not surprisingly, the processes for understanding and measuring operational risk lack the maturity of the credit risk management and market risk management processes. The risk considered as a variation of the expected risk requires a definition of the business and establishing where business losses may occur. Everything that is done to perfect the operational risk control system will be a great bonus for the bank. Thus, what is sought is the process of control of the operation on all fronts in order to mitigate the risk following a control process. The most important thing to note is that a methodology is based on building from what the organization wants to measure and going back to establish what data, information, and knowledge are necessary for a current evaluation (see Figure 5.3):

(1) Problem definition: Establish the bank's current situation, strategic plan, operating tactics, and performance evaluation structure.
(2) Identify map of organizational objectives: In the plan, identify what is sought up to the level of delivery and use of the bank's products and services.
(3) Develop the cause–effect matrix and its connections using networks.
(4) Identify organizational structure and relationship with risk control.
(5) Set what you want to control.
(6) Prioritize qualitative analysis and its connection to quantitative analysis.
(7) Establish standards based on best practices and related to the institution's development capacity.
(8) Establish how the variation of the indicators will be measured and how variance reduction goals will be set.

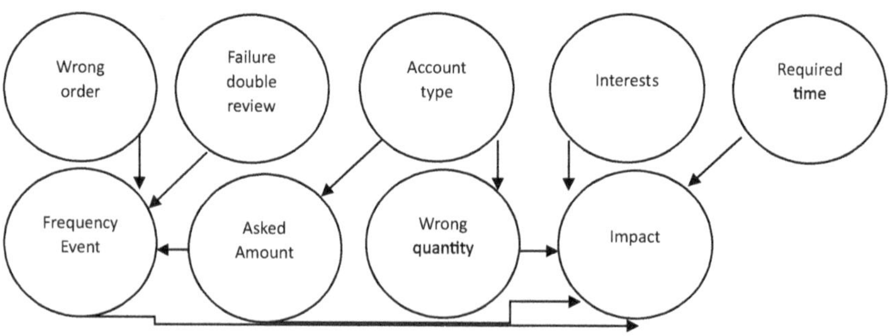

Figure 5.3. Operational risk analysis is based on the search for answers in a chain of events that can generate loss and its probability of occurrence.

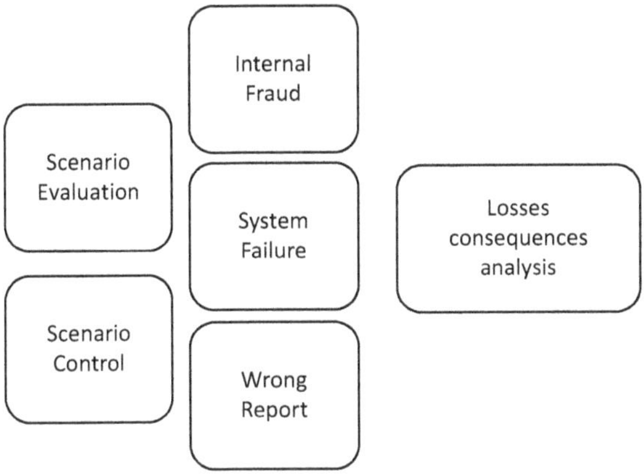

Exhibit 5.14 An example of operational risk is Fraud.

The following are sources of information for the different risks and processes involved as set by different business units:

(1) Interviews with bank officials.
(2) Identification of available databases and records kept.
(3) Observe what is being done at the level of the banking sector.

As illustrated in Exhibit 5.14, fraud as operational risk requires an analysis of scenarios where the risk can appear and data not only involve accounting records but also operation, customer, and supplier records.

5.4.1 *Data analysis methodology for operational risk*

The most important thing is to find a risk map and the relationships that the map has with the bank's operation, including products, services, and support processes. This involves a frame of reference for the identification of probabilities of occurrence of events, expected values of losses, and the location of the problem according to exposure levels as follows:

- Operational risk analysis has a more qualitative and subjective position than credit and market risk. The company's ability to relate strategy to operation is tested and mechanisms are determined to build from data to decision-making.

- Identification of risk exposures.
- Measurement and estimation of risk exposures.
- Search for instruments to change risk states.
- Assessing effects on exposures.
- Evaluate costs and benefits of instrument options.
- Determine how the risk mitigation strategy will be operated, avoided, transferred, mitigated, or maintained (see Exhibit 5.15).
- Evaluate the bank's performance from an operational risk perspective.

The functional system would contain the following features to be in line with Basel II–III standards:

(1) Dimensions of credit agreements, insurance, or any other product including collateral if existing and other factors might affect the loss given the occurrence of a non-payment (LGD).
(2) Establish the qualifications and criteria that are used for different lines of business and geographic location.
(3) Establish how basic functions would be in the event of a line service interruption — operational contingency plan requirements. Continuity and recovery plan for the operation in case of massive interruption.
(4) Determine the necessary elements of the calculations in Exhibit 5.16 that will be part of development of the company's risk management.

- Identify the data required for the creation of current and proposed management indicators based on risk and a cause–effect structure.
- Data quality, capacity and structure, dynamic data (continuously changing data), static data (e.g., some risk parameters), and hybrid

Impact	1 year	2 years	3 years	1 month	1 day	1 hour
100	5	6	9	3	5	1
80	4	6	7	1	2	3
60	1	2	3	5	4	4
40	4	7	8	7	4	5
20	6	3	4	5	6	3

Exhibit 5.15. Heat map for the potential risk impact.

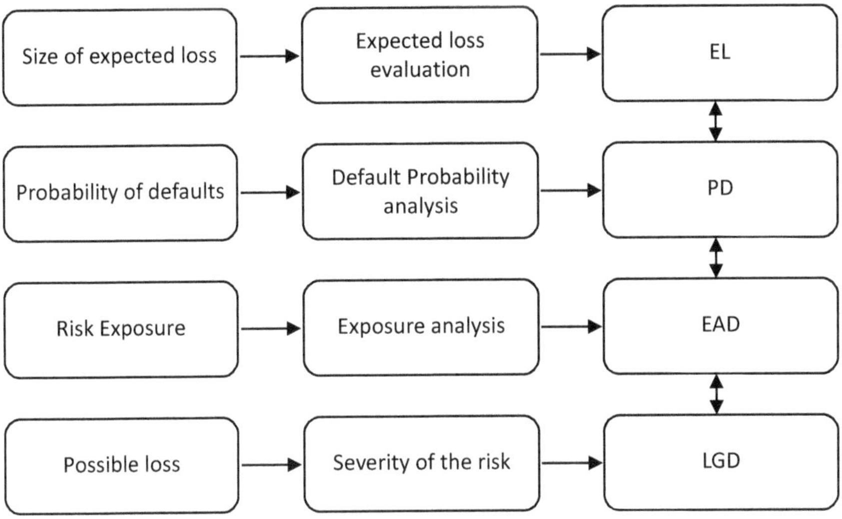

Exhibit 5.16 Metrics and data are always connected. Data are valuable depending on what should be measured.

data (derived from the previous two types, e.g., event, loss given default (LGD), and exposure at default (EAD)).

- Data Sources: A wide range of data sources are used in a bank. For example, in the case of exposure and collateral data, these would have to be derived from a combination of the front office of the client, back office, and middle office with decision support models.
- Determine how to integrate the required data with existing data and the bank's data architecture.
- The metadata's structure is fundamental; determine the level of detail that you want to cover, how the documentation will be maintained, and what will be the support structure, indicators, and data dictionary.
- Extraction of previous operational systems, transformation and aggregation, database loading, missing data handling, redundant data handling, and data feeder management are also important.

5.5. Cases to Study

This section is a summary of cases involving multiple aspects of strategic risks and development of organizations using digital transformation, data analytics, and Ai and fundamentally solving issues in creating intelligence. The issues and cases include stakeholder intelligence to review what is happening in organizations. The current cases of bank bankruptcies (2023) show that learning from past experiences is not well supported or understood by organizations and requires more attention from regulators, management, and other stakeholders. The cases include various sectors and problems from obsolescence to external factors, systemic risk that cannot be fully controllable, and resilience and managing losses that can be controlled by the management to reduce the total losses.

The following extracts of cases were presented by students of the Master in Risk Management University EAFIT Colombia.

Grancolombian Conglomerate Quintero, G. (2016). "Crisis Financiera decada de los ochenta: quiebra grupo Grancolombiano".	
General view	Grancolombian Conglomerate with main structure as follows (around 100 companies affiliated): Cingra and Inversiones Saturno, Capitalizadora Grancolombiana, Grancolombiana life insurer, and the Grancolombiana insurer.The portfolio companies: Inversiones y Valores, Indismetro, Administraciones y Construcciones, Inversiones y Negocios, Granvalores, and Graninversión. Financial Corporations and private savings Banco de Colombia and its Panamanian subsidiary, Granahorrar, Diners, and Granfinanciera, Colpafinsa, Continental de Inversiones and Artecto. Barcelona Inc. Carbohor, industrial and commercial sector: Tecimpre, Proindustrial, and Prisa, Cineco and real estate Cine Colombia, Medex ltda, Sedelan, Febo, Jupiter, Troya, and Inmobiliaria Internacional, Ulises ltda, Gestiones Ulises, and Promociones Ulises, and Construction companies.
Context	The share rice of a target company to buy Compañia Nacional de Chocolates move from \$20 to \$80 because of high demand and to get a 255 control required a lot of funds to invest.
Types of risks	• Low regulation for capital investment of financial institutions • Fraud-loans provided to relative companies to acquire shares and concentrate capital. In the 80"s financial institutions could lend money to shareholders as offence of the norm but not a crime and this was converted into a delinquency practice. • Liquidity/solvency risk • Self-loans • Parent risk • Credit Risk • Conflict of interest

Events and Mitigation	• Try to acquire control of Compañía Nacional de Chocolates • New regulation came asking for capitalization • SWAP for obtaining resources. To give the funds' shares of industrial companies, and receive in exchange shares of financial companies belonging to the funds • Issues to obtain the funds form Foreign Currency. Using a Panama subsidiary to obtain the funds
Possible Causes	• Lack of control and regulation, lack of good faith — criminal business operation • Financial groups as a way to invest in group members part of business units with similar activity (correlated) capital and reserves • Concentration of capital and the use of public funds to use for speculate • Use of allocation of credit products toward investment and allowing to partners to acquire credit up to 10 times the total equity of partners creating concentration of risk
References	• https://documents1.worldbank.org/curated/en/533291468766518413/pdf/multi-page.pdf • https://www.semana.com/edicion-impresa/caratula/articulo/la-quiebra-del-grupo-grancolombiano/182460/ • https://www.elespectador.com/especiales/la-caida-del-grupo-grancolombiano-333984/ • https://repositorio.uniandes.edu.co/bitstream/handle/1992/47284/grupo-grancolombiano.pdf?sequence=1 • https://mpra.ub.uni-muenchen.de/115662/1/MPRA_paper_115662.pdf • https://www.latinnews.com/index.php?option=com_content&view=article&id=80&Itemid=49&archive=670

SEARS Ramirez, A. and Rios, C.Y. (2021). Riesgo de Bancarota: Analisis Caso Sears.	
General view	SEARS was like the Amazon of its day at the beginning of 20th century. No digital transformation means to disappear. Introduces the catalog sales and additional services including credit.
Context	• Sears could not compete with e-commerce, • *August 2018, the volume of e-commerce purchases was US$127.3 billion in the US.* • *In 2015, Sears.com fell to $1.3 billion from* $2.6 billion in 2013 • 13% was Sears' last business in 2016, smaller than 20% of its competitors, Macy's or Kohl's.

Types of risks	Strategic Competitiveness
Events and Mitigation	• Underperformance • Sears stores fell nearly 14% in 2015, leading to the closure of 16 stores. • In 2016, sales were down 7.1%, the company closed another 50 stores and sold $300 million of assets. • In 2017, it closed 89 stores, which represented 13.2% of the total store count that year. • Sears planned to close 36 more stores in 2018, 6.2% of its total store count.
Possible Causes	Low adaptation and speed of reaction and being proactive to create mixed schema of operations with digital and in-place contact and transactions for customers.
References	• https://www.investopedia.com/news/downfall-of-sears/ • https://www.businessinsider.com/rise-and-fall-of-sears-bankruptcy-store-closings • https://www.cnn.com/2022/12/13/business/sears-hometown-bankruptcy/index.html • https://www.cnn.com/2018/10/15/business/sears-bankruptcy/index.html • https://www.economist.com/business/2018/10/20/the-collapse-of-an-american-retail-giant • https://publicaffairs-sme.com/PatriotFamily/wp-content/uploads/2015/01/Why-Sears-is-failing-and-closing-stores-Business-Insider.pdf • https://turnaround.org/sites/default/files/September%202020%20Runner%20up%20Paper_Downfall%20of%20Sears.pdf • BBC News Mundo. (15 de 10 de 2018). Sears en bancarrota: la icónica cadena de tiendas que fue emblema del “sueño americano” y acabó en la quiebra. Obtenido de https://www.bbc.com/mundo/noticias-45868508 • BBC News Mundo. (15 de 10 de 2018). Sears en bancarrota: la icónica cadena de tiendas que fue emblema del “sueño americano” y acabó en la quiebra. Obtenido de https://www.bbc.com/mundo/noticias-45868508 • Bits. (2021). Bits. Obtenido de www.bits.com.mx › importancia-del-balance-general. • CAAD Retail Design. (09 de 07 de 2019). Las 3 estrategias básicas para competir en el sector retail. Obtenido de CAAD: https://www.caad-design.com/las-3-estrategias-basicas-para-competir-en-el-sector-retail/

	• CAAD Retail Design. (10 de 08 de 2020). La sostenibilidad en el sector retail: ¿Tendencia o realidad? Obtenido de CAAD: https://www.caad-design.com/la-sostenibilidad-en-el-sector-retail- tendencia-o-realidad • Cardozo, L. (s.f.). Slide Share. Obtenido de https://www.slideshare.net/LuisCardozo24/importancia-de-los-estados-financieros-y-su-aplicacin • Deloitte. (2020). Las potencias globales del comercio minorista 2020. • Deloitte. (2020). Retail, el reto de prevalecer ante la disrupción. • Negri, C. C., & Marin, T. (03 de 2020). Del "apocalipsis del 'retail'" a actuar en la experiencia del cliente. Obtenido de Harvard Deusto: https://www.harvard-deusto.com/del-apocalipsis-del-retail-a- actuar-en-la-experiencia-del-cliente • Pasamón, F. (2020). El futuro del sector Retail. Obtenido de Deloitte: https://www2.deloitte.com/es/es/pages/consumer-business/articles/El-futuro-del-sector- Retail.html

AIG American International Group Corrales, J.M. and Zapata G.D. (2021). American International Group, Inc: un caso de estudio para la definición de herramientas de monitoreo de riesgos bajo la crisis financiera de 2008.	
General view	
Context	29th position in the Forbes Global 2000 United States government intervenes operation on September 16, 2008, providing a two-year loan of USD$85 billion (79.9% of the ownership of AIG) with an annual rate of 14%.
Types of risks	• Credit • Strategic • Liquidity • Model
Events and Mitigation	• Credit Default Swap (CDS), • CDOs Collateral Debt Obligation, wrong model assuming no correlation of mortgage markets. Tranche in a CDO can have its own risk profile which in the end generated deficiencies in the valuation of the CDOs
Possible Causes	• Subprime mortgages, wrong allocation of credit • Cash collateral received from borrowers was invested in illiquid instruments and at the end of 2007, 65% of the guarantees were invested in securities sensitive to house prices and mortgage defaults. • Super Senior Tranches, AIG executives valuation determined that the probability of default of the super senior tranches was zero (0), whereas CDS were risk-free

References	• McDonald, Robert, and Anna Paulson. 2015. "AIG in Hindsight." Journal of Economic Perspectives, 29 (2): 81-106. • Harrington, S.E. (2009), The Financial Crisis, Systemic Risk, and the Future of Insurance Regulation. Journal of Risk and Insurance, 76: 785-819. https://doi.org/10.1111/j.1539-6975.2009.01330.x • Bradford, D. K. (2008). The AIG Meltdown. Risk Management, 55(11), 14. • Sjostrom Jr, W. K. (2015). Afterword to the AIG Bailout. Wash. & Lee L. Rev., 72, 795. • Greider, W. (2010). The AIG bailout scandal. https://elischolar.library.yale.edu/cgi/viewcontent.cgi?article=10313&context=ypfs-documents • Chorafas, D. N. (2014). American International Group. In Banks, Bankers, and Bankruptcies under Crisis: Understanding Failures and Mergers during the Great Recession (pp. 109-126). New York: Palgrave Macmillan US.

Interbolsa S.A. Hincapie, C.C. (2016). Caso Interbolsa	
General view	• Brokerage company founded in 1990 in Medellín, Colombia. Commission firm acts in the market on his behalf but does so following the instructions given by his client. • Highest number and volume of transactions in the trading systems of the stock exchange (Stock Exchange, 2012).
Context	• Transactions related to the biggest textile companies (Fabricato) in the Colombian market. • Interbolsa was using Repos – high exposure with Fabricato operation • On November 2, 2012, Interbolsa was intervened by the Colombian financial regulator. Default to pay a loan with the Bancolombia bank
Types of risks	• Strategics • Fraud • Liquidity • Credit Default

Events and Mitigation	• The stock exchange organization requested a guarantee of the repo operations of 30%; • Share value reduced and the stock exchange increased the level of guarantee to 40%, the Fabricato share did not reflect the real price and that the repo operations were concentrated on a single person who had to allocate resources for clients and the organization's interest of its own operations.
Possible Causes	• Interbolsa's operations influence the share price and funds were used to perform operations not allowed in discounts of contracts to the partners. • Interbolsa Repo risk assessment was not appropriate according to Fabricato concentration. • Lack of control from the vigilance and regulatory bodies of the stock market. • on the stock market.
References	• Tito-Añamuro, J. A. (2015). Corrupción privada: un estudio de la ausencia de reglas de derecho privado, desde el caso Interbolsa. Vniversitas, (131), 433-466. • Restrepo, L. M. C., Gómez, M. C. V., & López, S. A. (2015). El caso Interbolsa: Analizado desde la problemática contable. Libre Empresa, 12(2), 141-162. • Gómez-González, J. E., & Velandia, L. F. M. (2014). Efectos de «ángeles caídos» en el mercado accionario colombiano: estudio de eventos del caso Interbolsa. Ensayos sobre política económica, 32(75), 23-27. • Aguilar Varela, J. M., & Gutierrez Orjuela, C. J. (2014). Base teórica del Caso Interbolsa (Bachelor's thesis, Universidad de La Sabana). • Leyva, N. C. (2019). Interbolsa y Grant Thornton errores metodológicos en la revisoría fiscal. Mundo FESC, 9(18), 69-76.

The Space Building Duque, O.M. (2016). Análisis del caso SPACE, desde el punto de vista del monitoreo de riesgos.	
General view	Space building project is built between 2011 and 2013
Context	Supervision organizations and local government were not providing the appropriate procedures to review quality of studies-design-structures for the project development

Types of risks	• Control • Fraud • Credit • Corruption
Events and Mitigation	• Lack of quality and operation control • Non-compliance of regulation • No earthquake standards followed • Monitoring was not carried out by the auditors during the construction stage • No verification by external agencies.
Possible Causes	Structural deficiencies in the building construction and rom the organizations point of view it was a lack of following the procedures and control the correct flow of supervision.
References	• Collazos, J. D. C., Perez, C. E. C., & Torres, B. A. (2019). Caso edificio Space. Tekhnê, 16(2), 51-60. • Y. GUALDRÓN, "Space: 12 muertos, 11 meses de pesquisas y ningún culpable," Medellín, 22-Sep-2014. • Final-Fase III, I. (2014). Concepto Técnico en Relación a las Causas más Probables del Colapso del Edificio Space. Universidad de los Andes, Facultad de Ingeniería, Bogotá DC–Colombia. • Aragón Grisales, J. (2023). Gestión de la comunicación en situaciones de crisis. Estudio de caso de la constructora Lérida CDO y el desplome de la torre 6 del Edificio Space en octubre de 2013. • Yela Garzón, C. A. (2020). Efectos jurídicos y económicos presentados por el desplome del Edificio Space en el mercado mobiliario, estudio de caso Región Suroccidente Colombiana. • Redacción Nacional, "Falta de capacidad estructural originó colapsó de la torre 6 del Space," Medellín, 03-Oct-2014. • NACIÓN, "El efecto del edificio Space," Medellín, 19-Oct-2013. • Redacción Economía y Negocios institucion., "Multa de $4.300 millones al grupo CDO," Medellín, 13-Jan-2016. • JUAN DAVID ORTIZ FRANCO., "¿Quién es Jorge Aristizábal, el diseñador de Space?," Medellín, 14-May-2014. • G. M. Muñoz., "Los efectos de la caída del edificio Space," Medellín, 11-Nov-2013. • Caracol Radio, "Nueva superintendencia vigilará a los curadores urbanos," Medellín, 21-Nov-2013.

General Motors Ordóñez, M.E. (2016). Análisis de la quiebra de la General Motors	
General view	Founded in 1908 In 1965, it had a 54% share of the automobile market and by 1990 more than half of its income came from sports vehicles; it also manufactured satellites and military equipment. By 1991, its sales had fallen by 14% and in response to this reduction in sales, the company decided to cut 15,000 jobs, reduce incentives to the other thousands of workers, and assets selling.
Context	By 1993, the company had already discontinued 14 of its new products and suspended contributions to workers' pension programs in order to maintain its cash flow. But the state forced companies to present liabilities for health and pension on the balance sheets, reaching a value for General Motors of US 52,000 million for 1992. Reduction in operation to 85% of installed capacity by the end of 2005, taking it to a 19% market share, by January 2009, when it filed for bankruptcy. Zero % financing, which increased sales, but plunged the company further into financial problems, since it was assuming part of the financing of the vehicles sold.
Types of risks	vertiginous growth, attention to changes in customer needs, innovation requirements, expensive fuel and only combustion cars, promotion with impact on medium-term results, employees cost, etc. The mere fact of having a large part of its employees unionized forced General Motors to take measures to address this problem, which was strengthened during the golden age of the company.
Events and Mitigation	• Market changes • Customers new needs-expectations • Huge competition foreigner car makers • Economic conditions in high volume markets • Speed to react • High load of internal problems-labor conditions
Possible Causes	• Marketing risk-offer acceptance by customers • Innovation risk • Strategic Risk-Competitiveness • Credit risk

References	• Nadal Alejandro. (2009)¿Quién llevó la General Motors a la quiebra? [Online] Disponible en http://www.archivochile.com/Debate/crisis_08_09/crisis00117.pdf • Adler, B. E. (2010). A reassessment of bankruptcy reorganization after Chrysler and General Motors. Am. Bankr. Inst. L. Rev., 18, 305. • Bosco, C., & Plante, C. (2013). Bankruptcy of General Motors. GSTF Journal on Business Review (GBR), 2(3). • Zywicki, T. J. (2019). The Chrysler and General Motors Bankruptcies. Research Handbook on Corporate Bankruptcy Law, Barry Adler ed, 18-31. • Goolsbee, A. D., & Krueger, A. B. (2015). A retrospective look at rescuing and restructuring General Motors and Chrysler. Journal of Economic Perspectives, 29(2), 3-24. • Rauh, J., & Zingales, L. (2009). Bankruptcy is best to save GM. The Economists' Voice, 6(4).

Groupe Societe General Ávila, M.E. and González, A. (2020). Groupe Societe Generale S.A. y BNP Paribas S.A.	
General view	• Groupe Societe Generale S.A. started in 2006 with a long-term credit rating of BBB- and short-term credit rating of F3, which changed at the end of that year to A and F2, respectively, and remained at those ratings until the end of 2008; then in 2009 until 2013, it remained at BBB; at F3 until 2011 and F2 until 2013. • Business definition Retail Banking and Specialized Financial Services, Global Investment Management and Services, and Corporate and Investment Banking.
Context	• In 2008, Societe Generale S.A. announced a fraud of 4,900 million euros, and additional losses of 1,100 million in mortgage assets and another 950 million in other movements to withstand the crisis. At the end of the third quarter of that year, the company announced a reduction of its profits by approximately 84% which generated a high volatility in its shares which had an annual average value of EUR 64,903 in 2006, EUR 71,965 in 2007, and EUR37,875 in 2008, reflecting a downward variation of 53% over the last two years, which is consistent with the crisis. • It was in 2011 the 4th largest bank in European Union

Types of risks	• Liquidity Risk • Strategic risk • Credit risk • Fraud Risk
Events and Mitigation	• Sub-prime mortgages • Unauthorized trading practice • Loss of over 7 Billions USD
Possible Causes	The financial crisis or the so-called real estate bubble that deepened in 2008 in the United States, due to tails of the American economy that arose from speculation on several financial indicators, which strongly hit the economies of the world in terms of profitability of real estate assets under which there were investments in the American stock markets, causing impact in other markets such as construction was an additional factor to the crisis in the automotive sector.
References	• Oji, C., & Makin, V. (2013). Moral Bankruptcy and Trading Losses at Société Générale. Wits Business School. • Canac, P., & Dykman, C. (2011). The tale of two banks: Société Générale and Barings. Journal of the International Academy for Case Studies, 17(7), 11. • Libaert, T. (1997). An Exceptional Fraud at Société Générale. Case Studies in Crisis Communication: International Perspectives on Hits and Misses, 331. • Véron, N. (2008). Europe and the US: A Tale of Two Financial Crises. Bruegel Blog, 7.

Enron Gómez, O.L. (2016). Lo que llevó a la quiebra a Enron y WorldCom: Análisis de casos	
General view	ENRON was an energy company from the United States of America and a combination of Houston Natural Gas and InterNorth
Context	Energy market starts to be part of market price transactions. Presentation of fraudulent profits. Diversification of thc organization. October 2001, the company declared losses ENRON securities collapsed in the stock market a share price as 10 years earlier, and in December 2001, the energy giant filed Chapter 11
Types of risks	• Fraud • Credit • Strategic • Corruption

Events and Mitigation	• New energy market is emerging • High speed to grow in the market • Multiple business were connected to the energy business • Risk management practice with start on the holistic view
Possible Causes	• Inappropriate management and management group – board of directors wrongdoing. • Excess of ambition-abuse of power-bad faith • Lack of control and confusion in the market because makeup of financial reports and wrong auditing reports • Slow intervention of regulators
References	• Fusaro, P. C., & Miller, R. M. (2002). What went wrong at Enron: Everyone's guide to the largest bankruptcy in US history. John Wiley & Sons. • Li, Y. (2010). The case analysis of the scandal of Enron. International Journal of business and management, 5(10), 37. • Lucci, J. P. (2003). Enron-The bankruptcy heard around the world and the international richochet of Sarbanes-Oxley. Alb. L. Rev., 67, 211. • Deakin, S., & Konzelmann, S. J. (2004). Learning from enron. Corporate Governance: An International Review, 12(2), 134-142. • Mayoral, J. M., & Sánchez-Segura, A. (2008). Gobierno Corporativo Y Calidad de La Información Contable: Evidencia Empírica Española/Corporate Governance And Earnings Quality: Evidence From Spanish Companies. Revista de Contabilidad, 11(1), 67. • Rapoport, M., & Brenta, N. (2010). La crisis económica mundial: ¿El desenlace de cuarenta años de inestabilidad?. problemas del desarrollo. revista latinoamericana de economía, 41(163), 7-30. • Rapoport, M. (2009). Diez razones de la crisis internacional. • Sociedades, D. (2004). Causas de la liquidación obligatoria de sociedades. estrategias para prevenir la crisis. • Zamagni, S. (2009). Lecciones de una crisis anunciada. Ensayos de Política Económica, nro, 3.

International Airlines Morales, E., Morales, M.V. and Correa, S.A. (2017). Diagnóstico del monitoreo de riesgos en cuatro aerolíneas internacionales	
General view	Time of terrorism actions around the world. Airlines companies reduced the demand. The level of passengers felt at the levels of 6 to seven years before the terrorist events. Cost of operation continue growing and the income/revenue of the airlines was descending. No preparation to have industry contingency plans.

Context	• Compliance with the laws and regulations of the aviation authorities and high taxes, fees, and airport charges increased LUV's operating costs and expenses, exposing it to liquidity risk. • Operating in regions such as the northwestern United States exacerbated this exposure due to fare payments based on congestion in the airspace of this region ("Southwest Airlines Co. SWOT Analysis," 2016). • The emergence of large transportation corporations from airline mergers, which have substantially greater financial resources, "more favorable hedges against rising fuel prices, and lower cost structures" than LUV, also exposed it to considerable financial risk ("Southwest Airlines Co. SWOT Analysis," 2016). • Context The high competition existing in routes, services, products, fares, and frequent flyer programs exposed DAL to a high market risk; new companies offer low costs on domestic and regional routes within the United States, and companies such as American Airlines and Southwest Airlines are among the competitors. Likewise, the company competes with foreign firms, both on routes within the United States and internationally ("Delta Air Lines, Inc. SWOT Analysis," 2016).
Types of risks	• Strategic • Operational • Systemic • Credit • Liquidity
Events and Mitigation	Consumption and operation affected by external circumstances. No preparedness to operate under collaboration conditions.
Possible Causes	• Black Swans-September 11 • High regulations in some regions to fly • Consumption limitations • Silo operation-software – costs of airports and logistic • Fuel and supplies
References	• Greer, C. F., & Moreland, K. D. (2003). United Airlines' and American Airlines' online crisis communication following the September 11 terrorist attacks. Public relations review, 29(4), 427-441. • Assaf, A. (2009). Are US airlines really in crisis?. Tourism Management, 30(6), 916-921.

	• Flouris, T., & Walker, T. J. (2005). The financial performance of low-cost and full-service airlines in times of crisis. Canadian Journal of Administrative Sciences/Revue Canadienne des Sciences de l'Administration, 22(1), 3-20. • Álvarez, V. (2016). El mercado aeronaútico en Estado Unidos. Estudios de Mercado, 1-3. • American Airlines Group Inc. SWOT Analysis. (2016). American Airlines Group Inc SWOT Analysis, 1-9. • Avianca. (2016). Avianca. Retrieved from http://www.avianca.com/es-ec/ • Buitrago, N., & Ocampo, D. (2015). Pensamiento estratégico y gerencial global. In U. EAN (Ed.). Bogotá. • Delta Air Lines, Inc. SWOT Analysis. (2016). Delta Air Lines, Inc. SWOT Analysis, 1-9. • Gonzalez, A. (2016). Estudio sobre el Mercado Aéreo de Transporte de Pasajeros en Latinoamérica. CRC América Latina, 98. • Southwest Airlines Co. SWOT Analysis. (2016). Southwest Airlines Co. SWOT Analysis, 1-10.

References

Aaker, D., *et al.* (1998). *Marketing Research.* John Wiley & Sons, Inc., New York.

Aaker, D. A., Kuma, V., & Day, G. S. (2000). *Marketing Research* (7th edn.). John Wiley & Sons, Inc., New York.

Abell, D. (1980). *Defining the Business: The Starting Point of Strategic Planning.* Englewood Cliffs: Prentice Hall.

Abrams, C. E., Känel, J. V., Müller, S., Pfitzmann, B., & Ruschka-Taylor, S. (2007). Optimized enterprise risk management. *IBM Systems Journal*, 46, 219–234.

Ackoff, R. L. (2007). Greeting. *Kybernetes*, 36(9/10), https://doi.org/10.1108/k.2007.06736iaa.002.

Adamo, J. M. (2001). *Data Mining for Association Rules and Sequential Patterns: Sequential and Parallel Algorithms.* Springer, New York.

Agarwal, P. K., Gurjar, J., Agarwal, A. K. & Birla, R. (2015). Application of artificial intelligence for development of intelligent transport system in smart cities. *International Journal of Transportation Engineering and Traffic Systems*, 1(1), 20–30.

Agbatogun, A. O. (2013). Interactive digital technologies' use in Southwest Nigerian universities. *Educational Technology Research and Development*, 61(2), 333–357. https://eric.ed.gov/?id=EJ997632.

Agrawal, S., De Smet, A., Poplawski, P., & Reich, A. (2020). Beyond hiring: How companies are reskilling to address talent gaps. McKinsey & Company. https://www.mckinsey.com/businessfunctions/people-and-organizational-performance/our-insights/beyond-hiring-how-companies-arereskilling-to-address-talent-gaps.

Alavi, M. & Leidner, D. E. (2001). Review: Knowledge management and knowledge management systems: Conceptual foundations and research issues. *MIS Quarterly*, 25(1), 107–136. https://doi.org/10.2307/3250961.

Albers, E., Giacobbe, M., & Gotelaere, J. (2005). Building a bridge between hospital risk and finance to support capital spending plans. *Journal of Health Care Finance*, 32(2), 1–7.

Albino, V., Beardi, U., & Dangelico, R. M. (2015). Smart cities: Definitions, performance, and initiatives. *Journal of Urban Technology*, 22(1), 3–21. http://dx.doi.org/10.1080/10630732.2014.942092.

Alexander, C. (1998). Risk management and analysis: Measuring and Modelling Financial Risk. John Wiley, Chicheste, England, New York.

Allam, Z. & Dhunny, Z. A. (2019). On big data, artificial intelligence and smart cities. *Cities*, 89(2019), 80–91. https://fardapaper.ir/mohavaha/uploads/2019/03/Fardapaper-On-big-data-artificial-intelligence-and-smart-cities.pdf

Alpaydin, E. (2014). *Introduction to Machine Learning* (3rd edn.). The MIT Press, Cambridge, Massachusetts, London, England.

Amankwaaa, E. F. & Blay, K. B. (2018). Cities at risk? Exploring the synergies between smartphones and everyday vulnerabilities. *Cities*, 83, 129–139. https://doi.org/10.1016/j.cities.2018.06.015.

Amrein-Beardsley, A. & Holloway, J. (2019). Value-added models for teacher evaluation and accountability: Common sense assumptions. *Educational Policy*, 33(3), 516–542. https://doi.org/10.1177/0895904817719519.

Analytics magazine revenue management & digital marketing. http://analytics-magazine.org/revenue-management-a-digital-marketing/.

Andersen, T. J. (2008). The performance relationship of effective risk management: Exploring the firm-specific investment rationale. *Long Range Planning*, 41(2), 155–176. https://doi.org/10.1016/j.lrp.2008.01.002.

Andersen, T. J. & Sax, J. (2020). *Strategic Risk Management: A Research Overview*. Routledge. State of the Art in Business Research https://doi.org/10.4324/9780429456381.

Anderson, J. T., Gibson, S., Luchtenberg, K. F., et al. (2022). How much are borrowers willing to pay to remove uncertainty surrounding mortgage defaults? *Journal of Real Estate Finance and Economics*, 64, 500–522. https://doi.org/10.1007/s11146-020-09810-4.

Anthony, R. N. & Govindarajan, V. (2007). *Management Control Systems* (12th edn.). Boston: McGraw-Hill/Irwin, APRESS. ISBN-13 (pbk): 978-1-4842-5027-3.

Apte, C. V., Natarajan, R., Pednault, E. P. D., & Tipu, F. A. (2002). A probabilistic estimation framework for predictive modeling analytics. *IBM Systems Journal*, 41(3), 438–448.

Argyris, C. (July–August 1994). Good communication that blocks learning. *Harvard Business Review*. https://hbr.org/1994/07/good-communication-that-blocks-learning.

Argote, L. (2013). Organization learning: A theoretical framework. In: *Organizational Learning*. Boston, MA: Springer. https://doi.org/10.1007/978-1-4614-5251-5_2.

Argyris, C. (2003). Actionable knowledge. In: Tsoukas, H. and Kndsen, C. (Eds.), *Organisation Theory*. Oxford: Oxford University Press.

Armstrong, G. & Kotler, P. (2013). *Fundamentos de Mercadotecnia* (11th edn.). Prentice Hall, Mexico. https://frrq.cvg.utn.edu.ar/pluginfile.php/14584/mod_resource/content/1/Fundamentos%20del%20Marketing-Kotler.pdf.

Arora, R. (2002). Implementing KM — A balanced scorecard approach. *Journal of Knowledge Management*, 6(3), 240–249. https://doi.org/10.1108/13673270210434340.

Arrow, K. (1963). Uncertainty and the welfare economics of medical care. *American Economic Review*, 53(5), 941–73. https://assets.aeaweb.org/asset-server/files/9442.pdf.

Avila, M. E. & Gonzalez, A. (2020). Analysis de la crisis compañias Group Societe Generale S.A. y BNP Paribas S.A.

Aven, T. (2003). *Foundation of Risk Analysis*, John Wiley, Chichester.

Avery, H. (November 2, 2007). Hedge fund strategies: Don't shoot the quant guys! Euromoney.

Babbie, E. R. (1998). *The Practice of Social Research* (8th edn.). Wadsworth Publishing Co., Belmont. https://www.worldcat.org/title/practice-of-social-research/oclc/37132582.

Baden-Fuller, C., Ravazzolo, F., & Schweizer, T. S. (2000). Making and measuring reputations: The research of European Business Schools. *Long Range Planning*, 33(5), 621–650. https://doi.org/10.1016/S0024-6301(00)00064-9 .

Baepler, P. & Murdoch, C. L. (2010). Academic analytics and data mining in higher education. *International Journal for the Scholarship of Teaching and Learning*, 4(2), Article 17. https://doi.org/10.20429/ijsotl.2010.040217.

Bailey, K. (1978). *Methods of Social Research* (1st edn.). The Free Press, New York.

Bailey, K. (2007). *Methods of Social Research* (4th edn.). The Free Press, New York.

Baloh, P., Desouza, K. C., & Hackney, R. (2012). Contextualizing organizational interventions of knowledge management systems: A design science perspective. *Journal of the American Society for Information Science and Technology*, 63(5), 948–966. https://doi.org/10.1002/asi.22599.

Baltzan, P., Detlor, B., & Welsh, C. (2012). *Business Driven Information Systems* (3rd edn.). MCGrawHill-Ryerson.

Banham, R. (2004). Enterprising views of risk management. *Journal of Accountancy*, 197(6), 65–72.

Bennett, D., Collinson, G., Edbury, M., Surkovic, E., & Wardle, J. (2014). Annual report of the government chief scientific adviser, innovation: Managing risk, not avoiding it. UK. https://assets.publishing.service.gov.uk/government/

uploads/system/uploads/attachment_data/file/381906/14-1190b-innovation-managing-risk-evidence.pdf.

Beretta, E., Santangelo, A., Lepri, B., Vetro, A., & De Martin, J. C. (2019). The invisible power of fairness. How machine learning shapes democracy. In M. J. Marie-Jean Meurs & F. Rudzicz (Eds.), *Advances in Artificial Intelligence: 32nd Canadian Conference on Artificial Intelligence,* Canadian AI, Kingston, ON, Canada. https://link.springer.com/book/10.1007/978-3-030-18305-9.

Berg, B. L. (1998). *Qualitative Research Methods for the Social Sciences* (1st edn.). Needham Heights.

Berg, B. L. (2001). *Qualitative Research Methods for the Social Sciences* (4th edn.). Allyn and Bacon, Needham Heightsh: A Pearson Education Company.

Bernstein, P. L. (2000). Risk management, financial markets and insurance: The hidden linkages. Geneva papers on risk and insurance. *Issues and Practice*, 25(4), 629–636. https://www.jstor.org/stable/41952556.

Bertini, M. & Koenigsberg, O. (September–October 2021). The pitfalls of pricing algorithms: Be mindful of how they can hurt your brand. *Harvard Business Review*. https://hbr.org/2021/09/the-pitfalls-of-pricing-algorithms

Bessis, J. (1998). *Risk Management in Banking*. John Wiley & sons, Chichester, England.

Bessis, J. (2015). *Risk Management in Banking* (4th edn.). John Wiley & sons, Chichester, England. https://www.wiley.com/en-us/Risk+Management+in+Banking%2C+4th+Edition-p-9781118660218.

Best, P. (1998). *Implementing Value at Risk*. John Wiley & Sons, Inc., New York.

Best, P. (2000). *Implementing Value at Risk*. John Wiley & Sons, Inc., New York. https://www.wiley.com/en-gb/Implementing+Value+at+Risk-p-9780470865965.

Blackman, R. (July–August 2022). Why you need an AI ethics committee: Expert oversight will help you safeguard your data and your brand. *Harvard Business Review*. https://hbr.org/2022/07/why-you-need-an-ai-ethics-committee.

Block C. (March 2022). 12 Reasons your digital transformation will fail. *Forbes*. https://www.forbes.com/sites/forbescoachescouncil/2022/03/16/12-reasons-your-digital-transformation-will-fail/?sh=54e614e61f1e.

Boda, G., Lõrincz, J., & Szlávik, P. (2008). *How to be More Efficient in Managing Intellectual Capital: An Overview of Various Techniques*. The ICFAI University Press.

Bodie, Z., Kane, A., & Marcus, A. J. (1997). *Investments*. Irwin-McGraw Hill, Toronto.

Bodie, Z., Kane, A., & Marcus, A. (2001). *Investments: Finance* (5th edn.). McGraw-Hill/Irwin, Toronto. https://books.mec.biz/tmp/books/KCNEMTXSWCHUN6GXX8RL.pdf.

Bodie, Z., Kane, A., & Marcus, A. (2006). *Investments* (7th edn.). McGraw-Hill/Irwin Series in Finance, Insurance, and Real Estate, Toronto.

Bolman, L. & Deal, T. (2003). *Reframing Organisations*. San Francisco: Jossey Bass Publishers a Willey Imprint.

Bonnet, D. & Wade, M. R. (February 2022). Unpacking the digital transformation at IKEA. *Innovation*, https://www.imd.org/ibyimd/innovation/unpacking-the-digital-transformation-at-ikea/.

Bosua, R. & Scheepers, R. (2007). Towards a model to explain knowledge sharing in complex organisational environments. *Knowledge Management Research and Practice*, 5(2), 93–109.

Bouska, A. S. (1989). Exposure Bases Revisited, Volume LXXVI, Part 1 No. 145, Proceedings. https://www.casact.org/sites/default/files/2021-02/pubs_proceed_proceed89_89001.pdf.

Bowers, N. L., Gerber, H. U., & Hickman J. C. (1997). Actuarial Mathematics (2nd edn.). *Society of Actuaries*. Schaumburg IL. https://docviewer.xdocs.net/view.php.

Bowling, D. & Rieger, L. (2005). Success factors for implementing enterprise risk management. *Bank Accounting and Finance*, 18(3), 21–26.

Brealey, R. A., Myers, S. C., & Allen, F. (2010). Principios de finanzas corporativas (9th edn.). McGraw Hill Interamericana, España. https://www.economicas.unsa.edu.ar/afinan/informacion_general/book/princ/de/finanzas/corporativas/9ed/myers.pdf.

Brown, B. (2001). Step by step enterprise risk management. *Risk Management*, 48(9), 43–50.

Brown S. (2022). 10 capabilities to accelerate digital transformation. Insights from MIT Experts. https://hbr.org/2004/12/making-real-options-really-work.

Buckley, S. & Giannakopoulos, P. (2012). Technology and tools supporting CoPs. In S. Buckley & M. Jakovljevic (Eds.), *Knowledge Management Innovations for Interdisciplinary Innovation* (1st edn., pp. 316–345). IGI Global, Hershey, PA. https://www.igi-global.com/chapter/technology-tools-supporting-cops/68333.

Bursk, J. F. & Chapman, E. C. (1963). *New Decision-Making Tools for Managers* (1st edn.). Harvard University Press.

Burstein, F., Zyngier, S., & Rateb, Z. (2002). Knowledge management in the financial services sector: Understandings and trends in Australia. In *Proceedings of the 3rd European Conference on Knowledge Management*, September, pp. 113–125.

Burton, R. & Obel, B. (1995). *Strategic Organisational Diagnosis and Design*. Boston: Kluwer Academic Publishers.

Burton, B. & Morello, D. (2006). Future worker 2015: Extreme individualization. Gartner Research, Portals, Content & Collaboration Summit 2006.

Button, K. J. (1979). Models for decision-making in public sector. OMEGA. *The International Journal of Management Science*, 7(5), 399–409. https://ideas.repec.org/a/eee/jomega/v7y1979i5p399-409.html.

Candelon, F., di Carlo, R. C., De Bondt, M., & Evgeniou, T. (September–October 2021). AI regulation is coming: How to prepare for the inevitable. *Harvard Business Review*. https://hbr.org/2021/09/ai-regulation-is-coming.

Carbonell, G. (ed.). (1990). *Machine Learning: Paradigms and Methods*. Cambridge, MA: MIT Press.

Cardwell, D. (1994). *The Fontana History of Technology*. Fontana Press, HarperCollins Publishers, London.

Carenys, J. (2010). Management control systems: A historical perspective. *International Bulletin of Business Administration*, 37–54.

Carrico, C. S., Hogan, S. M., Dyson, R. G., & Athanassopoulos, A. D. (1997). Data envelopment analysis and university selection. *The Journal of the Operational Research Society,* 48(12), 1163–1177. https://doi.org/10.2307/3010747.

Carroll, J. M. (1984). *Managing Risk a Computer Aided Strategy*. Burterworths, Boston.

Carroll, J. & Broadhead, R. (2001). *Get a Digital Life: An Internet reality check*. Stoddart, Toronto.

Chambers, M. & Dinsmore, T. W. (2014). *Advanced Analytics Methodologies: Driving Business with Analytics*. Pearson Education.

Chamorro-Premuzic, T. (2020). Can surveillance AI make the workplace safe? *MIT Sloan Management Review*, 62(1), 13–15.

Chapman, P., Clinton, J., Kerber, R., Khabaza, T., Reinartz, T. P., Daimlerchrysler, C., Shearer, R., & Wirth (2000). *CRISP-DM 1.0: Step-by-step Data Mining Guide*.

Charam, R. (2007). *Know-How: The 8 Skills That Separate People Who Perform From Those Who Don't*. Crown Business, New York.

Cheng, F., Ming, Y., & Qu, H. (2021). DECE: Decision explorer with counterfactual explanations for machine learning models. *IEEE Transactions on Visualization and Computer Graphics*, 27(2), 1438–1447. https://doi.org/10.1109/TVCG.2020.3030342.

Cheng, M. M., Humphreys, K. A., & Zhang, Y. Y. (2018). The interplay between strategic risk profiles and presentation format on managers' strategic judgments using the balanced scorecard. *Accounting, Organizations and Society,* 70(C), 92–105, https://doi.org/10.1016/j.aos.2018.05.009.

Cleverly, W. & Cleverly, J. (2005). Scorecards and dashboards using financial metrics to improve performance. *Healthcare Financial Management*, 59(7), 64–69. https://pubmed.ncbi.nlm.nih.gov/16060101/.

CLSI GP26-A3. (2004). *Application of a Quality, Management System Model for Laboratory Services; Approved Guideline* (3rd edn.). https://webstore.ansi.org/preview-pages/CLSI/preview_GP26-A3.pdf.

CLSI HS1. (2004). *A Quality Management System Model for Health Care; Approved Guideline*. https://standards.globalspec.com/std/1537966/CLSI%20HS1.

Collaris, D. & Van Wijk, J. (2022). StrategyAtlas: Strategy analysis for machine learning interpretability. *IEEE Transactions on Visualization and Computer Graphics*, 1–1. https://doi.org/10.1109/TVCG.2022.3146806.

Collaris, D. & Van Wijk, J. J. (2020). ExplainExplore: Visual exploration of machine learning explanations. IEEE Pacific Visualization Symposium (PacificVis), 26–35. https://doi.org/10.1109/PacificVis48177.2020.7090.

Collins, J. M. & Ruefli, T. W. (1992). Strategic risk: An ordinal approach. *Management Science,* 38(12), 1707–1731. http://www.jstor.org/stable/2632706.

Corrales, J. M. & Zapata, G. D. (2021). American International Group, Inc: un caso de estudio para la definición de herramientas de monitoreo de riesgos bajo la crisis financiera de 2008.

Crawford, M. & Benedetto A. D. (2003). New Products Management. (10th edn.). McGraw Hill, Boston. https://www.academia.edu/25415016/New/Products/Management/Crawford/and/B/1.

Crouhy, M., Galai, D., & Mark, R. (2000, December). One firm, one view. Risk, Special Report.

Cumming, C. M. & Hirtle, B. J. (2001). *The Challenges of Risk Management in Diversified Financial Companies*, Vol. 7, No. 1. Federal Reserve Bank of New York: Economic Policy Review, pp. 1–17. https://www.newyorkfed.org/medialibrary/media/research/epr/01v07n1/0103cumm.pdf.

Curley, M., *et al.* (2006). The IT transformation at Intel. *MIS Quarterly Executive*, 5(4). https://aisel.aisnet.org/misqe/vol5/iss4/5/.

da Cruz, N. F. & Marques, R. C. (2014). Revisiting the determinants of local government performance. *Omega,* 44(C), 91–103. https://www.sciencedirect.com/science/article/pii/S0305048313000923.

Daft, R. (1992). *Organisation Theory and Design*. St. Paul, MN: West Publisher.

Dai, L., Wang, Z. & Yang, Z. (2012). Next-generation digital television terrestrial broadcasting systems: Key technologies and research trends. *IEEE Communications Magazine*, 50, 150–158. https://ieeexplore.ieee.org/stamp/stamp.jsp?tp=&arnumber=6211500&tag=1.

Damodaran, L. (2001). Human factors in the digital world enhancing life. *Human-Computer Studies*, 55(4), 377–403. https://doi.org/10.1006/ijhc.2001.0490.

DAP BC. (2021). Diagnostic accreditation program accreditation standards. www.dap.org. Website information. https://www.cpsbc.ca/files/pdf/DAP-AS-Laboratory-Medicine-V1.5.pdf.

Dasgupta, S. & Tam, E. (2005). Indicators and framework for assessing sustainable infrastructure. *Canadian Journal of Civil Engineering*, 32(1), 30–44. http://dx.doi.org/10.1139/l04-101.

Daugherty, P. R., Wilson, H. J., & Chowdhury, R. (2018). *Using Artificial Intelligence to Promote Diversity*. MIT Sloan Management Review.

Davenport, T. H. (2006). *Competing on analytics. Harvard Business Review*, 84, 107–134.

Davenport, T. H. & Harris, J. (2005). Automated decision-making comes of age. *MIT Sloan Management Review*, 46(4), 83–89.

Davenport, T. H. & Redman, T. C. (May 2020). Digital transformation comes down to talent in 4 key areas. *Harvard Business Review*, https://hbr.org/2020/05/digital-transformation-comes-down-to-talent-in-4-key-areas.

Davenport, T. H. & Westerman, G. (March 2018). Why so many high-profile digital transformations fail. *Harvard Business Review.* https://hbr.org/2018/03/why-so-many-high-profile-digital-transformations-fail.

Davenport, T., Guha, A., Grewal, D., & Bressgott, T. (2020). How artificial intelligence will change the future of marketing. *Journal of Academy of Marketing Science*, 48, 24–42. https://doi.org/10.1007/s11747-019-00696-0.

De Cremer, D. & Kasparov, G. (March 18, 2021) AI should augment human intelligence, not replace it. *Harvard Business Review Digital Articles*, 3/18/2021, p1–8. 8p.

Degagne, C., Leandri, C., & Puchley, T. (January 2004). Linking knowledge and risk management controlling the information flood, business. Pricewaterhowse Coopers. www.pwc.com/extweb/newcoth.nsf.

Delacruz, E. (2009). Old world teaching meets the new digital cultural creatives. *International Journal of Art & Design of Education*. 28(3), 261–268. https://doi.org/10.1111/j.1476-8070.2009.01620.x.

Deloitte. (2021). A digital path to third-party oversight: Third-party risk management (TPRM) global survey 2021. https://www2.deloitte.com/content/dam/Deloitte/uk/Documents/risk/deloitte-uk-global-tprm-survey-report-2021.pdf.

Devaraj, S. & Kohli, R. (2003). Performance impacts of information technology: Is actual usage the missing link? *Management Science*, 49, 273–289. 10.1287/mnsc.49.3.273.12736.

Diaz, V. (2010). Web 2.0 and emerging technologies in online learning. *New Directions for Community Colleges,* 2010(150), 57–66. Special Issue: Online Education.

Dickinson, G. (2001). Enterprise risk management: Its origins and conceptual foundation. *The Geneva Papers on Risk and Insurance*, 26(3), 360–366.

https://www.actuaries.org.uk/system/files/documents/pdf/dickinson-g-2001-enterprise-risk-management-its-origins-and-conceptual-foundation-3.pdf.

Dicuonzo, G., Donofrio, F., & Galeone, G. (2021). Big data and artificial intelligence to support risk management: A systematic literature review. In M. S. Chiucchi, R. Lombardi, & D. Mancini (Eds.), *Intellectual Capital, Smart Technologies and Digitalization: Emerging Issues and Opportunities* (pp. 119–130), Springer. https://doi.org/10.1007/978-3-030-80737-5.

Ding, C., Kavuri, A. S. & Milne, A. (2021). Lessons from the rise and fall of Chinese peer-to-peer lending. *Journal of Bank Regulation*, 22(2), 133–143. https://doi.org/10.1057/s41261-020-00132-2.

Dixon, B. R., Bouma, G. D., & Atkinson, G. B. J. (1987). *A Handbook of Social Science Research*. Oxford University Press, New York.

Dock, B. (2005). Clinical practice: Improving the accuracy of specimen labeling. *Clinical Laboratory Science*, 18(4), 210–212. http://clsjournal.ascls.org/content/ascls/18/4/210.full.pdf.

Dock, B. (2005). Specimen labeling Failure Mode and Effects Analysis (FMEA). *Clinical Laboratory Science*, 18(4), 210–212. http://clsjournal.ascls.org/content/ascls/18/4/210.full.pdf.

Doherty, N. (2000). *Integrated Risk Management: Techniques and Strategies for Managing Corporate Risk*. New York: McGraw-Hill Inc.

Dong, Y., Firth, M., Hou, W., & Yang, W. (2016). Evaluating the performance of Chinese commercial banks: A comparative analysis of different types of banks. *European Journal of Operational Research*, 252(1), 280–295. https://doi.org/10.1016/j.ejor.2015.12.038..

Doumpos, M. & Cohen, S. (2014). Applying data envelopment analysis on accounting data to assess and optimize the efficiency of Greek local governments. *Omega,* 46, 74–85. https://doi.org/10.1016/j.omega.2014.02.004.

Doumpos, M., Zopounidis, C., Gounopoulos, D., Platanakis, E., & Zhang, W. (2023). Operational research and artificial intelligence methods in banking. *European Journal of Operational Research*, 306(1), 1–16.

Drucker, P. F. (1968). Decision-making and the effective executive. *The Bulletin of the National Association of Secondary School Principals*, 52(328), 24–39.

Dutton, W. H., Carusi, A., & Peltu, M. (2006). Fostering multidisciplinary engagement: Communication challenges for social research on emerging digital technologies. *Prometheus*. 24(2), 129–149. https://doi.org/10.1080/08109020600714910.

Duque, O. M. (2016). Analisis del caso SPACE, desde el punto de vista del monitoreo de riesgo.

Dyagilev, K. & Saria, S. (2016). Learning (predictive) risk scores in the presence of censoring due to interventions. *Machine Learning*, 102, 323–348. https://doi.org/10.1007/s10994-015-5527-7.

Dzinkowski, R. (June 2002). Knowledge for all: Knowledge sharing at the world bank. *Financial Times Mastering Management*. http://www.ftmastering.com/mmo (last accessed November 11, 2008).

Earl, M. (2001). Regarding the knowledge as a process and KM. *Journal of Management Information Systems*, 18(1), 215–233.

EBSCO SWOT. *Analysis Database: Business Source Complete*.

Eden, C. & Huxham, C. (1996). Action research for management research. *British Journal of Management*, 7(1), 75–86. https://doi.org/10.1111/j.1467-8551.1996.tb00107.x.

Editorial. (2020). Special issue, data intelligence and risk analytics. *Industrial Management & Data Systems*, 120(2), 249–252. https://www.proquest.com/docview/2343224940?parentSessionId=ckEgfyI0NNpAaby%2F6v%2FHF%2FBeu1Jfw6awPAncR%2BOEL2A%3D.

Edwards, J. S. (2005). Business processes and knowledge management. In M. Khosrow-Pour (Ed.), *Encyclopedia of Information Science and Technology* (2nd edn., pp. 471–476). IGI Global. https://doi.org/10.4018/978-1-60566-026-4.ch078

EFFRA: European Factories of the Future Research Association, https://www.effra.eu/.

Elenurm, T. (2012). Knowledge management and innovative learning. In S. Buckley & M. Jakovljevic (Eds.), *Knowledge Management Innovations for interdisciplinary Innovation* (1st edn., pp. 108–131). IGI Global Hershey, PA https://www.igi-global.com/chapter/knowledge-management-innovative-learning/68323.

Eppens, E., Gould, F., Schmidt, C., Moore, J., & Weaherford, L. (1998). *Introductory Management Science: Decision Modeling with Spreadsheets*. New Jersey: Prentice Hall.

Erhardt, R. J. & Smith, R. L. (2014). Weather derivative risk measures for extreme events. *North American Actuarial Journal,* 18(3), 379–393. DOI: 10.1080/10920277.2014.910472.

Etzioni, A. (1964). *Modern Organisations*. Englewood Cliffs, NJ: Prentice Hall.

European Commission. https://research-and-innovation.ec.europa.eu/knowledge-publications-tools-and-data/publications/all-publications/annexes-annual-reports-2009-2014-directorate-general-research-and-innovation_en; https://commission.europa.eu/index_en?wt-search=yes.

European Parliamentary Research Service. (2020). The ethics of artificial intelligence: Issues and initiatives. Scientific Foresight Unit (STOA), European Union. https://www.europarl.europa.eu/RegData/etudes/STUD/2020/634452/EPRS_STU(2020)634452_EN.pdf.

Fairchild, A. M. (2002). Knowledge management metrics via a balanced scorecard methodology. In *Proceedings of the 35th Annual Hawaii International Conference on System Sciences*, Big Island, HI, USA, pp. 3173–3180. doi: 10.1109/HICSS.2002.994356.

Fang, C., Wailes, E., & Cramer, G. (August 5, 1998). China's rural and urban household survey data: Collection, availability, and problems. In *Presented at the Free Section Entitled Availability and Discrepancy of China's Agricultural Statistics, AAEA Annual Meeting*, Salt Lake City. https://www.card.iastate.edu/products/publications/pdf/98wp202.pdf.

Fang, H., Gu, Q., Xiong, W., & Zhou, L.-A. (2016). Demystifying the Chinese Housing Boom. *NBER Macroeconomics Annual*, 30(1), 105–166. http://dx.doi.org/10.1086/685953.

Fang, H., Gu, Q., Xiong, W., & Zhou, L.-A. (2016). Demystifying the Chinese Housing Boom. *NBER Macroeconomics Annual*, 30(1), 105–166. https://www.journals.uchicago.edu/doi/10.1086/685953#.

Feynman, R. (1968). https://www.feynmanlectures.caltech.edu/.

Figlewski, S., Silber, W., & Subrahmanyam, M. G. (Eds.). (1990). Financial Options from theory to practice. Salomon Brothers, New York. https://archive.org/details/financialoptions00step/mode/2up.

Fitzgerald, M., Kruschwitz N., Bonnet D., & Welch M. (2013). Digital Transformation Global Executive Study and Research Project MIT's Center for Digital Business (CDB) and Capgemini Consulting.

Fourie, L. & Shilawa, J. (2004). The value of concept maps for Knowledge Management in the banking and insurance industry: A German case study. In: *Proceedings of the First International Conference on Concept Mapping*, Pamplona, Spain.

Fowler, B. & Vegas, E. (2021). *How England Implemented Its Computer Science Education Program.* Brookings Institution. https://www.brookings.edu/wp-content/uploads/2021/01/How-England-implemented-its-computer-science-education-program.pdf.

Frees, E. (2020). https://openacttexts.github.io/Loss-Data-Analytics/.

Frigo, M. L. & Anderson, R. J. (2011). Strategic risk management: A foundation for improving enterprise risk management and governance. *The Journal of Corporate Accounting & Finance*, 22(3), 81–88. http://dx.doi.org/10.1002/jcaf.20677.

Froot, K. A., Scharfstein, D. S. & Stein, J. C. A framework for risk management. *Harvard Business Review*, 72(6), 91–102.

Gartner (2023). Top strategic technology trends 2023 report. https://www.gartner.com/en/information-technology/insights/top-technology-trends/top-technology-trends-2023-gov.

Galloway, D. & Funston, R. (2000). The challenges of enterprise risk management. *Balance Sheet*, 8(8), 22–25.

Gates, S. (2006). Incorporating strategic risk into enterprise risk management: A survey of current corporate practice. *Journal of Applied Corporate Finance*, 18(4), 81–90. https://doi.org/10.1111/j.1745-6622.2006.00114.x.

Gibson, D. & Ifenthaler, D. (2020). Adoption of learning analytics. In D. Ifenthaler & D. Gibson (Eds.), *Adoption of Data Analytics in Higher*

Education Learning and Teaching. Advances in Analytics for Learning and Teaching. Springer, Cham. https://doi.org/10.1007/978-3-030-47392-1_1.
Gomez, O. L. (2016). Lo que llevo a la quiebra a Enron y WorldCom: Analisis de casos.
Goldratt, E. M. & Cox, J. (1986). *The Goal: A Process of Ongoing Improvement* (2nd edn.). National Productivity Institute; Avraham Y. Goldratt Institute.
Goovaerts, M. J., de Vylder, F. & Haezendonck, J. (1984). *Insurance Premiums: Theory and Applications*. North-Holland, Amsterdam.
Govindarajan, V. & Immelt, J. R. (2019). *The Only Way Manufacturers Can Survive*. MIT Sloan Management School, Spring Issue Opinion & Analysis March 12, 2019.
Greene, W. H. (1990). *Econometric Analysis*. New York: Macmillan.
Greenacre, M. J. (1984). *Theory and Applications of Correspondence Analysis*. London: Academic Press. http://www.carme-n.org/?sec=books5.
Grudin, J. (2006). Enterprise knowledge management and emerging technologies. In *Proceedings of the 39th Annual Hawaii International Conference on System Sciences (HICSS'06)*, Kauai, HI, USA. https://doi.org/10.1109/HICSS.2006.156.
Guiltinan, J. & Paul, G. (2000). *Administracion de Marketing*. McGraw Hill, Mexico.
Gulati, R. (2007). Silo busting: How to execute on the promise of customer focus. *Harvard Business Review*, 85(5), 98–108, 145. PMID: 17494254.
Guoping, Z. & Zuoxu, X. (2007). On the bankruptcy of private higher education institutions in China. *Frontiers of Education in China*, 2, 103–118.
Hájek, P. (2011). Municipal credit rating modelling by neural networks. *Decision Support Systems,* 5(1), 108–118. https://doi.org/10.1016/j.dss.2010.11.033.
Hamilton, S. & Zhu, X. (2017). Funding and financing smart cities. *The Journal of Government Financial Management*, 66(1), 26–33.
Hammond, J. S., Keeney, R. L., & Raiffa, H. (2006). The hidden traps in decision making. *Harvard Business Review*, 84(1), 118.
Hatch, J. (2018). Better teachers are needed to improve science education: The latest training techniques emphasize classroom practice and design thinking. *Nature*, 562(7725), S2–S4. https://doi.org/10.1038/d41586-018-06830-2.
Heizer, J., Render, B., & Munson, C. (2017). *Operations Management: Sustainability and Supply Chain Management* (12th edn.). Pearson. https://www.pearson.com/us/higher-education/product/Heizer-Operations-Management-Sustainability-and-Supply-Chain-Management-12th-Edition/9780134130422.html.
Hincapie, C. C. (2016). Caso Interbolsa.
Hipkin, I. (2010). Production competence and knowledge generation for technology transfer: A comparison between UK and South African Case Studies. In

M. Al-Shammari (Ed.), *Knowledge Management in Emerging Economies: Social, Organizational and Cultural Implementation* (pp. 66–78). IGI Global,Hershey,PA.https://www.igi-global.com/chapter/production-competence-knowledge-generation-technology/46841.

Hitt, L. M. & Brynjolfsson, E. (1996). Productivity, business profitability, and consumer surplus: Three different measures of information technology value. *MIS Quarterly*, 20. 121–142. https://doi.org/10.2307/249475.

Hogg, R. & Craig, A. (1994). *Introduction to Mathematical Statistics* (5th edn.). Prentice Hall. https://www.amazon.com/Introduction-Mathematical-Statistics-Robert-Hogg/dp/0023557222.

Hogg, R., McKean, J. W., & Craig, A. (2019) *Introduction to Mathematical Statistics* (8th edn.). Pearson Education. https://minerva.it.manchester.ac.uk/~saralees/statbook2.pdf.

Hormozi, A. & Giles, S. (2004). Data mining a competitive weapon for banking and retail industries. *Information Systems Management*, 21(2), 62–71.

Hsiao, Ch., Shen, Y., & Bian, W. (2015). Evaluating the effectiveness of China's financial reform — The efficiency of China's domestic banks. *China Economic Review*, 35, 70–82. https://doi.org/10.1016/j.chieco.2015.05.006.

Hu, Q. & Huang, C. (2006). Using the balanced scorecard to achieve sustained it-business alignment: A case study. *Communications of the Association for Information Systems*, 17. https://doi.org/10.17705/1CAIS.01708.

Huang, C. D. & Hu, Q. (2004). Integrating web services with competitive strategies: The balanced scorecard approach. *Communications of the Association for Information Systems,* 13(1). https://doi.org/10.17705/1CAIS.01306.

Huang, S.-M., Ku, C.-Y., Chu, Y.-T., & Hsueh, H.-Y. (2002). A study of value factors for adopting information technology in professional service industry: A demonstrative case of accounting firms in Taiwan. *Review of Pacific Basin Financial Markets and Policies*, 5(4), 509–519. https://doi.org/10.1142/S0219091502000882.

Hull, J. C. (2012). *Options Futures and Other Derivatives* (8th edn.). Prentice Hall. https://faculty.ksu.edu.sa/sites/default/files/options_futures_and_other_derivatives_8th_ed_part1.pdf.

IEEE's Ethically Aligned Design (1st edn.). (Mach 2019). A vision for prioritizing human well-being with autonomous and intelligent systems. https://sagroups.ieee.org/global-initiative/wp-content/uploads/sites/542/2023/01/ead1e-overview.pdf.

Ifenthaler, D. & Gibson, D. (2020). *Advances in Analytics for Learning and Teaching*. Springer.

Igan, D. & Pinheiro, M. (2010). *Exposure to real estate in bank portfolios. Journal of Real Estate Research*, 32(1), 47–74. https://doi.org/10.1080/10835547.2010.12091268.

Islam, M. R., Zhang, J., Ashmafee, Md. H., Razzak, I., Zhou, J., Wang, X., & Xu, G. (2021). ExVis: Explainable visual decision support system for risk management. In *8th International Conference on Behavioral and Social Computing (BESC)*, pp. 1–5. https://doi.org/10.1109/BESC53957.2021.9635491.

ISO/IEC JTC 1 Information Technology. (2015). Smart cities — Preliminary report 2014. ISO, Geneva, Switzerland. https://www.iso.org/files/live/sites/isoorg/files/developing_standards/docs/en/smart_cities_report-jtc1.pdf.

Ittner, C. D. & Larcker, D. F. (November 2003). Coming up short on nonfinacial performance measurement. *Harvard Business Review*. https://hbr.org/2003/11/coming-up-short-on-nonfinancial-performance-measurement.

Jackson, W. (2002). *Methods: Doing Social Research* (3rd edn.). Prentice Hall, Toronto. https://www.amazon.ca/Methods-Doing-Social-Research-3rd/dp/0130445495.

Jakhria, P. (2014). Difficult risks and capital models: A report from the extreme events working party abstract of the London Discussion. *British Actuarial Journal*, 19(3), 617–635. https://doi.org/10.1017/S1357321713000482.

James, G., Witten, D., Hastie, T., & Tibshirani, R. (2013). *An Introduction to Statistical Learning*. Springer Texts in Statistics (2nd edn., Vol. 112, p. 18). New York: Springer. https://doi.org/10.1007/978-1-0716-1418-1-1.

Jin, B. H. & Li, Y. M. (2012). Analysis of emerging technology adoption for the digital content market. *Information Technology and Management*, 13(3), 149–165. https://doi.org/10.1007/s10799-011-0113-6.

John, C. & Rubinstein, M. (1985). *Options Markets*. Prentice Hall, Englinwood Cliffs, NJ. https://afajof.org/wp-content/uploads/files/historical-texts/cox-rubinstein-ocr-1985.pdf.

Johnson, R. and Wichern, D. (1998). *Applied Multivariate Statistical Analysis*. Prentice Hall: Upper Sadle River.

Jones, R. (2001). "Measuring the benefits of knowledge management at the FSA", City University, http://www.km4dev.org/index.php/articles/downloads/307.

Joshi, M. P., Su, N., Austin, R. D., & Sundaram, A. D. (March 2021). Why so many data science projects fail to deliver: Organizations can gain more business value from advanced analytics by recognizing and overcoming five common obstacles. *MIT Sloan Management Review*. https://sloanreview.mit.edu/article/why-so-many-data-science-projects-fail-to-deliver/.

Kaplan, R. S. & Norton, D. P. (January–February 1992). The balanced scorecard-measures that drive performance. *Harvard Business Review*, 70(1), 71–79. https://www.hbs.edu/faculty/Pages/item.aspx?num=9161.

Kaplan, R. S. & Norton, D. P. (2000). *The Strategy-Focused Organization: How Balanced Scorecard Companies Thrive in the New Business Environment.*

Harvard Business School Press, Boston, MA. https://www.hbs.edu/faculty/Pages/item.aspx?num=5595.

Kaplan, R. S. & Norton, D. P. (July 1999). The Balanced Scorecard: Measures that drive performance. *Harvard Business Review*.

Kaplan, R. S., & Norton, D. P. (September 2000). Having trouble with your Strategy? Then Map It. *Harvard Business Review*, https://hbr.org/2000/09/having-trouble-with-your-strategy-then-map-it.

Kaplan, R. S. & Norton, D. P. (January 2005).The balanced scorecard: Measures that drive performance. (cover story). *Harvard Business Review*, 83(7), 172–180. https://hbsp.harvard.edu/product/R0507Q-PDF-ENG.

Karimi, J. & Konsynski, B. R. (2002). Information technology infrastructure-organizational structure relationship. In R. D. Galliers, D. E. Leidner, & B. Baker (Eds.), *Strategic Information Management* (3rd edn., pp. 431–453). Oxford: Butterworth-Heinemann. https://doi.org/10.4324/9780080481135.

Kellison, S. G. (1991). *The Theory of Interest* (2nd edn.). Irwin, Homewood, IL. https://adams.marmot.org/Record/.b17730314.

Kessler, D. (2001). Anticipating and managing risks in the 21st century. *Geneva Papers on Risk & Insurance*, 26(1), 1–7. https://doi.org/10.1111/1468-0440.00088.

Keyes, J. (2005). *Implementing the IT Balanced Scorecard: Aligning IT with Corporate Strategy*, Auerbach Publications.

Khanagha, S., Volberda, H., Sidhu, J., & Oshri, I. (2013). Management innovation and adoption of emerging technologies: The Case of cloud computing. *European Management Review*, 10(1), 51–67. https://doi.org/10.1111/emre.12004.

Kidd, W. & Murray, J. (2013). Using emerging technologies to develop professional learning in teachers have some issues. *Professional Development in Education*, 39(2), 165–167. https://doi.org/10.1080/19415257.2013.771087.

Kim, W. C. & Mauborgne, R. (January 2003). Fair process: Managing in the knowledge economy. *Harvard Business Review*. https://hbr.org/2003/01/fair-process-managing-in-the-knowledge-economy.

Kliem, R. L. & Ludim, I. S. (1997). *Reducing Project Risk* (1st edn.). Gower Publishing Ltd., Hampshire, England. https://doi.org/10.4324/9781315245089.

Knowledge@Wharton (2018). https://knowledge.wharton.upenn.edu/article/blockchain-will-impact-financial-sector/.

Kolmogorov, A. N. (1993). On works in information theory and some of its applications. In A. N. Shiryayev (ed.), *Selected Works of A. N. Kolmogorov. Mathematics and Its Applications*, Vol. 27. Springer, Dordrecht. https://doi.org/10.1007/978-94-017-2973-4_14.

Koss, R. & Shi, X. (2018). Stabilizing China's housing market. IMF Working Paper No. 18/89. Available at SSRN: https://ssrn.com/abstract=3182517.

Kourtit, K. & Nijkamp, P. (2018). Big data dashboards as smart decision support tools for I-cities — An experiment on stockholm. *Land Use Policy*, 71, 24–35. https://doi.org/10.1016/j.landusepol.2017.10.019.

Kovner, A. R. & Rundall, T. G. (2006). Evidence-based management reconsidered. *Frontiers of Health Services Management,* 22(3), 3–22. DOI: 10.1097/01974520-200601000-00002.

Krishnamoorthy, C. S. & Rajeev, S. (1996). *Artificial Intelligence and Expert Systems for Engineers*. CRC Press/Taylor & Francis, Boca Raton. https://www.routledge.com/Artificial-Intelligence-and-Expert-Systems-for-Engineers/Krishnamoorthy-Rajeev/p/book/9780849391255.

Kuang, L. & Liu, L. (2012). Discrimination against rural-to-urban migrants: The role of the Hukou System in China. *PLoS ONE*, 7(11), e46932. https://doi.org/10.1371/journal.pone.0046932.

Kwok, Y.-K. (2008). *Mathematical Models of Financial Derivatives* (2nd edn.). Springer, Singapore. https://accelerator086.github.io/accelerator086-Blogs-Books/Mathematical%20Models%20of%20Financial%20Derivatives%20-%20Yue%20Kuen%20Kwok.pdf.

Lam, J. (March 25, 2000). Enterprise-wide risk management and the role of the chief risk officer. White paper, ERisk.com.

Lebovitz, S., Levina, N., & Lifshitz-Assaf, H. (2021). Is AI ground truth really true? The dangers of training and evaluating AI tools based on experts' know-what. *MIS Quarterly,* 45(3), 1501–1526. https://doi.org/10.25300/MISQ/2021/16564.

Lee, M. K. O. & Turban, E. (2001). A trust model for consumer internet shopping. *International Journal of Electronic Commerce*, 6, 75–91.

Lehaney, B., Clarke, S., Coakes, E., & Jack, G. (2004). *Beyond Knowledge Management*. Idea Group Publishing, Hershey. https://doi.org/10.4018/978-1-59140-180-30.

Lennerholt, C., Van Laere, J., & Söderström, E. (2021). User-related challenges of self-service business intelligence. *Information Systems Management*, 38(4), 309–323. https://doi.org/10.1080/10580530.2020.1814458.

Leonard, D. A. & Sensiper, S. (1998). The role of tacit knowledge in group innovation. *California Management Review*, 40 (3), 112+. DOI: 10.2307/41165946.

Leoni, L., Ardolino, M., Elbaz, J., Gueli, G., & Bacchetti, A. (2022). The mediating role of knowledge management processes in the effective use of artificial intelligence in manufacturing firms. *International Journal of Operations & Production Management*, 42(13), 411–437.

Levine, R. (Spring, 2006). Risk management systems: Understanding the need. *Information Systems Management*, 21, 31–37. https://doi.org/10.1201/1078/44118.21.2.20040301/80419.5.

Li, J., Li, M., Wang, X., & Thatcher, J. B. (2021). Strategic directions for AI: The role of CIOS and boards of directors. *MIS Quarterly*, 45(3), 1603–1643. https://www.econbiz.de/Record/strategic-directions-for-ai-the-role-of-cios-and-boards-of-directors-jingyu/10012631449.

Liebenberg, A. & Hoyt, R. (2003). The determinants of enterprise risk management: Evidence from the appointment of chief risk officers. *Risk Management and Insurance Review*, 6(1), 37–51.

Liebowitz, J. & Suen, C. Y. (2000). Developing knowledge management metrics for measuring intellectual capital. *Journal of Intellectual Capital*, 1(1), 54–67. https://doi.org/10.1108/14691930010324160.

Lin, N. (2015). *Applied Business Analytics: Integrating Business Process, Big Data, and Advanced Analytics*. Pearson Education.

Linton, J. D. (2004). Perspective: Ranking business schools on the management of technology. *The journal of Product Innovation Management*, 21(6), 416–430. https://doi.org/10.1111/j.0737-6782.2004.00095.x.

Liu, L. G. (2014). Is China's property market heading toward collapse? Peterson institute for international economics, *Policy Brief*, Number PB 14-2. https://www.piie.com/sites/default/files/publications/pb/pb14-21.pdf.

Machina, M. J. (1982). Expected utility analysis without the independence axiom. *Econometrica,* 50(2), 277–323. http://dx.doi.org/10.2307/1912631.

Machina, M. J. (1987). Choice under uncertainty: Problems solved and unsolved. *Journal of Economic Perspectives*, 1(1), 121–154. DOI: 10.1257/jep.1.1.121.

Machina, M. J. (1995). Non expected utility and the robustness of the classic insurance paradigm. *Geneva Papers on Risk and Insurance Therory,* 20(1), 9–50. https://www.jstor.org/stable/41953307.

Maister, D. H., Galford, R., Green, C. W. (2000). *The Trusted Advisor*. Free Press.

Majchrzak, A., Beath, C. M., Lim, R. A., & Chin, W. W. (2005). Managing client dialogues during information systems design to facilitate client learning. *MIS Quarterly*, 29(4), 653–672. https://doi.org/10.2307/25148704.

Mandamadiotis, A., Eleftherakis, S., Glenis, A., Skoutas, D., Stavrakas, Y., & Koutrika, G. (2021). DatAgent: The imminent age of intelligent data assistants. *Proceedings of the VLDB Endowment*, 14(12), 2815–2818. https://doi.org/10.14778/3476311.3476352.

March, J. G. & Shapira, Z. (1987). Managerial perspectives on risk and risk taking. *Management Science*, 33(11), 1404–1418. https://doi.org/10.1287/mnsc.33.11.1404.

Marchetti, A. M. (2012). *Enterprise Risk Management Best Practices: From Assessment to Ongoing Compliance*. John Wiley & Sons, Inc. https://www.perlego.com/book/1002211/enterprise-risk-management-best-practices-from-assessment-to-ongoing-compliance-pdf.

Marshall, C., Prusak, L., & Shpilberg, D. (1996). Financial risk and need for superior knowledge management. *California Management Review*, 38(3), 77–101.

Masterson, F. (2012). Knowledge management in practice: Using wikis to facilitate project-based learning. In S. Buckley & M. Jakovljevic (Eds.), *Knowledge Management Innovations for interdisciplinary Innovation* (1st edn., pp. 385–401). IGI Global, Hershey, PA https://www.igi-global.com/chapter/knowledge-management-practice/68336.

Matin, H. Z., Alvani, S. M., Jandaghi, G. R., & Pashazadeh, Y. (2010). Designing and clarifying knowledge sharing model in administrative agencies to improve the performance. *European Journal of Economics, Finance and Administrative Sciences*, 22(1).

Mayer-Schönberger, V. & Ramge, T. (February 2022). *The Data Boom Is Here — It's Just Not Evenly Distributed.* MIT Sloan Management Review, https://sloanreview.mit.edu/article/the-data-boom-is-here-its-just-not-evenly-distributed/

McKibben, D. (2004). *Banks evolve in their approach to enterprise risk management.* Gartner G2 Report, pp. 1–10.

McKinsey Company. (August 2022). McKinsey technology trends outlook 2022 report. https://www.mckinsey.com/~/media/mckinsey/business%20functions/mckinsey%20digital/our%20insights/the%20top%20trends%20in%20tech%202022/mckinsey-tech-trends-outlook-2022-full-report.pdf.

McNeil, A., Frey, R., & Embretchts, P. (2005). *Quantitative Risk Management Princeton Series in Finance.*

McNichols, T. J. (2013). (1977) *Executive Policy and Strategic Planning* (Subsequent edition). McGraw Hill, New York. https://www.amazon.com/-/es/Thomas-J-McNichols/dp/0070456755.

Merchant. (2012). *Management Control Systems PowerPoints on the Web* (3rd edn.). Pearson Education Ltd.

Merton, R. C. (April 2013). Innovation risk. *Harvard Business Review*, 48–56. https://hbr.org/2013/04/innovation-risk-how-to-make-smarter-decisions.

Meulbroek, L. (2002). The promise and challenge of integrated risk management. *Risk Management and Insurance Review*, 5(1), 55–66. https://doi.org/10.1111/1098-1616.00006.

Meyer, M. (2001). *Continuous Stochastic Calculus with Applications to Finance.* Chapman & Hall, Boca Raton, Florida. http://www.untag-smd.ac.id/files/Perpustakaan_Digital_1/FINANCE%20Continuous%20stochastic%20calculus%20with%20applications%20to%20finance.pdf.

Michalczyk, S., Nadj, M., Azarfar, D., Maedche, A., & Gröger, C. (2020). A state-of-the-art overview and future research avenues of self-service business intelligence & analytics. In *28th European Conference on Information*

Systems (ECIS 2020), Online. https://publikationen.bibliothek.kit.edu/1000119927.

Michalczyk, S., Nadj, M., Beier, H., Maedche, A. (2021). Designing a self-service analytics system for supply base optimization. In S. Nurcan & A. Korthaus (Eds.), *Intelligent Information Systems* (pp. 154–161). CAiSE 2021. Lecture Notes in Business Information Processing, vol 424. Springer, Cham. https://doi.org/10.1007/978-3-030-79108-7_18.

Miller, K. D. & Bromiley, P. (1990). Strategic risk and corporate performance: An analysis of alternative risk measures. *Academy of Management Journal*, 33(4), 756–779. https://escholarship.org/uc/item/5rs559v6.

Mintzberg, H., Lampel, J., & Ahlstrand, B. (1998). *Strategy Safari: A Guided Tour through the Wilds of Strategic Management.* Upper Saddle River: Prentice Hall.

Mishkin, F. S. (2016). *The Economics of Money, Banking and Financial Markets* (11th edn.). Pearson, Addison Wesley, Boston. https://www.pearson.com/en-us/subject-catalog/p/Mishkin-Economics-of-Money-Banking-and-Financial-Markets-The-11th-Edition/P200000007697/9780133859829.

Mitchell, T. M. (1997). *Machine Learning.* McGraw-Hill. http://www.cs.cmu.edu/~tom/mlbook.html.

Mladenić, D., Lavrac, N., Bohanec, M., & Moyle, S. (2003). Data mining and decision support: Integration and collaboration. 10.1007/978-1-4615-0286-9.

Moody's. (2019). Research announcement: Moody's — Largest US cities take proactive steps to mitigate credit risk from climate change. https://www.moodys.com/research/Moodys-Largest-US-cities-take-proactive-steps-to-mitigate-credit–PBM_1158519.

Morales, L. & Aldana, L. M. (2021). Análisis de la quiebra de Avianca Holdings S.A.

Morales, E. deJ., Morales, M. V., & Correa, S. (2020). Diagnóstico del monitoreo de riesgos en cuatro aerolíneas internacionales.

Morgan, G. (1997). *Images of Organisation.* Thousand Oaks: Sage Publications.

Morse, J. M. & Richards, L. (2002). *Readme First for a User's Guide to Qualitative Methods.* Sage Publications, Thousand Oaks, CA.

Mossin, J. (1968). Aspects of rational insurance purchasing. *Journal of Political Economy*, 79(4), 553–568. https://doi.org/10.1086/259427

Mougayar, W. (1998). *Opening Digital Markets: Battle Plans and Business Strategies for Internet Commerce* (2nd edn.). McGraw Hill, New York. https://www.worldcat.org/title/37695660.

Mukora, A., Winksel, M., H. F. Jeffrey,H. F., & Mueller, M. (2009). Learning curves for emerging energy technologies. *Proceedings of the Institution of Civil Engineers — Energy*, 162(4), 151–159. https://doi.org/10.1680/ener.2009.162.4.151.

Musa, S. (2016). Smart city roadmap. [Online]. http://www.academia.edu/21181336/Smart/City/Roadmap.

Nasbitt, J., Naisbitt, N., & Philips, D. (1999). *High Tech, High Touch*. Broadway Books, New York. https://www.abebooks.com/9780767903837/High-Tech-Touch-Technology-Search-0767903838/plp.

Neeley, T. & Leonardi, P. (May–June 2022). Developing a digital mindset: How to lead your organization into the age of data, algorithms, and AI. *Harvard Business Review*, 100(3), 50–55.

Neftci, S. N. (2000). *An Introduction to the Mathematics of Financial Derivatives* (2nd edn.). Academic Press, San Diego. https://www.econbiz.de/Record/an-introduction-to-the-mathematics-of-financial-derivatives-neftci-salih/10004593318.

Negroponte, N. (1995). *Being Digital* (1st edn.). Alfred A. Knopf Inc., New York. https://www.abebooks.com/book-search/title/being-digital/author/negro-ponte/first-edition/.

Ng, K.-S., Hung, W.-T., & Wong, W.-G. (2002). An algorithm for assessing the risk of traffic accidents. *Journal of Safety Research*, 33(3), 387–410.

Nonaka, I. & Takeuchi, H. (1995). *The Knowledge-creating Company: How Japanese Companies Creates the Dynamics of Innovation*. New York: Oxford University Press.

OECD Economic Outlook (2021). *Volume 2021 Issue 1: Preliminary Version*. OECD. https://www.oecd.org/economy/outlook/OECD-economic-outlook-general-assessment-macroeconomic-situation-may-2021.pdf.

OECD Economic Surveys (April 2019). China, Overview. https://www.oecd.org/economy/surveys/china-2019-OECD-economic-survey-overview.pdf.

Oldfield, G. & Santomero, A. (1997). Risk management in financial institutions. *Sloan Management Review*, 39(1), 33–47.

Olson, D. L. & Wu, D. D. (2017). *New Frontiers in Enterprise Risk Management* (2nd edn.). Springer-Verlag, Berlin, Heidelberg. https://doi.org/10.1007/978-3-662-53785-5.

Ong, M. (2006). *Risk Management: A Modern Perspective*. Academic Press: London MA.

Ordoñez, M. E. (2016). Analisis de la quiebra de la General Motors.

Orlikowski, W. & Thompson, S. (2010). *Leveraging the Web for Customer Engagement: A Case Study of BT's Debatescape*. MIT Sloan School of Management WP No. 4935-11 and CISR WP No. 380. http://hdl.handle.net/1721.1/68552.

Panjer, H. H., Boyle P. P., & Cox, S. H. (Eds.). (1998). *Financial Economics. Actuarial foundation*. Schaumburg, IL.

Parente, S. (November-December 2000). Beyond the hype: A taxonomy of e-health business models. *Health Affairs,* 19(6), 89–102.

Paul, W., *et al.* (1995). *The Mathematics of Financial Derivatives a Student Introduction*. Cambridge University Press, New York.

Peng, A. T.-J. & Lee, Y. S. (2005). Healthcare intellectual capital: A framework at the Hospital level and the Alliance level. In *Proceedings of 6th European Conference on Knowledge Management*, ECKM, pp. 412–420. https://nccur.lib.nccu.edu.tw/handle/140.119/76803.

Perry, M. (2012). Innovation in higher education in Israel: Public Policy Implications. In S. Buckley & M. Jakovljevic (Eds.), *Knowledge Management Innovations for interdisciplinary Innovation* (1st edn., pp. 35–50). IGI Global, Hershey, PA. https://www.igi-global.com/chapter/innovation-higher-education-israel/68319.

Petzel, T. E. (1989). *Financial Futures and Options*. Quorum Books, New York. https://archive.org/details/financialfutures0000petz.

Pfeffer, J. & Sutton, R. (2006). Hard facts, dangerous half-truths, and total nonsense profiting from evidence-based management. *Strategy & Leadership*, 34, 35–42. DOI: 10.1108/10878570610652617.

Porter, M. E. (1980). *Competitive Strategy: Techniques for Analyzing Industries and Competitors*. New York: Free Press. (Republished with a new introduction, 1998.)

Porter, M. E., Sachs, J. D., & Mcarthur, J. W. (2001). Competitiveness and stages of economics development. Global Competitiveness Report 2001–2002. https://citeseerx.ist.psu.edu/document?repid=rep1&type=pdf&doi=fee0516424fa3a2f492b5775edaa9e0ed9856176.

Poutre, C. & Morales, M. (2021). Exploring optimal trading rules in a high-frequency portfolio, lecture notes in artificial intelligence 11489. M.-J. Meurs & F. Rudzicz (Eds.), *Advances in Artificial Intelligence*.

Protiviti Global Business Consulting (2021). Executive perspectives on top risks for 2021 and 2030 — The future of work. https://www.protiviti.com/us-en/survey/executive-perspectives-top-risks-2021-and-2030-future-work.

PWC. (2021). CRO and risk management leader. https://www.pwc.com/us/en/library/risk-management-leader.html.PWC.

QMPLS ONT. https://www.qmpls.org Website information (Free).

Quaadgras, A., Taveras, J., & Ross, J. W. (2012). *Transforming Supervalu by Exploiting Scale and Becoming Hyperlocal. MIT Sloan Center for Information Systems Research,* WP No. 387.

Quintero, G. (2016). Crisis Financiera decada de los ochenta: quiebra grupo Grancolombiano.

Raddan, G. H. (1990). *Developing new financial products: From Needs Analysis to Profitable Rollout*. Financial Sources Books, Naperville, IL. https://www.amazon.com/Developing-New-Financial-Products-Profitable/dp/0942061055.

Raiffa, H. (1968). *Decision Analysis: Introductory Lectures on Choices under Uncertainty*. Addison-Wesley.

Ramesh N. & Delen D., (2021). Digital Transformation: How to Beat the 90% Failure Rate? *IEEE Engineering Management Review*, 49(3), 22–25. Third Quarter. https://doi.org/10.1109/EMR.2021.3070139.

Ramirez, A. & Rios, C. Y. (2021). Riesgo de Bancarota: Analisis Caso Sears.

Ramli, N. A., Ismail, M. T., & Wooi, H. C. (2015). Measuring the accuracy of currency crisis prediction with combined classifiers in designing early warning system. *Machine Learning*, 101, 85–103. https://doi.org/10.1007/s10994-014-5447-y

Rathnam, R. G., Johnsen, J., & Wen, H. J. (2005). Alignment of business strategy and it strategy: A case study of a fortune 50 financial services company. *Journal of Computer Information Systems*, 45(2), 1–8. https://www.tandfonline.com/doi/abs/10.1080/08874417.2005.11645825.

Ray, G., Muhanna, W. A., & Barney, J. B. (2005). Information technology and the performance of the customer service process: A resource-based analysis. *MIS Quarterly*, 29(4), 625–652. https://dl.acm.org/doi/10.5555/2017274.2017278.

Robbins S. P. (1990). *Organization Theory: Structure, Design, and Applications*. Englewood Cliffs, NJ: Prentice Hall.

Robbins, C., *et al.* (June 2005). Risk factors. *Healthcare Financial Management*, 78–83.

Rockafellar, R. T. & Uryasev, S. (2000). Optimization of conditional value-at risk. *Journal of Risk*, 3, 21–41.

Rodriguez, E. (2002). Administración del Riesgo. Alfaomega, Bogotá. https://www.incubarhuila.co/books/administracion-del-riesgo-2/.

Rodriguez, E. (2004). Gerencia Matemática: la mente conceptual del gerente. Alfaomega, Bogotá. https://biblioteca.unimeta.edu.co/cgi-bin/koha/opac-detail.pl?biblionumber=9103.

Rodriguez, E. (2005). *Gerencia del Conocimiento*, Ed. Carrera 7a, Bogotá.

Rodriguez, E. (2006). Casos Administracion de Operaciones. Editorial Mayol, Bogotá. https://isbn.cloud/en/9789588307084/casos-de-administracion-de-operaciones/.

Rodriguez, E. (2007). Knowledge management applied to enterprise risk management in banking. In Proceedings of 8th European Conference on Knowledge Management, ECKM (pp. 813–819), Barcelona, Instituto Tecnologico de Cataluna Spain. https://research.aston.ac.uk/en/publications/knowledge-management-applied-to-enterprise-risk-management-is-the.

Rodriguez, E. (2008). A bottom-up strategy for a KM implementation at EDC export development Canada. In J. Liebowitz (Ed.), *Making Cents Out of Knowledge Management* (Chapter 10), Scarecrow Press Inc., Lanham, MD. https://biu.primo.exlibrisgroup.com/discovery/fulldisplay?vid=972BIU_INST:972BIU&search_scope=MyInstitution&tab=LibraryCatalog&docid=alma990023843200205776&context=L.

Rodriguez, E. (2010). Knowledge management applied to enterprise risk management: Country risk. In *Proceedings KMAC Knowledge Management Aston*

Conference, Aston Business School, Operations Research Society, Birmingham UK. https://publications.aston.ac.uk/id/eprint/15785/1/Rodriguez%2C/Eduardo/2010.pdf.

Rodriguez, E., Edwards, J. S. & Ramirez, G. (2019). Competencies for the design, implementation, and adoption of the analytics process. In S. Vowels & K. L. Goldberg (Eds.), *Teaching Data Analytics: Pedagogy and Program Design* (Chapter 8), CRC Press. https://www.routledge.com/Teaching-Data-Analytics-Pedagogy-and-Program-Design/Vowels-Goldberg/p/book/9781032091891.

Rollett, H. (2003). *Knowledge Management: Process and Technologies*. Boston: Kluwer Academic Publishers.

Ross, J. W. & Beath, C. B. (2010). USAA: Organizing for innovation and superior customer service. MIT Sloan Center for Information Systems Research. WP No. 382. https://cisr.mit.edu/publication/MIT_CISRwp382_USAA_RossBeath.

Ross, S. M. (2014). *Introduction to Probability Models* (11th edn.). Academic Press, San Diego, CA. http://mitran-lab.amath.unc.edu/courses/MATH768/biblio/introduction-to-prob-models-11th-edition.PDF.

Russell, S. & Norvig, P. (2021). *Artificial Intelligence: A Modern Approach* (4th edn.). Pearson. https://www.pearson.com/en-us/subject-catalog/p/artificial-intelligence-a-modern-approach/P200000003500/9780137505135.

S&P Global (December 3 2018). Residential mortgage backed securities. https://gcrratings.com/wp-content/uploads/2019/09/GCR-RMBS-Criteria-update-2018.pdf.

Sadgrove, K. (2005). *The Complete Guide to Business Risk Management*. Gower Publishing, Ltd.: London.

Säljö, R. (2010). Digital tools and challenges to institutional traditions of learning: Technologies, social memory and the performative nature of learning. *Journal of Computer Assisted Learning*, 26(1), 53–64. https://doi.org/10.1111/j.1365-2729.2009.00341.x.

Samoff, J. & Stromquist, N. (2001). Managing knowledge and storing wisdom? New forms of foreign aid? *Development and Change*, 32(4), 631–656.

Santomero, A. M. & Babbel, D. F. (1997). Financial risk management by insurers: An analysis of the process. *Journal of risk and insurance*, 64(2), 231–270. https://www.jstor.org/stable/pdf/253730.pdf.

Sarykalin, S., Serraino, G. & Uryasev, S. (2008). Value-at-risk vs conditional value-at-risk in risk management and optimization. *Tutorials in Operations Research*. 10.1287/educ.1080.0052.

Saunders, M., Lewis, P., & Thornhill, A. (2012). *Research Methods for Business Students* (6th edn.). Prentice Hall, Upper Saddle River. https://gibsoncollege.edu.et/wp-content/uploads/2022/01/Research-Methods-for-Business-Students-by-Mark-Saunders-Philip-Lewis-Adrian-Thornhill-z-lib.org-1.pdf.

Scheer, D. (2012). Risk governance and emerging technologies: Learning from case study integration. *Journal of Risk Research*, 16(3–4), 355–368. https://doi.org/10.1080/13669877.2012.729519.

Schlesinger, H. (March 1997) Insurance demand without the expected utility paradigm. *Journal of Risk & Insurance*, 64(1), 19–39. https://doi.org/10.2307/253910.

Sears, H. D. (2009). Bon secours health system integrates lean six sigma and knowledge transfer to drive clinical and operational excellence. *Global Business and Organizational Excellence*, 28, 31–45. https://doi.org/10.1002/joe.20286.

Sharda, R., Delen, D., Turban, E., Aronson, J. E., Liang, T.-P., & King, D. D. (2015). *Business Intelligence and Analytics: Systems for Decision Support* (10th edn.). Pearson.

Sharman, R. (May/June 2002). Enterprise risk management — The KPMG approach. *The British Journal of Administrative Management*, 26–28.

Shaw, J. (2005). Managing all your enterprise's risks. *Risk Management*, 52(9), 22–30.

Shiryayev, A. N. (ed.) (1993). To the logical foundations of the theory of information and probability theory. In *Selected Works of A. N. Kolmogorov. Mathematics and Its Applications*, Vol. 27. Dordrecht: Springer. https://doi.org/10.1007/978-94-017-2973-4_12.

Silva, P., Maçãs, C., Polisciuc, E., & Machado, P. (2021). Visualisation tool to support fraud detection. In *25th International Conference Information Visualisation (IV)*, pp. 77–87. https://doi.org/10.1109/IV53921.2021.00022.

Simões, A., Ferreira, F., Castro, H., Senna, P., Silva, D., & Dalmarco, G. (2021). Adoption of digital technologies during the COVID-19 pandemic: Lessons learned from collaborative Academia-Industry R&D case studies. In *IEEE 19th International Conference on Industrial Informatics (INDIN)* (pp. 1–7), Palma de Mallorca, Spain. https://doi.org/10.1109/INDIN45523.2021.9557470.

Simons, R. (1999). How risky is your company. *Harvard Business Review*, 77(3), 85–94.

Simpson, P. (2017). Smart cities: Understanding the challenges and opportunities. SmartCitiesWorld/Philips. https://smartcitiesworld.net/AcuCustom/Sitename/DAM/012/Understanding_the_Challenges_and_Opportunities_of_Smart_Citi.pdf.

Singh, T. & Premarajan, R. (2007). Antecedents to knowledge transfer: Trust and culture. *South Asian Journal of Management*, 14(1), 93–104.

Slywotzky, A. & Drzik, J. (2005). Countering the biggest risk of all. *Harvard Business Review*, 83(4), 78–88.

Smith B. J. & Colgate, M. (2007). Customer value creation: A practical framework. *Journal of Marketing Theory and Practice*, 15(1), 7–23. https://www.jstor.org/stable/40470272.

Smith, H. & McKeen, J. (September 2006). IT in 2010: The next frontier. *MIS Quartely Executive*, 5(3), 125–136.

Sodhi, Z., Flatt, J., & Landry, J. N. (2018). Getting to the open smart city [online], evergreen and open north for future cities Canada. https://futurecitiescanada.ca/downloads/2018/Getting/to/Open/Smart.City.pdf.

Stackpole, T. (2021). Inside IKEA's Digital Transformation, Strategy HBR, online June 4.

Stanford, N. (2007). *Guide to Organisation Design*. London: The Economist Newspaper Ltd.

Stanley Isanzu, J. (2017). The impact of credit risk on the financial performance of Chinese banks. *Journal of International Business Research and Marketing*, 2(3).

Stavros, Z. (1993). *Financial Optimization*. Cambridge University Press, Cambridge, UK.

Stehr, N. (2002). *Knowledge and Economic Conduct: The Social Foundations of the Modern Economy*. University of Toronto Press. https://doi.org/10.3138/9781442676527.

Strategy & PWC (2012). Driving analytics into action. https://www.strategyand.pwc.com

Stulz, R. M. (2022). Rethinking risk management. *Journal of Applied Corporate Finance*, 34, 32–46. https://doi.org/10.1111/jacf.12486.

Sturma, T., Gerlach, P., Pumplun, L., Mesbah, N., Peters, F., Tauchert, C., Nan, N., & Buxmann, P. (2021). Coordinating human and machine learning for effective organizational learning. *MIS Quarterly*, 45(3), 1581–1602.

Sullivan, C. & Krents, S. (November 2006). Avoiding the pitfalls of strategic planning. *Healthcare Financial Management*, 63–67.

Sutcliffe, K. & Weber, K. (2003). The high cost of accurate knowledge. *Harvard Business Review*, 81(5), 74–82.

Sutherland, B. (November–December 2006). When hazards go unchecked: A call to integrate an organization's risk management activities. *Journal of Health Care Compliance*, 39–40.

Taleb, N. (2007). *The Black Swan: The Impact of the Highly Improbable*, Random House, New York.

Tan, Y. (2016). The impacts of risk and competition on bank profitability in China. *The Journal of International Financial Markets, Institutions & Money*, 40, 85–110.

Tanriverdi, H. & Ruefli, T. W. (2004). The role of information technology in risk/return relations of firms. *Journal of the Association for Information Systems*, 5(11). DOI: 10.17705/1jais.0006.

Tapscott, D. & Caston, A. (1993). *Paradigm Shift: The New Promise of Information Technology*. McGraw Hill, New York.

Taulli, T. (2019). Artificial intelligence basics a non-technical introduction, APRESS, ISBN-13 (pbk): 978-1-4842-5027-3.

Tardivo, G. & Viassone, M. (2010). Creating an innovative social assistential performance management system: Beyond the economic-financial perspective: Empirical research findings. *Journal of Financial Management & Analysis*, 23(2), 99.

Te'eni, D. (2006). Organisational communication. In: D. Schwartz (Ed.), *Encyclopedia of Knowledge Management* (pp. 734–740). Idea Group Reference.

The Economist Intelligence Unit. (2006). Foresight 2020 economic, industry and corporate trends. https://graphics.eiu.com/files/ad_pdfs/eiuForesight2020_WP.pdf.

Thunström, A. O. (June 30, 2022). We asked GPT-3 to write an academic paper about itself—Then we tried to get it published. https://www.scientificamerican.com/article/we-asked-gpt-3-to-write-an-academic-paper-about-itself-mdash-then-we-tried-to-get-it-published/.

Transfusion Burgmeier, J. (June 2002). *Joint Commission Journal on Quality Improvement*, 28(6), 331–339.

Trieu, V.-H., Burton-Jones, A., Green, P., & Cockcroft, S. (2022). Applying and extending the theory of effective use in a business intelligence context. *MIS Quarterly*, 46, 645–678. https://doi.org/10.25300/MISQ/2022/14880.

Tsai, Y. S., Rates, D., Moreno-Marcos, P. M., Muñoz-Merino, P. J., Jivet, I., Scheffel, M., Rachsler, H., Delgado, C., & Gašević, D. (October 2020). Learning analytics in European higher education — Trends and barriers. *Computers & Education*, 155, 103933.

Tsoukas, H. & Knudsen, C. (2003). *Oxford handbook of Organisation Theory*. Oxford University Press.

Uchupalanam, K. (December 2000). Competition and IT-based innovation in banking services. *International Journal of Information Management*, 4(4).

Ullah, I., Fayaz, M., & Kim, D.-H. (2018). Analytical modeling for underground risk assessment in smart cities. *Applied Sciences*, 8(6), 921–939. https://doi.org/10.3390/app8060921.

UNESCO. (November 2021). https://en.unesco.org/artificial-intelligence/ethics.

University of California Berkley Understanding Science. https://undsci.berkeley.edu/understanding-science-101/what-has-science-done-for-you-lately/science-and-technology-on-fast-forward/.

Urrutia, I. & Eriksen, S. (2005). Insights from research application of the balanced scorecard in Spanish private health-care management. *Measuring Business Excellence*, 9(4), 16–26.

Ustun, B. & Rudin, C. (2016). Supersparse linear integer models for optimized medical scoring systems. *Machine Learning*, 102, 349–391. https://doi.org/10.1007/s10994-015-5528-6.

Uzzi, B. & Lancaster, R. (2003). Relational embeddedness and learning: The case of bank loan managers and their clients. *Management Science*, 49(4), 383–399.

Van Aken, J. E. & Romme, A. G. L. (2012). A design science approach to evidence-based management. In D. M. Rousseau (Ed.), *The Oxford Handbook of Evidence-Based Management* (pp. 43–57). Oxford University Press, Oxford.

Van de Bosch, F., *et al.* (January–February 2005). How knowledge accumulation has changed strategy consulting: Strategic options for established strategy consulting firms. Strategic Change.

Van Deventer, D. R. (1997). *Financial Risk Analysis*. Irwin.

Van Deventer, D. R., Imai, K., & Mesler, M. (2013). *Advanced Financial Risk Management (2nd edn.). Tools and Techniques for Integrated Credit Risk and Interest Rate Risk Management.* John Wiley & Sons Pte. Ltd., Singapore.

Van Greuning, H. & Bratanovic, S. (2003). *Analyzing and Managing Banking Risk: Framework for Assessing Corporate Governance and Financial Risk.* Washington: The World Bank.

Venkataraman, R. & Pinto, J. K. (2018). *Operations Management* (1st edn.). SAGE.

Vikson R. G. & Zimba W. T. (1975). *Stochastic Optimization Models in Finance*. Academic Press, New York.

von Krogh G., Ichijo, K. & Nonaka, I. (2000). *Enabling Knowledge Creation*. Oxford University Press: New York.

Von Krogh, G. & Roos, J. (1995). *Organizational Epistemology*. Springer: New York.

von Neumann, J., Morgenstern, O., & Rubinstein, A. (1944). *Theory of Games and Economic Behavior* (60th Anniversary Commemorative Edition). Princeton University Press. http://www.jstor.org/stable/j.ctt1r2gkx.

Wagner, L. & Van Belle, J. P. (2010). Web mining for strategic competitive intelligence: South African experiences and a practical methodology. In M. Al-Shammari (Ed.), *Knowledge Management in Emerging Economies: Social, Organizational and Cultural Implementation* (pp. 1–19). IGI Global, Hershey, PA. https://www.igi-global.com/chapter/web-mining-strategic-competitive-intelligence/46838.

Walton, M. (1986). *The Deming Method.*

Warren, B. (2002). What is missing from the RMIS design? Why enterprise risk management is not working. *Risk Management Magazine*, 49(10), 30–34.

Wayne Adachi, W. & Lodolce, A. E. (2005). Use of failure mode and effects analysis in improving the safety of i.v. drug administration. *American Journal of Health-System Pharmacy*, 62(9), 917–920. https://doi.org/10.1093/ajhp/62.9.917.

Wegmann, G. (2008). The balanced scorecard as a knowledge management tool: A French experience in a semi-public insurance company. Working Papers CREGO 1080902, Université de Bourgogne — CREGO EA7317 Centre de recherches en gestion des organisations.

Weill, P. & Broadbent, M. (1998). *Leveraging the New Infrastructure: How Market Leaders Capitalize on Information Technology*. Harvard Business School Press, Boston.

Wiener, N. (1961). *Cybernetics: Or, Control and Communication in the Animal and the Machine*. MIT Press.

Wilson, E. O. (1998). *Consilience: The Unity of Knowledge*. New York: Alfred Knopf.

Wimmer, R. & Dominick, J. (1994). *Mass Media Research: An Introduction*. Wadsworth Publishing Co., Belmont.

Winston Wayne, L. (1998). *Financial Models Using Simulation & Optimization*. Palisade Corp, Newfield, New York.

Wixon, B. H. & Ross, J. W. (2012). The US securities and exchange commission: Working smarter to protect investors and ensure efficient markets. MIT Sloan Center for Information Systems Research. WP No. 388.

Woetzel, J., Remes, J., Boland, B., Lv, K., Sinha, S., Strube, G., Means, J., Law, J., Cadena, A., & von der Tann, V. (2018). *Smart Cities: Digital Solutions for a More Livable Future*. McKinsey Global Institute. https://www.mckinsey.com/capabilities/operations/our-insights/smart-cities-digital-solutions-for-a-more-livable-future.

World Economic Forum. (2021). *The Global Risks Report 2021*. (16th edn.). https://report-files.weforum.org/docs/WEF_The_Global_Risks_Report_2021.pdf.

Wu, A. (2005). The integration between balanced scorecard and intellectual capital. *Journal of Intellectual Capital*, 6(5), 267–284.

Wu, A., Wang, Y., Zhou, M., He, X., Zhang, H., Qu, H., & Zhang, D. (2022). MultiVision: Designing analytical dashboards with deep learning based recommendation. *IEEE Transactions on Visualization and Computer Graphics*, 28(1), 162–172. https://doi.org/10.1109/TVCG.2021.3114826.

Xiaowei Li & Weida Kuang. (2012). Prepayment behavior of China's mortgage borrowers: Evidence from the loan-level data. *International Journal of Housing Markets and Analysis*, 5(1).

Xie, X., Du, F., & Wu, Y. (2021). A visual analytics approach for exploratory causal analysis: Exploration, validation, and applications. *IEEE Transactions on Visualization and Computer Graphics*, 27(2), 1448–1458. https://doi.org/10.1109/TVCG.2020.3028957.

Yahoo Finance. https://ca.finance.yahoo.com/.

Young, G. & Hasler, D. (2010). Managing reputational risks. *Strategic Finance*, 92(5), 37–46.

Zack, M. (1999). Developing a knowledge strategy. *California Management Review*, 41(3), 125–145.

Zech, J. (January 2001). Rethinking risk management: The combination of financial and industrial risk. *Geneva Papers*, 26(1).

Zhang, D., Cai, J., Liu, J., & Kutan, A. M. (2018). Real estate investments and financial stability: Evidence from regional commercial banks in China. *The*

European Journal of Finance, 24(16), 1388–1408. https://doi.org/10.1080/1351847X.2016.1154083.

Zhao, D., Chen, Y. F., & Shen, J. H. (2020). Mortgage payments and household consumption in urban China. *Economic Modelling*, 93, 100–111. https://doi.org/10.1016/j.econmod.2020.07.008.

Zhou, W., Arner, D. W., Buckley, R. P. (2015). *Regulation of Digital Financial Services in China: Last Mover or First Mover?* HKU Scholars Hub.

Zhu, K., Kraemer, K. L., Xu, S., & Dedrick, J. (2004). Information technology payoff in E-business environments: An international perspective on value creation of E-Business in the financial services industry. *Journal of Management Information Systems*. https://doi.org/10.1080/07421222.2004.11045797.

Zikmund, W. (2000). *Business Research Methods*. The Dryden Press Harcourt College Publishers, Orland.

Zschech, P., Horn, R., Höschele, D., Janiesch, C., & Heinrich, K. (2020). Intelligent user assistance for automated data mining method selection. *Business & Information Systems Engineering*, 62(3), 227–247. https://doi.org/10.1007/s12599-020-00642-3.

The thirteenth five-year plan for the development of Wenzhou's financial industry. http://zjjcmspublic.oss-cn-hangzhou-zwynet-d01-a.internet.cloud.zj.gov.cn/jcms_files/jcms1/web1825/site/attach/0/160929085756837.pdf.

Index

www.ingramcontent.com/pod-product-compliance
Lightning Source LLC
LaVergne TN
LVHW011656200926
848484LV00004B/961